It Came from 1957

It Came from 1957

It Came from 1957

*A Critical Guide to the
Year's Science Fiction,
Fantasy and Horror Films*

ROB CRAIG

McFarland & Company, Inc., Publishers
Jefferson, North Carolina, and London

LIBRARY OF CONGRESS CATALOGUING-IN-PUBLICATION DATA

Craig, Rob, 1954–
It came from 1957 : a critical guide to the year's science
fiction, fantasy and horror films / Rob Craig.
pages cm
Includes bibliographical references and index.

ISBN 978-0-7864-7777-7
softcover : acid free paper ∞

1. Motion pictures—United States—History.
2. Motion picture industry—United States—History—20th century.
3. Science fiction films—United States—History and criticism.
4. Fantasy films—Japan—United States—History and criticism.
5. Horror films—United States—History and criticism.
6. Nineteen fifty-seven, A.D.   I. Title.
PN1993.5.U6C68 2013   791.430973—dc23   2013034565

BRITISH LIBRARY CATALOGUING DATA ARE AVAILABLE

On the cover: poster artwork from *The Brain from
Planet Arous*, 1957 (Howco International Pictures/Photofest)

Manufactured in the United States of America

*McFarland & Company, Inc., Publishers
Box 611, Jefferson, North Carolina 28640
www.mcfarlandpub.com*

For Mother

Table of Contents

Preface

Just like every other red-blooded American youngster growing up in the 1950s, I was obsessed with television — almost from birth if dim memory serves. I couldn't have known — nor cared less — that television was designed and promoted specifically as a mass brainwashing tool by industry and government, in order to create generations of obedient, politically conservative citizens and rabid, debt-happy consumers, a function at which it succeeded beyond anyone's wildest dreams. Television was to me a mysterious, beautiful, and at times frightening "magic eye," an hypnotic portal opening into an apparently boundless alternate universe of art, entertainment, and education.

To a rapt child, *everything* on television was fascinating — even the commercials, as was intended — yet I soon found myself gravitating to the "longer form" of feature films, finding these extended stories completely mesmerizing, if a bit challenging at times to the attention span. Being a weirdo, I, of course, soon narrowed my focus to the "weird" movies: low-budget comedies, creaky early talkies, and primarily horror and science-fiction movies. Indeed, those horror and "sci-fi" movies I considered "good" I ended up watching over and over again, as many films shown on television in the late 1950s and early 1960s received multiple airings within a short space of time (due to their syndication rental terms, I would later find out). To me, a good weird movie had to have — in no particular order — a good title, a fantastic story, believable characters, a memorable monster or villain, and (oddly enough, perhaps) a memorable music score.

A common factor in movies I enjoyed most was the haunting specter of the split atom, in the form of either A-bombs, monsters, mutants, radioactive poisons, or atomically decimated wastelands. Now, the awesome promise and ghastly threat which the atomic age uneasily juggled certainly resonated with every single man, woman and child in the world, and I was no exception. But this immense socio-political reality affected me in a most personal way. Before my birth, my mother had been a successful chemist who worked for several years at National Union Radio in New Jersey, one of many small concerns subcontracted by the giant Radio Corporation of America to come up with a feasible design and manufacturing process for mass producing color television tubes. Mom and her colleagues were eventually successful in this venture, and the formulation they submitted became a major part of what eventually ended up as the "industry standard" for consumer-grade cathode ray tubes for color television receivers. For her efforts, my mother was awarded coholder status on U.S. patents for the process.

Thanks to her auspicious work in the field, Mom was approached soon after by the

Atomic Energy Commission to join the staff of chemists working at the AEC wing of the newly-expanded Brookhaven National Laboratories in Long Island, New York. She was about to accept this lofty position, which would have put her at the cutting edge of atomic energy research, when it was announced that she was pregnant — with me. Eschewing career for family, as did so many bright, promising women of the decade, my mother became a full-time caretaker, ending her potentially-illustrious career. In later years my mother would jokingly thank me for "saving her from the atom," as she put it — and I thanked her in turn for "inventing television" — but I always sensed her sadness that her opportunity to become something really grand had passed her by.

Simultaneously, my father worked as a senior editor for McGraw-Hill Publishing in Manhattan. One of his most auspicious projects was the publication of a series of large-format, photo-filled books promoting all possible "non-lethal" uses of atomic energy, a program hastily concocted by the AEC and President Eisenhower, and dubbed the "Atoms for Peace" program. Of course, I pored over these amazing volumes countless times during my youth, eventually saddened by the observation that the grand promises in the tracts had never managed to come to fruition.

Being the quintessential nerd then (as today), I kept a log book of many of the movies I saw on TV, scribbling some cursory (often misspelled) credits, a short synopsis, and notes on the music, the monsters, etc. Going through the notebook at some point in the mid-1960s, I noted that a large number of my favorite films were produced in 1957 — a seemingly important year, although I did not for decades have the slightest idea why. I much later found out that 1957 was a record year for the theatrical release of science fiction, horror and fantasy films in the United States. The "official" number in early genre film reference books was around 45, but subsequent research has uncovered an impressive — and indeed curious — *57* releases which fall into the "weird" genre for that remarkable year.

I have been highly entertained, for several decades now, by others' writings on the 1950s horror–science fiction canon, which were lumped in many cases into catch-all genre categories such as "trash film," "psychotronic film" and "paracinema." But to me, these films will always be simply known as "weird movies," since my parents repeatedly informed me that only a "weirdo" could like them. Film watching is a highly subjective experience, which says as much about the viewer as about the text. Like one's definition of or criteria for beauty or art, although there may be a general consensus one may adopt or reject, one's response to a cultural text such as a film relies on many factors, at least half of which emanate from the recipient of the experience. As much as I was thrilled when a writer or reviewer applauded a movie I also enjoyed, I was even more intrigued by how often my high opinion of certain films differed wildly from the low opinion of others, even those who loved the genre overall. Often I would find one of my "top ten" favorite pictures of the period (Roger Corman's extraordinary *War of the Satellites*, 1958, for example) to be a film almost everyone else — in print at least — either dismissed offhand or vociferously despised, and this "disparity of aesthetic perception" became a keen mystery for me. Alas, for many years I just thought I was "wrong" in my opinions, now I know that I was just "weird" in my love for "weird" movies, even among fellow "weirdos."

Yet my opinion on genre films still tends to vary widely from the general consensus. For instance, to this day I still cannot fathom how such an overproduced, underwritten, f/x-burdened, narratively insipid, imagination-barren franchise such as *Star Wars* could boast such an immense fan-base, counting among its members many bright, educated SF fans whose opinions I otherwise respect. (When I once confessed to a friend this frustrating observation — that so many intelligent people were prone to fall for simplistic, blatantly propagandistic science fiction treacle such as *Star Wars*— he shrugged his shoulders and quipped, "Brains ain't taste....") Indeed, "taste" is a most subjective — and, in critical circles, reviled — barometer of a cultural text's objective aesthetic and cultural value. A viewer can like any film he wants, for any reason or no reason at all. The trouble arises when people start to say that if they gravitate towards something, it must therefore be "good," whereas films they dislike must somehow be "bad." This is subjectivity at its worst, and, sadly, it seems to even creep into some otherwise well-constructed critical writing.

This work is not intended to be — nor does it pretend to be — an objective critical analysis of the subject, drawing on the current thought about same. It is simply a fan's interpretation of a unique body of texts, and what resonates about the films. Each movie discussed is worthy in its own way; all of them address and reflect some of the socio-political topics of the day, and many are exceptional for their genre and cultural moment. In my opinion, this group of films is an utterly unique collection of cultural artifacts, particularly given that they were all available for public viewing in the U.S. within a twelve-month period in a most astounding year, one which tipped the scales in American culture.

Introduction

Nineteen fifty-seven was truly a "fantastic" year in the history of motion pictures in the United States. In that calendar year at least 57 films in the science-fiction, horror and/or fantasy genres were released theatrically, a record unmatched to this day. There were several reasons for this short-lived "gold rush" of fantastic films, some of which overlapped. Cultural interest in all things scientific peaked after the end of World War II, reaching a crescendo in the early 1960s. Rapid advances in technology made for amazing daily headlines, and popular entertainment was quick to cash in on these trends. Most conspicuously, the ominous specter of the atomic bomb, with its unparalleled horrors and grim promise, loomed large over the world following the obliteration of Hiroshima and Nagasaki by nuclear weapons. Simultaneously, the U.S. and the U.S.S.R. were in a race to launch missiles — and soon people — into outer space; one of the most ancient dreams of mankind was finally within its grasp. Science Fiction as an entertainment genre had been gaining popularity since the early days of the century, with Hugo Gernsback and his "scientifiction" pulp magazines, and the post–World War II era, with its rapidly-evolving technology, feeding into this popularity, making the genre by far the fastest-selling one in both magazines and books for a large portion of the 1950s.

Intersecting with these interests was the coming of age of a new generation of Americans, birthed towards the end of the second World War and becoming a growing mass of teenaged consumers by about the mid–1950s. The movie studios particularly noted that this rapidly growing consumer base was the most likely to leave the comfort of their parents' homes to go out to the movies, either on a date or just to pass a weekend night, and beginning around 1956, moviemakers began to court this group aggressively, via films geared specifically to that demographic. The relatively new phenomenon known as the "drive-in," in which folks could drive their cars right into the "theater," was fast becoming all the rage, and the teenaged moviegoer was by far the most conspicuous inhabitant of this new form of movie viewing. The drive-ins and their young clientèle were one of the few areas of the film business of the 1950s which was making any headway into the incessant encroachment of television, which by mid-decade was seriously hurting the movie industry, drawing away a major portion of their previous audience. Put bluntly, the studios knew that teenagers were their best short-term customers, and teenagers liked "monster movies," so "monster movies" is what they gave them.

What is surprising is that, considering the juvenile audience the studios were catering to, the majority of the fantastic films released at this time (with some notable exceptions) were not particularly "dumbed-down" for their audience (although some may take exception to that observation). Indeed, the year 1957 produced some remarkably mature melodramas of a fantastic nature, and touched on several adult themes that belied their intended recipients.

A large number of the films discussed were released in pre-packaged "double bills," wherein two features were marketed nation-wide as a single promotional unit. Although double- and triple-features existed previously in the movie industry, this catering to a specific youth market created a unique, and rather short-lived, phenomenon of the packaged double bill, in which the two films were marketed, produced, and often even conceived as parts of a whole. Nineteen fifty-seven boasted the release of at least 24 pre-packaged double bills of the "fantastic" or "horror-chiller" variety, and many more in other genres. Several of these double bills were created by the same production teams, thus sharing many aesthetic and thematic qualities, making the pairing of the two films even more of a holistic viewing experience.

Yet the fantastic films of 1957 may have ultimately served a larger purpose than garnering quick cash for savvy producers, for they also (intentionally or not) vividly addressed many of the threats, fears, anxieties and misgivings which had built up in a decade ostensibly dedicated to ignoring and denying same, giving their original theatrical, and subsequent television, audiences an opportunity to meditate on taboo concepts and topics of the age. The patent silliness, utter banality and crushing conformity which appeared to dominate the 1950s was, of course, revealed to be a not terribly effective mask attempting to hide, through forced and manufactured frivolity, the truly deep and disturbing fears, prejudices and neuroses which haunted the nation's collective psyche. These dark forces began to emerge in mid-decade, in historical events and cultural trends which for a time seemed poised to completely undermine society's systemic, if half-hearted, efforts to construct a fabricated deceit of happy conformity. A journey into the dark heart of the decade may well find its most insightful and articulate expression in its fantastic films, many of which successfully expressed the subconscious dread of the era through highly-accessible (if at times simplistic) allegory. That journey culminates with 1957, when a veritable "tidal wave of terror" (as one of the posters put it) was unleashed, allowing a stampede of grotesque id-monsters to escape onto the nation's screens and into the very heart of the society it was terrifying while attempting to entertain. One might even consider the fantastic films of 1957 a mass cultural exorcism in which some of the most heinous sins and taboo fears of the culture were safely symbolized, ignited and vanquished, that society might learn, heal and move courageously onward towards that black hole of destiny: the future.

ONE

The Marvels of the Atomic Age

Alamogordo. Hiroshima. Nagasaki. The "atomic age" ignited with three cataclysmic detonations, a "holy trinity" of "unholy" events unparalleled in history, and judged by the world as either a great new hope for mankind or the "beginning of the end." Whether these unprecedented violations of the natural world ended the Second World War or merely took advantage of its imminent demise is a matter of hot debate even today, but history has shown that once kindled, the mighty atom would not be extinguished. Thus, the period immediately following the ignition of these unearthly flames, including the decade obsessed by them, was dubbed "the atomic age." The label is apt, for this period of time not only trembled under the granite thumb of this awesome new source of annihilation, but simultaneously glorified and fetishized same, granting it the potential to radically — and constructively — change life on earth as we know it.

The Allies' conquest of their chosen enemies, culminating in the end of World War II, allowed them a socio-political dominance over *the planet*— especially on the part of the United States — which still functions today, although somewhat unsteadily. Positioned for the first time in history as a world empire, the United States proceeded to flex its muscles both abroad and at home, attempting to fashion an ever more oppressive and conformism-oriented environment for its citizens. In this pursuit, the U.S. had as its leader for most of the 1950s former military commander Dwight D. Eisenhower, a man who seemed to symbolize both the promise of new hope and the stultifying forces of dogmatic regression.

While he was easily elected for two terms as president, and was known as the "Man of Peace," according to historian David Halberstam, Eisenhower was also seen as part of "an administration of older men no longer in touch, unaware of how quickly the world was changing."[1] In a sense, Eisenhower represented, in human form, one of the key dichotomies of the decade, in which rapidly advancing technology was awkwardly attempting to coexist with political ideology forged in a more innocent time. Halberstam notes, "While the country was exploding in terms of science, technology and business, and had assumed a new international role as the most powerful nation on earth, the minds of the governing class were rooted in a simpler day. Many of the tensions of the era stemmed from this contradiction."[2]

The Soviet Union was declared an enemy of the United States, probably for convenience as much as for any actual transgression on the part of the other would-be world empire; but when the U.S.S.R. successfully detonated their first atomic bomb in 1949, the "Cold War" was officially on, a cause celebre for both sides which served to keep a vibrant — and lucrative — military-industrial cabal cranking out new war technologies at a fever pace, while also acting as a powerful motivation to keep the populace fearful, obedient, and goal-oriented. Thus, the fifties was a grimly conservative decade, ruled almost entirely by the paranoid, isolationist dogma of the Republican Party. Progressive ideas and their thinkers were demonized, attacked, and (often successfully) ostracized or destroyed. The entire decade was crushed under the iron fist of an inflexible foreign policy aimed at both promulgating and exploiting a largely fictional Cold War in which an ungodly, even alien, "evil empire" was bent on destroying the U.S.

Thus, "anti-communism" was the primary political force of the decade, itself gaining energy from the long-held, highly delusional notion of America as being somehow unique, special, even "better" than any other nation. The American collective unconscious, greatly aided and abetted by government and media propaganda efforts, was woefully paranoid, firmly convinced that multiple sinister conspiracies were at work, endlessly striving to undermine and sabotage the newly-won American way of life. Communism was America's bogeyman, endlessly kindled into conflagration by accelerating nuclear proliferation on both sides. From the perspective of the Cold War, the 1950s started off with a bang. Within the first two months of 1950, several citizens — including Klaus Fuchs, Julius and Ethel Rosenberg, Morton Sobell, and Harry Gold — were accused of being Soviet spies and stealing the U.S.' atomic secrets. The Rosenbergs were sentenced to death and summarily executed, a grim reminder to all of the antediluvian tendencies still dominating this supposedly "enlightened" era of peace and prosperity. Also, liberal pacifist Alger Hiss found himself bafflingly convicted of consorting with the Soviet enemy. Soon after, Senator Joseph McCarthy introduced into Congress accusations of Soviet spies working in the government, business and entertainment industry, igniting the "Red Scare," which created a chilling atmosphere of paranoia and mistrust throughout the nation. To cap off this inauspicious beginning of a most troubled decade, in June, North Korea invaded South Korea, and the U.S. joined the South in solidarity against the North Korean Communist factions.

As their ascendancy to the throne of earthly power was largely based on new and fearsome technological weapons development, science, industry and the military forged ahead with their unholy alliance, beginning an association with greatly-expanding powers and unfortunate future consequences for all world citizens, a union which soon earned the infamous label of "the military-industrial complex." Thus, the notion of "peace," so new and so hard-won, was aggressively put on the back burner so that new adversaries could haunt the dreams of citizens, terrifying them into accepting a runaway military-industrial machine. Early in the decade, Secretary of State John Foster Dulles introduced the concept of "massive retaliation," a theory of military overkill against potential enemies which largely paved the way for the rapidly-blossoming Cold War ethos and increased military spending, including expensive ongoing projects such as the Strategic Air Command. As well, "little wars" were courted and waged to keep the military machine in readiness and operational and to justify ever-accelerating military spending. Although, politically speaking, the U.S. entered the Korean War reluctantly, as some military commanders saw it as the potential start of World War III, hotter heads prevailed, and several years and untold lives were sacrificed so that the U.S. military could maintain its cruel hegemony, both at home and abroad. Meanwhile, another small war, in a tiny country called Vietnam, was bubbling under the surface during the entire decade, preparing to burst into world consciousness some years later. Among considerations for both Korea and Vietnam at one time was the use of atomic bombs to decimate the areas, a sure sign that the U.S. military had reached a moral crossroads which it was completely unprepared to navigate.[3]

With plans unchallenged and expenditures unchecked, military defense spending became by far the largest factor in the 1950s economy. The military-industrial complex was perhaps the biggest single political-government force to rule the 1950s — by mid-decade, the aircraft industry was the United States' single largest employer. C. Wright Mills even penned a popular book, *The Power Elite*, which chronicled the increasing influence of the giant corporation in America. President Eisenhower was famously wary of the growth of this merger of military might with scientific insight and industrial might, built in large part on fabricated threats and imaginary enemies, but by and large found no support for his misgivings. According to David Halberstam, "Eisenhower's last three years as President saw him virtually alone on this issue, standing up to a powerful array of critics in insisting that America had more than enough defense, that there was no missile gap, and that the nation's security was not in jeopardy."[4]

The Atomic Dawn

J. Robert Oppenheimer, considered the "father" of the atomic bomb, and later one of its first political casualties, considered the use of these weapons on civilian populations to be a grievous error of state: "Hiroshima was a blunder and Nagasaki was a crime." Meanwhile, Republican hawks such as Senator Brien McMahon countered, "The bombing of Hiroshima… was the greatest event in world history since the birth of Jesus Christ."[5] (The highly disturbed McMahon also lobbied for the atomic bombing of Japan's Imperial Navy *after* the decimated nation had surrendered unconditionally.)[6] Considerations of ethics aside, the military-industrial cabal formed in haste during the Manhattan Project, which had by the end of the war built up an ominous, soon-to-be self-perpetuating infrastructure, made sure that the development and deployment (if only in simulated combat conditions) of ever-more powerful thermonuclear weapons of destruction would continue in earnest. The first major postwar exercise on the part of the U.S. military was Operation Crossroads, designed to test the effects of atomic bombing on a fleet of naval ships stationed near a tiny Pacific atoll named Bikini, about 2,000 miles southwest of Hawaii. Forty-two thousand personnel, 200 ships, and 150 airplanes were involved in this experiment, in which two weapons were detonated, with data collected afterwards to assess the impact on the surrounding region and the military hardware. Crossroads was also the infamous operation in which 109 mice, 3,030 rats, 146 pigs, 57 guinea pigs and 176 goats were imprisoned on the naval vessels, to be used as (by definition involuntary) "test subjects" to see the effects of radioactive decimation on mammalian life forms.[7] According to official Operation Crossroads publicity material, "Pigs were chosen because their skin and hair are fairly comparable to man's, and their bodily fluids are ample for analysis. Four goats were chosen because of their psychoneurotic tendencies." What is not mentioned in this sterile analysis of these animals' kinship to humans is that the experiments originally included a group of beagle dogs, a notion soon dropped due to unprecedented protesting by citizens, who fortunately got wind of it before the tests were launched.[8]

The Soviets detonated their first nuclear device in September 1949, thus launching the

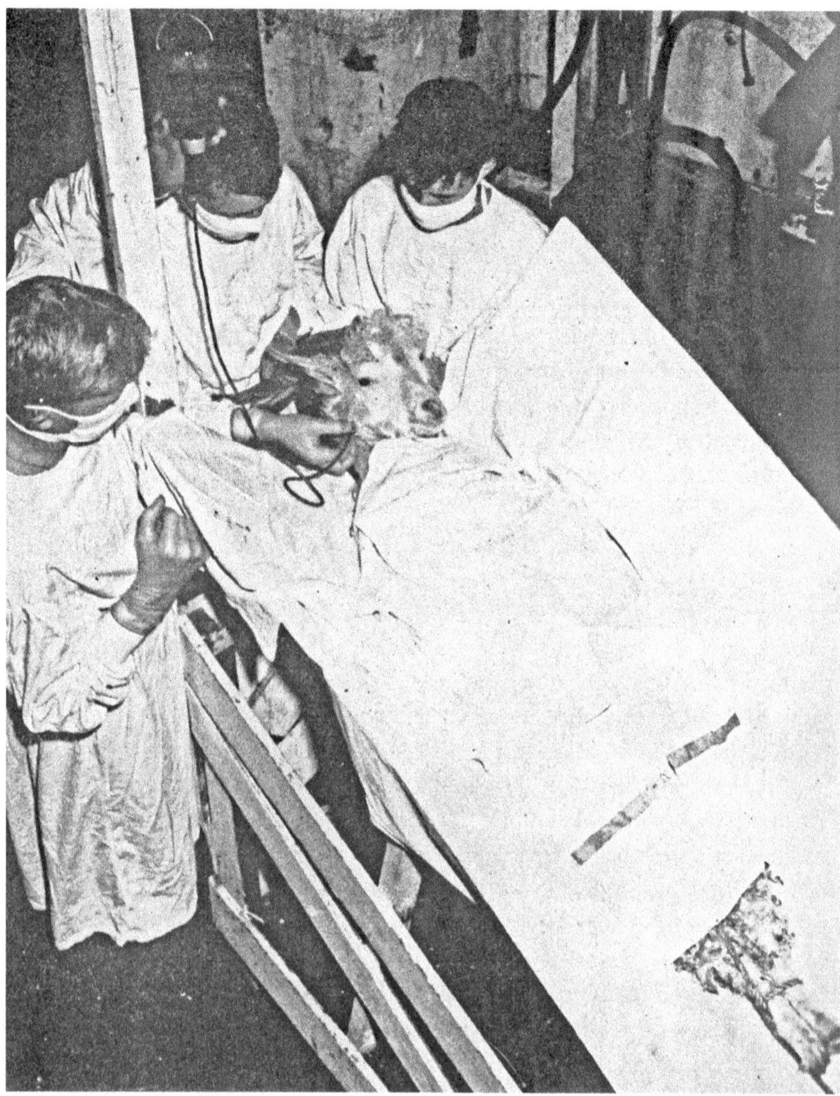

One of the goats used as a test subject to observe the effects of radiation exposure in the U.S. Navy's 1946 exercise Operation Crossroads is examined by doctors in a gruesome promotional photograph which could have easily come from Nazi Germany. The original caption read: "Of the animals used at Bikini about 35 percent were killed—10 percent by the air blast, 15 percent by radioactivity, and 10 percent by research workers after the tests."

Cold War in earnest and assuring that the 1950s would be one of deep secrets and high anxiety, the fear of global annihilation being the main agenda on the public's mind. The success of Operation Crossroads, the increasing gains of the Soviets, and the desire on the part of U.S. military and business interests to design and test increasingly powerful nuclear devices led to the creation of a bomb testing site in the United States, in the bleak deserts of Nevada. From 1951 through 1958, seven major test series were conducted in Nevada, as follows: Ranger (1951), Buster-Jangle (1951), Tumbler-Snapper (1952), Upshot-Knothole (1953), Teapot (1955), Plumbbob (1957) and Hardtack II (1958). All told, over 120 thermonuclear devices were detonated on American soil, with several volumes written on the deleterious environmental and health effects of the massive radiation released; as well, over 150,000 military personnel were exposed at various distances to radioactive releases from the bombs.[9]

Meanwhile, over roughly the same time period, the U.S.S.R. set off at least 50 similar devices. It seems obvious in hindsight that even at their most productive, the Soviet Union was in no position (or, arguably, mindset) to launch a preemptive attack on the United States, or any other declared enemy. However, this did not stop U.S. interests promulgating exactly that myth, so that their production and testing of such devices, and the vast amount of money being spent on same, could continue unmolested. To this end, many dubious reports were commissioned in order to discover the threat against all freedom-loving peoples; one such study, "Deterrence and Survival in the Nuclear Age," suggested a fearsome defense gap between the U.S. and the Soviet Union which, in fact, did not exist.

As fearsome as the atomic bomb was, certain minds were already thinking about building a "bigger, better" bomb that could kill even more people in one fell swoop. By 1949, after the Soviets had detonated their first atomic device, there was fierce debate behind closed doors over whether to proceed with a fusion-based thermonuclear weapon (originally called "the Super") which would offer immeasurably more destructive yield than the currently available fission-based devices. J. Robert Oppenheimer, co-inventor of the atomic bombs used on Hiroshima and Nagasaki, went on record as being morally opposed to the development of the "Super" bomb, a project which he considered tantamount to "genocide."[10] Yet Oppenheimer's partner in the Manhattan Project, Edward Teller, as well as the rabidly pro-nuclear Lewis Strauss, were formidable proponents of the development of what would eventually be labeled the "hydrogen bomb"; and by late 1949 the pressure to proceed with this diabolical new weapon of genocide was strong enough to convince President Truman to okay its development. After expenditures of over $2 billion, the first thermonuclear fusion device was detonated at Eniwetok, an atoll in the Pacific Ocean, on November 1, 1952. Part of "Operation Ivy," the "Mike" shot constituted the first use of a megaton-range hydrogen device (resultant yield = 10.4 megatons). The resulting fireball was over three miles wide, and the recorded fallout was extraordinary, even surpassing its creators' predictions. By November of 1955, the Soviets had conducted their first successful H-bomb blast in their ongoing attempt to "keep up with the Joneses," and the nuclear arms race was begun in earnest, a race with no winners and no perceivable finish line.

Atoms for Peace...

In the preface to a U.S. government publication called *Atoms for Peace*—which compiled the information culled from the International Conference on the Peaceful Uses of Atomic Energy, held in Geneva, Switzerland, in August 1955—Lewis Strauss, chairman of the recently-formed Atomic Energy Commission, proudly pontificated: "It is our sincere hope that this material will be of practical value to the men and women of science and engineering in whose hands the great power of the atom is becoming a benign force for world peace."[11] And so it was hoped that this so-called "Atoms for Peace" program—which promised everything from submarines, planes, trains and automobiles, even heart pumps and wristwatches, all fueled by the mighty atom—might take some of the taint off the split atom's only verified use thus far, as a weapon of horrible mass destruction.

Lewis Strauss and Edward Teller, two pro-nuclear "hawks," became the new guard of the atomic weapons program, along with the emergence of programs such as the Strategic Air Command, whose sole function was the delivery of atomic weapons to foreign lands. Strauss soon become head of the Atomic Energy Commission, a government agency ostensibly set up to monitor the safe use and logical parameters of nuclear technology, but soon seen as little more than the PR arm of the fledgling civilian atomic energy industry, whose interests it unflaggingly championed. Yet even while Strauss gushed on about the bountiful "peaceful" uses of atomic energy, he was simultaneously orchestrating decidedly "anti-peaceful" projects, such as the aerial surveillance of Soviet Russia, an early stealth program intended to gain secret knowledge of ongoing U.S.S.R. military operations.[12] Still, the use of atomic energy for peaceful consumer purposes was a highly visible mantra of the decade, and everyone for a time seemed to jump on the bandwagon; as Douglas T. Miller and Marion Nowak noted in their treatise on the era, "RCA's David Sarnoff predicted small atomic generators for every home, to provide a lifetime of power."[13]

Yet perhaps the most ludicrous — but seriously considered — fantasy in the entire "Atoms for Peace" program was Project Plowshare, begun circa 1953, which posited the use of atomic bombs to excavate tunnels, dig canals and modify other land masses for utilitarian purpose. In hindsight, the use of massive, mega-kiloton bombs to clear land and dig holes is quantifiably absurd, tantamount to using a shotgun to open a can of beans, but so obsessed were those in the "nuclear priesthood" with finding any perceivable use of atom bombs other than in the grotesque eradication of human life, that even this impossibly stupid idea was discussed in serious scientific circles for a time. Despite the obvious "overkill" of the concept, what finally killed the idea was the insurmountable problem of containing the released radioactive poisons that would contaminate the area to be cultivated, leaving it unsuitable indefinitely for any human use. The stubbornness of this same elementary problem of containing leaked radioactivity was the death knell (thankfully) for most of the consumer-oriented "Atoms for Peace" concepts involving planes, trains and automobiles, and personal appliances such as stoves, watches and pacemakers.

Yet the fearsome specter of "the Mighty Atom" still haunted the American populace in the form of the constant fear — fanned constantly by government and industry — of atomic attack from an unseen enemy (usually, but not always, the Soviet Union). In some ways the entire 1950s could be seen as a "decade of fear" in which Americans (and certainly other nations as well) lived in chronic terror that something horrendous from above would drop on them unexpectedly, disintegrating them, their loved ones, and everything they knew. The fact that some citizens saw clearly enough to realize that this fear was largely a guilt response to the cruel fate which the United States, in their name, had recently realized on a foreign nation and her citizens did little to relieve the nagging suspicion that "the enemy," being godless Communists disdainful of human life, might do exactly the same to them, at any time, without warning. The 1950s thus simmered in a continual atomic culture of fear, with extraordinary emphasis laid on dubious preemptive notions such as personal fallout shelters and civil-defense attack preparation.

Yet comments on the aftermath — and, to some, the inevitability — of a dreaded "nuclear war" were peppered throughout the media, surely as much to instill fear as to educate. For instance, in mid-decade, civil defense administrator Val Peterson was quoted as stating, "If nuclear war occurs, it is going to be stark, elemental, brutal, filthy and miserable."[14] Herman

The atomic age spawned many things, including a short-lived consumer industry — offering everything from Geiger counters to fallout shelters — promising to protect the populace against the ravages of (presumably enemy) radioactive fallout. This advertisement from a 1955 issue of *Popular Mechanics* offered flimsy vinyl coveralls to protect its wearer against the ravages of atomic attack — a dubious claim at best.

Kahn, a Rand scientist, was one of the first to publish books casually predicting ghastly destruction of all life due to all-out thermonuclear war. Children especially were indoctrinated in atomic attack preparation via the now-campy exercises known as "Duck and Cover." In these foolish and surely ineffectual drills, youngsters were encouraged to hide under their beds or school desks if inside, or to fall to the ground if outside, all the while crouching and covering their heads with their hands. One cannot help but see in these ritual submissive postures some rather curious allusions to the superstitious devout falling on their knees in abject submission to a diabolically cruel Old Testament god; in this sense, then, fear of nuclear destruction segues almost seamlessly into a devout (if timorous) worship of the split atom as an omnipotent, if dreadful, man-hating deity.

As well, the private atomic fallout shelter became a viable consumer notion circa 1950. These strange and creepy miniature domiciles took on many different shapes and constructions, but the most popular one, sold widely and given impressive media coverage, was a concrete tank, not dissimilar to an underground fuel storage tank, with a porthole on top. This tank would be sunk into the ground in the homeowner's back yard, with only the escape hatch at ground level. Inside the bunker, a family would theoretically exist comfortably for days or weeks — with food, water, air and light — until the nuclear Armageddon above ground subsided, and it was safe to come outside again. The diabolical father of the H-Bomb, Edward Teller, stated categorically that "it is necessary to provide every person in the U.S. with a shelter."[15] Yet, curiously, the U.S. government — which had introduced the idea of the family fallout shelter — refused to provide funding for the project, leaving it up to the individual homeowner to take the financial risk of purchasing protection for his family should World War III break out. Thus, only the most well-heeled were able to take this golden opportunity to save themselves, and to hell with their neighbors. Yet many observed that the private fallout shelter was not only an elitist notion, it was, in fact, completely ill-conceived and would surely be ineffective in its intended usage. As many in Hiroshima and Nagasaki found out, the home bomb shelter is worthless against the all-consuming ravages of thermonuclear warfare. Those in these ill-fated cities who did as instructed by their government, and dug deep trenches under their houses as ersatz "bomb shelters," were among the first to be roasted alive by the diabolical heat of the atomic explosions, which incinerated the ground for up to ten feet beneath the surface.[16] Bertrand Russell later confirmed this eventuality: "In a firestorm, the misinformed refugees in deep shelters would either be incinerated or die from lack of oxygen."[17] Equally ludicrous was the so-called "personal fallout suit" advertised in magazines by many mail-order establishments, usually nothing more than heavily-lined canvas overalls and a headpiece with a flimsy plastic windshield. Needless to say, these suits could not possibly protect wearers from anything but perhaps a chest X-ray, and to suggest otherwise was more than disingenuous.

Meanwhile, the military did its utmost to keep the public alarmed and fearful. In 1948 a "trial" atomic bomb run was flown over Dayton, Ohio, and was subsequently declared an unmitigated disaster, in that the entire city would be summarily destroyed. In 1951, in a military project called Operation Wakeup, planes dropped leaflets over Los Angeles, explaining them to be ciphers for a surprise atomic attack, which would have, of course, killed anyone who picked up and read the note. Eventually worn out from the continual "bombardment" of atomic nightmares, Americans uneasily learned to "love the bomb," as they could not in any other way comprehend or justify its awful existence. Thus the mantra of "the bomb" was used as mass psychological leverage to keep a potentially unruly or critical populace in line; in this way the U.S. scared its own citizens into obedience as much as it threatened other nations. As Miller and Nowak note, "Americans were manipulated by and through the bomb. They backed away from the threats of war and McCarthyism, and rushed instead into dreams of domesticity, religion, material conformity. Their leaders encouraged this turning away from both political power and autonomy."[18]

The cultural resonance of this continual assault on the people's fears of annihilation led to its appropriation in culture; bestselling doomsday fiction such as Nevil Shute's *On the Beach* and Walter Miller's *A Canticle for Leibowiz* obsessed on the potential horrors of atomic warfare. And indeed, the contradiction inherent in "loving the bomb" is the cause of much of the narrative tension seen in many of the films we will be discussing. Ambivalence, if not outright aversion, about the use of atomic weapons on civilian populations is peppered throughout the year's fantastic films. Yes these films also often obsess on and some might say even glorify the awful magic of the split atom, portraying atomic energy as a modern-day genie in an uncorkable bottle. The amount of screen time spent ruminating on, and endlessly showing stock footage of, the horrible beauty of the rising mushroom cloud amounts in the end to little short of a fetish, an objectification of something that, while ostensibly denounced in the films' narratives, was alternately being worshiped. As the massive amount of military footage used in the fantastic films of 1957 must have been approved for release by the military-industrial complex, one may only assume that the use of such footage served its creators in one form or another: perhaps it was meant to do nothing more sinister than scare the pants off the movie-going public, or perhaps it was meant to covertly increase fascination with, and thus tolerance toward, this newfound trigger for Armageddon.

Incredible Melting Man

One of the primary fears that people naturally intuited about this newly-harnessed power was the possibility of defect, deformity and death which radioactivity might cause, either in immediate consequence of an atomic weapons blast or, more insidiously, through long-term effects of the many highly-poisonous gases thus released (euphemistically named "fallout" by the powers that be). Indeed, if the American public had been made aware of the unspeakable devastation which the atom bombs dropped on two Japanese cities had wreaked on the thousands of innocent citizens residing there, they would have been enraged at their government for utilizing such a barbaric and cruel weapon — even on a proclaimed "enemy" — and would likely have vetoed any attempt to push atomic power during peacetime in the service of electrical generation or any other, highly suspect utilization. But all of the information gathered on the aftermath of the first atomic bombings — a database which grew to hundreds of volumes — was kept a closely guarded secret for many years, ostensibly in the interests of "national security," but more importantly so that the world at large would not understand the horror of what the United States had done to defenseless men, women and children.

According to official reports, many persons in both Hiroshima and Nagasaki were instantly killed by "flash burns" — an intense blast of searingly hot radiation emanating from the bomb upon detonation that in essence roasted them alive.[19] Ironically speaking, these may have been the lucky ones, as they probably did not know what hit them, and had but a fraction of a second to endure what must surely have been unbearable pain. Less lucky were the many thousands who "survived" the initial explosion and were thus subjected to waves of intense heat, surges of lethal radioactive gases, and blasts of wind of a velocity far greater that those of hurricane force. Those who did not then shortly die from falling debris, the many fires which raged throughout the target site, or severe trauma from blast injury, were subjected to the slow, painful death due to intense skin burns and the scourge of radioactivity. Official U.S. reports detailed the death suffered by thousands of Japanese citizens from radiation poisoning, which usually followed a similar pattern: loss of hair, bleeding of the skin, inflammation of the mouth and eyes, internal hemorrhage, chronic vomiting and bloody diarrhea. These symptoms were invariably accompanied by high fever and resulted, almost invariably, in death.[20]

According to Samuel Glasstone, who authored many radiation studies for the U.S. government, "Very large doses of whole-body radiation, e.g., 5,000 roentgens or more, result in very rapid injury to the central nervous system. The symptoms are hyperexcitability, ataxia (lack of muscular coordination), respiratory distress, and intermittent stupor. There is almost immediate incapacitation, and death is certain in a few hours to a week or so after the acute exposure."[21] What this clinical, if disturbing, description of death by radiation poisoning does not convey is the acute pain and sheer terror suffered by the victims, as one has to read between the lines in order to intuit the immeasurable suffering visited on this group of unlucky humans in that hot, fateful August of 1945.

Total initial casualties from the atomic bombing of Hiroshima are estimated at over 100,000, with over 100,000 more severely wounded; many of these likely perished some time later due to injuries inflicted by the bomb. As for Nagasaki, which also suffered the ravages of a 20-kiloton atomic device, official estimates, based on the reported population of the city pre-detonation, are 36,000 to 39,000 dead, and 25,000 to 40,000 injured.[22] Yet even with a concerted effort on the part of the military to downplay this mass murder of Japanese citizens, and the subsequent, widely chronicled deleterious effects of radiation, people intuited that there was more to the story than was being told, and by mid-decade there was growing evidence, from various quarters, that something was radically changing the environment in ways not known before the uncorking of the atomic genie. Cancer, virtually unknown before the atomic age, was by 1957 claiming over 250,000 lives a year. Some observers also blamed a polio epidemic in the early 1950s on fallout from atomic testing.

One unfortunate incident which did receive fairly wide publicity — even prompting an official rebuttal from the head of the Atomic Energy Commission — did confirm growing public concern about the health consequences of exposure to even minimal or "secondhand" radioactive fallout. One of the largest so-called "Super" hydrogen bombs was tested on March 1, 1954. The fallout was extraordinary — even by predicted scientific standards — blanketing many areas of the nearby (inhabited) Marshall Islands with dense clouds of radioactive mist. Yet the worst of the fallout drifted slowly out to sea and eventually enveloped the crew of a Japanese fishing vessel, *Fukuru Maru* (aka Lucky Dragon), which was trawling for tuna a hundred miles east of Bikini Atoll, the site of the nuclear testing. The crew of the *Fukuru Maru* later reported that they experienced shock waves and menacing, thick clouds shortly after the bomb blast.[23] The crew of the Japanese fishing vessel, upon returning home, all suffered the symptoms of severe radiation sickness: nausea, fever, aches and skin lesions. One crew member, Aikichi Kuboyama, fell terribly ill, becoming the central figure to be associated with the accident. Kuboyama died from his illness on September 23, 1954. Ralph Lapp even wrote a bestselling book, *Voyage of the Lucky Dragon*, about the fate of the *Fukuru Maru* and its men. Faced with anger and questions from a growing segment of the population, AEC head Lewis Strauss was forced to make a public statement; as expected, he dismissed the tragedy as a conspiracy by America's enemies in an attempt to undermine the atomic energy program. Yet the fate of Aikichi Kuboyama lived on in popular memory by turning up as the narrative basis for one of 1957's most popular and talked-about fantastic films, *The Incredible Shrinking Man*, which had its protagonist suffer a suspiciously similar exposure before becoming the titular disintegrating person.

At this same time, the AEC had done statistical health studies which suggested that as many as 13,000 instances of genetic birth defects could likely cite radioactive fallout from the testing of nuclear weapons as a major source. Of course, this information was kept from the public, and only shared with concerned industry professionals. Strontium-90 is one of the most dangerous fallout products of atomic testing, one which targets bone marrow, and is thus extremely deleterious to the growth and well-being of young mammals. Yet the AEC continued its stonewalling, forcing the free press to bring some version of the truth to light: "In 1959, *Nation* magazine reported the AEC was refusing to make public a report ("Project Sunshine") showing that Strontium-90 levels in the bones of American babies up to age four had doubled in the one-year period ending December 1957."[24]

Around mid-decade, the popular media took up the issue of radioactive fallout with increasing vigor, accurately reflecting the populace's fears regarding the ability of atomic energy to distort and mangle human (and other) life. As noted by Miller and Nowak:

> The possibility of deformity grew ever more prominent in the mass consciousness. Many photo magazines carried pictorial essays on horrifying laboratory experiments. One such feature, in the *National Geographic*, showed lab mice with huge malignant tumors, induced experimentally. *Life* showed photos of disfigured survivors of Hiroshima and Nagasaki. But these things, while real, did not quite answer the most fearful public questions: could fallout create human monsters? Did fallout cause congenital or genetic damage?[25]

Soon, popular culture took hold of the more fanciful aspects of this specter of self-induced defect and deformity, creating fictional platforms (stories, novels, comic books and films, primarily) which vividly brought to life people's worst — largely repressed — nightmares about the "marvels" of the atomic age:

> The fiction of holocaust and deformity was one expression of (atomic-age) fears. The novels and comics that predicted genetic monsters represent a degree of rebellion against officialdom. By fantasizing a future filled with freaks and horrors, Americans rejected the nuclear safety message.[26]

The unholy mixture of guilt, fear and fascination towards this ungodly force so recently uncapped by man is well illustrated by the preponderance of fantastic films in the 1950s that reference the mutation of men, animals, plants, and even rocks, often directly due to exposure to atomic radiation (and even when not based on such exposure, surely symbolized by same). This mutation often takes the rather simplistic, if vivid, form of gigantism, in which things of normal size are expanded to grotesque proportions due to foolhardy radiological experimentation. These unleashed "giants" stand as metaphors for the devastating potential of out-of-control nuclear energy, a most concrete fear of the day. In 1957, giant mutant creatures (usually, but not always, birthed by reckless atomic experiments) appear in *Attack of the Crab Monsters, The Monster from Green Hell, The Monster That Challenged the World, The Giant Claw, Beginning of the End, X: The Unknown, The Cyclops, From Hell It Came, The Amazing Colossal Man, Rodan, the Flying Monster, The Deadly Mantis* and *The Monolith Monsters.*

The preponderance of "atomic mutant" films in the fifties has a curious significance, considering their target audience. Inundated as they were by the radioactive fallout of hundreds of bomb blasts on their own soil, the baby boom generation was the first group of radioactive mutants in the history of the world. The population was, in effect, an epidemic-scale scientific experiment to see how a contaminated sampling of beings would function. It is now well-known that constant low levels of radioactivity impact most gravely the newborn and the young, so it is exactly this population which would be most adversely affected by any changes to their physiology due to this new assault on their bodies. And as history later proved, the general consensus was that this group was the first generation to burn out and suffer massive failure in their socio-economic endeavors. It was also the first generation successfully trained as a mass to become obedient consumers and debt slaves. So, in effect, as children and teenagers watched the gruesome deformed atomic mutants slither across their movie and television screens, they were seeing their diseased, mutating bodies reflected back at them, reinforcing a certain combination of self-loathing and fascination with deformity that subsequently became obsessions of that unlucky generation. Teenagers in 1957 surely saw a reflection of themselves in films such as *I Was a Teenage Werewolf, I Was a Teenage Frankenstein, Blood of Dracula* and *Teenage Monster,* in which personal dissolution of the young protagonist is triggered by a malevolent elder who, if not using radioactive elements directly, certainly represents an authoritative establishment who recklessly uses Science on unwitting innocents in diabolical experiments which further their own nefarious personal and political agendas.

Allied with this horror of mutated freaks of nature is the fear of dissolution and transformation of the personal self, also due to tinkering with diabolical nuclear forces beyond anyone's capacity to control. That this radical mutation of the personal self often took the form of severe bodily deformity also hints at Man's guilt towards his unleashed Leviathan of the Atom. This fear of a scientific horror without end is embraced in many fantastic films of 1957, in which the scenario clearly paints a picture of the immanent destruction of planet earth, often triggered by reckless human events. *The Incredible Shrinking Man* and *The Amazing Colossal Man* are the two fantastic films of 1957 which, in starkly allegorical terms, depict the painful and inevitable dissolution of the individual in a world rendered uninhabitable due to the never-ending scourge of atomic radiation. As well, *Not of This Earth, The 27th Day, Enemy from Space, The Brain from Planet Arous, 1000 Years from Now* and *Invasion, U.S.A.* all reference a civilization rendered desolate by the foolhardy use of atomic weapons.

It may have been wishful thinking, naïveté, or deliberate government-sponsored propaganda that the earth is saved from annihilation in many of the year's fright films only by the efforts of the U.S. military, seen at this moment by the country (and possibly some of the world) as the savior of the planet and the only bulwark of Man against monstrous tyrants like the just-deposed Hitler and "paper tiger" enemies like the Soviet Union. The U.S. military-industrial complex, which would soon become a hydra-headed monster of infamy, was in its infancy during the mid-to-late 1950s, so the insistence upon virtual hero-worship of the military in fantastic films of this time period is highly suspect. The preeminence of the military as the "hero" in many fifties fantastic films may in fact have been purposeful disinformation, a propaganda campaign on the part of various government and business interests, with the help of obliging Hollywood producers, to paint themselves as saviors of modern civilization rather than its probable destroyers.

The Devil in Your Own Back Yard!

One of the main thrusts of the aforementioned "Atoms for Peace" campaign, one which took root and forced itself upon the world, was the potential for using an atomic chain reaction to generate electrical power. Hyman Rickover, a Navy admiral, had succeeded in developing a pressurized water-based atomic reactor for use in the propulsion of military submarines — in itself one of the most advantageous and effective uses of atomic energy for non-lethal purposes. Sadly, this reactor system, inherently designed for use in a confined space in order to power one relatively small vehicle, was adopted as the basic blueprint for a proposed series of civilian power plants nationwide. These electricity-generating power plants would contain a nuclear reactor which would create and sustain an atomic chain reaction in the service of turning cauldrons of water into steam; this pressurized steam would then spin steam turbines, which would then generate vast amounts of electrical power for the surrounding area.

On paper this looked a good concept, perhaps, but in practice, as history has shown, it is one riddled with conceptual and practical design flaws, some of which were known at the time and many others of which were revealed later, sometimes in catastrophic ways. For starters, the "scaling up" of Rickover's efficient "little" naval reactors to sometimes obscene proportions increased exponentially the potential risk for various catastrophic failures. Secondly, the extraordinarily complex system of valves, pipes and filters needed to safely and efficiently operate one of these raging behemoths was prone to mishap and failure merely from a statistical point of view, based on the number of overlapping systems which had to perform perfectly in concord for indefinite periods of time. Third, the basic absurdity of placing such a volatile — and largely untested — new technology next to or near large population centers seems in hindsight an almost diabolical game of "Russian Roulette" played by government and industry with the nation's (and eventually the world's) citizens.

Yet the final nail in the coffin for this doomed industry came from a dangerous, shortsighted decision made early in the program's development. While the pressurized-water system which Rickover had overseen was by and large safe and efficient, it had, as one of its demonstrable downsides, extreme expense in design, construction and maintenance, largely due to the intricacies of maintaining a safe environment utilizing huge amounts of pressurized water within a highly radioactive atmosphere. Scientists at the Atomic Energy Commission, along with engineers at General Electric and Westinghouse, soon came up with a reactor design that simplified Rickover's PWR concept and utilized a large basin of boiling water as the turbine propulsion source, as opposed to pressurized steam. The primary advantage of such a system was its relative cost in design, construction and operation, which promised to be significantly less than that associated with the creation and maintenance of PWR units.

However, the inherent faults in boiling-water reactor (BWR) design were numerous, almost all of them involving the underlying integrity of the unit and its ability to operate safely in areas which might be adversely impacted by leaks of radioactive steam. Worse yet, a corruption of the reactor's containment was a conceivable consequence, which might leak deadly radioactive poisons into the atmosphere, airborne toxins that could negatively impact the environment for long periods. Regardless of these possibly fatal flaws, the BWR design was the one chosen for immediate implementation, and work proceeded at a feverish pace to bring these atomic "monsters" to life right in America's own back yard. From its inception, the civilian atomic power plant program was fraught with faulty science, bad statistics, secretive dealings hidden from the public, and in many cases outright lies. From the beginning — and likely as an official policy of the AEC — both the reality of atomic power's promises and the dangers of its potential failings were either highly manipulated or outright ignored. Propaganda pieces of the day trumpeted the glories of electricity "too cheap to meter," all but ignoring the potential for catastrophic accident should these impossibly complex machines malfunction. By 1957, a big push was on for convincing the public of the necessity, and safety, of atomic power plants.

One of many ways in which the public was manipulated regarding the real nature of atomic power was through the deliberate obfuscation of fact, both through false statements of inherent safety and the convenient omission of unsavory details about the units. One example involves the necessity of power plants having smoke stacks in order to continually vent radioactive effluents, a potential "smoking gun" which the AEC and the atomic industry desperately wanted to minimize if not eradicate entirely. Their solution was to act as if these stacks did not exist. As Miller and Nowak note:

> In manipulating facts, nuclear interests could also manipulate people. One minor example concerned the artists' conceptions of planned atomic facilities, which often showed the future plant to be free of smokestacks. In fossil-fuel plants, these stacks notoriously dispersed unpleasant pollutants into the air. To depict nuclear power plants as lacking such stacks was a very subtle deletion. Yet when the plant was completed, it would have stacks. These would then be explained as for "ventilation purposes only."[27]

Of course, these stacks "ventilated" radioactive gases constantly. Indeed, it was not until the early 1960s when it was finally revealed that the omnipresent stacks at nuclear facilities regularly released significantly radioactive effluents into the atmosphere, constant low-level emissions which many say have had a notable, deleterious impact on the environment. Should one desire to give the atomic industry the benefit of the doubt and assume they were unsure whether atomic power plants would generate radioactive effluents that would need to be released into the atmosphere, a quick look at the literature of the time gives lie to that comforting notion. A 1949 article in *Astounding Science Fiction* magazine, for example, describes the construction and operation of the new atomic pile at Brookhaven National Laboratories in New York:

> The laboratory workers around the pile naturally have no desire to breathe in any of the "hot" hot air coming from the pile — the heat the thermometers read they don't mind; it's the "hot" signaled by ionization chambers and Geiger-tubes that they object to. The stack is designed to exhaust the air, contaminated with radioisotopes from its passage through the heart of the atomic furnace, at a height where it will be harmlessly carried away. The reactor will not be operated unless the wind-direction and air conditions are favorable — i.e., will carry the exhaust in a safe direction.[28]

Considering the admission that the reactor is "contaminated with radioisotopes from its passage through the heart of the atomic furnace," what is amazing about this passage is the cavalier attitude taken towards these highly radioactive particles. Assuming that the "hot" particles will be "harmlessly carried away" by the wind is a most short-sighted viewpoint, as the still-hot particles are obviously entering the environment via this delivery system. Further, the notion that the wind "will carry the exhaust in a safe direction" begs the question: what is a safe direction? Away from the plant? Away from population areas? The extraordinary naiveté in this passage suggests both the blindness and arrogance of the nascent atomic power industry, which chose not to address the dangers it was creating as long as its deleterious effects left the immediate area of their creation, a most sinister and chilling illustration of the "out of sight, out of mind" mentality of the atomic power industry.

As disturbing as was the known but unaddressed eventuality of atomic power plants releasing low-level radioactivity into the environment, there was the even more distressing notion advanced by scientists that the atomic reactor, under constant, intense pressure, might under certain conditions rupture and explode. The industry had already taken great pains to convince the public that atomic reactors could not "blow up" like an atomic bomb, a statement which is ostensibly true: under no circumstances could an atomic reactor *detonate* like a thermo-nuclear weapon because the design principle is entirely different. Yet this reassurance is disingenuous because it denies the possibility that a *conventional* explosion, either through a chemical reaction or an untoward accumulation of pressurized gases, could happen at an atomic reactor, breaching the nuclear containment and releasing a large amount of highly radioactive particles into the surrounding community. This was perhaps the greatest "dirty secret" of the nascent atomic power industry, and great efforts were made to deny or downplay this assuredly unsettling possibly.

Yet so concerned was the industry about this very same potentiality that in 1957 the AEC commissioned a report which would detail the potential consequences of just such an accident at a civilian atomic power plant. The report was carried out by the Brookhaven National Laboratories in New York. The results, when submitted, were horrifying and immediately suppressed; to this day the contents of this report remain obscure. The gist of the report was that following such a catastrophic accident a large number of deaths, a greater number of injuries, and an inordinate amount of property and infrastructure damage could be expected.

The goal for the AEC and the reactor manufacturers became, then, not to correct the inherent design flaws in the atomic reactor program, but to aggressively attempt to underestimate or obscure them, to avoid undesired objection to the fast expansion of the nascent nuclear power industry. Hundreds of books and thousands of documents have since chronicled the systematic efforts on the part of the AEC and the reactor manufacturers to obfuscate, sabotage and suppress in order to squelch undesirable criticism in their quest to foist atomic energy on the public, whether they wanted it or not. Even when such morally dubious — and often illegal — antics did eventually reach the public, it was invariably too late to have an impact. Miller and Nowak note:

> Some exposes of AEC suppression only made the papers too late to have any effect. Such was the case in 1956, when AEC chairman Lewis Strauss suppressed a report that opposed the building of the Fermi reactor. Fermi was slated for the highly populated Detroit area, on a major watershed. Strauss kept the report secret until the construction permit had been approved and building commenced.[29]

The commercial atomic power plant project went forward at full speed, pestered only by occasional objections from concerned citizens and honorable judges, none of which were able to stop this hellish atomic juggernaut from gaining a stronghold in the U.S., and eventually the world. It was late in that pivotal year of 1957 when the first prototype civilian atomic power plant "went critical" (i.e., maintained a sustained chain reaction in order to generate electricity). Located in Shippingport, Pennsylvania, a mere 25 miles from Pittsburgh, this historic joint project of the Atomic Energy Commission, Westinghouse, and Duquesne Lighting Company was heralded as a showcase for the bright future of the atomic power industry. An early study, collated from samples of water in the Ohio River after it had passed through the power planet, noted virtually "zero releases" of radioactive effluents and was thus submitted as evidence of atomic power's negligible impact on the environment.[30]

Yet from the start, this claim of a supposed prototype of a "safe" atomic reactor was disingenuous on several levels, the first being that the highly specialized pressurized-water reactor used at Shippingport was unlike the designs proposed for use in any other commercial power plants, and so its operation was not comparable to future projects. According to Ernest Sternglass, a dedicated nuclear physicist who finally brought the tragic lies about this poster child of the atomic age to light, "The Shippingport reactor was in fact a prototype naval propulsion plant owned by the Navy and the AEC, and not a commercial power plant at all."[31] In the early 1970s, Sternglass uncovered some unsettling health statistics from the area directly surrounding the Shippingport plant, including significant increases in infant mortality rates, along with higher-than-average incidence of lung and pancreatic cancer among local citizens in the area.[32] Sternglass subsequently analyzed reports commissioned by the plant's owners, which chronicled radiation levels in the surrounding region. Sternglass was horrified to discover data which verified abnormally high rates of various gamma- and beta-emitting radionuclides, including high levels of strontium–90 and cesium–137, in nearby soil and water samples.

Sternglass concluded that the plant's own data suggested that "the Shippingport plant must have been the source of radioactivity in the environment many thousands of times as great as had been claimed in the official reports to state and federal agencies."[33] Of course, when Sternglass announced these findings publicly, they were immediately attacked by the AEC and Duquesne Lighting, who vociferously defended their dubious official data, stating categorically that the radiation levels in the water discharged into the Ohio River from the plant were absolutely minimal. Sternglass then clarified the situation: "The radioactivity did not come from the direct liquid discharges, but through the run-off of unreported gaseous releases that has settled on the land." That is, the bulk of the radioactive releases were airborne discharges of radioactive gases, conveniently ignored and unreported by those charged with monitoring public health.[34] As Sternglass described the situation: "It was the airborne gaseous activity and the run-off into the rivers serving as drinking-water supplies that had apparently carried the more damaging short-lived beta-ray-emitting chemicals rapidly into the critical organs of the people, in addition to the other pathways via the milk, the vegetables, the fruit, the fish and the meat that were most important for the long-lived strontium–90 and cesium–137."[35]

In the subsequent highly contentious hearings that followed, the AEC and their hired "independent" consultants rigorously defended their earlier claims of Shippingport's benign impact on the environment, applying many tactics in an attempt to discredit Sternglass and his findings. Yet in the end, even one of the consultants hired by the AEC to defend their official statements was forced to concede that "the Shippingport area may not be the greatest place to live...."[36] Yet so important was the reputation of this flagship atomic power plant to the future of the industry that every possible step was taken to bury or otherwise minimize publicity surrounding these hearings and their often-dire revelations. This may also explain why a serious early accident at Shippingport was kept from all public records, its details and impact remaining obscure even today.[37]

A Nightmare Come True!

As mentioned, a dominant theme of the 1950s was the vacillation between fear and fascination towards the potential of atomic energy as both healer and destroyer, residing uneasily alongside a wide vein of attendant guilt towards same. Perhaps not ironically, in our main year of interest, 1957, the atomic menace yielded several historical atrocities not far removed from the fantastic scenarios depicted onscreen. Above-ground atomic and hydrogen bomb testing by the U.S. military reached a fever pitch during 1957, with a massive series of tests collected in an operation called "Plumbbob." The series of 29 thermonuclear explosions (dubbed "shots"), launched from May 28 to October 7, 1957, eerily coincided with the "release" of the bulk of the fantastic films of the year, many of which, as will be seen, dealt directly with the threat of nuclear energy run amok. Indeed, the final test, "Shot Morgan," was ignited on October 7, conceivably at the same moment that an atomic reactor halfway across the globe fell victim to a runaway nuclear conflagration, as will be discussed shortly. The cumulative tests under the operation called "Plumbbob" led to a record amount of radioactive fallout, which contaminated not only populaces near the test sites but all over the country, and indeed measurable the world over. Some years later it would be discovered that mass

The dread many males felt in the atomic decade was taboo to express outwardly, so was sublimated in popular culture. In the movies, man's misgivings towards his "brave new world" were expressed in several ways. First was the "screaming woman," an omnipresent fixture in the thriller and horror genres, whose vocal release exorcised the audiences' collective angst. Second was the tradition of the film clown, such as the inimitable Huntz Hall, whose grotesque cowardice safely vented emotions considered unmanly (even "un–American"). Here, Hall is pictured as he appeared in the 1957 "Bowery Boys" comedy-fantasy *Looking for Danger.*

health problems in the U.S. could be directly linked to the fallout spewing from the 1957 bomb tests. Yet even more disturbing was the assignment of some 16,000 troops brought in to "observe" several of the detonations, and to perform combat maneuvers shortly after the blasts in the direct path of the radioactive clouds of death. A large number of these soldiers later contracted various life-threatening illnesses — leukemia most prominently — and successfully sued the federal government for compensation, as it was eventually proven that their exposure to dangerous radioactive fallout in 1957 was a primary cause of their debilitation.[38]

And in yet more gruesome cases of "life imitating art," two catastrophic radiological accidents — both occurring at hastily-constructed plutonium manufacturing facilities within a week of each other in late 1957 — threatened to dwarf even the most horrific nightmare fables of unleashed atomic energy being shown at that very moment on the nation's movie screens. In the late afternoon of September 29 of that fateful year, a cataclysmic chemical explosion shattered the Mayak plutonium manufacturing facility, ensconced deep within a top-secret military complex known as Chelyabinsk-65 near the Southern Ural Mountains in the U.S.S.R. The horrific accident spewed an incalculable amount of radioactive particles into the atmosphere, drenching the nearby environment. Due to the Cold War, this world-shaking disaster — seen by some as surpassing even the environmental impact of the Chernobyl disaster in 1986 — went unreported by U.S.S.R. sources and was thus unknown at the time to world media. However, the U.S. government apparently soon became aware of the accident, as it launched a U-2 spy plane mission to the area to assess the damage. Reports which surfaced much later describe the accident as one of unparalleled devastation, causing many casualties and contaminating the land and air for miles around, a contamination which continues to this day.[39]

Indeed, a most ominous development regarding the accident, reported decades later by survivors, is that at the time only *some* of the nearby residents were evacuated and/or relocated; others, chosen perhaps along racial lines and seen by some as "human guinea pigs," were encouraged to stay at their current location and are subject, to this day, to yearly health inspections by mysterious "doctors" who come and go quickly — often without a word of explanation.[40] Equally disturbing, according to a Greenpeace report on the disaster, was the discovery that maps of the region published in the 1970s — some years after the accident — exclude over 30 villages formerly located near Chelyabinsk-65, suggesting that entire towns were "disappeared" in the interest of national security. The fate of the inhabitants, of course, remains unknown.[41]

Meanwhile, a mere week later, in a sleepy town called Seascale in the United Kingdom, a crudely-constructed plutonium factory dubbed Windscale suffered a critical accident when its uranium pile became overheated, and all attempts to quench the rapidly-spreading atomic fire seemed doomed. The potentially catastrophic accident began on October 7 and continued for almost a week, when, as a last resort, the pile was drowned with water. This partial meltdown of a uranium pile led to a massive release of radioactive isotopes into the environment, particularly the deadly Iodine-131.[42] The release was considered so potentially hazardous to the region that drastic emergency measures were taken, the most notable of which was the government-mandated destruction of all fresh milk in the area for weeks afterwards.[43] Although the Windscale accident created nowhere near the devastation caused by the Mayak disaster, it doesn't take a nuclear physicist to realize that had the Mayak explosion occurred at Windscale, in the heart of a thriving nation, it would have easily decimated that nation, killing off much of the population and for all practical purposes rendering that country obsolete. Windscale, it could be said, was a "near-miss," an accident which could have been—and by some accounts was destined at one point to become—much, much worse. This playing of "Russian Roulette" with a force so obviously beyond the capacity of its creators to safely corral is a theme which unwary teenagers were concurrently seeing brought to life on movie screens all over the nation, blissfully unaware at the time that real-life horrors shockingly like those depicted in these lurid pulp melodramas were unfolding virtually in their own backyard.

Earth vs. the Flying Saucers

Certainly one of the most "fantastic" socio-cultural phenomena of the atomic age, tailor-made for a most "fantastic" decade, was the "appearance" of so-called "unidentified flying objects" in the skies. In 1947, a mere two years after a trio of atomic explosions rocked the world into a new era of fear and uncertainty, there occurred a triad of major sightings of "UFOs," within weeks of each other, events which started the "flying saucer" craze that dominated much of the 1950s. On June 21, 1947, several eyewitnesses saw six UFOs at Maury Cliffs, near Tacoma, Washington, one of which ejected slag material out of one of its portholes. Three days later, on June 24, pilot Kenneth Arnold claims he spotted a string of UFOs near Mt. Rainier, Washington. On July 8, in Roswell, New Mexico, an official military press release claimed that a "flying disc," and its occupant, had been captured—a statement which was quickly, and vehemently, denied in ensuing days.

Controversy rages to this day on the truth of these and a myriad of subsequent sightings. There are those who believe the entire phenomenon to be merely a case of opportunistic braggarts seeking fame and attention for themselves, and making up such stories out of whole cloth for potential gain. Those of a psychological bent have surmised that UFO sightings are a form of mass hallucination, a collectively suffered mental diversion of the unbearable guilt, fear and anxiety which dominated the time period, due to the great acceleration of bizarre and dangerous technologies, and the diminishing value of the individual in a group-oriented society. Further, there were/are those who believed the sighted craft to be real, but were actually experimental flying craft designed and flown by terrestrial creators such as the United States and Soviet Russia.

Then there is the final hypothesis on these most uncanny apparitions, and the one which most concerns our discussion of the fantastic films of the 1950s. This is the belief that these observed flying craft, which admittedly looked nothing whatever like any known earth-bound technology, and which flew at speeds and in patterns unachievable by existing man-made aircraft, actually were transportation vehicles of extraterrestrial origin—that is, spaceships "not of this earth." This notion of the earth being at least surveilled, and possibly invaded, by "aliens from outer space" was a wild notion to be sure, but one which caught the popular imagination by storm, in a way not seen in similar cultural phenomena of the day. Indeed, UFO culture has had a staying power far belying its accumulated ability to prove or disprove this historical archive of incidents as evidence of otherworldly visitation. Although the U.S. government has traditionally taken great pains to dismiss all UFO sightings as illusory, disingenuous, or mistaken, popular culture took the "flying saucer" phenomenon to heart, and it became somewhat of a cause celebre in the 1950s. Publisher Ray Palmer managed to start an auspicious career by printing the full story of Kenneth Arnold's 1947 "flying saucer" sightings in a magazine called *Fate*, which soon become a veritable icon for what was labeled "crackpot culture." Pulp science fiction authors took the UFO paradigm to heart, with many a short story and novel appearing to capitalize on the notion of visitors from outer space.

Popular cinema, being a pulp-oriented, highly-visual medium, took to the flying saucer craze most readily, creating in the 1950s a string of popular movies which dealt — either peripherally or overtly — with visitation from outer space. These included: *The Flying Saucer* (1950); *The Day the Earth Stood Still* (1951); *The Thing from Another World* (1951); *The Man from Planet X* (1951); *Phantom from Space* (1953); *It Came from Outer Space* (1953); *Killers from Space* (1954); *This Island Earth* (1955); *Invasion of the Body Snatchers* (1956); *Unidentified Flying Object* (1956); *It Conquered the World* (1956); and *Earth vs. the Flying Saucers* (1956). In our year of interest, 1957, there were three movies which dealt with invasion from other worlds: *Invasion of the Saucer Men*, *Not of This Earth* and *Kronos*. The decade ended with movies such as *Terror from the Year 5,000* (1958), *Attack of the 50 Foot Woman* (1958), *The Astounding She-Monster* (1958), *I Married a Monster from Outer Space* (1958) and *The Cosmic Man* (1959), all dealing with the subject in increasingly silly ways.

A major sighting, widely reported and documented at the time, occurred in July 1952 when groups of glowing orange "fireballs" flew over Washington, D.C., on two consecutive weekends. This threat to the nation's capital prompted the military to issue "shoot-down" orders, putting an entire jet squadron on 24-hour alert. Some days later, the military back-tracked, denied preparing any defensive measures, and dismissed the entire incident — witnessed by dozens of people — as a case of "temperature inversion." Nonetheless, this significant event, which created major headlines across the nation for weeks, made an indelible cultural impact and was the inspiration for at least two films: *Earth vs. the Flying Saucers* (1956) and *Plan Nine from Outer Space* (1959).

A major theme in many of the above-mentioned films is the alien visitors' especial interest in observing military installations. This narrative trope has a most interesting historical analog, according to several sources who maintain that UFOs did often tend to appear near U.S. military bases — especially those which were storing atomic weapons and/or working on nuclear technology. Historian Robert Hastings, in his exhaustive work on the subject, *UFOs and Nukes: Extraordinary Encounters at Nuclear Weapons Sites*, collected an astonishing database of official and anecdotal reports, historical documentation and eyewitness interviews, covering hundreds of "close encounters" with UFOs on or near U.S. military installations, most of which happened to be harboring and/or manufacturing nuclear weaponry.

As seen with the Washington, D.C., sightings, 1952 appears to have been a busy year for UFO activity, with another event, chronicled by Hastings, worth noting. On May 10, 1952, a group of "flying disks" were sighted over the Savannah River Plant, an atomic weapons development facility.[44] Most germane to our discussion, however, are three portentous "close encounters" which occurred between the Military-Industrial Complex and flying craft "of unknown origin" in 1957. As discussed earlier, the U.S. military conducted one of its largest series of nuclear weapons tests in the Spring and Summer of 1957. Dubbed "Operation Plumbbob," these tests included some of the highest-yield thermonuclear devices ever manufactured, and a few of these subsequently released extraordinary amounts of radioactive fallout into the environment worldwide. After "Shot Diablo," a 17-kiloton explosion detonated on July 15, a UFO was tracked on radar by the Air Force.[45] Three days after the Plumbbob "Morgan" shot on October 7, which saturated the area with unusually high amounts of radioactive fallout, a "huge fireball" of unknown origin crashed on the Utah-Colorado border.[46] And on November 7 of that year, three bright aerial objects hovered over the Pantex plant near Amarillo, Texas, used for the manufacture of nuclear weapons, an event observed by civilian and military employees as well as law enforcement officials.[47] As Hastings is quick to point out, these events are only some of over 100 such sightings which occurred on or near nuclear-related military and industrial facilities during the 1950s and early 1960s.

If one believes these incidents to be by and large historically accurate, one might postulate that the trio of atomic explosions in 1945 made inhabitants of other worlds aware of the Earth, concerned with our ability to harness such an awesome and fearful power. These otherworldly beings then traveled to Earth, reaching us first in 1947, in order to keep tabs on our development in nuclear weaponry. Further, these beings may have had on their agenda an attempt to warn us in some way of our folly in playing with such an unholy source of purely destructive energy, a power obviously far beyond our moral power to safely contain. Indeed, one of the main themes of many of the above-mentioned films, and others in the genre, is exactly this: a morally and intellectually superior alien race arrives on Earth to either warn us about the dangers of atomic energy or to intervene in an effort to change our ways before we either blow up ourselves, or — in some scenarios — annihilate the entire universe.

The Wizard War

As has been chronicled extensively, the original impetus for the development and deployment of the atomic bomb was the desire on the part of scientists and the military to manifest this weapon before it could be successfully developed by Nazi Germany. Although the Third Reich in fact never had the slimmest chance of creating "the bomb" (thankfully due to Hitler's myopic disinterest in the idea), faulty but consistent military intelligence coming from Germany suggested otherwise; and the primarily Jewish cabal of scientists involved in the creation of this mega-weapon for the Allies had good reason to fear the consequences should the "Madman of Berlin" get hold of such a horrible weapon of mass destruction. By the time the Manhattan Project had created their super-bombs, Germany had already been defeated and was no longer a threat; the subsequent use of the bombs on Japan was virtually — and unconscionably — an afterthought. It may thus be ironic that one of the most important scientists to be smuggled out of Germany when that nation collapsed under the weight of its own short-sighted self-love was Wernher von Braun, one of Germany's top scientists and inventor of the first long-range liquid-fueled rockets. Von Braun's most successful creation was the V-2, a rocket, first tested in 1942, which soon had been improved so that they could conceivably hit targets as far away (from Germany) as New York City. After intense debriefing, the former Nazi was invited to become the head of a U.S. space program; and, utilizing his advanced technology in the field, the United States began adopting his various rocket designs for use not as weapons but as transportation vehicles for the exploration of outer space and other planets.

This ostensibly altruistic goal of science galvanized the populace, and the soon-dubbed "space race" became one of the most reported and popular projects of the entire decade. Many in the U.S. space program felt that it might be possible to send a man to the moon by 1970—a goal eventually surpassed — and in 1962, an ever-optimistic Von Braun predicted that man would go to Mars by 2010. Yet the United States' apparent lead in the race for outer space received a near-mortal blow in October of 1957 when the Soviets launched an intercontinental ballistic missile, with a small satellite atop, called Sputnik. This first orbiting space satellite put the U.S.' comparative advances to shame, an embarrassment exacerbated a mere month later when, in November, the Russians successfully launched Sputnik II, which carried a small dog, Laika, as the first space traveler. Even worse, the first U.S. attempt to launch a similar space satellite, in December of that fateful year, burst into flames on the launch pad, a resounding failure. The hasty experiment was labeled "Kaputnik" and "Flopnik" by the press, and ensured that the "space race" was now on at a fever pitch. The father of the H-bomb, Edward Teller, called the Soviet Sputniks "a technological Pearl Harbor," and encouraged the U.S. to step up its own program post-haste.[48] Indeed, soon after Sputnik, the U.S. and Soviet space programs accelerated so rapidly, with a new technological marvel seemingly coming out every week, that it prompted British prime minister Winston Churchill to dub the space race "the wizard war," a telling allusion to the more sinister aspects of runaway scientific and technological advancement.[49] And as we shall see, space exploration became one of the most enduring narrative motifs of the fantastic films of the decade, although, curiously, featuring only peripherally in the specific fantastic film offerings of 1957.

Suburbia and the Idiot Box

The post–World War II "baby boom" created, over a short period of time, a significant increase in the U.S. population, and soon the cities and farm homesteads could no longer contain them. Entrepreneur William Levitt captured the spirit of the moment well as he designed and built planned communities with hundreds of units—all similar—and his "Levittowns" really started the postwar building boom. Young couples and families in record numbers migrated from both city and farm to these and similar housing communities, which in aggregate would soon earn the nickname "Suburbia," in promise and theory a "sub-urban utopia." This expansion outwards from tightly-concentrated population centers simultaneously created the need for affordable personal transportation, and the 1950s is thus also the decade of the personal automobile. Motor vehicles dominated the cultural landscape of the 1950s, with almost 74 million registered vehicles by decade's end. The big automobile manufacturers, with the monstrous General Motors leading the pack, forced bigger and faster cars on Americans, and soon automobile travel in itself became a sort of American pastime, a bona fide cultural lifestyle. Of course, as the U.S. became increasingly obsessed with the personal automobile, the nation's public transportation—already in a precarious state — was allowed to further wither and in many cases die. To compensate, a great effort was made to improve and increase the network of roadways in America, a project given its major impetus in 1956 with the National Defense Highway Act, which spurred construction of the interstate highway system, a phenomenon that greatly increased citizens' mobility even while—to some observers—it aggravated a sense of social estrangement. One important offshoot of the new automobile lifestyle which concerns our discussion is the drive-in theater, a specifically postwar phenomenon directly inspired by the ascendancy of the automobile and the highway system, along with the exodus to the suburbs. In the 1950s the number of drive-in theaters expanded exponentially, and as the main patrons of these outdoor cinemas were teenagers and young families, many of the fantastic films of 1957 — designed primarily for the youth market — were screened here.

A discussion of the culture of the 1950s would not be complete without mentioning television, one of the key consumer appliances of the 20th century. Seen by some in the 1940s as a mere novelty analog to the hugely successful radio industry, increased picture quality and improved methods of lower-cost mass productions dictated that television would be *the* paramount consumer product of the 1950s. The growth of television as a desired mass-entertainment commodity was truly startling, as Miller and Nowak note: "In 1946, 7,000 sets existed in the United States. In 1948, there were 148,000. By 1950, 4.4 million families had a TV, and people bought them at an acceleratingly feverish rate — 20,000 *a day* by 1956."[50] Yet the early promise of the magical box which had the

The drive-in movie business hit its stride in the 1950s due to the increasing mobility of the populace, in part thanks to more cars and better highways. All sorts of gimmicks were thus offered to theater owners in order to enhance the drive-in patron's experience. Among them were these portable car canopies, guaranteed to eliminate the need for windshield wipers, even in a downpour.

potential to bring high art and culture into the living room of each and every home in America was sabotaged (possibly from its inception) by ruthless corporate and government interests, which made sure that the soon-to-be-called "idiot box" was used in the service of business and industry and the governing class, and only used sporadically as a gateway to education and high culture.

Even by mid-decade, television had already been largely corrupted as a conformist propaganda outlet for American business and government. Programming swiftly morphed from live broadcasts to pre-recorded ones; production shifted from New York City (with its profound Broadway influence) to Los Angeles (with its emphasis on canned motion picture–like content). The variety of programming (especially the progressive "arts & humanities" aspects: opera, documentary, intellectual discourse, etc.) was quickly jettisoned to feature primarily escapist fare like westerns, sitcoms and crime shows. Hollywood, the government and advertising agencies were primarily responsible for this radical suppression of TV's potential for eclectic, entertaining and educational programming in order to forge the medium into a platform for the ruthless saturation advertising of mass consumer products — and mass ideology. Even more insidious were various efforts at mass programming or behavior modification during this period, with television seen as an ideal platform in which to, essentially, "brainwash" its viewers into increasingly ruler-friendly behaviors. The dumbing-down of content in itself was a form of cultural reprogramming, encouraging passive, non-critical thought over independent thinking, especially where that thinking might cast a harsh light on current political and cultural agenda.

Yet business and government had even more nefarious concepts in mind to bring citizens into line with their increasingly consumerist agenda. According to observers such as Aldous Huxley, subliminal advertising was widely in use in television and movie theaters by the Autumn of 1957. Huxley notes, "By means of specially designed tachitoscopes words or images were to be flashed for a millisecond or less upon the screens of television sets and motion picture theaters *during* (not before or after) the program."[51] The steadfast refusal of most people to believe in this assault on the minds of the populace — and the constant, vehement denials of the use of such psychological conditioning on the part of those doing it — begs the question of why a mass educational medium of such great potential seems to have, rather, turned its users, in generation after generation, into unthinking, lethargic, mentally-challenged consumers of junk food, junk appliances, and junk ideology.

As will be discussed shortly, the motion picture industry had accurately seen the emergence of television as the preferred means of mass entertainment and thus one of the most dire threats to its existence. By mid-decade the major movie studios by and large gave up trying to fight television, and tried to come to terms with this entertainment colossus in their own way. First, several major studios, including Universal, Paramount and Warner Brothers, opened up production units designed specifically for the creation of television programming, including features and series. Second, these same studios (and many other, minor concerns) began to release their back catalog of feature films to television for syndication, a venture which would prove to be extremely lucrative, in some cases becoming a major revenue stream for the studios. Finally, where the motion picture studios could not compete with television, they made a concerted effort to offer more daring subject matter in their theatrical releases, content usually of a violent and/or sexual nature which television would or could not cover. Although it may seem almost laughable today, when the movies have become television perennials, it might be stated that some of the fantastic films of the late 1950s were considered too violent, gory, sexually provocative or otherwise risqué to be shown on television, as at the time of their original theatrical release, this was likely true.

Teenagers from Outer Space

The 1950s saw the ascendancy of American adolescent youth, dubbed for the first time "teenagers," as an important segment of the population — and a most important demographic of cultural consumerism. By mid-decade, there were over 13 million teenagers residing in the United States.

Some even saw the 1950s as "the decade of the teenager." Miller and Nowak note,

"Youth occupied a unique place in fifties America. Teens were perceived as different from other human beings and so were more set apart by a generation gap."[52] Indeed, the basic creed of being a teenager in 1950s America was that of being misunderstood by their guardians. Perhaps being thrust headlong into a mass conformist culture was overwhelming for most young minds; or perhaps implicit differences between elders and their charges, always present but largely unaddressed, came to the fore during this era when psychological analysis first became fashionable. Yet in a highly regimented society such as the U.S., outlets for free expression were rare, and so came out with American adolescents in reactionary, impulsive ways. Two of the few forms of "acceptable" youth rebellion were delinquency (primarily for males) and mental illness (primarily for females). Criminal (read: unruly) teenagers were often sent to reform schools, i.e., youth prisons. The decade saw a sharp rise in school dropouts and juvenile delinquency, emblematic of serious distress within the emerging youth community.

Never shy in exploiting a trend for profit, American business immediately saw the need to create a separate, aggressively pursued "youth market," with the music and movie businesses among the first which took to the new teen culture with a vengeance:

> Still, it was only when Madison Avenue and the luxury industries got hold of the larger concept of unique youth that it changed. Fifties mass culture was, after all, dominated by business. And business generally expected people to indulge themselves with conspicuous consumption. Teens were no exception. Ads saturated the nation, and one of their major targets was young America. In these ads, youth became not the time when one's special character was molded but, instead, the time when one could expect to be totally indulged.[53]

Indeed, in retrospect, fifties culture was largely effective in primarily molding its youth not into a generation of critical thinkers, but rather into a herd of conspicuously apolitical mass consumers.

One of the most vibrant and indelible corporate-hijacked expressions of teenage angst was the emergence of rock 'n' roll music, which first reached a mainstream audience in mid-decade. Popular culture shifted radically with the birth of the rock 'n' roll era, with instant stars such as Elvis Presley, Chuck Berry and Little Richard belting out fast-paced, aggressive tunes that seemed to embody the very spirit of disenfranchised, psychologically imprisoned youth. This explosion of wildly expressive musical creativity coincided neatly with an enormous expansion of the radio industry; by mid-decade there were over 111 million radio sets in the U.S., and teen-oriented "Top 40" radio programming began in earnest. All too soon, however, rock 'n' roll music — which had as its igniting creative spark the musical legacy of black culture — was appropriated (read: "tamed") by white corporate America. Soon, squeaky-clean cover artists such as Ricky Nelson and Pat Boone were recording "safe" imitations of raucous original hits by Fats Domino, Chuck Berry and Bo Diddley. In 1957 the long-running musical television series *American Bandstand* premiered, further co-opting the renegade rock 'n' roll movement into a white, middle-class, establishment-friendly agenda. And as a response to what was seen as the contamination of America's youth by low racial or subversive foreign influences, white America targeted the early rock 'n' roll movement, especially the black artists and their promoters. The infamous "Payola" scandals, for instance, martyred popular disc jockey Alan Freed, a maverick loner who promoted racial equality by fearlessly exposing his largely white radio audience to obscure and emerging black musicians, a persecution which precipitated his ruin. Meanwhile, these same inves-

GEORGE WALDMAN FILMS
GEORGE J. WALDMAN
630 Ninth Avenue
NEW YORK 36, N. Y.

AMERICAN INTERNATIONAL PICTURES
JOHN SCHAEFFER
235 No. 13th Street
PHILADELPHIA 7, PENNSYLVANIA

AMERICAN INTERNATIONAL PICTURES
JEROME SANDY
1015 New Jersey Avenue, N.W.
WASHINGTON I, D. C.

SCREEN GUILD PRODUCTIONS
MILTON BRAUMAN
415 Van Braam Street
PITTSBURGH 19, PENNSYLVANIA

GEORGE WALDMAN FILMS
GEORGE J. WALDMAN
505 Pearl Street
BUFFALO, N. Y.

American International Pictures was the first studio to overtly court the emerging teenage movie-consumer demographic by the aggressive marketing of youth-centric, pre-packaged double bills such as this release—*Reform School Girl* and *Rock Around the World*—from the summer of 1957.

tigative committees left completely untouched such sleazy corporate sharks as Dick Clark—creator of the aforementioned *American Bandstand*—who segregated black recording artists on his program, relentlessly promoted white hegemony in his music listening audience, and who had highly dubious, if not technically illegal, financial interests in all aspects of the recording industry. Aptly standing as a symbol for the demise of "real" music in an age of crushing homogeneity, legendary black singer Little Richard officially "left" the music business in late 1957, thinking that the Soviet Sputnik launch was a sign from God of an impending biblical Armageddon that would crush America.

Although the "teen film" emerged as a separate genre circa 1950, it was not until mid-decade that the youth market became visible and formidable. Films about juvenile delinquents and young rebels, in which these delinquents and rebels were at least partly heroic, began to emerge. Soon, the youth of America had two bona fide film heroes portraying these brave new antiheroes: Marlon Brando and James Dean. Marlon Brando portrayed a death-defying, authority-hating rebel motorcyclist in *The Wild One* (1951), and James Dean played a moody, sensitive teenage outlaw in *Rebel Without a Cause* (1955). In these and many other films, the teenage hero suffers a profound, even heartbreaking alienation from both peers and community, but most of all from parents and other elders, on whom he blames both his own personal angst and the general insanity of a world gone mad. This powerful, if somewhat simplistic, view of heroic youthful suffering found ready acceptance among the new youth audience. As Miller and Nowak note:

> For thousands of adolescent Americans, the film rebels (particularly Brando and Dean) personified their own feelings of alienation. They were seen as figures of moral purity rebelling against an inhuman environment, as individuals incapable of conforming in a society dominated by conformity and social compromise.[54]

In a sense, then, James Dean's tragic death in 1955 symbolized the dire fate of the innocent 1950s teenager, soon to be catapulted headlong into the gruesome real world of adult responsibility. For many, Dean's death was a metaphorical falling off of a very high cliff into that

The "teenaged monster" was one of the prime archetypes of late-1950s youth culture, illustrated overtly in such 1957 films as *I Was a Teenage Werewolf*, *I Was a Teenage Frankenstein*, *Blood of Dracula*, and *Teenage Monster* (shown above), but addressed obliquely in many other forms, from the specter of juvenile delinquency to the unruly lyrics of the new-fangled "rock 'n' roll" music.

fearful black void called "the future," and back into a world primarily run by lunatic old people.

This fear of impotent and morally or mentally challenged authority was a main theme for fifties youth. When looking over a culture geared towards teenagers, one prominent issue is that of the weak, frightened, ineffectual or otherwise failed father figure. This lack of a strong, abiding patriarch ably acts as a metaphor for a perceived lack of sane adult leadership, an understandable concern in a society seemingly hell-bent on world destruction. In the place of such a powerful and protective leader of the community is substituted something akin to mob rule, with its inevitably dire consequences. Historian W. T. Lhamon, Jr., in his treatise on the decade, notes:

> In films, records, plays and novels — all the narrative arts — this basic problem appears: the father is gone, is illegitimate, is corrupt, cannot stand up to women or his children, is effete, is mortally ill. He left, was killed, committed suicide, miraculously died. His messages to his dependents are faint, quaint, or nonexistent. In his absence, peer pressure, or brotherly love, or mob rule, or participatory structures emerge.[55]

To contradict this prevalent notion of inadequate authority, television — culture's most effective mass propaganda tool — attempted almost obsessively to glorify and worship the father figure as a benign, even passive but always potent leader of the family, and thus society at large. Yet the movie business continued to exploit and glorify the ecstatic triumphs and tragic joys of teenage rebellion, astride the demonizing of parents and authority figures, in hits such as *Rebel Without a Cause, East of Eden, The Wild One* and *The Blackboard Jungle* (1955). This trend hit full stride in 1957 with such fantastic films as *I Was a Teenage Werewolf, I Was a Teenage Frankenstein, Blood of Dracula* and *Teenage Monster*. These "quickie" releases expressed — in simplistic allegorical form — some of the basic generational themes developed fully in the more "mature" films aimed at general audiences.

The Good Citizen

As might be expected in any newly-positioned world empire, a concerted effort was mounted in the 1950s to manage acceptable behavior and establish allowable social boundaries for the swelling mass of American citizens. The "mass dream," as pushed by the media of the day, was working for a corporation, getting married and having babies. The middle class, a rapidly growing segment of the population, was richer than ever before, and the decade was a time of relative peace and affluence. The ideal role model for the American male became the corporate cipher or "company man," an obedient "yes man" dedicated to furthering the cause of American business enterprise for the good of his company and the nation. Yet this suffocating, other-directed goal for the modern male seemingly created more problems than it solved — in terms of stress, substance abuse and mental breakdown — for by mid-decade this "role model" was being critically assailed, and outright parodied, in popular books of the time such as David Riesman's *The Lonely Crowd*, William Whyte's *The Organization Man* and Sloan Wilson's *The Man in the Grey Flannel Suit*. The general consensus in these works was that the corporate lifestyle was personally unfulfilling, perhaps even deleterious to the individual. As will be discussed, the fate of the postwar American woman was even more dire, as she was directed to be a perky and optimistic servant and nursemaid to husband and children, and have all of her existential needs met within the confines of her clapboard kingdom. In short, much-touted suburbia was being increasingly seen as a conformist prison for the soul. But freedom of expression was not encouraged in postwar America, so this self-awareness, if addressed, lead not to emancipation but increased suffering. As Miller and Nowak note, "Many people suffered from the conflict between the desire for personal autonomy and the pressures for collective conformity."[56] Yet the powerful socio-cultural forces which demanded and endorsed harsh conformity were formidable and all-encompassing; as Aldous Huxley noted of the decade in 1958, "Its basic assumption is that the social whole has greater worth and significance than its individual parts, that inborn biological differences should be sacrificed to cultural uniformity, that the rights of the collectivity take precedence over what the eighteenth century called the Rights of Man."[57]

Indeed, the role of the individual vs. the collective in the advancement of society has been a controversial debate among philosophers and social engineers since man attempted to live harmoniously with his fellows. Huxley, for one, unceasingly championed the incorruptible and inimitable power of the unique individual to forge works which benefited society, and had little good to say about a society that denigrated the role — and sanctity — of the individual for the good of the group:

> The social whole, whose value is assumed to be greater than that of its component parts, is not an organism in the sense that a hive or a termitary may be thought of as an organism. It is merely an organization, a piece of social machinery. There can be no value except in relation to life and awareness. An organization is neither conscious nor alive. Its value is instrumental and derivative. It is not good in itself; it is good only to the extent that it promotes the good of the individuals who are the parts of the collective whole. To give organizations precedence over persons is to subordinate ends to means. What happens when ends are subordinate to means was clearly demonstrated by Hitler and Stalin.[58]

This belief lies in sharp contrast to the views of certain psychologists of the period, such as B.F. Skinner, who maintained that an individual who took credit for his own accomplishments was erroneous, as he was merely channeling the collective accumulated energies of his peers and surrounding environment. This debate rages on even today, but had a particularly reverberant dissemination during the 1950s, when the good of the social whole was perceived as paramount, yet individuals still strove to achieve and express themselves on their own terms. One of the ways in which Americans dealt with this ostensibly insoluble dilemma was to turn away from it altogether through escape. Miller and Nowak note:

> People turned away from thinking about harsh realities. They turned instead to a nostalgic vision: the happy family huddling together against the visceral terror of modern times. A mock-Victorian vision of life became the great fifties American dream — Mom the homemaker, Dad the breadwinner, smiling determinedly in their traditional roles.[59]

Indeed, the very notions of autonomy and free expression became a psychological bogeyman to many, a Pandora's box better left locked and sealed. Americans decided en masse not to dwell consciously on the terrifying and precarious nature of the world around them, and by doing this, of course, undermined their potential to act on these problems and change them.

For one, Americans in the fifties returned to an obsession with organized religion, with church attendance reaching record proportions for much of the decade. This suggests a terrified and confused populace that has been reduced to burying their collective heads in the sand rather than tackling difficult issues on an intellectual and political level, seeking comfort in the ignorant superstition of religious dogma. This was a dangerous regression to an infantile state of a large, potentially problematic populace, which assured that the military-industrial complex could carry on its nefarious mission of increased industrialization and world conquest with an absolute minimum of scrutiny or protest until it was by and large beyond redress, which is exactly what happened. In addition, other forms of fantasy escape, such as alcoholism and addiction to prescription tranquilizers, reached epidemic proportions during the decade, especially among the cherished and courted middle class.

Of course, the awkward, stifling, largely artificial posturing of social conformity merely suppressed other, more autonomous energies going on within the individual and various informal groupings at the time. As seen elsewhere, the social upheaval which bubbled just under the surface of forced tranquility and anxious conformity achieved many sporadic outlets about mid-decade — the youth culture in general for one, and specifically the birth of the counterculture. Perhaps not surprisingly, several of the fantastic films of 1957 feature the dialectic of the outsider-individual straining against a conformist society as a main or peripheral theme. *Unnatural, Not of This Earth, The Incredible Shrinking Man, She-Devil, The Vampire, I Was a Teenage Werewolf, Daughter of Dr. Jekyll, The Disembodied, The Amazing Colossal Man, The Invisible Boy, Fright* and *Blood of Dracula* all touch upon this easily-identifiable problem of modern living.

Astounding She-Monsters

Women in the 1950s had a tough row to hoe. The stiflingly conservative cultural climate of the decade effectively sabotaged women's hard-won advancements in the workplace and political arena, relegating them to roles as virtual prisoners in tiny clapboard domiciles. In many cases, with husband and children off in their own, highly nurturing social environments, life in the suburbs for a woman was little more than solitary confinement, with television being her sole social contact — and a highly dubious one at that. Television, for the most part, presented an homogenized view of the American middle class as WASP archetypes, both reflecting and influencing the social conformity of the era, and offering women as role models who were, by and large, unthinking patrist flunkies. David Halberstam describes the desired female archetype of the era succinctly:

> A postwar definition of femininity evolved. To be feminine, the American woman first and foremost did not work. If she did, that made her competitive with men, which made her hard and aggressive and almost surely doomed to loneliness. Instead, she devotedly raised her family, supported her husband, kept her house spotless and efficient, got dinner ready on time, and remained attractive and optimistic; each hair was in place. According to studies, she was prettier than her mother, she was slimmer, and she even smelled better than her mother.[60]

Television — primarily a male propaganda tool, after all — pushed endless examples of this "ideal woman," but perhaps the most noxious and indelible was that of Betty Furness, corporate America's role model for the perfect suburban cipher — repressed, other-directed, obedient, perky, and obsessed with high-priced gadgetry for the home. In her weekly shilling of shiny kitchen appliances from military-industrial giant Westinghouse, and her at-times virtually obscene stroking and fondling of the machines she was promoting, this binary of "woman and machine" was illustrated almost as a sexually-fueled fetish ritual. The machines themselves came to represent phallo-centric technocratic culture, her gleefully mindless worship of them something of a surrogate sex act — a "techno-porn," if you will.

This forced conscription was, of course, accepted only reluctantly — and at great personal cost — by the majority of women of the era. The new isolation of the suburban housewife lead to an epidemic of female depression, alcoholism and insanity. Betty Freidan noted among many of the women she interviewed for her groundbreaking feminist manifesto *The Feminine Mystique* a pervasive "emotional malaise, bordering on depression."[61] As Miller and Nowak note, "Around mid-decade, many magazines began running articles about the astounding number of problems affluent American women were suffering."[62] These "problems" included everything from mild neurosis to chronic depression, guilt feelings to suicide, abortion to alcoholism, adultery to divorce. Of course, the prescribed answers given to "cure" these "problems" was not to contemplate or explore their root causes — many of which might be traced to repression of various expression-oriented goals — but to have another kid, try a new cake recipe, or put more effort into conscientious homemaking. Indeed, since one of womankind's "sacred" roles in 1950s culture was as a "baby factory" — a notion which eerily echoed the greatly accelerating consumer-based mass production of industrial society — if a woman did not have children she was "sick, damaged, perverted."[63]

This notion of a woman's sexuality being channeled into its only accepted function — the furthering of the human race — was an old one, faithfully trotted out by repressive regimes for millennia; yet it is somewhat disheartening that it took hardy root in a culture which, in some ways, was simultaneously poised to blossom into collective enlightenment. The decade worshiped the institution of marriage as almost a sacred tenet, this itself being a repressive sociocultural mechanism for control. During the era, sexuality in adult women was demonized and suppressed, an apt metaphor also for the suppression of other forms of expansive expression. In short, a woman's role in the 1950s was simply to serve patriarchy — as servant, slave and nursemaid — and most assuredly not to rebel against this sentence.

Yet within this wholesale war against womankind were murmurs of something greater, emerging slowly, even timidly, and most assuredly not without the expected counterattack. Books such as Simone de Beauvoir's *The Second Sex* became surprisingly popular, offering some hint of how women could be something other than slaves for a demonic phallocentric empire. A fiction bestseller, *Peyton Place*, by Grace Metalious, was released in paperback in 1957. It described small town America as a hypocritical hotbed of sexual and political subversion, a revolution in waiting lurking beneath its calm exterior, and was seen in retrospect by some observers as an early proto-feminist document. Planned Parenthood pioneer Margaret Sanger appeared on the Mike Wallace television show also in 1957, promoting birth control education; she was vilified by both the audience and the press. As expected, conformist 1950s culture responded viciously to any perceived autonomy in women. Especially pilloried were so-called "career women," such as the aforementioned De Beauvoir, Metalious and Sanger — i.e., smart women who spoke their mind.

Career women were, after all, portrayed in popular culture (television and the women's magazines especially) as hard, cold and emotionally empty — and possibly subversive as well. Subversive they were, in fact, for they desired to undermine a noxious culture which desired to rule the planet with scientific horrors inconceivable to a sane society. Burgeoning examples of early feminist thought were thus marginalized as a form of psychological disease. Some (male-dictated) studies of mid-decade even declared that the more educated a woman was the more chance she had of having a "sexual disorder"—whatever that nebulous term was supposed to suggest.[64]

Most frightening to patrist culture, for several reasons, was the notion of the intelligent woman who attempted to forge her own career. Thus, women were discouraged even from pursuing education beyond that which was needed to effectively feed the faces and wipe the butts of their charges. The pursuit of higher education for women was critiqued in journals of the day as being not only irresponsible and useless, but actually harmful to women. In addition to the obvious threat of adding women to the already competitive male-dominated workplace, especially in traditionally male vocations such as business and science, there was also the fear that if women "got smart" they might begin to see through the flimsy other-directed facade of a misogynist culture that encouraged them to become maids, mommies and manual laborers.

For our discussion, the archetype of the woman scientist is most important. A quick overview of the ephemera of the day might give one the impression that there were no female professionals in the scientific arena. As Eugenia Kaledin notes in her overview of the role of women in the 1950s, *Mothers and More*, "Leafing through the *New York Times* of the 1950s, it is hard to find the names of women scientists."[65] Yet, of course there were many successful female professionals working in many fields, including photography (Margaret Bourke-White), biology (Ethel Harvey), physics (Maria Goeppert Mayer), astronomy (Cecilia Payne-Gaposchkin), nuclear medicine (Rosalyn Yalow), conservation (Rachel Carson), zoology (Ann Haven Morgan) and sex education (Margaret Sanger). The deliberate, systemic media silence regarding these extraordinary women could not wholly dampen the emergence of what would soon blossom forth as the feminist movement. As Kaledin notes:

> The 1950s became the decade when many women first confronted the reality that American society made no concessions to their problems as wives or mothers or divorcees or underpaid workers. The number of exceptional women out in the world, defined by their professions, served to remind the others at home of how frequently women's astonishing capabilities were thwarted by rigid institutional policies and inflexible attitudes. Seeing themselves as bearers of children who would live long, active lives, women began to understand that they had special needs, that society might do much more to make good use of their talents. To "underestimate" their power was to underestimate their capacity for change.[66]

Fortuitously, albeit curiously, one area in which what might be termed "proto-feminism" was illustrated was the science fiction and horror film genre, a subset most germane to our discussion. In many of these films, women were depicted as *both* subservient lackeys and brave, intelligent (and at least semi-autonomous) professionals. The appearance of the lackey archetype is expected, but what is intriguing and exciting is the narrative ascendancy of the female professional, often depicted in not wholly unflattering terms—in some ways a huge leap in pro-female cultural discourse. This (almost sudden) appearance of the "professional woman" in such films has been noted by several observers. One of the most astute analyses of the phenomenon is Bonnie Noonan's *Women Scientists in Fifties Science Fiction Films*, in which Noonan notes, "One characteristic of American B science fiction films from 1950 to 1963 or so is their depiction of professional women characters, particularly as assistants to scientists, students of science, and even as scientists in their own right."[67] Regarding the awkward dichotomy—not always resolved—of woman-as-follower vs. woman-as-leader in these texts, Noonan further observes, "The speculative films of the postwar era incorporated the percolating tensions between the role of woman as professional and her ability to fulfill the gender expectations that would relegate her to a private, domestic sphere."[68]

Indeed, while the feminist movement per se was still years away, and popular culture by and large resonated with the retrograde, punitive portrayal of woman as obedient servants of maledom, hints of radical change in the cultural depiction of women were slowly starting to seep through the cracks of culture, and it is noteworthy that many fantastic films of the era — and several from 1957 — have a pronounced (if at times contradictory) championing of female empowerment as a prominent subtextual theme. As well, many of the films' screenplays (perhaps unwittingly) portray searing indictments of patriarchy's subjugation and exploitation of womankind, relating modern-day atrocities to historical crimes such as the Catholic Church's genocidal campaigns against freethinking women, an assault on humanity which lasted well over a century and whose misogynist spirit still breathes today.

As for the fantastic films of 1957, three major themes emerge involving the destiny of a curious, intellectual (i.e., professional) woman who dares to stretch her prescribed gender requirements in various ways, and suffers for it. Heroic professional women — scientists and other "career women" — are featured prominently, and sympathetically (if in sometimes woefully sexist shades), in *Attack of the Crab Monsters, Not of This Earth, Beginning of the End, Kronos, From Hell It Came* and *The Monster That Challenged the World*. Powerful, enterprising women who overstep their contract with the male universe, and who subsequently meet their demise, appear in *Unnatural, Pharaoh's Curse, The Disembodied, Teenage Monster* and *Blood of Dracula*. Yet the darkest theme occurs in films which depict the fate of acquiescent (read: "traditional") women who allow themselves (or are coerced) to be victimized at the hands of a malevolent patriarchal overlord: *Voodoo Woman, The Undead, Fright, She-Devil, Daughter of Dr. Jekyll, Back from the Dead, Cat Girl, The Man Who Turned to Stone* and *The Brain from Planet Arous*. Yet all of these films — even allowing for the widely divergent fates of their heroines — offer an overarching theme, that being the risk awaiting any woman who dares (solicited or not) tinker with the entrenched male socio-political sphere. Even the professional woman who participates gladly, and with gratitude from her male "masters," in their foolhardy attempts to harness the powers of the gods suffers egregiously, inviting torture and destruction for her bold confidence. In short, the fantastic films of 1957 often showcase women who refuse to accept their proscribed roles as domestic nursemaids, manual laborers and sexual slaves, and thus anger the male deities who rule their expositional universe, inviting a potentially terrifying fate. As Noonan observes:

> To explode the boundaries of gender performance, particularly as that explosion would affect the ingrained and biologically rationalized structure of the American family, leads to an explosion of those who would dare to challenge those boundaries. If you want to live outside natural laws, you can't be saved. You can only bring about your own doom and that of the men who trust you.[69]

Yet even more enduring than the cautionary aspects of these films is the overarching motif of women attempting, at all costs, to break their gender-defined fetters and forge new roles for themselves, come what may. Even at risk of violence or death, the heroines of these films struggle to achieve some level of escape from obsolete — and demonstrably life-threatening — phallocentric dogma, and in so doing create life experiences which come dangerously close to what would, almost a decade later, blossom under the rubric of "female empowerment." Far more progressive than the plucky, wise-cracking "girl reporter" archetype of pulp fiction and B-movie tradition, who asserted herself only to win adulation and acceptance from male society, the "fantastic" heroine of 1957 demanded — and in some cases received — acceptance on her own terms, often in direct opposition to stated male objectives. Her reward for this challenge to patriarchal institutions might be anything from reluctant acceptance to extreme marginalization — with death a distinct possibility — but she was nonetheless allowed to express her desired terms of liberation, thus illustrating to her peers (and the movie audience) the possibility of such emancipating life arcs and their potential for world-shaking apotheosis.

1955: A Cultural Breaking Point

According to some observers, the fear, repression and conservatism of the 1950s, reaching unrestrainable proportions, exploded in mid-decade, with 1955 being the year in which American culture reached a perceivable "tipping point." Certain trends and events tend to back up this thesis. Nineteen fifty-five was the first year in which rock 'n' roll music dared enter the cultural mainstream, embraced by youth and vilified by elders, symbolizing a vivid and irrevocable break with past tradition. In the sweltering August of that year, black teenager Emmet Till was kidnapped and killed by southern rednecks, a heinous act which assured that racial issues could no longer be ghettoized and ignored, and would become of mainstream concern. In August as well, Billy Ray Taylor had an encounter with "aliens" in Kentucky, one of the first ground-based U.F.O. "visitations" to receive wide press coverage; the "encounter" suggests either an expression of mass hysteria reaching a breaking point, or a harbinger of an awesome new age of discovery and revelation. In September of that fateful year, teen idol James Dean died in a horrific automobile crash, chillingly illustrating American youth's collective death of innocence. And in December, Rosa Parks refused to give up her bus seat in Mobile, Alabama, to a white person, igniting the modern civil rights movement in earnest.

In his remarkable essay on the decade, *Deliberate Speed: The Origins of a Cultural Style in the American 1950s*, W.T. Lhamon, Jr. makes a strong case for various energies, both conscious and unconscious, forging new ground in the era, toiling indefatigably behind the scenes even within a repressive socio-political regime, and forcing a break with tradition about mid-decade, leading to a flamboyant ignition of liberal thought in arts and culture, and seen in awkward manifestations immediately but soon gaining steam to birth the modern counterculture movement which dominated the 1960s. As Lhamon observes:

> Far from there being no culture in the fifties, or its being the whining sound of lower-class resentment, the truth is that conditions in the fifties produced an aggressive and whole culture which was distinct from its predecessor and is not yet replaced. All the elements of the American contemporary culture were in place by the year 1955, when the civil rights movement began, when the TV takeover had reached the majority of the nation's homes, when rock 'n' roll surfaced, when the consumer society and its energy problems were as visible as the fallout and bomb shelters beginning to obsess American citizens, and when the baby boom's outriders started coming into their own. No wonder the sociologists David Riesman and Nathan Glazer confirmed that year "a decisive shift in the American Mind."[70]

Indeed, 1955 can be seen in retrospect as a flash-point of awareness in the American psyche, that moment of perceivable shift from the dogma of conservatism to the expansiveness of liberalism.

Notes Lhamon, "After 1955, the culture became demonstrably speedier in style, delivery, and cycles because it was inevitably starting to represent the megapolition, geographic, and demographic development of the postwar period."[71] This may partly explain why the fantastic films of the era, showcased by the 50-odd entries from 1957, created as they were as a youth-oriented answer to the conservative techno-military dogma of the era, came at times so close to something avant-garde, critical, even confrontational, oppositional to both general mainstream entertainment and most assuredly film narratives of the earlier portion of the decade. Some of the creators of the fantastic films seem to have had, even as a subconscious agenda, an oppositional, even revolutionary, perspective in their productions, taking extremely critical viewpoints on issues such as atomic energy, the role of the woman in society, and the sanctity of the individual within a mass-oriented social structure. Most of these films were created for the youth market as primarily an economic notion, to be sure, but their narrative import seemed also to tap into collective longings, anxieties, and objections regarding the fetid cultural swamp inhabited by their elders. Also around this time, American culture toyed with the notion of increased sexual expression, seen in various events such as the birth of the *Playboy* mythos and the release of—and controversy surrounding—the Alfred Kinsey reports on American sexual behavior. Yet the shift towards sexual expression — if not yet exactly sexual freedom — can also largely be attributed to an entire generation of children coming of age at this time, becoming sexual creatures themselves and thus deserving and demanding a say in the development and trajectory of their own culture.

Lhamon took the title for his book from the historical court ruling of May 31, 1955, when Justice Warren spoke on the desegregation of the public school system, advising all involved parties to enable this crucial revision of entrenched racial prejudice "with all deliberate speed." Lhamon finds Warren's curious wording a most apt metaphor for the momentous changes occurring nationwide in so many socio-cultural areas, stating, "The remarkably resonant phrase 'deliberate speed' echoes and evokes all of America's attempts to transform itself from an industrial to a post industrial society. The real importance of the phrase is how it caught and crested a welling American mood."[72] This "welling American mood," one which tentatively but definitively experimented with expansive personal and sexual freedom, unbounded artistic creativity and an often-articulate criticism of existing power structures and political agendas, is surprisingly well represented in the 1957 fantastic film canon, as we shall see.

Movies Are Still Your Best Entertainment

One of the more curious casualties of the postwar American experience in an otherwise bustling economy bursting with new technological advancement was the motion picture industry, which struggled throughout the decade to survive. Studio-based movie production declined radically during the decade, from 400 feature films in 1951 to 154 in 1960. As Miller and Nowak note, "From a record weekly attendance of 82 million in 1946, film audiences alarmingly plummeted to about 36 million by 1950. Labor troubles, higher production costs, adverse court rulings, highly publicized anticommunist hearings all hurt the movie industry."[73] The studios were forced to assume new roles, as financiers and distributors, subcontracting productions out to independent producer-directors. Significantly, the topic of our conversation, 1957, became one of the worst years in industry history, with the major Hollywood studios posting record losses of almost $16 million. Among many overlapping reasons for this precipitous decline in movie attendance, two major factors emerge. First, the late–1940s Supreme Court rulings which separated movie production from exhibition largely demolished the traditional Hollywood studio system, and the movie studios scrambled throughout the decade to regain a foothold in the theater distribution market, which was largely being taken over by smaller independent distributors. Most portentous, however, was the deleterious effect that television had on the industry. Television, at the start of the decade an amusing if peripheral novelty, by decade's end came to be seen as the great equalizer of the era. In addition to the proliferation of other home-based entertainment systems, such as tape recorders and hi-fi phonographs, television and her consumer-friendly electronic sisters forced movie theaters in the hundreds to cease operations.

Hollywood desperately tried to breathe new life into the business with gimmicks such as 3D and Cinemascope, neither of which made a lasting impact on theater attendance. The decade also saw the birth of the epic blockbuster, at first often based on bible stories, such as *The Ten Commandments* (1956). An ever more desperate Hollywood ruthlessly exploited cold-war fears with overt propaganda pieces such as *The Iron Curtain* (1948), *Conspirator* (1949), *Guilty of Treason* (1949), *I Married a Communist* (1950), *The Whip Hand* (1951), *I Was a Communist for the FBI* (1951), *The Steel Fist* (1952), *Never Let Me Go* (1952), *Man on a Tightrope,* (1953) *Red Planet Mars* (1952) and *Invasion USA* (1952). The proliferation of the drive-in movie theater during the 1950s did manage to capture the younger moviegoer, a segment which the industry increasingly courted and relied upon.

One of the more ingenious — if ill-fated — attempts to beat television at its own game was a short-lived early experiment in what was then called "pay television," which would some decades later morph into the highly successful cable television phenomenon, an offshoot of the movie industry that flourishes today. The first pay television system was dubbed "Telemovies" and offered homeowners first-run theatrical features piped directly into their living rooms for the modest fee of $9.99 per month. Overcoming the considerable technical and legal obstacles involved in "wiring" an entire community with coaxial cable, the Telemovies system finally had its inaugural broadcast on September 3, 1957, in Bartlesville, Oklahoma, with more than 300 homes participating in a viewing of a current theatrical release, *The Pajama Game.* Although early reports indicate enthusiasm for the project, it soon became evident that people were not willing to pay for television, even if it offered a first-run feature that they would have to pay to see in the theater.[74] The content, apparently, wasn't as important as the convenience of sitting at home and watching whatever was on the tube, gratis. Pay television, in various incarnations, limped along until finally gaining a foothold in the consumer marketplace in the late 1970s, becoming something of a household necessity by the mid–1980s.

Midnite Spook Party

One of the most curious phenomena to augment the fantastic film experience of the 1950s was the concurrent appearance of the so-called "Spook Show." Spook Show was the accepted industry term for the live performance on stage of various acts which might be loosely defined as horror-based. These acts generally began with a master of ceremonies (often a magician) who would dazzle the audience with visual trickery invariably annotated with hyperbolic narration. The act would also include actors dressed up as various movie monsters and horror icons, who would cavort about the stage accompanied by weird music, disorienting lighting and special effects trickery. The Spook Show has a history dating back to vaudeville days, and indeed was perhaps the last remaining vestige of that august theatrical art form, as the Spook Show tradition carried on well into the 1960s. Perhaps the first — at least one of the earliest — Spook Show producers was Elwin Charles Peck, aka "El-Wyn," whose popular "Midnite Spook Party" began life in the 1920s and ran successfully for decades.[75]

The Spook Show industry was peopled by a number of practitioners, many of whom offered their services over the course of decades and became famous (or infamous) in the entertainment industry. Some giants of the Spook Show phenomenon — and their most popular shows — are: Arthur Francisco Bull, aka "Francisco," and his "Midnight Spook Frolic"; Joe Karsten's "Dr. Macabre's Frightmare of Movie Monsters"; Phillip Morris, aka "Dr. Evil," and his "Terrors of the Unknown"; Raymond Corbin, aka "Ray-Mond," and his "Ray-Mond Voodoo Show"; Johnny Cates, aka "Dr. Satan," and his "Shrieks in the Night"; Wladyslaw Michaluk, aka "Kara-Kum," and his "The Crawling Thing from Planet 13"; Donn Davison, aka "The Mad Doctor," and his "Doctor Psycho's Asylum of the Occult"; Ormond McGill, aka Dr. Zomb," and his "Seance of Wonders;" John Calvert, aka "Dr. London," and his "Great London Ghost Show"; Jack Baker, aka "Dr. Silkini," and his "Asylum of Horrors"; and "Dr. Rome," aka "The Ghostmaster," and his "Chamber of Horrors."

Several of these performers and their traveling stage shows worked during the monster-movie craze of the 1950s. Often these "spook shows" would be scheduled late at night — on or near midnight — ostensibly to increase the allure of the program as being scary and otherworldly, but primarily to utilize the theater during a typically vacant time period, providing an opportunity for the theater owner to garner an extra source of income. According to some accounts, these Spook Shows were, as a group, quite lucrative and made their producers, and sponsors, a good deal of money. More importantly for our discussion, the Spook Show acted as an important cultural annotation of the monster movie craze for their audiences, who saw the live stage performances as in some ways augmenting the narrative message or "zeitgeist" of the films which they invariably accompanied. When the monsters seen onscreen threatened to "jump right out at you" in the audience, the entire experience, although consciously seen as stagecraft, subconsciously may give reality or credence to the fantastic parables depicted onscreen. In the atomic age of mutant radioactive monsters, the notion of "real" monsters attacking theatergoers in "real life" took on a particularly poignant edge, as concurrently with the horrific atomic experiments and their ungodly offspring that slithered across the safely contained movie screen, similar atrocities were occurring in the "real world," the fact of which the more astute teenage audience member might be subconsciously aware. Thus, the "spook show," at least in the 1950s, acted as a most efficacious refraction of malefic events happening right outside the sheltering safety of the dark, womb-like theater.

As for 1957, at least one Spook Show has been confirmed as being performed that year, and there were undoubtedly others. Jack Baker was one of the premier operators of these carnivalesque stage programs; according to Jim Ridenour, fellow Spook Show operator and

Although the live "spook show" had been around since vaudeville days, this carnivalesque industry enjoyed a renaissance in the 1950s due to the preponderance of horror and science fiction films aimed at the youth market. Here is an advertisement for "House of the Living Dead," a spook show which came to a Bridgeport, Connecticut, theater in March 1957. Note two references to current pop culture: the "materialization" of teen idol James Dean, killed in a tragic car crash in late 1955; and a crude illustration of Roger Corman's "crab monster," a prime icon of this most "fantastic" year. This spook show was produced (and likely performed by) Jack Baker, based in Toledo, Ohio, and considered one of the giants of the spook show business.

subsequent archivist of the genre, Baker "worked the spookers for forty-two years, made millions of dollars."[76] During the 1957 moviegoing season, Baker offered one of his "biggest" programs, "House of the Living Dead." Baker himself traveled the country with his show, performing under the nom-de-plume "Dr. Silkini." Savvy enough to address current trends in order to lure a wider audience, Baker added something especially timely to his "House of the Living Dead" program: "See the Materialization of James Dean." James Dean, of course, was the troubled, magnificent actor whose short life and tragic death in September of 1955 was already, in early 1957, becoming a modern myth in the making. As well, Dean was seen as perhaps Hollywood's most effective icon representing the teenage moviegoing demographic (with Marlon Brando a close second), so invoking the spirit and image of the recently deceased hero was a surefire attention-getter. How Baker managed to "materialize" James Dean is not known, but it probably involved some low-rent optical trickery and hoary f/x work; yet undoubtedly the highly ritual act served as an important catharsis to an audience likely still grieving for their fallen rebel hero.

As for the structure of the Spook Show itself, Ridenour offers a priceless recollection from his own experience as operator and attendee:

> The ideal spook show starts with a horror movie. This lets the hoodlums get tired and worn out. After the first movie ends, you immediately start the stage show. The stage show ends with a blackout where the theater is completely dark, and spooks, ghosts, bats, skeletons — luminescent paintings on fishing poles — "fly over" the heads of the audience. Once the lights come on, you immediately hit the screen with a second horror flick.[77]

Certainly one of the most anachronistic, and sexist, portions of the most popular spook shows — a hoary trope lifted entirely from the earliest days of stage magic — was the on-stage "dismembering" of a young woman. In various spook shows, the master of ceremonies would cut off a girl's appendage (heads and arms were most popular, with legs a distant third) with a buzz saw and proudly display the severed limb to a horrified audience.[78] This highly political act of violence towards women certainly reflected postwar society's overall misogyny, but acted more specifically as a grotesque allegory of the fate of those females who dared challenge the absolute rule of patriarchy, cannily symbolized by the omnipotent "doctor of horror" who presided over the performance, and who obviously held the power of life and death over all his charges.

Less violent — yet undoubtedly as effective as cautionary lesson — were the almost obligatory hypnotism acts included in these stage shows. With few exceptions, these hypnotism bits were phony, staged sketches using pre-chosen "foils" as their subjects, yet the notion of the father-figure/magician undermining the power of free will over his subjects (which were surely both male and female) could not but reinforce the desired hegemony of patriarchal omniscience in almost comically literal form, which desired to rule over all females, along with the weakest of males.

Fantastic Films of the Fifties

As might be expected from an era obsessed with science and technology, and all that these harnessed forces of the natural world might do for good or ill, perhaps the preeminent genre of that decade's popular culture — including fiction, comic books, television and movies — was science fiction. As a literary genre, science fiction had existed in some form since the latter 19th-century, with authors such as Edgar Allan Poe, Mary Shelley and H. G. Wells making great strides in the always popular but often marginalized genre. At its core, science fiction contains the basic elements of the fantasy genre, a tradition of oral — and later transcribed — folk tales (aka fairy tales) that go back almost to the beginning of recorded history, and were first captured in book form for a mass audience by folks such as Charles Perrault, the Grimm Brothers and E.T.A Hoffmann. With the emergence in the 19th century of medical and physical science as human disciplines, and the concurrent growth of the industrial revolution (with its promise of all forms of labor-saving machinery), science fiction took the basic concepts of the "fantastic" fairy tale universe and stitched them to then-current advances in science and industry. The result was an unusual and immediately popular cultural form which gained ascendancy until what is considered its literary "golden age," the mid–20th Century. As such, the time was right for the movie industry to take note of this hardy — and often highly visual — cultural genre and apply it to films made for an audience hungry for modern-age thrills. Certainly the main trigger for the birth of the "modern" science fiction film was the emergence of atomic weaponry as the equally awesome and fearsome progeny of the marriage of science and industry, but it was, as mentioned previously, the "space race," with its obvious political implications, that really ignited the genre.

The first science fiction films of this period all focused on outer space in some way. *Destination Moon* (1950, d: Byron Haskin, George Pal) paved the way for the science-fiction "spectacle," in which state-of-the-art special effects enhanced the fantastic narrative. A low-budget copy-cat of *Destination Moon* — *Rocketship XM* (1950, d: Kurt Neumann) — managed to cover the same narrative territory using a much smaller canvas, and is seen by some as the superior film, as it dealt with some of the human psychological problems that space travelers would surely encounter. Yet a third, somewhat obscure film more accurately portrayed the wariness, fear and paranoia of the time better than its more well-known cousins. *The Flying Saucer* (1950, d: Mikel Conrad) deals with an American spy who journeys to a remote section of Alaska in order to conduct surveillance on Soviet agents sequestered there, and is shocked to witness an Unidentified Flying Object racing around the skies. The intrepid intelligence agent soon uncovers a sinister government plot as he unlocks the strange secret of this weird "spacecraft."

The "space picture" gained immense popularity in subsequent years, soon settling into two basic subsets: earth expeditions to other planets, and strangers from outer space visiting earth, either for good or ill. Of the first, some of the more memorable are *Flight to Mars* (1951, d: Lesley Selander), *This Island Earth* (1955, d: Joseph Newman) and *Forbidden Planet* (1956, d: Fred McLeod Wilcox), the latter considered the magnum opus of the genre. The second narrative template, the "alien invasion" film, ruminated on the threat to the nation by any and all "foreigners" or "outsiders," generic catch-alls for everyone from Communists to free-thinkers. The masterpiece of the genre is considered by many to be *The Day the Earth Stood Still* (1951, d: Robert Wise), a film with such an impact on the industry it soon boasted legions of imitators, with *The Man from Planet X* (1951, d: Edgar G. Ulmer), *It Came from Outer Space* (1953, d: Jack Arnold), *It Conquered the World* (1956, d: Roger Corman) and *The Cosmic Man* (1959, d: Herbert Greene) some of the more successful treatments of the basic storyline. Yet possibly the greatest of all "alien invasion" movies of the period is *Invasion of the Body Snatchers* (1956, d: Don Siegal). In the film, average citizens are taken over by aliens, with many being none the wiser for the transformation, as the resultant mutant appears, for all intents and purposes, to be exactly like the original host — with one key difference: the alien clones have no emotions, or "soul." Seen primarily as yet another heavy-handed allegory about the threat to democracy from the creeping vines of insidious Communism, *Invasion of the Body Snatchers* also makes some harshly critical observations about the sterile, vapid nature of the postwar American lifestyle in general, and the new suburban experiment in particular. The message by film's end was quite clear: mass society destroys the individual.

Bursting onto the scene at about the same time, and paying homage in some ways to the popular "gothic" horror films of the 1930s and the 1940s (which brought to life such classic literary figures as Frankenstein, Dracula and the Invisible Man), the 1950s offered its own unique take on the notion of the unnatural or unearthly "beast" threatening the community, giving birth to a beloved and long-lived science-fiction/horror genre colloquially known as the "monster movie." This genre was arguably ignited by three films that set the style for the genre for years to come: *The Thing from Another World* (1951, d: Christian Nyby), *The Beast from 20,000 Fathoms* (1953, d: Eugene Lourie) and *Them!* (1954, d: Gordon Douglas). The latter two films featured a subsequently essential element of the monster-movie equation: gigantism. Mammoth creatures, much larger than man or any other extant mammal in the natural world, provided a vivid and quantifiable threat to mankind's infra-structures, often literally trampling over humanity's trinkets of civilization. Of course, the "giant monster" movie also owed something to the wonderful "great ape" movie *King Kong* (1933, d: Merian C. Cooper, Ernest Schoedsack) and its offspring *Son of Kong* (1933) and *Mighty Joe Young* (1949). The first three monster movies of the 1950s were, in retrospect, the best of the genre, but they did inaugurate a long-running series of increasingly bizarre — and thus to some wonderful — series of films featuring ever more grotesque and fanciful mammoths created primarily by the unleashed atom and other wayward energy sources. For sheer spectacle, the "giant monster" movie gave audiences the most for their money, and even if the plotlines of the films tended towards the simplistic (and unlikely), the sheer thrill of the fantastic stories usually overshadowed such concerns.

As noted earlier, the "giant monster" as drawn in 1950s cinema readily stood as an admittedly obvious, yet not ineffective, metaphor for the withering might of runaway atomic power, with its knack for creating hideous mutation and monstrous deformity. Certainly these films expressed — even if almost comically at times — collective anxiety about the dubi-ous promise and awful power of atomic energy, and were thus (quite possibly in spite of themselves) a rare forum for criticism of established policy in an era when such criticism was largely discouraged and marginalized. Yet the rampaging screen beast also starkly con-trasts with the intrinsically diminishing nature of the individual who was, in an increasingly mass-oriented technologically-based culture, becoming an ever smaller, exceedingly unim-portant entity. The logical conclusion of this inexorable diminution is grimly stated in 1957's *The Incredible Shrinking Man*, wherein the individual ultimately fades away to noth-ing, being erased completely from society's equation after having been declared — by forces far greater than he — completely superfluous.

Aside from the occasional critiques of atomic energy and suburbia, we may find that the overall message of the 1950s science fiction film is ultimately a conservative one. Aliens and monsters constantly threaten our world, symbols clearly meant to suggest the "godless

Communists" first and foremost — foreign, inscrutable forces of great malevolence. Any attempt to understand this invading force, to sympathize with it, is almost invariably foolish and ill-fated. Only the merciless extermination of these uninvited outsiders will suffice. The overriding message to the viewer is thus to always be suspicious of any intrusion from outside your socio-cultural comfort zone (i.e., your home and town), for it may well be an evil thing trying to conquer and annihilate you. Even more lamentable in these films is the observation that the U.S. military is often portrayed as heroic, many times saving the protagonists — and often the entire world — from destruction from the outside, through the use of excessive force (often with atomic weaponry). Many of these films shamelessly champion, romanticize and glorify the military-industrial complex, at times making these movies seem almost like baldfaced propaganda pieces for same.

Regarding the genre in general, Miller and Nowak make an interesting observation which reinforces the notion that these films by and large encouraged a timid, conservative world-view:

> Most of the science fiction films dealt with alien monsters who threatened American civilization. Many such monsters were brought forth by atomic explosions: either mutants created by radiation, or prehistoric brutes resuscitated by nuclear blasts. *The Beast* [sic], *The Blob*, *The Creature from the Black Lagoon*, the giant ants that emerge from the Los Angeles sewers in *Them*, *Godzilla* (a Japanese atomic mutant popular in America), *The Deadly Mantis*, *The Spider*, *The Crab Monsters* [sic] were just a few of the deadly atomic offspring stalking or slithering through post–Hiroshiman cinema.[79]

Oddly, the assumption in the above paragraph is that all the "beasts" mentioned were "deadly atomic offspring," when actually only about half of the creatures can boast misuse of atomic energy as their genesis. The Blob was from outer space, the Creature from the Black Lagoon was a prehistoric being whose existence in his environs seems to have been almost eternal, the Spider likewise just seemed to exist in its caves as some sort of generic natural anomaly, not bothersome until prodded outside its natural lair by man. Yet the essential point which the authors make is a valid one: the unleashed mutant-beast is made manifest by some human sin, some technocratic folly, even if it be so benign as exploring a forbidden location which should be left alone. Messing with Nature is a bad idea, whether it is done with an A-bomb or a fishing vessel or a spelunking team. All of these films — and most others in the genre — state that after Man has sinned he will be punished, again a very "Old Testament" ideology which works well for these morally simplistic atom-age fables.

Fantastic Fifty-Seven

The year of 1957 certainly was newsworthy, as many pivotal events coalesced to further disorient a nation (and world) teetering precariously between tradition and modernism. Nineteen fifty-seven was generally seen as a prosperous year for the U.S., yet almost a quarter of the population was living at poverty level, and the nation began a years-long economic recession. Following a traumatic civil rights riot in Little Rock, Arkansas, on Labor Day weekend, the U.S. Congress passed the first civil rights act in almost 100 years, setting the stage for a long-sought progressive impetus to racial relations. In medicine, a vaccine is first successfully used on a number of patients to treat the dreaded new disease, polio. Popular bestsellers included doomsday fiction, such as Nevil Shute's *On the Beach*, and lurid critiques of suburbia, such as Grace Metalious' *Peyton Place*. The year also saw "rock 'n' roll" becoming a significant force in the music industry, a sure sign that the youth demographic, and its avowedly anti-establishment stance, was finally getting some hard-earned attention from dominant cultural paradigms. As well, Jack Kerouac's groundbreaking "beat" novel *On the Road* was published, which, along with other brilliant new works of writing and poetry (such as Allen Ginsberg's *Howl*), was seen as officially inaugurating the counterculture (which, of course, would blossom forth in the next decade to undreamed-of heights). In contrast, Senator McCarthy, who had terrified the nation and ruined so many lives with his modern-day witch-hunts, died of acute alcoholism, perhaps a sign that the regressive forces that dominated the first part of the decade were losing momentum as the era attempted to progress beyond hateful, exclusionary xenophobia. Yet the Soviets, heretofore a distant second in developments in the nuclear arena, called our bluff by being the first to successfully launch an artificial space satellite, a momentous event that greatly accelerated the "race for space," and solidified the tensions and animosity simmering between the two world superpowers. Meanwhile, in the Nevada desert, the military continued to test a wide array of ever-larger weapons of mass destruction in an orgy of chronic detonation. The Operation Plumbbob tests of 1957 released such extraordinary amounts of radioactive poison into the world environment that the very next year a concerted effort was launched to stop such above-ground testing by a program and an industry increasingly seen as foolhardy and reckless. And finally — and perhaps portentously — President Eisenhower suffered a heart attack, some seeing this as symbolizing the potential demotion, and perhaps even the impending death, of the techno-military patriarchy which seemed compelled to bring the human race ever closer to its own annihilation.

It is in this tumultuous socio-political setting that the fantastic films of the year were unleashed on the nation, and an overview of these movies will reflect much of the zeitgeist of the moment. Chapters 2 and 3 are devoted to individual analysis of 57 fantastic films released theatrically in the United States during the calendar year of 1957. Although the aesthetic, narrative and thematic elements in the movies differ widely, there are certainly recurring motifs and concerns which apply to many, if not all, of the films. Virtually all of the pictures are contemporary in setting, with a very few taking place in the past or the future. Due to the somewhat marginalized nature of the horror, fantasy and science-fiction genres, most of the films are small-to-medium budgeted independent productions. Most of the films address atomic power in one way or the other. Many also address, obliquely or overtly, the Soviet menace and the threat of communism. Most curiously, no fantastic films of the year take place, either in whole or in part, in outer space, a common locale for fantastic films of the 1950s; all 1957 offerings are "home-bound" and thus important as allegory to the current cultural climate. However, many of these movies do feature "invaders" from other worlds. These "invaders" almost invariably serve as surrogates for a perceived Soviet/Communist menace. Personal dissolution and the pitfalls of societal conformity is a key theme throughout. And finally, there is a highly problematic — at times contradictory — yet intriguing depiction of women in many of the fantastic films of the year, especially showcasing the "professional" woman and the woman scientist, giving some early hints of a burgeoning feminist viewpoint wrestling with the dominant regressive, sexist gender roles.[80]

TWO

Films Released January Through June

The following discussion includes feature-length motion pictures released theatrically in the United States between January 1 and December 31, 1957, and which reasonably fall under the genres of horror, science-fiction or fantasy. The discussion will not include popular 1956 releases — such as *Forbidden Planet, Godzilla, King of the Monsters* and *Invasion of the Body Snatchers*—which were still in wide theatrical release during 1957; nor will it discuss genre films such as *Curucu, Beast of the Amazon, The Mole People* or *The Gamma People*, released in December of 1956 and so still in wide release in 1957. The discussion will, however, include several films produced earlier in the decade that received significant national re-release during the 1957 season as pre-packaged double bills. These include *Tobor the Great* (1954) plus *The Rocket Man* (1954); *1,000 Years from Now* (1952) plus *Invasion U.S.A.* (1953); *The Beast of Paradise Isle* (1953) plus *Creatures of the Jungle* (1954). Films are discussed in roughly chronological order, based on the month of their national theatrical release.

February

Unnatural: The Fruit of Evil

(original production, *Alraune*, 1952)
92 minutes (West Germany), Black and White
Produced by Carlton-Film, Deutsche Styria Film GmbH
Distributed in the U.S. by Distributors Corporation of America
Released in the United States in February, 1957
Directed by Arthur Maria Rabenalt
Story: Hanns Heinz Ewers (as "Hans Heinz Ewers," from his novel "Alraune")
Screenplay: Kurt Heuser
Produced by Günther Stapenhorst
Music by Werner Richard Heymann
Cinematography by Friedel Behn-Grund
Film Editing by Doris Zeltmann
Set Decoration: Robert Herlth
Costume Design by Herbert Ploberger
Unit Managers: Rudolf Fichtner, Gustl Gotzler
Production Manager: Otto Lehmann
Sound Department: Heinz Terworth, Klang-Film Eurocord
Still Photographer: Wolfgang Brünjes

Lyricist: Robert Gilbert
English Language Version: American Dubbing Company
Cast: Hildegard Knef (as "Hildegarde Neff") (Alraune), Erich von Stroheim (Jacob ten Brinken), Karlheinz Böhm (as "Carlheinz Böhm") (Frank Braun), Harry Meyen (Count Geroldingen), Rolf Henniger (Ralph Goutram), Harry Halm (Doctor Mohn), Hans Cossy (Mathieu), Gardy Brombacher (Lisbeth), Trude Hesterberg (Princess Wolkonski), Julia Koschka (Olga Wolkonski), Denise Vernac (Mlle. Duvaliere), Arno Ebert, Willem Holsboer

Published synopsis: Jacob ten Brinken is a wealthy scientist, who at the turn of the century busies himself with studying the problem of artificial insemination. He was expelled from his post at the University and sneered at by other men in his profession because of such studies. He finally brings to fruition his theories by actually producing life! The creature he has brought to life was fathered by a criminal about to be hanged. Her mother was a street walker. Ten Brinken names the girl Alraune after the mandrake root alraune, for according to the legend, it grows underneath the gallows and is said to bring its owner luck and riches but also death and ruin. Alraune grows into a lovely girl who fascinates everyone who comes into contact with her. Ten Brinken brought her up as his ward but withheld the circumstances of her origin from her. At her guardian's home, she eventually meets Frank Braun, a young medical student, who is the nephew of Ten Brinken; however, Braun feels an instinctive aversion to Alraune and Alraune then subsequently devotes herself to systematically making every man who comes within her orbit fall in love with her. After she accomplishes this purpose, she then proceeds to destroy her hapless victim. Upon her advice also, Ten Brinken buys up worthless acreage on which rich mineral springs are discovered. Around it he builds a fashionable watering and amusement resort where Alraune is the social leader. After a while Frank Braun returns and her love for his [sic] is redoubled, but love, as the legend has it, breaks the magic of the mandrake root. The mineral springs dry up, and Ten Brinken faces financial disaster. Finally, Alraune tells Ten Brinken that she loves Braun, and she wishes to leave the scientist. Ten Brinken, insanely jealous, tells her the secret of her origin. A violent struggle insues [sic] and Alraune meets death at the hand of the man who brought her to life.

Unnatural: The Fruit of Evil (1952) is the fifth screen adaptation of *Alraune*, a novel by Hanns Heinz Ewers first published in Germany in 1911. The novel takes as its narrative spark a legend dating from the Middle Ages regarding the *mandragora officinarum*, or "mandrake root," a plant with supposed magical properties. According to legend the root, with a roughly humanoid shape, was manifested from the semen of hanged men, as hanging was known to cause involuntary ejaculation among some. The dead man's ejaculate was then absorbed into the earth, allowing the root to acquire the criminal's (largely negative) energy. Ewers' novel works this premise into an interesting comparison of genetics versus environment in an attempt to pinpoint and predict human moral behavior. As well, the then-popular process of artificial insemination is a major theme of the work. In the novel, a reckless scientist artificially impregnates a prostitute with the semen of a hanged murderer. The woman subsequently births a malefic girl-child who appears to lack a soul. The girl is named Alraune, and the scientist adopts the evil youth. Alraune has an uncanny ability to lure men to their demise, and she uses sex to ruin several. Alraune finally learns of her "unnatural" origins and takes out her revenge on the professor, her ungodly "father." *Unnatural* follows the plot of the novel fairly faithfully, while the film's prologue honors its debt to the legend of the mandrake root:

> Since ancient times, the legend of the alraune or mandrake root has held a mystical fascination for mankind. The root, which flourishes under the gallows of a hanged man, is believed to endow its master with the power of producing good and evil... to enable him to possess the power of the gods. *Unnatural* is the story of one man's attempt to control destinies with the powers of the alraune root.

The alchemist-professor Ten Brinken is played by the notorious Erich von Stroheim (1885–1957), at one time considered one of the great silent film directors. Von Stroheim had all but retired from the profession by the time *Unnatural* was filmed in 1952, but did enjoy playing the occasional film role, often as a bigger-than-life version of himself, such as his star turn in Billy Wilder's *Sunset Boulevard* (1950, in which he played a down-and-out former movie director reduced to playing man-servant to a delusional movie star). In *Unnatural*, Von Stroheim exploits yet another aspect of his own personality — a megalomaniac alchemist with delusions of grandeur and a total lack of personal morality — and does so quite effectively. Alraune is played by Hildegard Knef (1925–2002), a German-born actress who achieved fame both in her native country and internationally. The same year she filmed *Unnatural*, Knef starred opposite Gregory Peck in *The Snows of Kilimanjaro* (1952, d: Henry King), an international hit considered to be Knef's "breakthrough" picture. Knef's sultry, smoking sexuality was perfect for her role in *Alraune*, and gives the film much of its palpable sexual tension.

In *Unnatural* (as undoubtedly in the original novel), Alraune and Ten Brinken share a most perverse father-daughter relationship, which sizzles with barely-repressed sexual tension and seems always ready to devolve into incest. Although she performs many malicious acts, some bordering on outright murder, in essence Alraune as portrayed in *Unnatural* is little more than an amoral "brat" of industrial society, born of permissive, ethically complicit parents and unleashed on a world which has no concept of how to contain her. Ten Brinken has even attempted to make Alraune "go straight" by sending her to a nunnery, but the slippery lass escapes the convent after being imprisoned for possessing "obscene literature" (which, according to Ten Brinken, was his own copy of the 1911 novel *Alraune* by Hanns Heinz Ewers!).

Newspaper advertisement for Distributor Corporation of America's February 1957 U.S. release of the German thriller *Unnatural: The Fruit of Evil* (1952).

The first time the viewer gets a clear view of Alraune, she is hiding in her father's basement laboratory — likely her birthplace — and is flanked by a menacing gorilla, nicely emphasizing her essentially bestial nature. It is revealed anon that Alraune's birth mother was a whore, and her biological father was a killer. Given this cruel legacy, what could the child become but a profane alchemical conglomeration of these morally corrupt environments? According to her adoptive father, Alraune has indeed inherited all of her parents' "evil characteristics"; she is even called at one point a "crime against nature." With the film coming hot on the heels of the epic failure called the "National Socialist" experiment, the viewer could easily see allusions here to Hitler's lamentable "Master Race" concept, an uber-eugenics nightmare which posited the creation of "perfect beings" from the forced mating of racially "pure" types; but, of course, it could produce nothing but broken, soulless monsters. Again the main symbol in the film — the mandrake root — functions nicely as shorthand for the "artificial" creation of soulless human monsters, for this unfortunate plant has, according to Ten Brinken, "the head, arms and legs of a man, but it has no soul," a description which could certainly be applied to his offspring — and indeed to himself. Even Alraune, the victim of diabolical tampering with nature, possesses occasional self-awareness regarding her "unnatural" physiology, at one point observing, "Funny, I never feel my own heart beating."

Artificial insemination in *Unnatural* is portrayed with a problematic, if not outright malevolent cast — any attempt to create new life outside the "laws of nature and God" creates nothing but soulless monsters who destroy all around them and in turn must be destroyed themselves. In other films of the postwar era, such as *Test Tube Babies* (1948, d: W. Merle Connell), the concept of artificial insemination is seen as a boon to mankind, giving previously "unfit" or "barren" mothers the chance to produce offspring. As Eric Schaefer observes in his seminal treatise on the "classical" exploitation film (*Bold! Daring! Shocking! True! A History of Exploitation Films, 1910–1959*), this embracing of scientific methods to increase fecundity — embraced rabidly in the "exploitation films" of the era — had definite and specific reasons to validate a society increasingly focused on production and consumption: "Here, employed in the service of sex, technology could be used to reorient the unproductive in order to affirm the economic status quo, increasingly based on the act of consumption."[1] Thus artificial insemination, which had been a viable procedure for decades (especially in the propagation of beef cattle), became a most curious and highly vaunted analog to increased industrial productivity — in the United States at least — and widely promoted as such in the mass media. In highly-traumatized postwar Germany, however, where *Unnatural* was "birthed," there was little but shame, revulsion and regret in the awareness that man can create his own monsters, as witnessed so recently by that country's horrid detour into neo-barbarism. Indeed, *Unnatural*'s avowedly morbid premise — punctuated succinctly by Friedel Behn-Grund's bleak noir cinematography and Werner Richard Heymann's mournful score — makes it in some ways a requiem for a crippled, decimated culture just beginning to lick its collective wounds and redress its crimes against humanity.

The decidedly unholy, ultimately nihilist union of parent and child in *Unnatural* could serve, as well, as an extremely dark allegory towards all human reproduction, even that perpetuated by two "normal" souls in typical carnal union. Alraune causes, during her short, fated life, as much consternation to her father as would any spoiled teenage daughter. Ten Brinken, stereotypical petit-tyrant, alternately lords over and genuflects to his manifested love object, as would any self-respecting middle-class patriarch. In the end, unable to sponsor her entrée into the adult world, Ten Brinken yanks his daughter back to the ethereal nothingness from whence she emerged. This death sentence, dictated by a "loving" parent to his hapless child, is indeed true of all parents, who are by definition the murderers of their own children. By sentencing their offspring to life via birth, every parent is also sentencing them to a likely gruesome, traumatic death at the tail end of the sorry debacle, which — it must be remembered — was *never* requested by its victim. Here may be where *Unnatural* works best, as a pitch-black allegory of "modern" parenthood, a grisly crime of delusional passion which has only suffering and destruction as its "fruit of evil." This sentiment is expressed nicely by the film's last three shots. The first shows the deceased Alraune dissolving into a hideous, grimacing skull before her father's horrified eyes, revealing that her grisly fate was indeed predetermined and likely universal. Next is an iconic close-up of the eerily-humanoid Mandrake root, grievous emblem of the atrocious human monster. Finally, Ten Brinken is led to the gallows to be hanged for the murder of his "child." The viewer may be certain that through this twisted patriarch's perverse ejaculation into the earth upon his death throes, he will assist in perpetuating the evil that is human reproduction into perpetuity.

Hal Roach, Jr.'s tiny releasing outfit, Distributors Corporation of America, released *Alraune* in an English-dubbed version to art house and grindhouse theaters in February of 1957, making this most unusual film the first fantastic picture of that most "unnatural" year. It is, however, unlikely that *Unnatural* had a large audience, likely languishing in the art-house ghetto. DCA would reach a far wider audience with their two 1957 drive-in double bills: *The Monster from Green Hell* and *Half Human*, and *Rodan, the Flying Monster* and *Hell in Korea*. As will be discussed later, producer-director Kurt Neumann almost certainly saw *Unnatural: The Fruit of Evil* in its limited early–1957 theatrical run, as his *She-Devil*, released later the same year, is a remarkably similar melodrama, following many of the major plotlines of the Alraune story faithfully.

Voodoo Island with *Pharaoh's Curse* (United Artists)

This early 1957 double-bill released by United Artists was produced by Bel-Air Productions, a film production outfit formed by Howard W. Koch, Aubrey Schenck and Edward Zabel. The following year Koch would make his "breakthrough" picture, *Frankenstein 1970*, with Boris Karloff. Koch soon graduated from "B" pictures to large "prestige" films like *The Manchurian Candidate* (1962), *Robin and the Seven Hoods* (1964), *The Odd Couple* (1968) and *On a Clear Day You Can See Forever* (1970). In addition, Koch made a name for himself in television, being responsible for many of the early Academy Awards telecasts.

Voodoo Island
aka *Silent Death*

76 minutes, Black and White
Produced by Aubrey Schenck Productions (as Oak Pictures Inc.), Bel-Air Productions
Distributed by United Artists
Directed by Reginald Le Borg
Screenplay: Richard H. Landau
Produced by Howard W. Koch
Executive Producer: Aubrey Schenck

Newspaper advertisement for *Voodoo Island* and *Pharaoh's Curse*, the first horror-thriller double bill of 1957, released by United Artists.

Music by Les Baxter
Cinematography by William Margulies
Film Editing: John F. Schreyer
Production Design: Jack T. Collis
Makeup Artist: Ted Coodley
Hair Stylist: Mary Westmoreland
Assistant Director: Paul Wurtzel
Property Master: Arden Cripe
Sound Re-Recordist: Charles Cooper
Sound Mixer: Joe Edmondson
Sound Editor: Charles G. Schelling
Special Effects: Louis DeWitt, Jack Rabin, Milt Rice
Camera Operator: Ben Colman
Lighting Technician: Joseph Edesa
Wardrobe: Angela Alexander, Wesley Jeffries
Music Editor: Carlo Lodato
Theremin: Samuel Hoffman
Script Supervisor: Kathleen Fagan
Cast: Boris Karloff (Phillip Knight), Beverly Tyler (Sarah Adams), Murvyn Vye (Barney Finch), Elisha Cook, Jr. (Martin Schuyler), Rhodes Reason (Matthew Gunn), Jean Engstrom (Claire Winter), Friedrich von Ledebur (Native Chief), Glenn Dixon (Mitchell), Owen Cunningham (Howard Carlton), Herbert Patterson (Dr. Wilding), Jerry Frank (Vickers), Adam West (Radio Operator)

Synopsis: An exploration party, seeking a locale for a posh new tourist resort, travels to a foreboding island only to encounter strange monsters and occult curses.

Voodoo Island is a crackling good horror-mystery prominently featuring "King of the Monsters" Boris Karloff in one of his best comeback roles. The credits roll over what appears to be a scale model of a tropical island with a large resort hotel on it; the viewer may consider this attractive but simplistic miniature by Jack Rabin and Louis DeWiit to signal the start of a cheap adventure utilizing obvious artifice, but as the camera pulls back to reveal a miniature replica of an upcoming island resort, one sees that *Voodoo Island* will be concerned with doubles, imitations and fakes, including many tricks of optical illusion. Indeed, Karloff's credit is superimposed over a small doll containing his likeness, subsequently revealed to be his voodoo double to be used for nefarious occult purposes. And before the expedition leaves for the real island, first seen in miniature, the model inexplicably starts to "bleed," clearly suggesting that "it" represents the spirit, if not the essence, of the real thing.

Karloff plays a cynical television host whose program showcases strange occult phenomena, only to later mock and debunk them. Coyly referencing his career as a monster in film, Karloff gleefully states, "The public *likes* to be scared!" His assistant is a cold duck of a woman conspicuously named "Adams"; as an emotionless archetypal feminist, she is more man than woman. In stark contrast is an alcoholic libertine named Winters, who remarkably reveals herself to be a lesbian, a rare thing in 1950s cinema. A chauvinist male immediately spots the Sapphic sister in the group, correctly calling her world "private, exclusive, special." Yet Winters and Adams, both "anti-man" until tamed by patriarchal forces later in the film, are in other ways diametrically opposed, not only in their opposite gender preferences but in their emotional make-up. In one of the film's most overtly sexist plot points, both the lesbian and the feminist are eventually "corrected" via attacks by exceedingly penis-like monster plants, absurd emblems of phallo-centric forces determined to rid the world of non-conforming females.

The bulk of the scenario ruminates on the inherent perils of imperialism, a common theme in genre films of the day, in which white capitalists seeking coarse profit invade a native population only to be felled by the collective zeitgeist of the invaded peoples, a political energizing most often symbolized by the unleashing of demonic occult powers far exceeding the whites' power to counter, and forcing the invading army to retreat with haste. Within this somewhat pedestrian framework, abundant nice touches prevail; walking dead men, superimposed voodoo dolls, and an abundance of overzealous, if clichéd, character development turn an ostensibly mediocre programmer into something quite memorable.

Pharaoh's Curse

Produced by Schenck-Koch Productions, Bel-Air Productions
Distributed by United Artists
66 minutes, Black and White
Directed by Lee Sholem
Screenplay: Richard H. Landau
Story: Richard H. Landau
Produced by Howard W. Koch
Executive Producer: Aubrey Schenck
Music by Les Baxter

Cinematography by William Margulies
Film Editing by George A. Gittens
Set Decoration: Clarence Steensen
Makeup Artist: Gordon Bau
Makeup Man: Ted Coodley
Hair Stylist: Mary Westmoreland
Assistant Director: Paul Wurtzel
Set Designer: Robert Kinoshita
Character Designer: Nick Volpe
Sound Editor: John A. Bushelman
Sound Re-Recording Technician: Charles Cooper
Sound Mixer: Joe Edmondson
Photographic Effects: Louis DeWitt, Jack Rabin
Lighting Technician: Joseph Edesa
Key Grip: Martin Kashuk
Casting: John G. Stephens
Wardrobe Mistress : Angela Alexander
Wardrobe Master: Wesley Jeffries
Supervising Editor: John F. Schreyer
Music Editor: Sam E. Waxman
Cast: Mark Dana (Captain Storm), Ziva Rodann (as Ziva Shapir) (Simira), Diane Brewster (Sylvia Quentin), George N. Neise (Robert Quentin), Alvaro Guillot (Numar), Ben Wright (Walter Andrews), Guy Prescott (Dr. Michael Farraday), Terence de Marney (Sgt. Smolett), Richard Peel (Sgt. Gromley), Kurt Katch (Hans Brecht), Robert Fortin (Claude Beauchamp), Ralph Clanton (Col. Cross)

Synopsis: In 1902, a British expedition travels to the site of an archeological dig, only to discover that the mummy entombed there has come to life with the help of a reincarnated Egyptian cat goddess.

This interesting take on a horror-film staple positions, along with its co-feature, two powerful women as the main engines of the scenario. The first is the estranged wife of the archaeologist who lobbies for her personal freedom against obstacles both man-made and supernatural. The second, a mysterious witch-like creature who claims to be the sister of the titular pharaoh, manifests virtually absolute power over the male collective and turns out to be an incarnation of Bast, the warrior-cat goddess of Egyptian mythology. It's a good example of the proto-feminist notion of female empowerment creeping into popular entertainment of the day, and one of a very few fantastic films of the year to be a period piece. *Film Bulletin* reviewed the movie in its February 18 issue, emphasizing its relative lack of abundant entertainment value:

In its category as supporting meller for a dual-bill bally program, this low-budget Bel-Air Production for UA will get by. Offering chills and thrills in lieu of a name cast and production values, Howard W. Koch's production will satisfy addicts of the eerie and supernatural. It's all wholly incredible and Lee Sholem directs strictly by the book, bringing the monster into close range whenever the plot stagnates. To counteract riots, British authorities dispatch Mark Dana to halt American archaeologist Neise from disturbing an ancient tomb. Diane Brewster, Neise's unhappy wife, goes along to join her husband. A spooky "cat goddess," Ziva Rodann, steps out of the desert to bring evil forebodings. When Neise cuts open the mummy, a native feels the pain and turns into walking mummy that feeds on human blood [sic]. Several members of the expedition, including Neise, are killed by the monster before Dana seals the tomb and returns to Cairo.[2]

March

ATTACK OF THE CRAB MONSTERS PLUS
NOT OF THIS EARTH (ALLIED ARTISTS)

Cinema's "fantastic" year got off to an auspicious start with the release of these two exceptional programmers from young producer-director Roger Corman. Corman, who was rapidly becoming a force as an independent producer-director, had, since 1954, made several similar genre pictures for James H. Nicholson and Samuel Z. Arkoff and their fledgling American International Pictures. Corman approached Allied Artists and proposed a pre-packaged science-fiction double bill aimed primarily at the coveted youth market. Allied Artists had achieved success the previous year with their genre releases *Invasion of the Body Snatchers* and *World Without End*. The company was at this time attempting to distance itself from its "poverty row" origins as Monogram Pictures Corporation, and so were winding down their programmer product (such as Westerns, and the "Bomba, the Jungle Boy" and "Bowery Boys" series) in order to emphasize big-budget, high-profile releases, such as 1957's *Love in the Afternoon*, starring Cary Grant and Audrey Hepburn, and *The Hunchback of Notre Dame*, starring Sophia Loren and Anthony Quinn, in an attempt to compete favorably at the box office with the major studios. In order to achieve this, the company needed low-cost, popular fare such as Corman's double bill to, in effect, float the major releases with their larger production and campaign budgets. This fantastic pair of chillers, proudly tagged "The Greatest Double Horror Show of All Time!" achieved this goal admirably. According to anecdotal accounts, including those of Corman, *Attack of the Crab Monsters* cost $70,000 to produce and eventually earned over $1 million in rentals, making it one of the most financially successful B-horror pictures of the decade.[3] Likewise, *Not of This Earth*—also with an under–$100,000 budget—purportedly grossed just under $1 million itself, making the double bill an exceptionally successful venture into the short-lived "all science-fiction" genre.[4] Certainly, Allied Artists was pleased with the result, as they rushed into production another science-shocker double bill—*From Hell It Came* and *The Disembodied*—released in late summer of 1957, and also picked up two other pictures—*The Cyclops* and *Daughter of Dr. Jekyll*—to flesh out their summer youth market schedule.

Attack of the Crab Monsters

62 minutes, Black and White
Produced by Los Altos Productions
Distributed by Allied Artists Pictures Corporation
Directed by Roger Corman
Screenplay: Charles B. Griffith
Produced by Roger Corman
Associate Producer: Charles B. Griffith
Music by Ronald Stein
Cinematography: Floyd Crosby
Film Editing: Charles Gross, Jr.
Makeup Artist: Curly Batson
Assistant Director: Maurice Vaccarino
Underwater Scenes: Charles B. Griffith
Second Assistant Director: Lindsley Parsons, Jr.

Rarely-seen combo poster for Roger Corman's fantastic pair of 1957 nightmare fables —*Attack of the Crab Monsters* and *Not of This Earth* —which Allied Artists modestly proclaimed as "The Greatest Double-Horror Show of All Time!"

Props: Karl Brainard
Chief Grip: Charles Hannawalt
Gaffer: Floyd Williams
Underwater Technician: Maitland Stuart
Titles: Paul Julian
Cast: Richard Garland (Dale Brewer), Pamela Duncan (Martha Hunter), Russell Johnson (Hank Chapman), Leslie Bradley (Dr. Karl Weigand), Mel Welles (Dr. Jules Deveroux), Richard Cutting (Dr. James Carson), Beach Dickerson (Ron Fellows), Tony Miller (Jack Sommers), Ed Nelson (Quinlan), Maitland Stuart (Mac), Charles B. Griffith (Tate), Robin Riley, Doug Roberts

Synopsis: Following a series of hydrogen bomb blasts in the Pacific, a group of scientists land on a desolate atoll to search for members of an earlier scientific expedition that disappeared without a trace some months previously. The group encounters giant crabs which eat people, devouring and absorbing their victims' brains and personalities.

Attack of the Crab Monsters is one of the most unusual science-fiction films of the 1950s. It boasts a bright, literate script, above-average performances, and a glorious music score. The film is engaging and fast-paced, utilizing brisk dialogue exchanges and quick cutting for maximum impact — thus, a somewhat complicated scenario is compacted into a little over an hour. Corman really tested the limits of his capacities as both producer and director with this high-concept film, which took the already tired "radioactive mutant" film genre, which boasted such pedestrian entries as *The Beast from 20,000 Fathoms* (1953), *Them!* (1954) and *Tarantula!* (1955), and created a mysterious, allegorical atomic-age nightmare fable. Unlike the average product of the day (such as the aforementioned), *Attack of the Crab Monsters* consistently ventures beyond the boundaries of similar films. Floyd Crosby's highly choreographed camera work leans towards the neo-realistic, featuring some arty, almost "European" shot compositions and utilizing some highly engaging dolly work. In a cutting edge move, the film also contains some actual gore, which is heavily reinforced by more referenced gore, putting the picture right on the fringe of acceptable culture of the day, in effect making it a grisly horror comic book or lurid pulp science-fiction story brought to life.

Charles Griffith's screenplay adds numerous laudable touches to the basic narrative template of man against monster, the most important of which is the addition of personality to the titular beast. The crab monster is not merely a dumb brute ripped from the ground due to atomic tests, stomping blindly over the countryside and trampling hapless villagers. The beast here is a character, and a formidable one at that, for it is a conscious, malevolent force with a frankly stated agenda — to eat and thus negate mankind. The crab monster plots strategies, lies in wait, and pounces upon its victims with a cleverness that is unnerving. Via the power of telepathy — one of Corman's main recurring themes at this time — the crab can both communicate its misanthropic agenda to the poor scientists trapped on the island and also lure unsuspecting victims to their demise. In so doing, the crab evokes the vocally-articulated spirits of the scientists it has devoured previously in order to confuse and sway the living scientists. In this way the film also succeeds as a sort of postmodern ghost story wherein the disembodied spirits of the dead also play their part, giving the movie a most decidedly Gothic edge. Finally, Griffith's taut script offers scenes that build up an almost unbearable tension, creating a narrative energy which propels the film nicely. Corman had dictated to Griffith that "in every scene there must be horror and suspense, so that there would never be a straight expository scene."[5] Combined with the rather complicated plot structure, this dramatic conceit makes for a most "spooky" picture, an unusual instance of Gothic fable subsumed within contemporary melodramatic trappings. The power of Griffith's screenplay is well illustrated by the fact that as a character the crab occupies a major portion of the scenario via its various attacks on humans, detonations of the landscape, and telepathic communications, even though the crab monster prop itself is onscreen for less than sixty seconds. The character of the crab monster expands far beyond its mere shell; indeed, it is an abiding—if malevolent—spirit hovering over the whole island, an omnipresent spectral being forever haunting the protagonists.

Attack of the Crab Monsters resonates thematically on several intriguing levels, three of which will be mentioned briefly here. As in many Corman pictures of this time period, the role of the female in society, especially the strong, autonomous female, is brought front and center, although not in the way one might at first expect. While Martha Hunter (Pamela Duncan) is a bright young female scientist (a not uncommon fixture in films of this type), she does not come across as an especially strong or unusual character—certainly no proto-feminist like her counterpart in *Not of this Earth*, Nadine Storey. In fact, Martha seems a classically-repressed character at times (subservient to the male collective in most important decisions), yet at others she appears to be on the edge of burgeoning autonomy (her brief flirtation with adultery, her insistence on joining the men in one of their later excursions into the crab caves). As with most other Corman females of the day, she is highly intu-itive—to the point of being psychic. It is Martha who first picks up the ethereal vibrations of the crab monster as it sends out counterfeit telepathic signals of missing group leader McLean. Yet Martha is equally aware, shortly after hearing the disembodied voice, that it is a fake, a ruse, a subterfuge with possibly devastating consequences.

Even with all this, Martha doesn't express the rage of the female against a repressive phallic hegemony. Yet the female principle, in some of its more nefarious aspects, is illustrated vividly—oddly enough, by the title monster. After quickly killing the first crab monster upon encountering it, throughout the rest of the story the scientists must deal with the remaining monster, who is specifically identified as a female. This is a most interesting conceit on the scenarist's part, as there would appear to be no reason to label this beast as female—or any gender at all—if not for the role the character plays in the subsequent proceedings.

This female freak's existence, no doubt fraught with pain and suffering, is solely due to the reckless, highly phallic intrusion of Man's monstrous weaponry on the natural (female) world—a rape of sorts. And as the crab absorbs the brains and knowledge of her tormentors, she surely becomes conscious of this assault against her, and knows who her enemies really are. Although there is only one woman to pick from amongst a primarily male group on the island, it may nonetheless be significant that the crab monster's victims are all male—for surely the male is the enemy. The crab monster thus embodies the female principle, rep-resentative of the natural world, as set against the hegemony of the male principle, represented by the wholly destructive power of atomic weaponry. (The brutal, rape-like violence of atom bomb blasts is only *referred to* in the film's theatrical release, but is vividly depicted via military stock footage of multiple A-bomb and H-bomb blasts in the syndicated tele-vision version, arguably seen by a far larger audience than the original theatrical one.) Fur-ther, atomic weapons' perpetual faux-semen—radioactive fallout—which decimates the natural world without mercy and lasts, in some cases, almost forever, can only lead to the monstrous birthing of generations of mutant monsters (human and other) in perpetuity.

Another salient point emphasized in the film is that this female crab is pregnant, poised to foist her offspring onto the world, surely with dire consequences for humankind. That this gruesome menace to mankind is an expectant mother — one of the decade's most fetishized and cherished cultural roles — is curious at least, perhaps perverse and possibly even subversive. This odd expositional conceit threatens to convey a somewhat critical view of the nurturing role of the fifties female (that role subliminally accented by the female scientist's ample bosom), perhaps suggesting that what modern mothers might unleash upon the world are armies of "little monsters." Even more provocatively, from certain angles the silhouette of the crab monster, with its raised limbs and cavernous open mouth, suggests the image of a woman preparing for intercourse (missionary position), her legs spread high in the air, her vagina invitingly open. This highly Freudian aspect of the crab monster prop may evoke images of the archetypal "devouring vagina," whose voracious, gnashing teeth threaten to castrate any male foolish enough to enter. Yet, as are we all, the crab monster's very existence is challenged by the horrific inroads of phallic culture via the burgeoning military-industrial complex, and its mascot — baleful emblem of patriarchal intimidation — the mushroom bomb that can easily kill us all. The crab monster expresses both the horror of subatomic molestation at the hands of careless male hands, and the rage to endure in this new terror-world of largely gender-based genocide, finally standing as one of Corman's more memorable "power females."

As mentioned previously, the demonization of the United States' chosen enemy, the Soviet Union, was a major theme running through the entire decade, leading to the routing out of supposed Communists (more often than not, just luckless liberals, progressives and idiosyncratic creative persons) and an aversion to anything smacking of socialist philosophy. In popular film, this aversion manifested itself in a recurring theme of alien outsiders turning American citizens into mindless, soulless "pod people" (as in one of the decade's purest examples of this theme, *Invasion of the Body Snatchers*). Many of 1957's fantastic film offerings used this motif as either main theme or subtext, and *Attack of the Crab Monsters* is a good example of the perceived evils of socialism. The crab monster's sole purpose, it seems, is to appropriate all available individuals into its own being, creating both a socialist commune of sorts and, most importantly, a "mass mind" which works as a single unit towards its stated agenda, the conquest of its environment. Thus the crab serves as a vivid metaphor for the West's perception of the Soviet Communist experiment as an attempt to squash all individualism, harvesting the populace as workers for the great project of Soviet expansion, the creation of a vast industrial state and the perpetuation of the Communist mindset out into the world, hopefully resulting in one group mind, all individual intelligence deformed into serving that great collective will, the august nation-state of Karl Marx's naïve fever dreams. (Although the film is in black and white, and the "color" of the crab is not mentioned, the crab as seen in the poster art is conspicuously pinkish-red, perhaps further emphasizing the monster's "Red Commie" leanings.)

Yet perhaps the most efficacious and resonant theme throughout the film is its harnessing of the scenario as a biblical parable, a tale of Man's fall from Grace and his redemption via the savior figure sent to save Man from his infernal destiny. Certainly, many "beasties" in science-fiction films can be seen as messengers of an angry god taking revenge on a fallen mankind by unleashing the bestial, but the poignant screenplay of *Attack of the Crab Monsters* takes this concept and elaborates on it remarkably. Drawing from both the Old and New Testaments in a somewhat random yet effective manner, the film's dramatic tension is greatly increased by this superimposition of various icons and parables of Christian mythology. Most conspicuously in this regard, the film opens with God himself as a character. As angry clouds roil in a tumultuous heaven — those clouds illustrative of Man's new creation, his atomic clouds of death — God makes a proclamation which announces his agenda and serves as the main subtextual thrust of the subsequent scenario:

> I will destroy man, whom I have created, from the face of the earth. Both Man and beast and the creeping thing, and the fowls of the air, for it repenteth me, that I have made Him.

This loose paraphrasing of familiar text from the Old Testament declares that Yahweh, the vengeful God of Moses and the Israelites, has decided that Man is fatally corrupted and completely unfixable, thus deserving of swift annihilation.

As the atomic scientists land on the island, one of them, positioned as a religious man by his propensity towards prayer during times of stress, ruminates out loud about the fate of the previous missing scientists — most particularly the final disposition of their "souls," a most romantic, even reckless comment for a scientist to make. Shortly after, the scientists sit together and listen as one of their number reads out loud the final entries of the lost scientist's journal. The assembled listen quietly, even reverently, as would rapt children listening to a teacher reading portions of the Bible. It is clear these learned men and women consider this journal a "sacred text," for it may contain clues to their own fate as written by one who is deceased, and who thus possesses the secrets of life and death. The scene, in effect, depicts an Old Testament Bible reading for moderns.

One of the first actions of the crab monster when it realizes it has a new group of enemies to vanquish is to use its immense geo-thermal abilities to create a vast network of caves and pits in which both to hide and to lure recalcitrant sinners. The crab monster is certainly positioned in the film as a devil figure, even moreso than its many generic predecessors. Due to the wildly expressionist face of the prop, with its gnarly limbs, snarling scowl and judgmental eyes, the monster *looks* like an angry devil, a cartoonish personification of supernatural malice like that which might have been painted by a religious artist in the high Middle Ages. From certain angles, two curious ridges on the crab's shell even look like the proverbial "horns" seen in certain depictions of demons. This conspicuous design conceit — in addition to making the monster look "creepy" — also clearly reinforces the beast's misanthropic ideology and nihilistic agenda. As if to dispel any doubts about the crab monster's supernatural agenda, the beast itself speaks (telepathically to the other characters and narratively to the viewer), thus expressing its aims quite succinctly. "We will rest in the caves and plan our assault upon the world of men!" As well, the crab monsters choose to live in deep underground caverns, creating a geographic landscape wherein luckless or reckless humans easily trip and fall into their seemingly bottomless pits. That is, the humans trapped on this allegorical island, succumbing to the sins of curiosity and bravado, tumble headlong into the inferno of Dante, the lair of the demonic, and thus participate to some degree in their own demise.

At mid-film, two of the characters, perhaps in some way swayed by the seductive power of the crab-demon, venture very close to breaking one of the Ten Commandments. Martha, who is betrothed to Dale, and Hank, bachelor for life, find themselves in the devil's lair,

Pamela Duncan and Richard Garland are attacked by the crab monster.

and at one point come breathlessly close to kissing each other. It is only the sudden awareness
of the demon beast that interrupts and defuses this act. This fortuitous turn of events in which
Man is saved from himself clearly suggests the demon's complicity in some grander scheme
ultimately orchestrated by his heavenly rival, a hunch which will prove accurate by film's end.

Bachelor Hank, having avoided sin by no particular effort of his own, seems now positioned to make a further "sacrifice," if you will, to save his fellows from the tortures of the
inferno. He has dared threaten the social order and, in light of subsequent actions, appears
ready to repent for his sins. At the film's finale, when only Martha, Dale and Hank are left
to fight the devil-crab, Hank decides to confront, attack and finally sacrifice himself to the
demon of old in order that the heterosexual paradigm, in the guise of Dale and Martha,
may continue, thus providing hope for the future of Mankind. Hank climbs high onto a
radio tower, shaking it loose in order to electrocute the crab — and, of course, himself. This
scenario will of course remind many of the star of Christian mythology — Jesus Christ and
his conscious sacrifice on the cross of Calvary in order to free Man from the burden of Sin.
Even more revealing, as Hank hangs, arguably "Christ-like," from the wobbling radio tower,
the final shot of the crab is a close-up in which the beast looks up at Hank and *winks*. This
extraordinary moment may remind us not only of the crab's complicity in the entire God-
wrought scenario, but more specifically of the concept of *felix culpa*, the theological notion
of "the happy fault," wherein certain at first apparently antithetical events or phenomena
eventually become clear as a cohesive part of God's overall "plan" or destination for fallen
Man. Here the crab is signaling to Hank that the brave hero is doing exactly what he is

supposed to do — indeed, what he was destined to do all along — in order to vanquish the threat to mankind and restore some semblance of a pre-apocalyptic social order, so that man may attempt to begin anew.

As savior and beast disintegrate back into their respective subatomic structures — each, in fact, returning to the state of grace inherent in all non-sentient phenomena — Dale and Martha embrace against a mammoth outcropping of rock. Here, of course, the couple serves as Adam-and-Eve figures, their hard-won atomic wasteland a post-modern Garden of Eden. In one of the most suggestive parting shots in all of fifties cinema, Dale and Martha continue to embrace, ever more passionately, as they concur over Hank's role as their surrogate Jesus: "He gave his life!" "I know!" In the film's final conceit, the new Adam and Eve begin to paw each other aggressively, incredibly seeming to be sexually aroused in this post-trauma environment. As the scene fades to black, the viewer may get the distinct impression that the couple are going to engage in coitus right on the rocks, next to the still-smoldering corpses of their savior and enemy. Put bluntly, Adam and Eve — suggestive of the recurring heterosexual paradigm — are about to sin again, starting anew the inexorable cycle of Man's fall from innocence into sin, a fall which will certainly invoke the need for more gods to chastise them, and more monsters to frighten them into repentance. And to finally cap the film's theological leanings, the score's finale is an ascendant three-note fanfare which suggests the omniscience of the holy trinity — Father, Son and Holy Ghost.

Speaking of ghosts, one way in which *Attack of the Crab Monsters* works as fantastic melodrama is in its attempt to fashion a modern ghost story. The story's very premise — to locate missing and presumably dead peers — positions it both in terms of a mystery and as a metaphysical allegory concerned with the destiny of deceased spirits. In the film's very first scene, one of the scientists muses specifically about the fate of the missing's "souls" — that is, the supernatural destination of their life spirits or "ghosts." The scientist even calls out loud to McLean, leader of the missing group, and soon that very spirit abides the caller's request, communicating with the living in an attempt to lure them into the crab's infernal pit. As the scientists are picked off one by one by the crab monsters, their spirits or "ghosts" are cleverly, if cynically, used by the beasts to lure yet others towards their demise. The crab monsters are able to telepathically communicate with the living, in effect performing all the functions of the historical ghost figure, through cagey use of their diabolical new atomic powers. Scenes which emphasize the "ghost story" motif are often accentuated by creepy organ music, nicely underscoring the Gothic tone of the scenario. By mid-film, the implication is that these luckless scientists are dealing with something even worse than ghosts, a woeful tearing of the boundary between life and death triggered by the atomic blasts. When Hank, the radio operator, quips, "What is this supposed to be — a ghost story?" Weigand, the nuclear physicist, who above all may know some of the more treacherous dangers of the split atom, retorts, "No, I do not believe in ghosts. We are dealing with a man who is dead, but whose voice and memory live. How this can be I do not know, but its implications are far more terrifying than any ghost could ever be..." What Weigand seems to be insinuating is that the force of the unleashed atom, Man's foolish uncorking of the genie's bottle, brings with it metaphysical horrors on a plane as yet unimagined, in effect erasing the heretofore stolid and cozy boundaries between life and death. The crab monster may finally symbolize the ghost of Man's lost innocence as he stumbles headlong into the atomic age, his own catastrophic inferno, his own pit of torture, remorse and eternal suffering.

As for the crab monster itself, the mammoth life-sized prop has been the subject of contempt and ridicule since the film's first release, disdained by fans of the genre even today. As the prop is one of the most accomplished monster designs of the decade, competing only with the mollusk from *The Monster That Challenged the World* for the most impressive life-sized monster prop of 1957, its rejection by film audiences suggests something more than mere dislike. Indeed, the crab monster prop is a magnificent pop sculpture, a fully mobile entity which successfully portrays a gigantic, lumbering beast with unusual physical agility and, more importantly, a sinister intelligence. Certainly the main complaint leveled against the crab monster is that it is not realistic, that it is in fact, of a somewhat "arty," even expressionistic design and thus not "believable." This accusation is true only in the most literal sense — the crab monster does not look anything like the little sand crabs seen scurrying about throughout the film. If Corman had wanted to achieve this literal transmutation of reality, he could have just as easily (and probably at less cost) used optical blow-ups of actual crabs (along the lines of what Bert I. Gordon did so well in his genre films such as *The Cyclops* and *Beginning of the End*). One likes to think that the reason the crab is not lifelike, and is in fact "fantastic-looking," is that it is not merely a nameless, faceless outside menace but an intrinsic and important character in the film, as significant to the narrative as the others. It is thus essential that the beast *look* like a character. It is also a stroke of genius on Corman's part that in several shots he saw fit to place the full-sized prop in the same space as one or more of the actors in order to reinforce the proximity between the two. The protagonist and antagonist occupying the same theatrical space, easily done when the "monster" is an actor in a suit, is far more narratively engaging when the antagonist is awesome, large and gruesome, as with the crab monster.

The main conceit of the crab monster prop, and its arguably brilliant design element (by a designer who remains anonymous to this day), is its "face." Specifically, the crab monster has a somewhat human face superimposed onto its body, including a snarling mouth with crooked teeth, a squat nose, and two bulbous, menacing eyes, replete with working eyelids. These human "features" make no sense if the crab is supposed to be merely a result of atomic gigantism, but makes perfect sense if the crab is supposed to be — as clearly indicated in the screenplay — a mutation which has somehow combined elements of its source crustacean with the brains (and presumably "spirits") of the humans it has eaten, explaining both the monster's supreme, almost supernatural intelligence and its profound hatred of Man. In short, the crab monster is part-crab, part-human. Thus, the monster's face expresses several overlapping emotions throughout the film: anger, hatred, agony, even perhaps dementia. Its expressiveness greatly augments the crab's role as a character in the film, much in the tradition of horror classics *Frankenstein* and *King Kong*, in which the highly expressive faces of the monsters articulate emotions (including rage and anguish). Recalling that the crab monster, in large part, symbolizes the collective will of its creator, its scornful visage reinforces its place as an angry, vengeful character in the narrative. As well, the crab's menacing grimace suggests the doleful face of a godhead who is disgusted with Man. Finally, the crab monster's face symbolizes the collective rage of Man at the end of history, trapped inside his self-made atomic hellscape, enveloped and absorbed by his foolish, sinful search for forbidden knowledge. In sum, the crab monster prop — an unsung icon of fifties pop culture — is a magnificent sculptural evocation of the decade's anxiety, fear, guilt, and certainly rage, a manifestation of the nation's collective unconscious brought to the surface in a maleficent countenance of unleashed communal angst.

Although the actual designer of the crab monster prop remains anonymous, the influence of Paul Blaisdell can easily be seen. Blaisdell, a California-based artist and designer, is an unsung genius of fifties creature design, woefully underused (and underpaid) during his all-too-short heyday, and virtually forgotten today. His utterly fantastic monster designs, usually fabricated as suits meant to be worn by actors, captured some of the more ethereal and expressionist aspects of the beings he was assigned to invoke. Three of his most memorable creations were the female demon in *The She-Creature*, the atomic mutant in *Day the World Ended*, and the Venusian in *It Conquered the World* (all 1956). Perhaps the most distinguishing feature of all these (and most other) Blaisdell designs was the depiction of a menacing face, known colloquially today as "the Blaisdell scowl." The extremely pictorial faces of these beasts almost invariably featured angry, judgmental eyes and a frowning mouth, often with teeth exposed, suggesting the countenance of a snarling, growling beast of prey about to attack. To the modern film buff, these admittedly expressionist designs are often seen as corny or quaint, but in fact they captured in stark relief much of the repressed anger and fear underscoring the decade in which they burst forth onto the screen. In these films and others, the scowling Blaisdell beast symbolized rage towards those who brought him into being, disdain towards those who would dare to vanquish them, and, even more universally, an expression of the largely unaddressed fear, rage and hatred that was lying within all during that decade of severe emotional denial. In short, to the mostly youthful audience who attended these films, the scowling beast represented their own subconscious, struggling to escape their constrictive, conformist societal roles and become the destructive beasts they largely felt themselves to be inside. A Freudian might say that these angry behemoths are illustrative of the viewer's Id, an unruly, death-fixated force which continually struggles to break the bonds of the repressive superego.

Regardless of perceived symbolism, the Blaisdell monsters are, to put it simply, cool, scary and quite memorable. The story of Blaisdell's use and abuse by poverty-row Hollywood is a story unto itself, told brilliantly in Randy Palmer's book *Paul Blaisdell, Monster Maker*. Regarding the film being discussed, it appears from accounts that Roger Corman, who had worked with Blaisdell previously, approached the artist with his plans for "Attack of the Giant Crab," as it was called then, but Blaisdell purportedly declined to participate in the project after reading the script.[6] Corman then went to another Hollywood prop house — a company called "Dice, Inc.," according to D. Earl Worth — and contracted with them to create the prop, which was eventually built of an aluminum frame with papier-mache covering the body proper, and filled out with Styrofoam forms.[7] Worth also claims that the prop cost Corman $400. Considering Blaisdell's track record in regards to being short-changed by cheapjack producers, it is likely that the $400 figure Corman eventually paid another outfit would have been more than acceptable to the designer, so one wonders why he did not accept this plum assignment, as a Blaisdell crab monster would have surely been most exciting. Yet Blaisdell seemed to have unerring bad luck in his dealings with producers, exemplified by what occurred with Allied Artists' follow-up to *Attack of the Crab Monsters* — *From Hell It Came* — in which an animated tree harasses scientists on a radioactive island in the Pacific. Producers Jack and Dan Milner paid Blaisdell a paltry sum to concoct sketches of what would become Tabanga, the monster tree, and then proceeded to take the sketches to another outfit for its creation. Thus, although the resulting tree monster prop is not a Blaisdell product, it is absolutely a Blaisdell creation (borne out by the trademark "Blaisdell scowl" that adorns Tabanga's trunk).[8]

Yet the eventual designer of the crab monster prop, whether through willful theft or unconscious allegiance, did the spirit of Blaisdell proud, as the "Blaisdell scowl" does reside on the prop, an artistic conceit which, although risible to unimaginative science-fiction literalists, in fact makes the beast all the more menacing and the film all the more memorable. Again, if the giant crab were a mere blow-up of a realistic creature, the result would have been disappointing, perhaps even catastrophic. One need only look at lackluster monster films of the same year like *The Deadly Mantis* and *The Land Unknown* for examples of tired, woefully uninspired beast designs which all but ruined their films' potential narrative impact. As mentioned earlier, the unique design of the crab monster, along with its ability to "speak" and thus interact with the others in the film, positions it not as a dumb, lumbering "other" but as an intrinsic character participating in the narrative on an equal basis with the entrapped humans.

Another unforgettable facet of *Attack of the Crab Monsters*, inexplicably neglected in most discussions of the film, is the haunting score by Ronald Stein. Using a small orchestra to full advantage, Stein manages to create a highly memorable, intensely evocative score which greatly aids both the desolate atmosphere and mysterious narrative development of the film. Two elements of Stein's score worth noting are the use of harps and strings in lush arrangements to evoke the mystery and wonder of the sea, and the use of woodwinds — especially mournful sole oboe and piccolo — to convey both the isolation of the trapped scientists and the desolation of their outpost at the end of the world. As well, a vivacious brass section, punctuated with muscular percussion, is used to convey the marauding advance of the mammoth crustacean, effortlessly creating an atmosphere of dire threat and ill omen. While many B-movie studios refused to credit their music composers (Columbia Pictures and Universal International being the most notorious), Corman clearly knew the importance of the score in lending an air of polish to a poverty-row product — in all his films during this time period, Corman proudly billed the music composer immediately before his own producer-director credit. Certainly Stein's score for this film, and his wonderfully avant-garde score for *Not of This Earth*, reinforced the dramatic power of their subjects substantially, and to some are what make these films timeless cultural artifacts.

One final flourish which gives *Attack of the Crab Monsters* — and its co-feature — an artistic polish that belies its frugal budget is the animated title sequence by designer Paul Julian (1914–1995). Julian made his career primarily in the creation of memorable, stylistic background paintings for many of the iconic Warner Brothers cartoons of the 1940s and 1950s. Julian went on to do the extremely abstract design for an animated version of Edgar Allan Poe's *The Tell-Tale Heart* (1953). Although comprehensive credits are elusive, it appears that from the mid–1950s to the early 1960s, Julian also tried his hand at creating animated title sequences for several feature films, covering roughly the same time period as the far more well-known title designer Saul Bass. While Bass lent his artistic and animation skills to high-visibility product like Alfred Hitchcock's *Vertigo* (1958) and *North by Northwest* (1959), Julian's equally impressive (and, to some, superior) animated sequences were obscured by being linked to the "throwaway" B-film ghetto; in fact, it appears that Roger Corman was one of a very few who utilized this underappreciated animator. Yet even with these relatively "minor" productions, Julian put forth his best efforts in creating title sequences that stand on their own as vivid animations bordering on the surreal.

Combining limited animation with highly stylized renderings and overlapping layers, Julian managed to create completely integral little "stories" with his animated titles, as demonstrated by the title sequence for this film, considered by some to be one of his best. As the sequence begins, the Allied Artists corporate logo appears over the misshapen, crumbling towers of a sunken freighter buried at the bottom of the sea, its sad fate a mystery. A school of frightened fish scurries past, and the camera pans over to a gaggle of grotesque sea-creatures, each with bulbous carcass, bulging eyes and willowy limbs. These "crab monsters" hover over the rusted carcass of the downed ship, staring at the viewer while seeming to protect the sunken vessel. Suddenly, a mammoth octopus with immense black tentacles appears. More terrified fish swim past. The octopus grabs the conning tower of the ship and flips it over, reasserting her hegemony of the sea. The story is simple but primal: Man's technology, his "civilization," intrudes into the natural world, inviting self-destruction, creating monsters and threatening the natives. But the grand scheme of nature has allies of any size to thwart a threat to its existence, and so enters the fairy tale villain — the "killer" octopus — to crush the evidence of man's encroachment while regaining primacy over the oceans, the lifeblood of the natural world. This, of course, mirrors the synopsis of the film proper, in which Man's cruel invasion upon the natural world destroys life, creates monsters, and forces Nature to assert herself to retain control of what is rightfully hers, even as Man summons his own destruction.

As was typical of the youth-targeted double bills of the late 1950s, the release title of the film was confirmed first, and then key art was commissioned, followed by the script and the actual production. In several accounts, Corman proudly stated that he came up with his iconic title with the help of a market research outfit, but it is just as likely that he was encouraged by Allied Artists to create a title similar to their big sci-fi hit *Invasion of the Body Snatchers*, released exactly one year previously to *Attack of the Crab Monsters* and boasting a remarkably similar title.[9] The poster art for this film and its co-feature *Not of This Earth*, like many poster artworks for B-level motion pictures, is colorful, vivid and lurid, bearing a striking (and not unintentional) resemblance to the equally lurid and colorful artwork created for the covers of pulp fiction magazines, a popular mass media of the time with which B-movies shared a great deal, both in spirit and target demographic. The poster art for *Attack of the Crab Monsters*, of course, prominently features the imposing giant crab menacing a lithe blond woman who hangs from a suspended rope, her one-piece bathing suit suggestively ripped about the waist by the monster's "razor-sharp" claw, which entraps her. The implication is that the crab is about to slice the poor screaming female in two, a most sordid eventuality which does not occur anywhere in the film. Still, the implication of sexually-fueled gore is telegraphed loud and clear, and likely lured more than a few curious youngsters into the theater, unaware that they were about to experience one of the most thought-provoking and creepy depictions of nuclear menace ever concocted.

After a lengthy theatrical run, *Attack of the Crab Monsters* had an even more auspicious afterlife on television, where it eventually reached a far larger audience than during its original theatrical run. Following the astounding success of Screen Gems' "Shock" feature film package, consisting of Universal horror classics such as *Frankenstein*, *Dracula* and *The Mummy*, and released to television in late 1957, other distributors and studios jumped into the fray, releasing their back catalog to television. Allied Artists created a memorable package of 22 genre features in its "Sci-Fi for the '60s" syndication package, available to stations in late 1962.

Many double-bill programmers of the late 1950s —*Attack of the Crab Monsters* included — ran a little over an hour and so were not acceptable for the typical 90-minute television feature time slot, the ideal program length for such venues being about 75 minutes. Allied was unique in the industry in spending significant funds to augment their short theatrical features so that they would clock in at 70-or-more minutes. To do this the films were given several additions. Most conspicuously, the revised television versions began not with the main credits but with a short scene from the movie, which would recur later in the film. This use of a pre-credits dramatic scene, known in the industry as a "teaser" or "grabber," was at the time becoming an oft-used device in television series to lure the audience into the story before the credits rolled. But while most television series used a new scene for their teaser, one which did not recur in the main portion of the scenario, Allied Artists simply duplicated an existing scene and placed it at the beginning of the film. This device thus not only grabbed the potential viewer but created a certain temporal distortion of the film experience itself; when one encountered the scene again later in the movie, a somewhat creepy sense of deja vu occurred, a feeling well in keeping with the fantastic nature of the scenarios.

After the main credits comes a newly-shot explanatory prologue "crawl" which introduces the main thrust of the story:

> You are about to land in
> a lonely zone of terror .. on
> an uncharted atoll in the
> Pacific!
> You are part of the Second
> Scientific Expedition
> dispatched to this mysterious
> bit of Coral reef and
> volcanic rock. The first group
> has disappeared without a
> trace! Your job is to find
> out why!
> There have been rumors
> about this strange atoll ..
> frightening rumors about
> happenings way out beyond
> the laws of nature...

This quaint technique of "annotating" the source film has its roots in similar tactics used to cheaply pad the running time of classic exploitation films of the 1930s and 1940s, while legitimizing the usually-lurid plots by claiming its educational value in illuminating the pressing need for social reform in the area being exploited and/or discussed (drug use, unwed mothers, venereal disease, the slave trade, etc.). There is more than a touch of the spirit of classic exploitation in the often-hyperbolic scripts for these adorable little segments, which effectively add to the overall otherworldly verisimilitude of the feature proper, and as well give the viewer an opportunity to hear the film's main musical theme restated. The identity of the author of these little snippets of commercial film "poetry" remains unknown, although anecdotal online claims have cited both producer-director Herbert L. Strock (*I Was a Teenage Werewolf,* et al). and film historian William K. Everson as possible authors. It is known that Everson was working for Allied Artists as an advertising copy editor at some point during this time period — and was also a published poet — so he may well have been the author of these strange little "postmodern haikus," but this possibility is unverifiable at present.

In several cases, such as with *Attack of the Crab Monsters* and *War of the Satellites* (1958), a stock-footage montage was added to expand the running time by another two or three minutes. In fact, *Attack of the Crab Monsters* features the best of these well-crafted montages, as a series of violent atomic blasts unleashes a ferocious typhoon which decimates an island paradise — that island being the one on which the story will take place. Finally, a cast listing was tacked onto the end of the film, again using the movie's main musical theme as accompaniment.

Oddly, one final "trick" Allied Artists used to stretch the running times of their films for television was a laboratory technique called "skip-framing," in which every 24th frame of film was optically printed twice in order to expand the movie's running time without having to add new material. The only trouble with this technique was that it was immediately visible — and quite annoying — as the film seemed to halt for a brief moment every second, lending the characters onscreen a very jerky quality, especially if they were walking or running. Also, simple math reveals that the amount of time gained with this ill-advised optical trick was minimal, so the use of it seems questionable at best. Sadly, this skip-framing virtually ruins the television prints of *Attack of the 50 Foot Woman* (1958) and *From Hell It Came,* and likely others which have been unavailable for viewing for some time.

Not of This Earth

Produced by Los Altos Productions
Distributed by Allied Artists Pictures Corporation
67 minutes, Black and White
Directed by Roger Corman
Screenplay: Charles B. Griffith, Mark Hanna
Produced by Roger Corman
Music by Ronald Stein
Cinematography: John J. Mescall
Film Editing: Charles Gross, Jr.
Makeup Artist: Curly Batson
Production Manager: Lou Place
Assistant Directors: Jan Boleslavsky, Charles B. Griffith, Lou Place
Property Master: Karl Brainard
Sound: Phillip Mitchell, Herman Lewis
Special Effects: Paul Blaisdell, Bob Burns
Key Grip: Charles Hanawalt
Assistant to Director: Tom Graeff
Location Scout: Charles B. Griffith
Titles: Paul Julian
Cast: Paul Birch (Paul Johnson), Beverly Garland (Nadine Storey), Morgan Jones (Harry Sherbourne), William Roerick (Dr. F.W. Rochelle), Jonathan Haze (Jeremy Perrin), Dick Miller (Joe Piper), Anna Lee Carroll (Davanna Woman), Pat Flynn (Simmons), Barbara Bohrer (Waitress), Roy Engel (Sgt. Walton), Tamar Cooper (Joanne), Harold Fong (Speciman), Lyle Latell, Gail Ganley (Girl),

Ralph Reed (Boy), John Clark (Man), Tom Graeff (Car Park Attendant), Charles B. Griffith (Man at Newsstand), Hank Mann (Bum)

Synopsis: An alien from the planet Davanna settles in a mansion in the Hollywood Hills to prepare for an intended invasion of earth. In order to do this, the alien must try to pass as an earthling so that he may kidnap people and extract their blood for testing on his home planet.

As extraordinary as its co-feature is, the bottom of "The Greatest Double-Horror Show of All Time!" manages to surpass it. *Not of This Earth* is an astounding example of allegorical melodrama, easily on a par with similar product such as *Invasion of the Body Snatchers* and *The Incredible Shrinking Man*. The accomplished screenplay again takes a shop-worn pulp sci-fi premise — an alien attempts to take over the world for his own people — and fashions something wholly modern which reflects and addresses many hot socio-cultural issues of the day. Among these are: the role of "the other," i.e., the outsider, in a conformist society; the specter of communism, threatening to absorb mankind into a socialist web of sub-servience; the existential alienation of the American middle-class, increasingly lost and alone amidst a sea of strangers; the encroachment of "big business" and its most visible victim, the corporate "company man," a cold, emotionless cipher who might even kill for "the organization"; the aloof father figure, emotionally absent and possibly even destructive to his underlings; the postwar suburban experiment seen not as a tranquil oasis of bliss but as a bloodthirsty house of horrors; and the ascendancy of the strong female archetype, the "proto-feminist." As well, the magnificent use of arcane language to symbolize a cold, calculating and very foreign evil conveys a certain anti-intellectual prejudice well in keeping with society at the time. The film is shot in a dark, almost "European" neo-realism, creating a gloomy and morbid atmosphere which augments the theme of alienation so prominent in the film. Finally, the dissonant, at times avant-garde score by Ronald Stein, one of his absolute finest, greatly adds to the "otherworldly" ambiance of the picture. Indeed, but for one fatal flaw, *Not of This Earth* might well have been the perfect fifties B-movie; and even with this egregious defect, it comes as close to perfection as a B-level programmer could probably get.

As with its co-feature, *Not of This Earth* benefits greatly from a brilliant animated title sequence by Paul Julian, creator of many background paintings for Warner Brothers and UPA cartoons. In this sequence the Allied Artists corporate logo is superimposed over a textural graphic of a decomposing human skull. A subliminal burst of blood splashes onscreen as the main title appears. Another skull, with the top of the cranium removed, is brought together, and the scene changes to an unearthly landscape, possibly a fanciful depiction of radiation-ravaged Davanna. Two glowing orbs, at first looking like hovering planets but soon seen as two disembodied eyes, float over the landscape, searching for something. Over the screenplay credit, a gnarled, groping hand descends, its bared fingernails drawing rivulets of blood which drip down the screen. The blood drops soon create a series of abstract splatters, which could not help but remind the astute viewer of the highly controversial "splatter paintings" of abstract artist Jackson Pollack, who had just died in August the previous year, mere weeks before this sequence was created. The music credit appears over what at first seems to be another alien-scape but soon becomes identifiable as a portion of a human skeleton, with spine, vertebrae and rib cage easily visible. The camera pans to the right, focusing on the skull attached to this skeleton, over Corman's producer-director credit. Suddenly, the skull rotates 180 degrees, and it is only then that the viewer realizes that he was looking at the skull, and presumably the entire skeleton, upside-down. Finally, the glowing orb-eyes flash every-so-briefly before fading again into the impenetrable darkness of the skull's gaping eye sockets. Aided considerably by Ronald Stein's spooky, dissonant theme music, which eschews a straight melodic structure for brief bursts of brass fanfare counterpointed by weird percussion, this creepy opening positions death as the main theme of the piece, specifically the dire fate of all flesh — to be stripped from its carcass, leaving only bleached bones to rot in the sunshine. The staring eyes, which feature prominently in the movie itself, suggest the power of a malevolent supernatural gaze to unnerve, perhaps even destroy, its target. And the consistent visual confusion shown between the alien landscapes and strikingly similar "landscapes" of crumpled bones suggests a thematic link between macrocosm and microcosm, between the self and society, between the temporal and the eternal.

In the opening sequence — surely positioned here to engage the movie's target demographic — two frisky teenagers make out in a jalopy parked on the side of a dark street late at night. After exchanging some delightful teen slang, the girl excuses herself and begins to walk home alone. She hears creepy footsteps in the distance. Out of nowhere a well-dressed older man appears, carrying a suitcase. The girl, attempting to be civil, says hello, but the silent man lifts his arm and removes his dark glasses, burning the poor teen to death with some sort of fiendish death ray eyes. The man then sets up some equipment in his briefcase, inserts a needle into the dead girl's veins, and extracts her blood. This strong opening scene sets up two main themes — the first being that this man, and whatever faction he represents, is nothing more than an atom-age vampire using modern scientific techniques to steal blood from hapless victims. Second, the clear distinction in age between the predator and victim introduces a widely popular theme in youth-oriented films of the day — the positioning of elders (parents, authority figures, etc.) as parasitic villains plotting to decimate youth's (figurative and literal) life blood. This motif of powerful, manipulative and destructive elders will turn up in several 1957 films, most conspicuously in *I Was a Teenage Werewolf*, *I Was a Teenage Frankenstein*, *The Man Who Turned to Stone* and *Blood of Dracula*, among others.

From the first moment the alien known as "Paul Johnson" enters the scene, he positions himself as an outsider. Parking his automobile at a no-parking zone in front of a hospital, he clearly sets himself up as someone who either does not understand or chooses not to obey the laws of society. His choice of a black Cadillac as his means of transportation is also significant, that vehicle being an ostentatious American status symbol emblematic of a certain inferred class distinction. This iconic vehicle was extremely popular among both gangsters and morticians, and Johnson looks a great deal like both. With his grim business suit, stiff demeanor, expressionless face, and occlusive dark glasses, Johnson looks alternately like an overworked businessman, an undertaker, and the head of an organized crime syndicate. But it is when Johnson speaks that his outsider status becomes most clear. His speech is intelligent and arcane, spoken in an unerring monotone, sounding equally like old English and the dialect of a university-trained foreigner using English as a second language. This singular character must be credited both to screenwriters Charles Griffith and Mark Hanna, who concocted a magnificent alternative language for the alien to speak, and to Paul Birch, whose woefully underappreciated performance leans towards the abstract and boasts no counterpart in fifties cinema.

Johnson enlists the aid of nurse Nadine Storey to maintain his failing health, and the two retire to a house Johnson has apparently rented, a beautiful Tudor mansion somewhere in the Hollywood hills. Nadine moves in with Johnson, setting up one of the most intriguing aspects of *Not of This Earth*— as an allegory to the new suburban experiment which overran the United States after World War II. In it, newly-married male-female couples left behind their extended families, and urban or rural community environments, to settle into small, single-family houses in new construction developments which grew exponentially outside of all major metropolitan areas and soon hosted a large portion of the American population. As the film plays out, Johnson and Nadine represent an ersatz married couple living in a virtually "haunted" house, and in many ways it works as a biting satire on the new middle-class suburban experiment. Even the way in which Johnson "picks" Nadine by hiring her from her employer suggests both the purchasing of a daughter from a father, a common practice in many historical periods, and more recently the phenomenon of lonely, isolated men choosing a "mail-order bride" in essence, purchasing a life partner. Reinforcing this notion of the male purchasing a mate and considering her his own property, Johnson attempts to lock Nadine in her room — until challenged by the autonomous female.

The third main character in this new atomic family is Jeremy, a reformed convict whom Johnson employs as chauffeur and all-around handyman. Alternately cocky and deferential, Jeremy is quickly identified as the "child" in the family, as he is impulsive, nosy and immature. As played brilliantly by Jonathan Haze, Jeremy comes across as a half-grown man-child, emotionally infantile and easily cowed by his surrogate father figure. Even when Nadine, his new "mommy," moves in, Jeremy treats her largely as a mother figure, as the

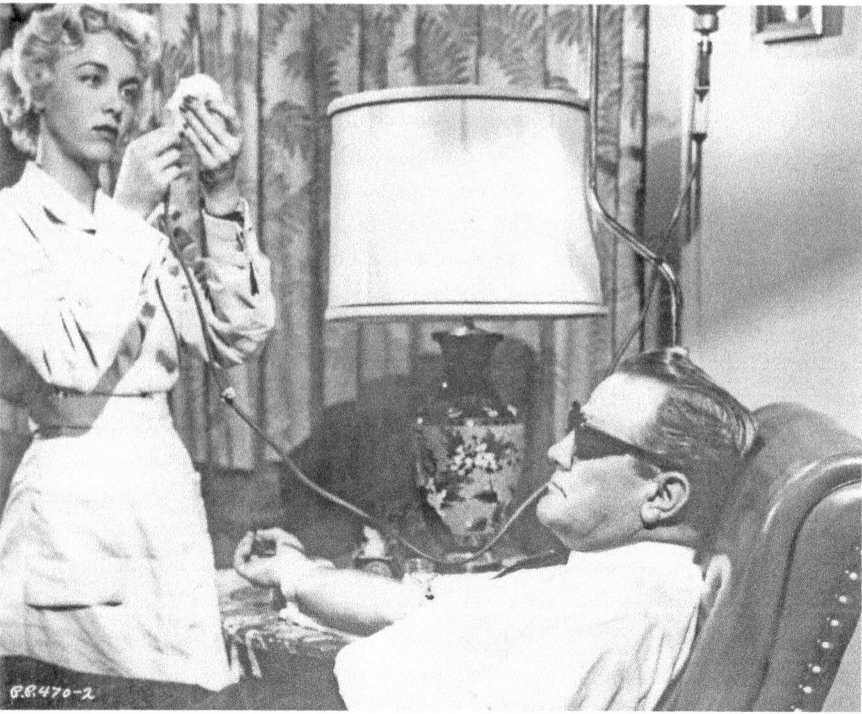

Registered nurse Beverly Garland unwittingly assists an alien invader, Paul Birch, in a scene from *Not of This Earth*.

relationships in this haunted household are not dictated by chronological age but by power dynamics, and Nadine, as Johnson's caretaker, immediately sets herself up as the most important person in the house.

When Johnson contacts his home planet the entire scene can be read as another parody of the middle-class suburban experiment. Johnson slumps down in an easy chair in his den, looking like a sacked-out businessman after a hard day at work, and uses a device which looks suspiciously like a television remote control to access his alien contact. Next to a mounted elk-head trophy, a closet door slides open, and inside hovers the disembodied head of his communicator. This hilarious "alien in the closet" motif eerily symbolizes the dark secrets which lie behind the phony suburban facade, the inevitable "skeletons in the closet" found within the American middle-class home. The scene also works as a satire on the invasive and conquering aspects of television, at this very moment first seen as a momentous cultural force. The scene also provides essential exposition, but does so with a delicious and biting wit which enhances it immensely. Johnson's dire opinion of the humans clarifies his antagonistic, even elitist agenda: "They are second-state, sub-human, weak and full of fright."

The character Paul Johnson — as brought to vivid life by Paul Birch and scenarists Griffith and Hanna — resonates on many levels, one of the reasons *Not of This Earth* entertains far more than the average science-fiction quickie. One of the most intriguing centers on the failed father figure, an especially salient theme considering the film's original theatrical audience, which was almost certainly a youthful one. Mid-fifties cinema obsessed on the curious role of the father or authority figure in modern life, specifically in how the tribal patriarch had somehow been compromised, diminished or weakened by the rigors of postwar social expansion and the forging of modern America. While television (which by definition was from its inception a propaganda outlet for government, manufacturing and heavy industry) portrayed the father figure conservatively as a harmless buffoon or staunch defender of the family unit, the less controlled film industry (drawing heavily from the literature and theater of the day) painted far more critical portraits of the father archetype and his increasingly problematic position in the postwar family hierarchy. One need look no further than *East of Eden* (1955, d: Elia Kazan), *Rebel Without a Cause* (1955, d: Nicholas Ray), and *Blackboard Jungle* (1955, d: Richard Brooks) — all released in that pivotal year of 1955 — to find examples of popular films with highly critical portrayals of father and/or authority figures completely at odds with their charges and peers. In *Deliberate Speed: The Origins of a Cultural Style in the American 1950s*, a salient analysis of the decade's cataclysmic sociocultural revolution, W.T. Lhamon, Jr. articulates the phenomenon:

> In films, records, plays and novels — all the narrative arts — this basic problem appears: the father is gone, is illegitimate, is corrupt, cannot stand up to women or his children, is effete, is mortally ill. He left, was killed, committed suicide, miraculously died. His messages to his dependents are faint, quaint, or nonexistent. In his absence, peer pressure, or brotherly love, or mob rule, or participatory structures emerge.[10]

Corman and company could not have been unaware of this popular motif, and so Paul Johnson comes across as (among other things) a purely malevolent father figure whose conformist demeanor hides the devastating subversive agenda he harbors. As mentioned, the film's original audience was largely comprised of teenagers going to the drive-in, so Johnson's role as evil patriarch was surely perceived, as least subliminally, by many viewers. To confirm that this theme is communicated to the audience, Johnson's very first victim is a teenage girl — a virgin most likely — which underscores the alien's position as an elder who is a distinct (indeed fatal) threat to youth. Lhamon notes that much of the culture of the mid-fifties reflected "adolescent anxiety about failed fathers," and it could be argued that *Not of This Earth* illustrates this trend brilliantly, if obliquely.[11] The underlying theme of this "failed father" motif, as seen in this film and elsewhere during the decade, is that even in a conservative, near-totalitarian environment such as 1950s America, when the iron fist of government and industry was everywhere to be felt, there still was an abiding sense in society that authority was deficient, incompetent or worse. As symbolized by Paul Johnson, authority in the mid-fifties was not merely aloof, otherworldly, or emotionally absent, but downright destructive to his community, an evil alien force which bodes ill will for all.

Surely, part of what makes Johnson such a menace is the disparity of his public persona as opposed to his actual person. From all outward appearances Johnson comes across as an upstanding — if a bit odd — member of the community. He is well-dressed, well-mannered, well-spoken, and apparently well-heeled. He lives in a beautiful house, drives a big Cadillac, and has servants attend to him. He appears to be the epitome of middle-class — or even upper middle-class — success. The public face of Johnson could, in fact, be used as the poster boy of the American success story as it was perceived in the 1950s — an intelligent, level-headed businessman, a solid citizen. In fact, Johnson could be seen as as somewhat devastating parody of the so-called "company man" which was alternately championed and later pilloried in the culture of the time, the obedient lackey of a large corporation who would figuratively — and in Johnson's case literally — kill for "the organization." Cold, calculating, emotionless, ruthless — these are all traits which could apply equally to Johnson or any ambitious businessman of the day. Indeed, the increasingly problematic fate of this odd postwar duck, "the company man," was dissected and probed in contemporary books such as Sloan Wilson's *The Man in the Gray Flannel Suit*, David Riesman's *The Lonely Crowd* and William Whyte's *The Organization Man*, which painted a critical, sometimes dire portrait of this creature who abandoned emotional expression and creative activity for humorless obedience to corporate agenda. These tomes and others — and certainly *Not of This Earth* — also depicted suburbia not as the purported wonderland of happy families but as a conformist prison which creates neurotics, if not outright monsters. The withering irony of Paul Johnson is that he presents himself — and is largely accepted as — a model citizen, when he is, in fact, a bloodthirsty parasite literally sapping the lifeblood from the community. This can certainly be seen as a none-too-subtle metaphor for the company man, whose obedience to the corporation — superficially seen as a boon to both economy and community — is eventually revealed to be a parasitic influence, as big business inevitably drains resources both economic and social from its host community, taking away much more than it ever purports to give.

Finally, the character of Paul Johnson — his coldness, his role as parasitic outsider in the community — mirrors well the potentially surreptitious role of the foreigner in domestic America, the "odd" alien as a threat to the status quo. The Davannan is clearly positioned as such in the film — another character goes out of his way to query, "Johnson's some kind of a foreigner, isn't he?" As evidence accrues regarding Johnson's actual intentions, curiosity turns to suspicion, which turns to all-out Cold War paranoia. Even his flunky Jeremy ponders, "Maybe he's makin' atom bombs down there in the basement!" — surely a very "Communist" activity. And Johnson himself is not averse to revealing his "identity" if it serves the purpose of terrorizing an intended target; as the Davannan attempts to lure a victim to destruction with his hypnotic powers, he declares, "My eyes are *alien!*" thus underscoring the power of "the alien" to subvert and bully an innocent. Johnson's early acceptance into the community, a coup challenged only after much blood has spilled, may remind us of the tragic tale of Alger Hiss. Hiss was a clerk in the State Department who was swept up in the postwar hysteria for finding "secret Communists" in high places, i.e., government. It is telling that almost all of those accused of being treasonous spies for the enemy just happened to be Democrats and/or highly educated liberals. In hindsight it appears that these ungodly freethinkers, such as the learned, liberal and erudite Hiss, were seen as dangerous ideological foes to the pro-military, uber-nationalistic, ultra-conservative zeitgeist of Washington D.C. at the time. Several staunch defenders of "the American Way," including Whittaker Chambers and Richard Milhous Nixon, although unable to prove one single charge of treason against Hiss, were, however, able to successfully charge him with perjury, and the poor sap was sentenced in 1951 to five years in prison. Although the blatant manipulation of justice towards crass political ends which went on at the time draws no direct parallel to Paul Johnson, the figure of Hiss may still function adequately as a metaphor for "the Secret Davannan" of *Not of This Earth*, a crafty oddball whose outward demeanor harbors an illicit agenda — the subjugation and conquest of his target community — and who skillfully uses the infiltration of societal institutions to accomplish this.

Likewise, the character of Nadine Storey pushes against gender stereotyping in significant ways. As played by Beverly Garland, she comes across as a strong proto-feminist archetype, a not uncommon occurrence in Corman pictures of this vintage.[12] Granted, the character begins her narrative life in a "safe," traditional female role — nurse — whose entire career is dedicated to working for and serving (primarily) males. Yet as the story progresses, we seen Nadine champing at the bit to break these archaic gender-centric fetters, emerging finally as something remarkably similar to a first-edition feminist. First, Nadine is sexually aggressive, as evidenced by her brazen undressing in the proximity of a co-worker, and her daring romp in her boss' pool. This confirms that Nadine is no wallflower — most likely not a virgin — and so already has challenged maledom's assigned roles for "good girls." Second, although Nadine begins the film in direct obedience to both her doctor and her employer, she severs ties with both when she sees that their agenda for her is unhealthy, if not downright fatal. Nadine's moment of true awakening comes near the film's climax when she screams loudly, finally "expressing" herself clearly and succinctly to her oppressor — a highly "feminist" action which disarms her would-be killer and allows her to narrowly escape his serpentine clutches. Finally, in the film's parting shot, Nadine has once and for all broken the hypnotic "spell" which powerful, malefic males often successfully cast over womankind, seeing perhaps for the first time the dangers ever-lurking for naïve women in patriarchal social systems. To punctuate for the audience this dawning awareness of who the enemy really is, while paying respects to her fallen employer at the graveside, Nadine identifies him in no uncertain terms: "He was a foreign thing come here to destroy us; thank god he tried too hard." Nadine could easily be speaking here of males in general when referring to "he," and to the collective of her fellow women as "us."

Significantly, Nadine was purportedly raised by an aunt and so, technically speaking, is an orphan, which may explain her fierce independence, as she was not the product of the conformist nuclear family so prominent at the time, with its incestuous, smothering mommy-daddy-baby motif. Simply put, she was raised by a strong woman, so she became one herself. As an independent woman, Nadine has important relationships with four males in the film: Johnson, her surrogate boss/husband; Jeremy, her surrogate son/brother/co-worker; the doctor, her second boss and professional colleague; and the cop, her romantic interest. With each of these males she originally allies herself, and with each of them at a key point in the scenario she breaks off relations with them, asserting her independence when each relationship threatens to become oppressive to her. Thus, throughout the film she is testing the limits of her place in the male-female power dynamic, laudable homework which will come in handy during her moment of truth as Johnson's hypno-slave. To clarify her expansive attempt at autonomy, one need only compare Nadine to the only other female character of note in the film — the poor exile from Davanna. This doomed woman managed to escape her torturous alien community only to be felled by an ill-advised obedience to male dictates, agreeing deferentially to submit to Johnson's ignorant transfusion of rabid blood, a heinous — if ostensibly innocent — act which summarily kills the poor woman and clearly underscores the fate awaiting any female foolish enough to put her faith in men.

As noted, *Not of This Earth* features many touches which playfully mock the suburban experiment of postwar America. Where the normal American refrigerator might contain vast plates of cooked, dead animal flesh, Johnson's contains beakers of human blood, perhaps useful as metaphor for the Western world's addiction to killing and eating non-human animals. As for the house itself, Johnson makes no bones about its function; when nurse Nadine comments politely, "You have a lovely house here, Mr. Johnson," its owner perfunctorily replies, "It is ... adequate, Miss Storey." When Johnson's surrogate family, Nadine and Jeremy,

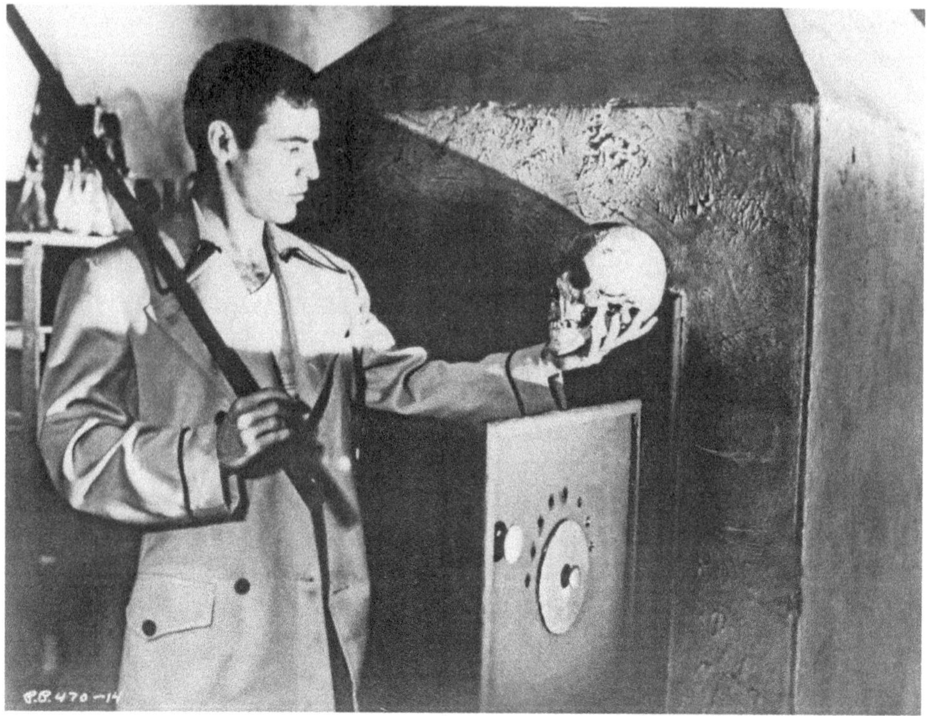

Jonathan Haze does his best Hamlet impression in Roger Corman's *Not of This Earth*.

finally gain the courage to look around their home, they venture into those very places posted as forbidden by their petty tyrant, attempting to uncover the "secrets" of their patriarch's unfathomable loyalties. As such, they act as surrogates for the youthful audience member who may be tempted to peek into closets and behind locked doors in order to find the damning flaws of the postwar suburban experiment in which they are at least pawns, if not guinea pigs. Johnson's off-limit basement contains assorted scientific equipment, such as rows of chemical beakers, and features a creepy black furnace which seems to constantly harbor a raging fire. This odd setting thus reinforces the traditional suburban basement — with its heating apparatus and home workshop paraphernalia — yet simultaneously alludes to something more sinister, such as ungodly human experimentation and the sacrifice of subjects to the fiery furnace, all under the control and sanction of the creepy, occlusive father figure. (In a nice touch, while in the basement Jeremy extracts a human skull from the furnace, holding it contemplatively before him like Hamlet, perhaps even lamenting the victim's tragic end as did Shakespeare's hero. This scene may even represent the first instance of overt Shakespearean reference in Corman's work, a motif which would occur with increasing regularity in films such as *The Undead, War of the Satellites* [1958], and *The Intruder* [1962], and which would become a dominant narrative subtext in the Edgar Allan Poe adaptations.)

Not of This Earth also offers light allegory in terms of the conceivable future of a world obsessed with atomic supremacy at all costs. It is revealed at the film's climax that Johnson's home planet, Davanna, is an atomic wasteland, and its dying citizens are all suffering from radiation poisoning — the main reason that Johnson was sent to scout a new location for his doomed race. The dire fate of a foolish, technologically-beholden species serves as a most poignant foreshadowing of the planet Earth's own horrible destiny, thanks to the irrevocable unleashing of the evil atom. Theorizing late in the film where a Davannan might have contracted such frightfully toxic blood, the doctor muses, "In a place where continuous nuclear detonations had taken place over a period of years." Even the most casually observant viewer could extrapolate this statement to mean the United States and the Soviet Union, where, even at this relatively early stage of their suicidal mission, hundreds of atmospheric and marine tests of thermonuclear weaponry were conducted on an alarmingly frequent basis, with the devastating ecological and biological impact of the cumulative fallout being only vaguely understood at the time. In short, the Earth is Davanna, and its legacy to current generations, as well as those unborn, will be horrible slow death by radiation. As the message of Davanna's fate is not predominant in *Not of This Earth*, it would be presumptuous to call the film either anti-war or anti-nuclear, yet the gloomy content is there for those who wish to contemplate it.

As does its co-feature, *Not of This Earth* boasts an impressive early score by Ronald Stein. This music, coming across at times as dangerously avant-garde for a mainstream film, vacillates wildly between lush and lean, between lyrical and discordant, forgoing a classic symphonic structure for a lean experimental one which borrows equally from the modern jazz idiom and the "musique concrete" movement. Quiet patches of near-silent meditation, created solely via violin, clarinet and xylophone, burst into highly expressionist moments with brass chorus, tense strings, screeching woodwinds and bold percussion (including a highly expositional use of the cymbal). The influence of one of Stein's mentors, Paul Hindemith (1895–1963) is evident in this grand score, which at times captures the dissonant, contrapuntal and expressionist flavor of Hindemith's early music, especially his *Kammermusik* series of the 1920s. As well, Stein followed Hindemith in the use of the liturgical music genre as muse for some melodies and arrangements, along with the juxtaposition of exotic, peculiar combinations of instruments for maximum aesthetic and narrative impact.

Unfortunately, the film stops dead in its tracks for a woeful scene which — to add insult to injury — is completely peripheral to the scenario and appears to have been hastily added in order the expand the film's lean running time. In the scene, a vacuum cleaner salesman visits the Johnson household and is summarily vanquished by the alien's death-ray eyes. The salesman is played by Dick Miller, who almost singlehandedly sabotaged other Corman films such as *War of the Satellites*, *Little Shop of Horrors* and *The Terror* with his amateurish mugging and sloppy line delivery. In this film Miller plays his character as a mangy cross between a beatnik, a Brooklyn thug and a hipster doofus. The supposedly hilarious counterpoint between Johnson's arcane speech and Miller's jive-talk merely trivializes what is already an obvious distinction between normal American speech and Johnson's singularly "foreign" dialect. This is one case in which Corman erred in letting an actor build a character without supervision, as the result is horrendous. The scene sharply contradicts the rest of the film's melancholy, bleak tone, threatening to turn it into a dreaded "horror-comedy." Still, so powerful is the rest of *Not of This Earth* that this ill-advised moment does not succeed in ruining the picture. Bafflingly, Corman is on record as stating that this sophomoric scene is his *favorite* in the film, and in his opinion is a main reason for the movie's warm reception from the audience.[13] This may be a case of the creator being too close to his work to see clearly what works and what does not. As mentioned, so powerful is the bleak, creepy and melancholy nature of *Not of This Earth* that even the slap-dash salesman scene cannot bring it down; yet one swoons at the thought of what the film might have achieved had it remained entirely humorless — and thus entirely horrific — as did one of its definite inspirations, *Invasion of the Body Snatchers*, a film which terrified largely because it refrained from relieving the audience's tension with cheap comic relief. To verify this observation, one need only glance at Corman's 1988 remake of *Not of This Earth*, which, loaded with cheap sexual and comedic references, is an embarrassment to the script, the original film, and the character Paul Johnson as uniquely essayed by Paul Birch.

Most conspicuous in Charles Griffith and Mark Hanna's script is the use of arcane language to symbolize a cold, calculating and very foreign evil. Although the unusual speeches given to Johnson are meant to suggest a superior alien intelligence, it further implies a general distrust of the intellectual tradition, fitting in well with the conservative, anti-intellectual mindset of the decade. This dialogue also offers some passable dry humor that's much more effective than the film's dire attempts at overt comedy. Rather than telling someone he intends to kill them, for instance, Johnson threatens, "I shall eliminate you." Ruminating on his house guest's reluctance to lock her bedroom door at night, Johnson muses, "In the place from which I come, no person would dare sleep in insecure quarters." But much of the delicious dialogue — likely attributable to Mark Hanna, who has a long list of such screenplays — is in the tradition of serious science-fiction literature. When the disembodied alien emissary brings Johnson up to date on the dire state of things on Davanna, he utters what is perhaps the film's most exquisite line: "The conquered enemies dwindle in the pens of pasture, and time constricts. It is soon that we shall all perish." Later, the emissary utters an even more poetic line: "There is destruction within the council of the northern orbit. Rule is dissolving. Independent action increases on a 73-degree tangent." When Johnson tutors a Davannan exile on how to communicate with the "sub-humans," he doesn't say "talk to them" but, "A clerk will speak to you vocally. You must remain in a state of lingual receptivity, and imitate his sounds and meanings." This marvelous effect of talking around a subject lends *Not of This Earth* a good deal of its somewhat cerebral quality. Elsewhere, when Johnson discusses medicine with Nadine, he poses a question about Uranium being attracted to cancer tissue, referencing one of the earliest uses of radioactive isotopes in ways other than to cruelly decimate an enemy population: "In the uranium method of cancer examination, it is true that the uranium flies to the cancerous area, but the books neglected to give me an explanation." Nadine confirms that as yet no-one has discovered the reason for this phenomenon. Johnson continues: "Then one assumption may be that since cancer attracts radioactivity, the cancer itself may be charged with the negative energy. Possibly that might lead to a cure; what do you think?" That this brilliant mind — which may have indeed found a profitable avenue of research in the attempt to conquer one of mankind's most malign illnesses — is seen as a creepy foreign monster clearly reinforces the anti-intellectual prejudice of the time. Corman utilized arcane and distorted language elsewhere to great effect during this period — *The Undead, Teenage Doll* and *War of the Satellites* being prime examples — and this love of purblind linguistics will evolve into the glorious dialogue that graces many of his Edgar Allan Poe films of the 1960s.

The unusual epilogue of *Not of This Earth* punctuates two main themes, cleverly reinforcing one. Johnson's funeral is attended apparently only by Nadine and Harry, who stand solemnly before the alien's tombstone, which curiously reads, "Here Lies a Man Who Was Not of This Earth." Harry offers, "In a way, I kind of feel sorry for him. Buried so far from home, so far from everyone he knew." He thus reinforces his allegiance to the overall patriarchal agenda — he feels sorry for this inhuman monster solely because he was a fellow male. But the clear-headed Nadine, a lucky survivor of this tyrant's heinous plot, knows better: "I can't feel sorry for him. He had no emotions as we know them. He was a foreign thing, come here to destroy us. Thank god he tried too hard." Certainly this notion of "a foreign thing come here to destroy us" references Johnson's placement in the film as an emblem of generic Communist threat, an agent sent to convert the liberties of democracy into totalitarian servitude through murder, brainwashing and enslavement. Yet the overarching theme of *Not of This Earth* is even more clearly underscored when Nadine and Harry leave the grave site, and another black-suited man with briefcase and dark glasses walks slowly toward the camera. It is Johnson's replacement, another emissary from Davanna, and an absolute assurance that the patriarchal conspiracy against humanity will continue ad nauseum.

Finally, *Not of This Earth* is enhanced by its overall gloomy, bleak atmosphere, which, as mentioned, is so powerfully oppressive that even the dreaded "vacuum cleaner salesman" scene can't ruin it. Much of the credit for this can be given to John J. Mescall's excellent cinematography, which makes the sunny Hollywood Hills somehow look like the gloomy back alleys of old Europe. Indeed, *Not of This Earth*, with its oddly-dressed main character, morbid atmosphere and strange dialogue, might almost pass as an unstated homage to European art cinema, which at this moment — with films like Roger Vadim's *And God Created Woman* (1957 U.S. release) — was having such an impact on the American movie business. By far the most "European" scene in the film occurs when Johnson encounters, somewhat to his surprise, another fellow traveler from Davanna, a young woman who is adorned with the same trademark sunglasses. The two look at each other longingly, saying not a word. They finally stop at a newsstand and begin a poignant telepathic conversation, covering their actions by appearing to browse the magazines. Yet to any outside observer — the audience included — this encounter looks like little more than a garden variety pick-up between two horny strangers. And Johnson does indeed "pick up" the Davanna woman, taking her to the doctor's office for a fatal transfusion of rabid blood. The poor woman is then sent off — like a cheap tart — to a nearby hotel to wait for Johnson to come to her, another classic set-up for two lovers who wish their illicit tryst to be discreet. The woman dies shortly after leaving Johnson, falling in the street and yelling "Davanna!" as her dying words. This poignant, melancholy sequence — the heart of *Not of This Earth*— seems to summon almost intuitively the existential alienation of European cinema of the time, as well as brutally illustrating the noxious effect that male social systems can have on the unwitting female.

So powerful is the film's bleak mise en scene and formidable — and cunning — villain that *Not of This Earth* manages to convey a sense of unnerving alienation and sheer horror with an absolute minimum of props or gimmicks. One of the few fantastic effects in *Not of This Earth* is an adorable little monster by Paul Blaisdell, a flying thing which looks descended from a spider and an octopus. It hovers over its intended victim, covering his head and sucking the blood out of his cranium. With its vaguely crustacean-like design, this blood-sucking creature subtextually links the film to its co-feature. And as with *Attack of the Crab Monsters, Not of This Earth* was granted an extensive afterlife via its syndication television release. As with other features in Allied Artists' "Sci-Fi for the '60s" package, a teaser, prologue crawl and cast listing were added to expand the film's short theatrical running time. The prologue crawl for *Not of This Earth* is one of the most lyrical in the entire series, replacing any expositional material with purely evocative, dreamy imagery:

> You are about to adventure
> into the Dimension of
> The Impossible!
> To enter this realm
> you must set your
> mind free from the earthly
> fetters that bind it!
> If the events you are about
> to witness are unbelievable,
> it is only because your
> Imagination is chained!
> Sit back, relax and believe..
> so that YOU may cross
> the brink of time and space..
> into that land you sometimes
> visit in your dreams!

VOODOO WOMAN WITH *THE UNDEAD*
(AMERICAN INTERNATIONAL)

American International Pictures was perhaps the first "major-minor" studio to emphasize both the youth market as their target demographic and the "packaged double bill" as their preferred product offering. Marketing research had discovered that the teens' favorite subject matters were rock 'n' roll musicals, "weird horror," crime dramas, and war films coming in at a distant fourth. AIP had something to offer in all these categories, with the "weird horror" genre being amply represented by this quirky double bill. *Motion Picture Herald* gave both films the expected perfunctory industry reviews:

[*Voodoo Woman*:] Marla English, Tom Conway, Touch Connors and others enact with anticipated professional proficiency a story that is an apparent natural lure for the action-horror fiction type of film fancier. Renegade scientist Tom Conway, accompanied by his wife, Mary Ellen Keyes, labors away at formulas and other data deep in the uncharted jungle country. Realizing he can't return to civilization, Conway develops a serum that enables him to turn a native girl into a monster. A twist of fate kills her off, and Conway then decides to use still another woman — this time adventuress Marla English. After much ranting and raving, in the best tradition of horror science, Miss English is destroyed, and the remnants of her violent escapades resume age-old patterns.[14]

[*The Undead*:] Roger Corman has packaged known ingredients of horror with enough deft touches to make *The Undead* box office. There are no marquee names here, but resourceful advertising can provoke word-of-mouth, stressing, of course, reincarnation and implied ramifications. By way of plot development: Van Dufour, termed a time experimentalist, wants to prove that life follows an unbroken chain. He takes Pamela Duncan back into time a thousand years. Along about here, Corman really gets his imagination working. It seems that Miss Duncan, in all her lithesome beauty, has been condemned to die in a medieval prison. Richard Garland, her romance of the era, wants to save her by selling his soul. Dufour projects himself back 1,000 years and tells Miss Duncan the truth. After some nail-biting situations, Dufour finds he can't return to modern living. The players are young and display considerable alacrity, despite the grimness of the material at hand.[15]

Voodoo Woman

75 minutes, Black and White
Produced by Carmel Productions
Distributed by American International Pictures
Directed by Edward L. Cahn
Screenplay: Russ Bender, V.I. Voss
Executive Producers: James H. Nicholson, Samuel Z. Arkoff
Produced by Alex Gordon
Music by John Blackburn, Darrell Calker
Cinematography: Frederick E. West
Film Editing: Ronald Sinclair
Production Design: Don Ament, Bartlett A. Carre
Set Decoration: Harry Reif
Costume Design: Robert Olivas
Makeup Artist: Carlie Taylor
Special Makeup: Harry Thomas
Assistant Director: Bartlett A. Carre
Monster Suit: Paul Blaisdell
Props: Karl Brainard, Richard M. Rubin
Sound: Robert Post
Script Supervisor: Judith Hart
Cast: Marla English (Marilyn Blanchard), Tom Conway (Dr. Roland Gerard), Touch Connors (Ted Bronson), Lance Fuller (Rick Brady), Mary Ellen Kay (Susan Gerard), Paul Dubov (Marcel Chateau), Martin Wilkins (Chaka), Norman Willis (Harry West), Otis Greene (Bobo), Emmett Smith (Gandor), Paul Blaisdell (the Monster), Giselle D'Arc (Yvette), Jean Davis (Zuranda)

Typically garish newspaper advertisement from American International's early 1957 double bill release targeting the teenage moviegoer, *Voodoo Woman* and *The Undead*.

Synopsis: In league with a corrupt tribal chief, a mad doctor manages to create a homicidal monster-woman using a combination of voodoo and science, all the while keeping his own depressed wife as a virtual prisoner.

Voodoo Woman is a sly treatise on the patriarchal exploitation of the female, cleverly disguised as a cheap monster movie. This rather amazing film is a good example of what early American International releases were capable of, combining adult themes with ludicrous pulp-fiction plots to remarkable effect, before AIP centered on the dreary "teenage monster" formula of subsequent years. *Day the World Ended*, *The She-Creature*, *It Conquered the World* and *The Undead* all held darker, adult themes within their pulp-fiction frameworks, in stark comparison to insipid, teenage-targeted Herman Cohen productions like *I Was a Teenage Werewolf.*

This most interesting combination of jungle B-picture and monster movie is sprinkled liberally throughout with some provocative sexual politics, played out via the travails of two female protagonists. One female is literally imprisoned by a brutal patriarch, while another uses her feminine wiles to try and play the male's game — to disastrous effect. This dialectical balancing of a victimized female with a predatory one is symbolically merged in the title creature, a young woman who, through a diabolical alliance between "White Man's Science and Black Voodoo," is forced to become a murderous tool for phallocentric interests.

The common genre theme of the horrible, involuntary transformation of the self is brightly brought to life in the scenario when the woman morphs into a vaguely prehistoric beast. This "Voodoo Woman," although created by patriarchal evil for its own use, stands as the alchemical "missing link" between the victimized and empowered female, a most peculiar proto-feminist fantasy. Even the malicious use of telepathy by the evil doctor against the conscripted creature underscores the brutal sway that an oppressive male-based socio-economic structure has over the female gender, wherein forces greater than the individual can endure force them to commit acts against their "better" nature. The ultimate victory of this emergent feminist archetype is cannily underscored in the film's magnificent parting shot wherein the beast, supposedly fallen to its death in a bubbling hot spring, climbs out again, apparently having conquered death to rise, phoenix-like, from the ashes of her former domination to lead womankind towards its hard-won emancipation.

Mad doctor Tom Conway commands the fearsome "Voodoo Woman" (costume designed and operated by Paul Blaisdell) to attack Marla English in *Voodoo Woman.*

Tom Conway is absolutely hilarious as the slimy-yet-charismatic "white overlord" whose complete self-absorbtion and lack of compassion for the natives, and the females he exploits, paints him as a cartoonish depiction of an "old school" tyrant. Also curious are two black characters: the corrupt voodoo chieftain, whose over-the-top mugging borders on parody, and "Bobo," a selfless servant whose devotion to his female charge costs him his life.

As with the same year's *The Disembodied*, the voodoo high priest swings a chicken over his head before submitting the poor fowl to sacrificial bloodletting; one may assume this was taken from apocryphal tales of actual voodoo ritual practice. The voodoo icon depicted throughout the film is a primitive cartoon of a snake piercing a magic circle, but it does convey, albeit in elementary fashion, a rudimentary yin/yang, male/female dichotomy. The title creature is another magnificent creation of Paul Blaisdell's, unfortunately used very conservatively here and almost always seen in deep shadow, a fault of the previous year's *The She-Creature* as well. *Voodoo Woman* was (very) loosely translated by Larry Buchanan a decade later for his micro-budget TV movie *Curse of the Swamp Creature* (1966).

The Undead

71 minutes, Black and White
Produced by Balboa Productions
Distributed by American International Pictures
Directed by Roger Corman
Screenplay: Charles B. Griffith, Mark Hanna
Produced by Roger Corman
Music by Ronald Stein
Cinematography: William A. Sickner
Editing: Frank Sullivan
Makeup Artist: Curly Batson
Assistant Director: Lou Place
Property Master: Karl Brainard
Sound: Robert Post
Key Grip: Charles Hannawalt
Choreographer: Chris Miller
Cast: Pamela Duncan (Diana Love/Helene), Richard Garland (Pendragon), Allison Hayes (Livia), Val Dufour (Quintus Ratcliff), Mel Welles (Smolkin), Dorothy Neumann (Meg Maud), Billy Barty (the Imp), Bruno VeSota (Scroop), Richard Devon (Satan), Maurice Manson (Prof. Ulbrecht Olinger), Aaron Saxon (Gobbo), Don Garrett (the Knight), Dick Miller (the Leper), Paul Blaisdell (Corpse)

Synopsis: An unscrupulous hypnotist convinces a prostitute to undergo past-life regression therapy, only to discover that in her previous existence the poor woman was destined to be killed as a witch. The hypnotist travels back in time in order to save his patient from this horrible fate.

It is common knowledge that in the postwar world of quickie exploitation pictures, if a filmmaker submitted a finished product with the agreed-upon running time, title, cast and main plot points, he could pretty much do whatever he fancied with the actual content. Some ran with this idea, creating interesting and fantastic melodramas which adhere in spirit to genre convention yet deviate wildly in narrative, aesthetics and structure. Perhaps the champion of these is Roger Corman, who with *The Undead* gave audiences more than they could possibly hope for in a drive-in second feature. Taking a page from the previous year's bestseller, *The Search for Bridey Murphy*, in which a hypnotist claims to have regressed a patient to an historically verifiable past life, Corman concocts an absolutely fantastic mythical world of demons, witches and goblins, a virtual parallel universe that evokes the spirit of Shakespeare and the Renaissance "mystery plays" of yore.

Essentially a light comedy with horror touches, the fantastic scenario begins in the present day and focuses on "Diana Love" (the wildly underrated Pamela Duncan), a devil-may-care whore who is amused by a hypnotist's sudden interest in her. In what amounts to a psychic rape, Diana succumbs to the doctor's dangerous and invasive mind-therapy, and soon Diana and the audience have travelled back to a spooky stage-bound netherworld full of bats and grave-robbers and witches and knights, roughly in line with the Middle Ages. In this incarnation Diana discovers that she has been accused of being a witch by her enemies and is due to be exterminated, a marvelous reference to the timeless patriarchal assault on independent and "uppity" women carried on with savage ferocity then and (more subtly, but no less effectively) today.

In Corman's highly symbolic fantasy world, the Devil is real and plays among the mortals as a living character. Also mesmerizing is Allison Hayes as a "real" witch who intends to frame Diana in order to snare a mortal man to love and conquer. The only false step in the whole film is Mel Welles' grating portrayal of a loudmouth mortician whose quasi-rhymic annotations of the proceedings nearly destroy the sublime quality of the basic scenario.

The focus of the film is the woman alternately known as "Diana Love" and Elaine,

Uncredited dancers come back from the dead to cavort in the ethereal void in Roger Corman's incredible *The Undead.*

two manifestations of the female as dictated by patriarchal culture. In the present, Diana represents Woman-as-Whore, a cherished patriarchal archetype whose entire existence is dedicated to the casual sexual servicing of the male gender; a more tragic figure one cannot imagine. Diana is named perhaps after her mythological namesake, the goddess Diana, hunter with a magic bow, said to be protector of all women, and a virgin who forsook marriage so as to devote her life and energies to her sisters.

Elaine, the historical wench accused of being a witch, is also bound by patriarchal law in terms of her forthcoming punishment as an enemy of mankind (i.e., a witch). As well, the magician responsible for Diana/Elaine's terrible tumbling through time is a male with obvious megalomaniacal inclinations. Indeed, as the film is bookended by the proclamations of a very male Devil, one may say that the entire *universe* of *The Undead* is borne of a duplicitous, malevolent male spirit.

When Elaine first hears the voice of her other self, pleading with her to summon courage, it strikes the startled naïf as some sort of hallucination or demonic possession — the tortured girl cannot imagine anyone, let alone that of a female, coming to her lowly rescue. Yet the voice soon stands for the powerful forces within all women struggling to free themselves from the strictures of patriarchal brainwashing. When Elaine finally must make a horrible decision — to end her current life for the chance of future lives spared — she mirrors the patriarchal female's act of sacrifice for the future of Womankind, in which she declares a life in subservience to male culture one not worth living, and thus unleashes not only the potential poets, doctors, and dancers within herself but within future generations of women unborn who, through her valiant sacrifice now, may have opportunities they could not otherwise imagine.

The deadly nature of patriarchal government is underscored in a remarkable scene wherein villagers gawk in rapt fascination while witches are brutally beheaded, illustrating that the subjugation and elimination of Woman in patriarchy serves as both political expedient and popular entertainment. In contrast, another memorable scene shows three black-clad female corpses materializing on top of their graves to perform a highly-synchronized dance routine before sinking back to their eternal homes, a sublime expression of female solidarity: beautiful and omniscient, inextinguishable even by death.

In a sardonic twist ending, the doctor, after going back in time to save Diana, discovers that he has changed the fabric of time and is now trapped in the past. The Devil chortles in glee at Man's insipid naivete and infantile greed, which leads him to fuck up in every single thing he does.

The Undead is an uncanny film in several senses. As it jumps from today to yesterday frequently, the viewer is constantly in a state of temporal disorientation. The spooky fog-machine netherworld of Diana's "past" is a marvelously expressionist forest primeval, claustrophobic and yet expansive, painted even grimmer by the fact that the entire exposition takes place during one long night, from approximately midnight till dawn. This highly evocative verisimilitude is augmented immeasurably by an absolutely mesmerizing score by Ronald Stein, one of his true masterworks. As well, *The Undead* is one of Corman's earliest experiments in radicalizing traditional B-movie verisimilitude by the use of exotic setting, historical character and arcane language. Similar experiments included *Teenage Doll* (1957), *Not of This Earth* and *War of the Satellites* (1958). Corman would soon synthesize these aesthetic tricks, applying them liberally to his singular series of horror films inspired by the morbid symbolist writings of Edgar Allan Poe; one could almost call *The Undead* the experimental prototype of the Poe series.

THE MAN WHO TURNED TO STONE WITH ZOMBIES OF MORA TAU (COLUMBIA)

Harry Cohn's Columbia Pictures, considered in the industry as either the poor cousin of the major studios or the whiz-kid of the poverty row studios, cranked out an impressive supply of both "A" and "B" movie material for theaters during the 1950s, and was still going strong as one of the biggest producers of theatrical short subjects, such as the long-running and ever-popular "Three Stooges" series, which was to end one year hence. "Quickie" drive-in double bills such as *The Man Who Turned to Stone/Zombies of Mora Tau*—licensed from independent producers such as Sam Katzman, who had been making successful genre films already for over a decade — continued to generate considerable profit for Columbia, both domestically and abroad (where almost half of Columbia's revenues accrued).[16]

The Man Who Turned to Stone

71 minutes, Black and White
Produced by Clover Productions
Distributed by Columbia Pictures Corporation
Directed by László Kardos (as Leslie Kardos)
Screenplay: Bernard Gordon (as Raymond T. Marcus)
Produced by Sam Katzman
Cinematography: Benjamin H. Kline
Film Editing: Charles Nelson
Art Direction: Paul Palmentola
Set Decoration: Sidney Clifford
Assistant Director: Sam Nelson
Sound: J.S. Westmoreland
Sound Editor: John H. Newman
Conductor: Ross DiMaggio
Stock Music: George Duning
Cast: Victor Jory (Dr. Murdock), William Hudson (Dr. Jess Rogers), Charlotte Austin (Carol Adams), Jean Willes (Tracy), Ann Doran (Mrs. Ford), Paul Cavanagh (Cooper), George Lynn (Dr. Freneau), Victor Varconi (Dr. Myer), Friedrich von Ledebur (Eric), Tina Carver (Big Marge Collins), Barbara Wilson (Anna Sherman), Don C. Harvey (Mr. Griffin), Jean Harvey (Matron)

Synopsis: At a reform school for delinquent teenagers a cabal of mad doctors drain the life energy of young women in order to achieve immortality.

Once again, Sam Katzman's Clover Productions refashions tired B-movie clichés into something surprising; here, various movie genres are deftly merged to create an unusual scenario which vividly, if problematically, addresses in microcosm the agenda of a punitive patriarchal social system that takes aim at, and mercilessly exploits, the females who fall within their clutches.

Essentially a "reform school girl" picture with a dollop of gothic horror, *The Man Who Turned to Stone* concocts a fabulously deranged scenario in which an elder clan overtly targets and conspires against the younger generation, making a clear statement to the teens in the audience about the essentially malevolent nature of the parental generation. Further, the patriarchal institution set up as the villain of the piece specifically targets for extermination "bad girls"—that is, young females who have demonstrably challenged male authority and who are now exiled in the "LaSalle Detention Home for Girls," a particularly transparent euphemism for "woman's prison." These "bad girls," who have in some way "hurt" male society, must be corrected and/or punished—and, ideally, exterminated. The young women who are the victims of this gender-based genocidal program are portrayed in a sympathetic light, even though their previous acts branded them as "criminal." In contrast, the elders are all gleefully amoral, monstrous quacks, an excitingly reckless portrait of deranged authority.

Certainly patriarchy's ongoing goal concerning the female is to bring her into line with male-centered goals, the most important of which is the obedient breeding of men's babies so that the noxious male-dominated socio-political system may endure into eternity. Barring that, females may be useful to men in terms of various forms of subservience—sexual, economic and intellectual among them. Finally, females who do not or will not conform to phallo-centric edicts (i.e., "feminists") must be targeted, corralled, contained, corrected or eliminated. *The Man Who Turned to Stone* successfully portrays this entire agenda in allegorical form, with the old-fart immortal "vampires" forcibly extracting the literal "life force" from the imprisoned females in order to maintain their own political hegemony in perpetuity. Once extracting all needed resources from the female "donor," killing her and trashing the body, they cover all traces of their gender-centric genocide.

Victor Jory and George Lynn subject Barbara Wilson to an ignominious death-by-electrocution as Ann Doran, Paul Cavanagh and Victor Varconi look on in Sam Katzman's *The Man Who Turned to Stone*.

Even the exploitation/murder of the females is significant, as they are forced into what appears to be a scalding acid bath, which immediately saps their energy and renders them lifeless, transferring their stolen "power" to the bodies of the diabolic ancients. Surely this highly ritualistic killing procedure harkens back to the patriarchal church's arresting and burning of "witches" — that is, any independent, free-thinking woman (and preferably one who owned substantial property which could be confiscated).

Although the bulk of the villainous group are men, reinforcing their role as a microcosmic patriarchy, there is one older female, portrayed perhaps as the most despicable and amoral of the bunch. She symbolizes the female who has thrown her lot in with patriarchal interests, and also manages to suggest an evil mother figure, a twisted, toxic woman who has lost all ability to nurture, protect or champion those sisters-in-spirit under her care.

When one of the vampires, who has sinned against the group, is finally "allowed" to die, his rapid decomposition into a gruesome visage alludes to parables such as Oscar Wilde's *The Picture of Dorian Gray*, in which the dissolution of the face-in-artifice reveals the previously hidden moral decay of the soul within. And as for the title, surely the transformation of men into mutants, monsters or stone-like corpses, one of the most prominent motifs in 1950s fantastic cinema, mirrors deep subconscious fears about individual and societal degradation due to the soul-crushing strictures of a deeply conformist society even then splitting at the seams, as well as concerns that an increasingly technocratic world would wreak havoc on the collective body of Man, creating a zoo of amoral atomic monsters unworthy of salvation or survival.

The ostensible heroes of the piece are a most oddly-drawn heterosexual couple, a social worker and a psychiatrist who, although attracted to each other, do not consummate their mutual feelings, remaining at a conspicuous, sexually-tense distance throughout the film. They don't appear, even by film's end, to have joined the ranks of heterosexual couples who will blindly carry on the patriarchal socio-political agenda, and this is curious and refreshing in a decade in which the consummation of couples in all media of popular culture seemed *de rigeur*. The film climaxes with a big fire that burns the villains' evil headquarters to the ground, forcing all the inmates to flee also (another curious allusion to the burning of "wayward" females in antiquity). Indeed, *The Man Who Turned to Stone* seems to consistently, if haphazardly, address the goal of male-dominated society: to perpetuate itself into "immortality" at all costs, with or without the female's consent or permission, and preferably "over her dead body."

Film Bulletin published a most curious — and sloppy — review of *The Man Who Turned to Stone* in their February 18 issue:

Inveterate horror film fans might work up some mild interest in this somber, grade C exploitation entry Sam Katzman's Clover Unit for Columbia release [sic]. It should serve adequately as a dualler in action and ballyhoo houses. The treatment is dated and the "scare" gimmicks obvious as Victory Jory, Ann Doran, Paul Cavanagh, and Frederick Ledebur (he played the aborigine in *Moby Dick*) depict scientists who are about 200 years old and live on by electrically drawing off the life force of women reformatory inmates. Director Leslie Kardos plays up the sadistic angle with screaming girls being carried off in the night by a half-man-half-ape character, and drained of their blood in a solution-filled vat. Prison director Jory and his assistants murder women inmates and list their death as cases of "heart attrack" [sic]. The welfare worked [sic] Charlotte Austin learns that girls are heard screaming in the night before they disappear. State psychiatrist William Hudson discovers the secret from Cavanagh who, unable to react to transfusions, leaves his diary. The ape-like Ledebur kidnaps Miss Austin, but she is saved by Hudson as the laboratory burns down with the mad scientists all inside.[17]

Zombies of Mora Tau

70 minutes, Black and White
Produced by Clover Productions
Distributed by Columbia Pictures Corporation
Directed by Edward L. Cahn
Story: George Plympton
Screenplay: Bernard Gordon (as Raymond T. Marcus)
Produced by Sam Katzman
Original Music: Mischa Bakaleinikoff
Cinematography: Benjamin H. Kline
Film Editing: Jack Ogilvie
Art Direction: Paul Palmentola
Set Decoration: Sidney Clifford
Assistant Director: Jerrold Bernstein
Sound: Josh Westmoreland
Conductor: Mischa Bakaleinikoff
Stock Music: George Antheil, Mario Castelnuovo-Tedesco, David Diamond, George Duning, Hugo Friedhofer, Lucien Moraweck, David Raksin, Miklós Rózsa, Marlin Skiles
Cast: Gregg Palmer (Jeff Clark), Allison Hayes (Mona Harrison), Autumn Russell (Jan Peters), Joel Ashley (George Harrison), Morris Ankrum (Dr. Jonathan Eggert), Marjorie Eaton (Grandmother Peters), Gene Roth (Chauffeur), Leonard Geer (Johnny), Karl Davis (Zombie), William Baskin (Zombie), Ray Corrigan (Sailor), Mel Curtis (Johnson), Frank Hagney (Capt. Jeremy Peters), Lewis Webb (Crewman)

Synopsis: In a remote part of Africa an army of the undead guard a long-buried treasure against its current exploiters. An old woman seems to hold power over the underwater zombies.

From the opening title prologue, to the moody nocturnal setting, to the crackling melodramatic dialogue, this surprisingly effective B-programmer seems an anachronism from the start. It is so reminiscent of the Halperin Brother's enduring walking-dead flick *White Zombie* (1932) that at times it almost seems positioned to make a claim as a remake; at other times, it looks virtually indistinguishable from a PRC horror quickie of the 1940s. There were precious few "zombie" movies in the science-obsessed 1950s, so *Zombies of Mora Tau* does stick out like a sore thumb. Credit Columbia indie producer Sam Katzman, who, if nothing else, certainly had his finger on the pulse of the nation regarding successful box-office "quickies" such as *Rock Around the Clock* (1956, d: Fred F. Sears), and director Edward L. Cahn, who helmed at least two other walking dead pictures at around the same time: *Creature with the Atom Brain* (1955) and *Invisible Invaders* (1959). (Indeed, a study of Cahn's "zombie trilogy" might be a rewarding project.)

Unsung femme fatale Allison Hayes is scintillating as always as a ne'er-do-well gold-digger; when she falls into an open grave and squeals "I know it's for me..." the revelation sends shivers up one's spine. Her main rival is a blonde twit who is the perfunctory love interest in the scenario. Yet the central character of the story is an elderly matron, well played by Marjorie Eaton, whose guiding hand leads the visiting explorers to an unlikely happy ending. This strong-willed matriarch can bring the zombies to a halt with a mere wave of her torch, and she later brings a near-dead sailor back to life with an herbal potion,

Uncredited zombie-men rise from the sea in Sam Katzman's *Zombies of Mora Tau*, paired by Columbia Pictures with Katzman's *The Man Who Turned to Stone*.

suggesting that this woman is a modern incarnation of the witch/crone figure of ancient history. When the matriarch first enters the dining room, she is flanked on each side by twin cameo portraits of revered women, further accentuating the omniscience of the female principle in this cursed community. As the elder female seems to have a completely symbiotic relationship with the army of deceased men, and fears not their fate nor their presence, one is not surprised when she intones, "Only fools are afraid of the grave..."

This film simply drips with atmosphere, starting with the aforementioned quirk wherein the entire movie seems to take place at night in some sort of accursed purgatory of lost souls. The film boasts some memorable images, including a scene of the zombie men simultaneously rising up in their coffins, and some highly effective underwater scenes which almost qualify it as some sort of fantastic noir ballet. The viewer first assumes that the underwater zombie scenes were merely filmed on a sound stage in front of a water-filled lens of some sort, but this conceit is disproved by amazing scenes of the zombies battling a diver in a suit, from which air bubbles are emerging, suggesting that these cleverly-crafted scenes were actually filmed underwater, giving them a truly unearthly quality.

It is always a pleasant surprise when a throwaway, "formula" picture can rise above its meager origins to become something greater than its intended genre or purpose, standing as both anomaly and icon of that genre. *Zombies of Mora Tau* is one of those anomalies, and with it Cahn and Katzman cannily resurrected a forgotten genre — the poverty-row horror quickie of the World War II years — and breathed new life into it, making the film a post-modern horror tale of note.

1,000 Years from Now with *Invasion U.S.A.* (American Pictures Company)

Prolific B-movie producer Albert Zugsmith (1910–1993) was never one to let a valuable property lie fallow (and he was assuredly aware of the ascending popularity of the science-fiction film, having been the producer of Universal-International's big 1957 hit *The Incredible Shrinking Man*), so he decided to mount a nationwide re-release for two of his earlier movies, both produced under his American Pictures banner. With the aid of a title change and lurid advertising, Zugsmith managed to sneak the creaky *Captive Woman* (under the far more evocative title *1,000 Years from Now*) and the wildly xenophobic *Invasion U.S.A.* onto drive-in screens in the Spring of 1957, where they presumably did adequate business among similar genre product. What American teens thought of these avowedly anti–Communist films, at a moment when the Cold War was just beginning to take a back seat to other national concerns, is anybody's guess, however. As for Zugsmith, he hit the big time with his late–1950s hits *High School Confidential* (1958) and *The Beat Generation* (1959).

1,000 Years from Now

(original production, *Captive Women*, 1952)
Produced by Albert Zugsmith Productions (as "American Pictures")
Distributed by RKO Radio Pictures (1952), American Pictures Company (1957)
64 minutes/Black and White
Directed by Stuart Gilmore
Screenplay: Jack Pollexfen, Aubrey Wisberg
Produced by Jack Pollexfen, Aubrey Wisberg
Associate Producer: Albert Zugsmith
Music by Charles Koff
Cinematography: Paul Ivano
Editing: Fred R. Feitshans, Jr.
Production Design: Theobold Holsopple
Set Decoration: Clarence Steensen
Costume Design: Yvonne Wood
Makeup Artist: Steven Clensos
Sound: Frank McWhorter
Special Effects by Irving Block, Louis DeWitt
Mechanical Effects: Rocky Cline
Cast: Robert Clarke (Robert), Margaret Field (Ruth), Gloria Saunders (Catherine), Ron Randell (Riddon), Stuart Randall (Gordon), Paula Dorety (Captive), Robert Bice (Bram), Chili Williams (Captive), William Schallert (Carver), Eric Colmar (Sabron), Douglas Evans (Jason), Marshall Bradford (Mutant Leader), Tom Daly (Durk)

Synopsis: In the year 3000 A.D., warring tribes battle for control of an atomically-decimated Manhattan. A rebel from one of the clans manages to infiltrate his enemy's lair.

Originally released in 1952 as *Captive Women*, the then-topical threat of total nuclear annihilation is the springboard for this very different, if anachronistic historical drama. By

An impressive poster tries valiantly to hide the fact that this 1957 release actually features reissues of two creaky Cold War thrillers from 1952 and 1953.

catapulting the scenario into the unforeseeable future, the filmmakers get away with what is essentially a biblical-era costume drama.

After a present-day teaser which meditates on the hopes of the United Nations and the horrors of Hiroshima, and concludes with a common thesis of 1950s cinema — that only an unfettered (U.S.) military can ensure a "free" world — the setting changes to over "1,000 years from now," as the re-release title claims, and offers a strangely compelling melodrama in which three factions vie for ascendancy in a creepy atomic wasteland. Robert Clarke is the noble warrior of moral conviction, while popular RKO bad guy William Schallert plays a ruthless mutant who sells out his people for the promise of short-lived power.

The story unfolds shortly after the "Black Century," when most of humanity succumbed to radiation poisoning, becoming mutants (dubbed "Mutates" by their peers). This sets the scene in a post-modern revisitation of the scourge of the Black Death, which decimated Europe during the 14th century. Then, as here, this scourge ravaged the dominant culture, whose survivors were forced to revert to a primitive barbarism to survive an increasingly hostile environment. The survivors' tireless efforts to leave their bitter past behind and forge ahead with a renewed attempt at a cultured civilization also vaguely echoes Europe's slow, painful evolution from the religion-poisoned Dark Ages to the hard-won dawn of the Age of Enlightenment at roughly the same time.

The "Upriver" men war against the "Norms," and everyone hates the dreaded "Mutates," who are seen as sub-human. As an "Upriver" hack states, "The only good Mutate is a dead Mutate!" a slur with obvious racial overtones. One of the reasons the Mutates are so hated is that they periodically steal Norm women for breeding, as their own bloodline is hopelessly tainted with gamma-ray poisoning; this amusing allegory to black men desiring white women is another racial pigeonholing of these poor souls. Throughout the film, the Mutates are indeed positioned as the civilization's lower, or slave, class, with the Norms and the Upriver groups vacillating between the merchant and ruling classes. Yet the hilariously-named Norms have their own problems. During a wedding which triggers much of the ensuing story, the priest offers the couple to "the Devil Goddess of the Seven Black Devils that we worship." Apparently, the Norms became devil worshippers when God forsook them in the historical atomic holocaust, an understandable if reactionary response to diabolical wholesale slaughter. As one of the Norms defends his dark god, "The Devil's works endure..." So true!

Alternating with some perfunctory but affable battle and intrigue sequences, the bulk of the film seems more concerned with long dialogue exchanges that dwell on various social, political and philosophical questions, making this truly a "thinking man's" science-fiction film, and reminding one of another meditative SF classic, *Creation of the Humanoids* (1962, d: Wesley Barry).

Another potentially inflammatory subject invoked is the new society's strict guidelines regarding breeding — in order to avoid unnecessary monstrosities — a discussion which touches on the controversial notion of eugenics. Likewise controversial is a debate regarding the populace's eventual fate, with one side propounding hope and survival, and the other advocating race extermination via mass suicide. Expectedly, the convoluted but always engaging scenario ends with a pro-life stance via a holy, "sacred" marriage, during which the priest intones, "What is conceived in love can only end in good..."

This fascinating production is entirely studio bound, with some impressively dank and claustrophobic sets that always seem to be in darkness, suggesting a malefic atomic purgatory. *1,000 Years from Now* is another noteworthy early co-production by Albert Zugsmith, Aubrey Wisberg and Jack Pollexfen, the team who also gave us *Port Sinister* (a film which also warranted a 1957 re-release, as discussed later).

Invasion U.S.A.

(originally released in 1952)
Produced by American Pictures
Distributed by Columbia Pictures (1952), American Pictures Company (1957)
73 minutes/Black and White
Directed by Alfred E. Green
Screenplay: Robert Smith
Story: Robert Smith, Franz Schulz (as "Franz Spencer")
Executive Producer: Joseph Justman
Associate Producer: Peter Miller
Produced by Robert Smith, Albert Zugsmith
Music by Albert Glasser
Cinematography: John L. Russell, Jr.
Art Director: James Sullivan
Set Decoration: John Sturtevant
Makeup Artist: Harry Thomas
Production Manager: Ralph E. Black
Assistant Director: Ralph E. Black
Sound: Frank McWhorter
Mechanical Effects: Rocky Cline
Special Photographic Effects: Jack Rabin
Wardrobe: Einar H. Bourman, De De Johnson
Supervising Editor: W. Donn Hayes
Dialogue Director: Robert Bice
Cast: Gerald Mohr (Vince Potter), Peggie Castle (Carla Sanford), Dan O'Herlihy (Mr. Ohman), Robert Bice (George Sylvester), Tom Kennedy (Bartender), Wade Crosby (Congressman Harroway), Erik Blythe (Ed Mulfory), Phyllis Coates (Mrs. Mulfory), Aram Katcher (Factory Window Washer), Knox Manning (Himself), Edward G. Robinson Jr. (Radio Dispatcher), Noel Neill (Airline Ticket Agent), Clarence A. Shoop (Army Major), Jack Carr (Plant Worker), John Crawford (Man in Bar), Richard Eyer (Blythe's Son), Franklyn Farnum (Man from Omaha), Ethan Laidlaw (Russian Sea Captain), Jack Lomas (Man in Bar), Frank Mills (Plant Worker), Jack Reitzen (Russian Invader), William Schallert (Newscaster), Bert Stevens (Plane Spotter)

Synopsis: Thanks to a mysterious hypnotist, patrons at a Manhattan bar are allowed to fantasize about the devastating effects of a potential atomic attack on America by the Soviet Union.

Alongside such notable competition as *The Next Voice You Hear...* (1950, d: William Wellman), *I Was a Communist for the F.B.I.* (1951, d: Gordon Douglas) and *Red Planet Mars* (1952, d: Harry Horner), *Invasion U.S.A.* stands as perhaps *the* quintessential (and certainly most notorious) example of a short-lived post-war B-movie genre which might be coined "Cold War Agit-Prop." In these overtly racist, wildly xenophobic melodramas, the "Free World" (i.e., the Axis Allies) is in constant danger of attack from "the Enemy," either specifically or allegorically portrayed as Communist Russia. In hindsight it is easy to see that the Cold War was largely a publicity stunt of the U.S. Military-Industrial complex, in order to justify its ominous presence and prohibitively expensive expansion. *Invasion U.S.A.* seems at times almost an advertisement for these interests.

The film opens with a bunch of stereotypical folks relaxing at a New York saloon. A reporter from a nearby TV station enters and poses a question to all the barflies. The question is, "Do you believe in the Universal Draft?" This was assumedly a concept being discussed in actual political circles at the time, which basically lobbied that, in addition to the involuntarily recruiting of young males as cannon fodder for the Military-Industrial complex's sought-after "endless war," the draft was positioned to conscript various business interests to produce, presumably at very low profit, products for the military, such as tanks and firearms. The bar patrons react viscerally to this totalitarian concept: "Draft Factories? That's Communist!" and "The people in this country will never put up with a police state!" The rest of the scenario goes on to prove that only personal and collective sacrifice to the government can stave off horrible attacks like the one described. The irony, of course, is that this Machiavellian concept, which never got anywhere (at least under that name) smacks of Communism, that supposedly "barbaric" socio-political system which the "free world" had vowed to fight against.

To reinforce this draconian thesis, a strange "seer" hypnotizes the bar patrons, causing them to suffer a mass hallucination in which they enter a horrible parallel universe that succumbs to the evils of a passive, voluntary Capitalism. The bulk of the film takes place in this "other world," in which the unthinkable happens: the Red Commies destroy America. Bringing to life one of those most dreaded fears of the Cold War is not only shamelessly opportunistic but also arguably cruel, and all to scare people into worshiping "big government." But *Invasion U.S.A.* wears its uber-conservative colors proudly and unapologetically, making it a most remarkable curio of a most paranoid postwar mindset. The subsequent invasion of America is primarily told through expertly-edited montages of military stock footage, including some impressive aerial dogfights. While generic, the invasion thus has a timely quality which must have scared audiences silly.

When "the Enemy" finally does the dirty deed and starts dropping A-bombs on major U.S. cities, one cannot help but think of the collective guilt Americans felt for the insensible bombing of the innocent civilian populations of Hiroshima and Nagasaki, still so fresh in memory. The destruction of everything the U.S. holds dear seems somehow a form of national remorse for acts which all knew, at root, were evil. Of course, this "guilt" is strictly subconscious, as the plot demands that America "punishes" the dirty Commies by dropping *three* bombs for every one of theirs, an accurate if inadvertent expression of selfish American "overkill." When the viewer finally sees "the Enemy," they are hilariously portrayed as an amalgam of cartoon stereotypes — basically America's idea of Russian Commies, but with a touch of Nazi and a hint of Asian thrown in for good measure.

As if the script wasn't heavy-handed enough to begin with, towards the film's conclusion another TV reporter (the ever-present William Schallert) states in no uncertain terms that this cruel fate suffered by America was directly due to its citizens not wanting a big, bad government and its bastard offspring, an unbridled Military-Industrial complex. The nuclear bombing of New York is rather impressively handled via a combination of nicely rendered miniatures and stock footage of fire-bombed cities (possibly including footage of Dresden, the cultural shrine of Germany, which was decimated by U.S. and British allies in one of the greatest unpunished war crimes of the century). This "parallel universe" horror show, this orgiastic stock-footage Armageddon, finally ends as the heroine leaps to her death rather than risk facing gang rape by the enemy. Back at the bar, the stunned patrons wonder: was it all a dream? Scared straight, they all now agree that the best course of action is to obey their government and devote all their labors to its worship and expansion. And if that ain't communism, what is? Mixed messages abound in this truly hallucinatory film, all the way up to the last frame: "The End" is superimposed over a cartoon bust of George Washington, the beloved "father" of America but also now known as a greedy land baron and vicious slave owner.

One of the more amusing aspects of the film is the stormy romance between the cad TV reporter (Gerald Mohr) and a reformed gold-digger (Peggie Castle). The sexual tension between the two mounts exponentially as the world situation deteriorates, until they finally consummate their lust for one another during a particularly ugly newscast — apparently "Doomsday" acts as aphrodisiac to some. Yet later, when the situation deteriorates further, we find that the reporter goes to give blood at a nearby blood bank, only to discover that his former paramour has enlisted as a nurse! The male's desire to offer his blood to the duty-bound woman, presumably replacing the seminal fluid shared during their former torrid romance, acts nicely as metaphor regarding the nature of personal sacrifice in traumatic times.

Associate producer Albert Zugsmith was also responsible for *Captive Women* (aka *1,000 Years from Now*) and *Port Sinister* (aka *Beast of Paradise Isle*), a busy beaver in early 1950s B-movies. Thirty years later, during the height of the noxious "Reagan Years," the lachrymose *Red Dawn* (1984, d: John Milius) mutated *Invasion U.S.A.*'s storyline into an adventure-love story for teenage idiots; and, of course, it was a smash hit.

THE ROCKET MAN PLUS TOBOR THE GREAT (REPUBLIC PICTURES)

Republic Pictures, undergoing severe financial difficulties in its last days, sought cheap product to keep its distribution channels flowing. In order to cash in on the current sci-fi trend, Republic took its earlier science-fiction film, *Tobor, the Great,* and coupled it with *The Rocket Man* (presumably leased from Twentieth Century–Fox) for a nationwide re-release in the Spring of 1957. It is doubtful whether these films, both of which feature child protagonists, were well-received by the teenage drive-in crowd, but they may have done reasonably well in suburban "Kiddie Matinee" situations.

The Rocket Man

(originally released in 1954)
Produced by Panoramic Productions
Distributed by Twentieth Century–Fox Film Corporation (1954)
79 minutes/Black and White
Directed by Oscar Rudolph
Screenplay: Lenny Bruce, George W. George
Story: Jack Henley, George F. Slavin
Produced by Leonard Goldstein
Music by Lionel Newman
Cinematography: John F. Seitz
Editing: Paul Weatherwax
Art Director: George Patrick

Set Decoration: Glen Daniels
Costume Design: Travilla
Makeup Artist: Louis Hippe
Assistant Director: Henry Weinberger
Sound: Eugene Grossman
Musical Director: Lionel Newman
Cast: Charles Coburn (Mayor Ed Johnson), Spring Byington (Justice Amelia Brown), Anne Francis (June Brown), John Agar (Tom Baxter), George Winslow (Timmy), Stanley Clements (Bob), Emory Parnell (Big Bill Watkins), June Clayworth (Harriet Snedley), Don Haggerty (Officer O'Brien), Beverly Garland (Ludine), Paul Brinegar (Dave Harris), Richard Cutting, Jack Daly (Loan Company Manager), Byron Foulger (Card Player), Harry Harvey (Rally Chairman), Ralph Moody (Farrow), Howard Negley (Poker Player), Lillian Powell (Mrs. Lloyd), Lawrence Ryle (Captain Talray), Dale Van Sickel (Man at Rally)

Synopsis: An orphan is taken in by a kindly woman in a small town rocked by corrupt politics. Meanwhile, a spaceman empowers the youngster with a magical ray gun that causes people to reveal their darkest secrets.

The Rocket Man is a most unusual entry in the 1950s fantastic film canon, as it represents a style of comedy prominent in the 1940s, but with a light science-fiction overlay. The

Original poster art for *The Rocket Man* (1954), a light comedy-fantasy that was given a nationwide re-release in the spring of 1957, coupled with another 1954 fantasy, *Tobor the Great*.

result is a most odd duck, appealing not wholly to kids or adults, which may be why it is ignored or maligned by buffs of the era, and has yet to land a legit video or DVD release. This appears to be the sole movie credit for director Oscar Rudolph, a prolific director of television. Rudolph shows a master's touch for the fine art of light comedy, knowing when to let the actors go wild with their performance and when to let the screenplay carry the film.

The star of the show, a 7 year old named Timmy, is a most troubled soul. He is a world-weary pessimist and a thief, having seen nothing but pain and suffering his whole short life. It is thus no wonder that he has had a lapse of mental clarity and fully believes himself to be a man from outer space, no kin to the horrible earth-creatures which surround him. When a real spaceman appears out of nowhere to enable Timmy to manifest positive change in his community, Timmy doesn't bat an eye, so powerful is his inner fantasy world. The super ray gun that the "Rocket Man" gives Timmy allows the child to right all wrongs, surely a powerful metaphor for the young lad's ensuing sexual and moral maturity into adulthood.

Timmy's benefactor in this quest to fight evil is a kindly woman named Amelia Brown, who also happens to be judge for her small town. Thus, the whole scenario unfolds around a benevolent matriarchy, a most unusual thing in postwar cinema. A woman (indeed, an *older* woman) seen as the power figure in a U.S. community seems either a throwback or a very avant-garde idea, and gives the film much of its energy. It is significant also that Ms. Brown is a widow — that is, *without man* — completely encompassing the female principle of old by making her, in a sense, a reincarnation of a high priestess of antiquity.

Her foe, the evil politician who encapsulates everything noxious about patriarchal society, is felled simply by Timmy's shooting him with his ray gun, which forces the thug to reveal his actual misanthropic agenda before the startled populace. In a marvelous parting shot, Timmy tells everyone that spacemen eat green cheese, which provokes riotous laughter among the dullard grown-ups. Cut to our Rocket Man happily eating a green cheese sandwich, reinforcing the potential of creative fantasy to alter reality. *The Rocket Man* is an amazing film that prophesies the emergence of female empowerment as an issue in later 1950s B-cinema.

Tobor the Great

(originally released in 1954)
Produced by Dudley Pictures Corporation
Distributed by Republic Pictures
77 minutes/Black and White
Directed by Lee Sholem
Story: Carl Dudley
Screenplay: Philip MacDonald
Produced by Richard Goldstone
Executive Producer: Carl Dudley
Music by Howard Jackson, William Lava
Cinematography: John L. Russell
Editing: Basil Wrangell
Art Director: Gabriel Scognamillo
Set Decoration: Edward G. Boyle, John McCarthy, Jr.
Makeup Supervisor: Bob Mark
Production Manager: Orville Fouse

Assistant Director: Herb Mendelson
Sound: T.A. Carman, Howard Wilson
Special Effects: Howard Lydecker, Theodore Lydecker, Melbourne A. Arnold
Orchestrators: Michael Heindorf, Charles Maxwell, Clifford Vaughan
Cast: Charles Drake (Dr. Ralph Harrison), Karin Booth (Janice Roberts), Billy Chapin (Brian
    Roberts), Taylor Holmes (Prof. Arnold Nordstrom), Steven Geray (Spy Chief), Henry Kulky (Spy
    Henchman), Franz Roehn (Karl), Hal Baylor (Spy Henchman), Peter Brocco (Dr. Gustav), Jack
    Daly (Scientist), Franklyn Farnum (Government Representative), Norman Field (Commissioner),
    Art Gilmore (Airport Announcer), Maurice Hill (Scientist), Alan Reynolds (Reporter), William
    Schallert (Reporter), Robert Shayne (General), Charles Sherlock (Military Man), Lew Smith
    (Tobor), Lyle Talbot (Admiral), Emmett Vogan (Congressman), Helen Winston (Secretary)

Synopsis: A kindly scientist creates a marvelous "automatic man" that can do amazing, almost-human
    things. The marvelous robot comes to its master's rescue when he is kidnapped by foreign spies.

This affable if simplistic film starts off with a model shot of a spinning earth, with the
narrator intoning, "This is a story of the future — the *near* future!" Following this, the earth
appears to explode via a stock shot of the H-bomb going off, a somewhat overt illustration
of the "fear of the atom" so prevalent in cinema of the day. In the ensuing scenario, three
generations of scientists (boy, young adult, elder) all work for the common good of man,
focusing especially on the "race for space," which many at the time thought would decide
who would rule the world — the good guys ("us") or the bad guys ("the Commies").

This concept of the generational continuance of an altruistic scientific community
delineates in base form the essential momentum of patriarchy, which demands that each
generation builds upon yet follows the blueprint forged by its elders. The elder scientist has
created a robot he proudly dubs Tobor ("Robot" spelled backwards), calling his magnificent
creation "an electronic simulacrum of a man." Tobor is indeed an impressive mechanical
man-in-suit design, quite a popular icon in the immediate postwar years. The elder's grand-
son is especially taken by this metallic beast, and the relationship between he and the mecha-
man takes center stage.

The paradigm of "boy and robot," of which *Tobor the Great* may be the first cinematic
example, is curious. In this film, as in *The Invisible Boy* (1957) and *The Colossus of New York*
(1958), a young boy becomes emotionally (and some might say even sexually) attached to
a mechanical man designed and/or sponsored by his father, acting in effect as both surrogate
father figure and perhaps surrogate sibling. Yet the creation from nothing of an "animated"
beast by these brilliant patriarchs reminds us of Rottwang's creation of Maria in *Metropolis*
(1927, d: Fritz Lang). Might these handsome "clockwork men" be more intended as subliminal sex objects for the youngsters of America — in effect, techno-erotic icons that exem-
plify the sexually-charged "fetishization" of technology which culture aggressively pushed
during the postwar years? Indeed, when the kid first sets eyes on Tobor, he gasps breathlessly,
"Tobor, you're *beautiful!*" a rather odd reaction from a scientist but a perfectly natural one
from a lover or admirer. Indeed, at film's end, after Tobor rescues the kid and the old man
from the enemy, the mighty mechanical man takes the boy in his arms, where the boy
swooningly coos, "Tobor, you're *wonderful!*" If that ain't love, what is?

As with *The Rocket Man*, the other 1954 picture that was paired with this film in a
1957 re-release, a very phallic ray gun is used as a metaphoric prop to suggest the young
male's impending sexual (and hopefully moral) maturity into adulthood. In *Tobor*, the kid
significantly uses the ray gun to telepathically control his "robot-lover." This strictly "emo-

Tobor the robot, "an electronic simulacrum of a man," carries little Billy Chapin in his arms as its creator, Taylor Holmes, looks on approvingly in *Tobor the Great,* a 1954 film that received wide reissue in 1957.

tional" connection between parties could certainly be seen as another psycho-sexual symbol. The use of the robot as a character leads to some amusingly anachronistic scenes, such as the clunky metal-man driving off in a jeep or ripping apart an automobile piece by piece.

Also amusing (in an ironic sense) is a scene wherein Tobor demonstrates his ability to perform menial office chores by sitting in front of a typewriter and banging out the sentence "Tobor is robot spelled backwards" over and over, ad infinitum. The modern viewer cannot help but think of Jack re-typing, "All Work and No Play Makes Jack a Dull Boy" in Stanley Kubrick's brilliant *The Shining* (1980), which in that case signaled the author's burgeoning madness. Thus, the viewer might think that Tobor is likewise ready to "snap," perhaps even driven to lunatic violence by the existential implications of his given name being a crass reversal of his "species" label.

The woefully simplistic subplot involves actual Commie spies first infiltrating the good doctor's lair (conspicuously, via the problematic societal loophole of state secrets — the press). Whereas most later-decade genre films used the fear of Communist invasion in metaphoric terms, with aliens and monsters taking the symbolic place of the actual "enemy," this early Cold War agitprop makes no bones about who the bad guys are.

One unusual aspect of the film occurs when the Commies kidnap the elder scientist and the young boy; the nasty spies virtually torture the child, first by knocking him around and then by threatening to burn him alive via a blowtorch. This is a somewhat strong "endangerment towards a child" scene for the era. Apparently, *Tobor the Great* was the intended prototype for a television series that never materialized, although the feature, which separates nicely into three roughly half-hour segments, might have been compiled so as to provide three episodes of the proposed series.

April

The Incredible Shrinking Man

81 minutes, Black and White
Produced by Universal International Pictures
Distributed by Universal Pictures
Directed by Jack Arnold
Story: Richard Alan Simmons
Screenplay: Richard Matheson (from his novel *The Shrinking Man*)
Produced by Albert Zugsmith
Music: Irving Gertz, Earl E. Lawrence, Hans J. Salter, Herman Stein
Cinematography: Ellis W. Carter
Film Editing: Albrecht Joseph
Art Direction: Robert Clatworthy, Alexander Golitzen
Set Decoration: Russell A. Gausman, Ruby R. Levitt
Costume Design: Jay A. Morley, Jr., Martha Bunch, Rydo Loshak
Hair Stylist: Joan St. Oegger
Makeup Artist: Bud Westmore
Hairdresser: Virginia Jones
Makeup Artist: Jack Kevan
Unit Manager: Lew Leary
Assistant Directors: William Holland, Wilbur Mosier
Props: Floyd Farrington
Prop Masters: Ed Keyes, Roy Neel
Prop Maker: Whitey McMahon
Sound: Leslie I. Carey, Robert Pritchard
Sound Recordist: Donald Cunliffe
Sound Editor: Bob Hirsch
Cable Man: Henry Janssen
Sound Editor: George Ohanian
Mike Man: Roger A. Parish
Special Effects: Cleo E. Baker, Fred Knoth
Optical Effects: Everett H. Broussard, Roswell A. Hoffmann
Special Photography: Clifford Stine
Camera Operator: William Dodds
Key Grip: Stanley Guliver
Co-grip: Jim Hilbert
Best Boy: Everett Lehman
Special Photography: Tom McCrory
Gaffer: Tom Ouellette
Assistant Camera: Robert Pierce
Still Photographer: William Walling
Wardrobe: Martha Bunch, Rydo Loshak
Music Supervisor: Joseph Gershenson
Trumpet Soloist: Ray Anthony
Music Supervisor: Harris Ashburn

Coordinator: Ray Gockel
Script Supervisor: Dorothy Hughes
Cast: Grant Williams (Scott Carey), Randy Stuart (Louise Carey), April Kent (Clarice), Paul Langton (Charlie Carey), Raymond Bailey (Doctor Thomas Silver), William Schallert (Doctor Arthur Bramson), Frank J. Scannell (Barker), Helene Marshall (Nurse), Diana Darrin (Nurse), Billy Curtis (Midget), John Hiestand (Newscaster), Joe La Barba (Joe the Milkman), Regis Parton, Luce Potter

Synopsis: After being exposed to atomic fallout, a young man finds himself inexorably shrinking. Medical science can find no remedy for this remarkable atomic mutation, as its unfortunate victim shrinks ever smaller.

One of the most profound movies of the decade, and certainly the top fantastic film of the year in terms of intelligence and emotional impact, this atom-age fable, very much a nightmare rendering of Perrault's "Tom Thumb," brilliantly elucidates several key themes of the day, primarily a righteous fear of the terrible split-atom, and an equal fear of the dissolution of self. Scott's battle with a house cat and a spider, both rendered giant by his escalating diminutiveness, qualify as cheap "monster movie" thrills, but also register the sheer terror of puny man against a "natural world" he can no longer control. Likewise, Scott's transformation into a child-like man echoes great sexual fear on the part of the postwar male, who feared that his role in heterosexual society was ever-shrinking due to woman's emancipation, increasing technology, and an ever-expanding population which made each individual, by extension, less important to society. The existential issues raised by the scenario are largely unaddressed in the film's "chiller-diller" storyline but are a vital part of the film's mournful subtext, as Scott slowly shrivels until he is an invisible, subatomic non-entity. The final parting shot, as Scott walks bravely forward into a world which now completely engulfs him, brilliantly shows the ancient mystical point of view that everything in the universe is connected, part of one great cosmic whole, and that an individual ego cannot be extinguished even by death, for it is forever part of the transcendent omniscience of eternal life.

Early in the film occurs a scene which is among the most memorable in a consistently memorable film, and is the catalyst for the protagonist's slow, painful disintegration into subatomic particles. Scott Carey (Grant Williams) and his wife Louise (Randy Stuart) decide to take a relaxing voyage on the Pacific Ocean on their small yacht. Far out at sea, Louise goes below-deck to fix some drinks for the pair, leaving Scott sunning himself on the front deck. Suddenly, an ominous fog moves rapidly towards the vessel, surrounding it and completely enveloping Scott. The fog seems to contain some sort of metallic mist, which falls on Scott and attaches to his skin. Being inside, Louise seems to have escaped the deadly drizzle. Returning home later, Scott begins to feel the cruel metamorphosis transforming his body into an unwitting experiment for the evil forces of the split atom. Yet this creepy, unforgettable scene becomes all the more haunting when one realizes that it was based on a true incident. The first "Super" hydrogen bomb was tested by the U.S. military on March 1, 1954. The fallout was recorded as extraordinary — even in official military accounts — devastating many areas of the Marshall Islands and poisoning congregations of natives in the surrounding area. In yet another cruel irony of fate, the worst of the radioactive fallout was destined to target the Japanese, who had so recently been devastated by the twin atomic attacks on Hiroshima and Nagasaki. Trawling for tuna a hundred miles east of Bikini Atoll,

Early trade advertisement for Universal-International's *The Incredible Shrinking Man*, one of the most successful fantastic films of 1957.

the crew of a Japanese fishing vessel, *Fukuryu Maru* (Lucky Dragon), experienced shock waves and menacing clouds shortly after the "Super" bomb blast. According to David Halberstam, "Two hours later the sky changed. Suddenly a giant fog appeared and a light drizzle began. But this was no ordinary rain, for it contained tiny bits of ash."[18] Returning to Japan, the *Fukuryu Maru* crew all fell ill, suffering the major symptoms of severe radiation sickness:

nausea, fever, aches and skin lesions. One crew member, Aikichi Kuboyama, fell terribly ill and became the central figure associated with the accident. Over the course of the next few months, Kuboyama's condition deteriorated — prompting him at one point to scream, "My body feels like it is being burned with electricity!" — and he died in agony on September 23, 1954. As was typical for the period, there was very little coverage of the incident in the U.S. news media, and when some stories did trickle out, they were immediately attacked by various Washington legislators — including AEC chairman Lewis Strauss — who vociferously dismissed the tragedy as a fabrication, a Communist plot to discredit the nascent U.S. atomic energy program.[19] Yet the story did live on, finding a relatively wide audience a few years later when embedded in the plot of this popular science-fiction film. Was this a way for the scenarists to sneak subversive, potentially anti-nuclear information into popular culture? More likely, it was a way to safely address or "rewrite" — and thus largely nullify — the actual incident. Couched in fictional terms and conspicuously ignoring the racist angle of the actual event, this reworking of a real-life tragedy gave audiences a brief glimpse of the horrors of the atom, a vicarious thrill ride viewed from the comfort and safety of theater seats. Yet Scott Carey's demise does, in broad allegorical terms, mirror the horror-death of real-life martyr Aikichi Kuboyama, who was also "disintegrated" by the byproducts of atomic fission, albeit in a much more gruesome way. One might even be tempted to call *The Incredible Shrinking Man* an unwitting tribute to Kuboyama, surely one of the unsung heroes of the atomic age.

As grim and avant-garde as the ending of *The Incredible Shrinking Man* is, it likely caused consternation with audiences weaned on happy endings. Witness this most amusing observation by Mel Danner, manager of the Circle Theater in Waynoka, Oklahoma (population 2,018): "Good picture, but had the wrong ending. That's what the patrons said. He should have come back to his natural size."[20]

KRONOS WITH *SHE DEVIL* (TWENTIETH CENTURY–FOX)

German-born Kurt Neumann (1908–1958) was a filmmaker who came to the U.S. in the early 1930s, soon making a name for himself as a competent director of low-budget melodrama. Neumann entered the world of science-fiction in 1950 with *Rocketship XM*, and he directed both *Kronos* and *She Devil* for Regal Films, the B-level production arm of Twentieth Century–Fox. Shortly before his untimely death the next year, Neumann would direct one more thriller for Twentieth Century–Fox, the boxoffice smash *The Fly* (1958).

Kronos

78 minutes, Black and White
Produced by Regal Films
Distributed by Twentieth Century–Fox Film Corporation
Released in April
Directed by Kurt Neumann
Story: Irving Block
Screenplay: Lawrence Louis Goldman
Executive Producer: E.J. Baumgarten
Produced by Irving Block, Louis DeWitt, Kurt Neumann, Jack Rabin
Music by Paul Sawtell, Bert Shefter

Cinematography: Karl Struss
Editing: Jodie Copelan
Production Design: Theobold Holsopple
Set Decoration: Chester L. Bayhi, Walter M. Scott
Hair Dresser: Madine Danks
Makeup Artist: Louis Hippe
Production Manager: Herbert Mendelson
Property Master: Max Goldman
Sound: James Mobley
Special Effects: Irving Block, Louis DeWitt, Jack Rabin, William Reinhold, Menrad von Mulldorfer,
    Gene Warren, Wah Chang
Wardrobe: Richard Staub, Mary Tate
Dialogue Coach: Clarence J. Marks
Script Supervisor: Mai Dietrich
Cast: Jeff Morrow (Dr. Leslie Gaskell), Barbara Lawrence (Vera Hunter), John Emery (Dr. Hubbell
    Eliot), George O'Hanlon (Dr. Arnold Culver), Morris Ankrum (Dr. Albert Stern), Kenneth Alton
    (McCrary), John Parrish (Gen. Perry), Jose Gonzales-Gonzales (Manuel Ramirez) Richard Harrison
    (Pilot), Marjorie Stapp (Nurse), Robert Shayne (Air Force General), Don Eitner (Weather Oper-
    ator), Gordon Mills (Sergeant), John Halloran (Security Guard), Robert Stevenson (Newscaster),
    Baxter Ward (Newscaster)

Synopsis: A monstrous machine from outer space threatens to destroy the earth by absorbing all its
    energy sources. The alien presence takes over a preeminent scientist to further its nefarious plans.

Hands-down the most clever and "abstract" sci-fi film of the year, *Kronos* shows the
standard SF film formula at its best, with a great cast, intelligent yet gripping screenplay,
and a most memorable "beastie" which nicely symbolizes the runaway technocracy of postwar
man.

At a sinister top-secret government complex, scientists fawn over a super-computer
dubbed "Susie," underscoring the fetish-nature of man's technological "toys," a theme
brought to vivid life with the unleashing of the title "monster." The popular sci-fi theme
of being taken over by an alien presence is referenced here, with a scientist turned into an
intermediary of the invading force. The loss of one's will, and thus moral freedom, which
these all-too-frequent alien takeovers illustrated, related to popular fears about the "Communist" lifestyle, which U.S. propaganda interests portrayed as one of soulless, emotionless
drudgery towards a massive technological moloch to scare the public into blindly loving
the U.S.A., as well as deflecting critical scrutiny away from some similar disturbing trends
occurring right here at home.

For no immediately apparent reason, like the same year's *The Black Scorpion*, part of
the film is set in Mexico and features one or more sympathetic "Latin-flavored" characters.
Was this perhaps the movie studios' sorry nod to the postwar influx of Puerto Rican immigrants to U.S. shores? This seems likely, as *Kronos* even takes its only comic detour to show
one of the scientists gagging on hot Mexican food — apparently the "earthy" spices of Mexican cooking are too much for the bland palette of wimpy Caucasians.

But the star of *Kronos* is without a doubt the magnificent machine-monster created by
Mssrs. Rabin, Block and DeWitt, an extraordinary contraption that is all the more creepy
because it is non-organic, without soul, and thus obviously without conscience or mercy.
Alternately awkward, beautiful and menacing. Kronos may be best described as a mammoth,
two-tiered monolith "box" with piston "legs" and a globe-like "head." As an aesthetically-

Trade advertisement for Kurt Neumann's impressive double bill, *Kronos* and *She Devil*, which managed to juggle male and female energies admirably in a most thrilling sci-fi drive-in package.

pleasing abstraction of various elements of both architectural and industrial design (with an assured nod to the "Bauhaus" school), Kronos comes across as a "pure" symbol of technology, as both fetish-object and myth-infused manifestation of out-of-control human impulses writ large.

The bizarre monolith is dubbed "Kronos" by earthlings in a sly reference to the Titan of Greek mythology who overthrew his own father to obtain omnipotence. Certainly this metaphor of the "creation destroying the creator" applies to Mankind, who will surely be felled by his own technological excesses.

As it turns out, Kronos is an "energy accumulator," and its sole purpose is to suck up all the earth's energy resources and spirit them off to its home planet. As a greedy, insatiable consumer of energy, Kronos symbolizes mankind in general, the Western Hemisphere in particular, and, most importantly, the serpentine military-industrial complex, which even today threatens to absorb all resources — natural, technological and human — for its own nefarious purposes. When Kronos begins its attack on the earth, it becomes a vaguely humanoid thing, with stomping piston-feet and a bleeping, glowing head-globe — these scenes are well-depicted via a combination of exquisite miniatures and adequate animation sequences. Less effective is a giant prop piston that clumsily stomps down on some Mexican peasants in a few brief studio shots. Augmenting the visuals are impressive optical and audio effects, the sum of which makes Kronos a most peculiar yet fearsome foe.

The military unwittingly "feeds" Kronos by sending it the ill-advised gift of an H-bomb, which the monster machine laps up gratefully. First the bomb is shown exploding (via military stock footage), and then the scene is shown again but in reverse, with the monstrous mushroom cloud collapsing in on itself. One might posit that this curious scene of a bomb "unexploding" mirrors a subconscious wish on the part of Mankind to erase the atomic age, to once and for all put that awful nuclear genie back in the bottle which humanity so foolishly uncorked.

Yet the most frightening moment in this sequence is a vision accidentally caught by the military photographer — as the H-bomb explodes, and the massive, mushroom-shaped dust cloud expands to grotesque proportions, the grimacing face of what appears to be a demon can clearly be seen in the cloud for almost a full second before it is re-absorbed into the atomic vapor. As optical doctoring of film was in its infancy at the time, one must assume that the demon-face actually "appeared" in the original explosion, a revelation of fearsome portent. Are those who see the "face" in the cloud suffering from hallucination brought on by deep-seated subconscious guilt about their inherent complicity in the bringing forth of this monstrous killer of life? Another possibility is even more sinister — dark supernatural forces from within the structure of the bomb itself manifested into a visual symbol that one could witness in order to announce that Man had finally become the evil thing which his potential for destruction had always suggested was his ultimate destiny and doom.

It is clear that Roger Corman saw, and was impressed by, *Kronos*, for much was borrowed for his 1958 SF potboiler *War of the Satellites*, not the least of which were the scenarist, Lawrence Louis Goldman, and the f/x team of Rabin, Block and DeWitt. But even *Satellites'* animated credits sequence borrows heavily from Kronos' credits sequence, and both screenplays feature floating balls of alien light that take over human minds. Even Walter Greene's fantastic score for *War of the Satellites* seems inspired by Paul Sawtell and Burt Shefter's somewhat similar score.

She Devil

77 minutes, Black and White
Produced by Regal Films
Distributed by Twentieth Century–Fox Film Corporation
Directed by Kurt Neumann
Story: Stanley G. Weinbaum (from his story "The Adaptive Ultimate")
Screenplay: Carroll Young, Kurt Neumann
Produced by Kurt Neumann
Music by Paul Sawtell, Bert Shefter
Cinematography by Karl Struss
Editing: Carl Pierson
Production Design: Theobold Holsopple
Set Decoration: Chester L. Bayhi, Walter M. Scott
Hair Stylist: Madine Danks
Makeup Artist: Louis Hippe
Assistant Director: Herbert E. Mendelson
Property Master: Max Goldman
Sound: Eugene Grossman
Wardrobe Supervisors: Norma Koch, Wesley Sherrard
Cast: Mari Blanchard (Kyra Zelas), Jack Kelly (Dr. Dan Scott), Albert Dekker (Dr. Richard Bach), John Archer (Barton Kendall), Fay Baker (Evelyn Kendall), Blossom Rock (Hannah), Paul Cavanagh (Sugar Daddy), George Baxter (Store Manager), Helen Jay (Blond Nurse), Joan Bradshaw (Redhead), X Brands (First Doctor), Tod Griffin (Intern)

Synopsis: Two doctors inject a dying woman with an experimental serum that turns her into an murderous she-beast. The woman asserts her independence, wreaking havoc on the community.

In this astounding B-melodrama, a surrogate father-son duo effectively conspire against the entire female gender, pretty much summing up the agenda of patriarchy in a nutshell. The two encounter a young, apparently homeless woman dying of tuberculosis, whose imminent death signals both the end of innocence and the demise of the servile, pre-feminist archetype. Through the reckless injection of a diabolical experimental serum, an act which, through the forced puncturing of the flesh and the injection of a faux-seminal fluid, amounts to rape, the dying Kyra is quickly transformed into a confident, healthy, even arrogant "new woman," a post-modern take on the male myth of the "man-eater."

The frightfully bold Kyra makes it plain early on that she can do anything she wants, and intends to. This powerful new female is the feminist model, as seen from the perspective of the terrified male collective, who views female autonomy as both politically threatening and sexually devastating. The new Kyra is, in fact, an egotistical sociopath without any redeeming qualities, and actually expresses the suppressed *male* desire for complete freedom to conquer her world. Kyra's uncanny ability to change her hair color at will represents both her animistic ability to adapt, chameleon-like, to threatening surroundings, and the radical sea change her sexual politics have undergone.

In stark contrast is the doctor's maid, a buffoonish cartoon of a woman (well played by Blossom Rock), whose position literalizes the pre-feminist role of complete, if begrudging, subservience to the male collective. Of course, Kyra's actions spiral out of control to include theft and murder, and the males' Faustian bargain turns sour all too quickly. To complicate matters, the younger scientist has fallen hopelessly in love with his new creation, evil or not. After Kyra leaves the residence of her co-creators, she teases them by sending over a huge, saucy portrait of her, mocking the man who loves her with this pathetic substitute for the real thing, and underscoring the fact that the males had fetishized the woman as an ideal fantasy object, easy to control, and not a real person, perhaps uncontrollable. Finally, Kyra is coerced back into the clutches of her creators only to be given another rape-injection, which erases her new role and indeed causes her wheezing, painful death. Surely patriarchy cannot allow such monstrous freedom-loving creatures to exist!

She Devil expertly mingles several sources into one of the most powerful films of the year. Firstly, there is the story of Pygmalion, the sculptor of Greek mythology who fell in love with his statue of Galatea and begged the gods to give her life, only to regret it later. In German legend the mad genius Faust makes a deal with the devil, Mephistopheles, in exchange for unlimited creative power. Mephistopheles helps Faust seduce a beautiful innocent, Gretchen, who is eventually destroyed and sent to Heaven. In Offenbach's opera *Tales of Hoffmann*, two scientists named Spalanzani and Coppélius create a magnificent female automaton named Olympia, and the wandering poet Hoffmann falls hopelessly in love with her, causing his downfall. In *She Devil*, scenarists Carroll Young and Kurt Neumann cleverly update these concepts to forge a most interesting cultural foreshadowing of the nascent feminist movement.

As mentioned previously, it is almost certain that Young and Neumann were familiar with the *Alraune* novel, the Mandrake Root legend, and the 1952 film *Unnatural* while they were conceiving *She Devil*, as the basic plotline is so similar. Eschewing artificial insemination for more recent medical trends, the elder patriarch nonetheless "creates" a soulless female monster with his pseudo-scientific machinations, then becomes as much victim as benefactor of the resultant she-beast. As well, a younger male acts as co-conspirator and love interest of the ungodly she-thing. Finally, both scenarios end with the elder causing the death of the doomed female, an act simultaneously merciful and misogynistic. Granted, many of these narrative points also appear in the credited source story "The Adaptive Ulti-mate," by Stanley G. Weinbaum (1902–1935). Weinbaum was a prolific fiction writer, and this story was first published in the November 1935 edition of *Astounding Science-Fiction* magazine under the pseudonym John Jessel. Although unverifiable, it would be extremely unlikely that Weinbaum was unfamiliar with Ewer's 1911 *Alraune* novel, and it is highly conceivable that some of that novel's "spirit" found its way into Weinbaum's "modern" update.

May

MONSTER FROM GREEN HELL WITH HALF HUMAN (DISTRIBUTORS CORPORATION OF AMERICA)[21]

Hal Roach's tiny distribution outfit DCA had perhaps its "biggest" year in 1957. In addition to picking up *Unnatural: The Fruits of Evil* and *Rodan, the Flying Monster* for U.S. release, it acquired other independent productions, such as these two, for release to suburban drive-in and urban grindhouse theaters. While Roach's primary focus at the time was tel-evision production, the theatrical arm managed to make an impact in the marketplace. Other 1957 DCA double bills aimed at the youth market included *Teenage Bad Girl/Teenage Wolf Pack*, a combo of British and German juvenile delinquency films.[22] DCA also distrib-uted a good number of British melodramas in 1957, as well as such eclectic fare as Vittorio de Sica's *Gold of Naples* and *Mademoiselle Striptease*, starring French sex kitten Brigitte Bardot. As well, the Alan Freed 31 rock 'n' roll omnibus *Rock, Rock, Rock*, released in late December 1956, pulled strong boxoffice throughout 1957.[23]

Monster from Green Hell

Produced by Gross-Krasne Productions
Distributed by Distributors Corporation of America
71 minutes, Black and White
Stock Footage: *Stanley and Livingston* (1939)
Directed by Kenneth G. Crane
Screenplay: Endre Bohem, Louis Vittes
Executive Producers: Philip N. Krasne, Jack J. Gross
Produced by Al Zimbalist
Associate Producer: Sol Dolgin
Music by Albert Glasser
Cinematography: Ray Flin
Film Editing: Kenneth G. Crane
Production Design: Ernst Fegté
Set Decoration: G.W. Berntsen
Costume Design: Joseph Dimmitt
Makeup Artist: Louis Haszillo
Production Manager: Byron Roberts

Assistant Director: John Greenwald
Property Master: Robert R. Benton
Sound: Stanley Cooley, Robert Roderick
Sound Editor: Charles Diltz
Special Effects: Jess Davison
Visual Effects: Louis DeWitt
Special Photographic Effects: Jack Rabin, Irving Block, Jack Cosgrove, Wah Chang
Stop-Motion Animator: Gene Warren
Music Editor: Robert Post
Script Supervisor: Doris Moody
Cast: Jim Davis (Dr. Quent Brady), Robert Griffin (Dan Morgan), Joel Fluellen (Arobi), Barbara
 Turner (Lorna Lorentz), Eduardo Ciannelli (Mahri), Vladimir Sokoloff (Dr. Lorentz), Tim Huntley
 (Territorial Agent), LaVerne Jones (Kuana), Frederic Potler (Radar Operator)

Synopsis: An expedition to locate a missing astronaut encounters mammoth radioactive wasps in
 Africa.

This low-budget SF film comes close to the perfect "generic" monster movie; although
it is engaging and has its moments, it lacks a certain abiding personality. The scenario boasts
a curiously ethnocentric focus, as "White Science" rather specifically harasses the poor black
population of Africa via the giant wasps who eat the natives.

The rambling narrative spends a great deal of time on the scientists' safari to "Green
Hell," and even more time as the group tries to traverse a cave in which they are trapped—
both of these scenes being economically padded with stock footage from either *Stanley and
Livingstone* (1939, d: Henry King) or *King Solomon's Mines* (1950, d: Compton Bennett,
Andrew Marton). In between are sparse but impressive f/x scenes by Jack Rabin and Irving
Block, including some professional stop-motion scenes and a full-scale mock-up of a wasp
head that is easily the equal of the mock-up ant in the overrated *Them!* (1954, d: Gordon
Douglas).

Thanks to tight cropping and judicious editing, some of the wasp attack scenes are
quite effective. One interesting theme, which also figures prominently in *Attack of the Crab
Monsters*, is the notion of the wasps' breeding to create armies of unstoppable monsters; yet
it would be wishful thinking to assume that this plot point was added as a sly protest against
unbridled human procreation.

The biggest letdown in the film is the hasty, awkward finale, in which stock shots of
volcanic lava are superimposed over f/x shots of the wasps, with creepy "screaming" dominating the soundtrack. The assumption is that the exploding volcano has swallowed up the
wasps in its molten lava, but the effect is confusing and unconvincing. *Rodan, the Flying
Monster* crafted the same finale in far better fashion. Skid-row producer Al Zimbalist was
also responsible for two other peculiar '50s SF quickies, *Cat Women of the Moon* (1954, d:
Arthur Hilton) and *King Dinosaur* (1955, d: Bert I. Gordon).

The production of *The Monster from Green Hell* has an interesting genesis. Jack Gross,
a former producer at Universal Pictures, and Philip Krassne, a producer at Monogram Pictures (responsible for the popular *Cisco Kid* film series), decided to form their own production
company, primarily to enter the lucrative television syndication game. The resulting corporation, Gross-Krasne Productions, then created two television series, both shot and
released in 1957.[24] *Adventures of a Jungle Boy* was the first, which—according to TV historian
Hal Erickson—was "designed to capitalize on 1957 headlines concerning the efforts of

several African nations to declare independence." The series was purportedly filmed in Kenya, as was Gross-Krasne's follow-up series, *African Patrol*.[25] It is thus exceedingly curious that Gross-Krasne's only known feature film property also takes place in Africa, and was also produced and released in 1957. It seems entirely conceivable that certain scenes for this "monster movie" were filmed in Kenya simultaneously with the production of the two television series, and a comparison of the settings and stock characters in each might prove rewarding.

Half Human

(original production, *Jujin Yuki Otoko*, 1955)
Produced by Toho Company
Distributed by Distributors Corporation of America
63 minutes, Black and White
Directed by Kenneth G. Crane, Ishirô Honda
Original Screenplay: Takeo Murata
Produced by Robert B. Homel (U.S. version)
Produced by Minoru Sakamoto, Tomoyuki Tanaka
Cinematography: Lucien N. Andriot, Tadashi Iimura
Editing: Kenneth G. Crane
Casting: Lynn Stalmaster
Production Design: Tatsuo Kita, Nicolai Remisoff
Art Department
Property Master (U.S. sequences): Sam Heiligman
Sound Director: Jack Wiler
Direstor of Special Effects: Eiji Tsuburaya
Wardrobe (U.S. sequences): Morrie Friedman
Cast: John Carradine (Dr. John Rayburn), Momoko Kôchi (the Girl), Akira Takarada (the Boy), Akemi Negishi (the Mountain Girl), Russell Thorson (Prof. Philip Osborne), Robert Karnes (Prof. Alan Templeton), Sacho Sakai (Third Member of Ski Party), Nobuo Nakamura (Prof. Tanaka), Kokuten Kôdô (Old Tribe Leader), Morris Ankrum (Dr. Carl Jordan), Kenji Kasahara (Murdered Skier)

Synopsis: An expedition to the snowy mountains of Japan discovers a strange creature that appears to be the missing link between modern man and prehistoric ape. The body of the creature's slain child is brought to the United States for scientific examination.

Half Human is a most interesting, if not terribly engaging, film; it is an early example of a cinematic "hybrid"—a new film created by the use of foreign-lensed source material with additional footage shot in the United States. The prototype of this curious sub-genre is probably *Godzilla, King of the Monsters* (1956), the English-language release of the 1954 Japanese thriller *Gojira* (d: Ishiro Honda). The impressive success of *Godzilla*, which deftly framed the Japanese narrative with inserted scenes of American actor Raymond Burr, is probably what encouraged producer Robert B. Homel to attempt a similar concoction here. Alas, the result is somewhat stillborn, and the hybrid concept quickly became a cynical way for skid-row producers (such as Jerry Warren, who would turn the formula into a veritable art form) to take cheaply-acquired foreign film footage boasting relatively high productive values and crudely stitch on U.S. scenes featuring one or more bankable box-office names. The resultant unwieldy monstrosities usually appealed more to the distribution and marketing people than to the poor audiences who suffered through them.

In *Half Human*, the core melodrama is framed by newly-shot footage featuring John Carradine as a scientist who "explains" the Japanese footage to two colleagues. The Japanese footage is not dubbed, the bulk of it being merely narrated (or, more rightly, annotated) by Carradine. Indeed, long patches of exposition don't even boast that editorial conceit, and the effect is somewhat alienating, like watching a story being told rather than watching a story unfold. The Japanese "mountain man," when seen, is fairly effective; although it is a man-in-suit creation, like Gojira and most other Japan movie monsters, the use of a man-sized suit in a normal-sized environment increases the believability level significantly.

The scenario pits a group of young Japanese urbanites against a tribe of wizened elders, with the mysterious "mountain man" being a "missing link" of sorts between generations. A young man is kidnapped by the elders and used as a sacrifice to their gods, hung by a rope from a mountain top and prey to vultures. The elders are portrayed here as distinctly opportunistic if not downright malevolent. The "mountain man" rescues the young man from his fate, thus aligning himself with the young group, the new order (and also, sub-textually, with the teenaged audience). It is emphasized early on that the "mountain man" is especially attracted to the one young woman in the youthful expedition; in fact, during a later attack on a village, the female is the only one the monster does not kill. The beast may be instinctually beholden to the female principle, which he knows intuitively to be the true power source of the natural world.

The second half of the film shifts focus somewhat, as it is revealed that the monster had a son, which was captured and killed and brought all the way to Carradine's offices, where it is examined in autopsy by all parties. Considering the low budget of the enterprise, the prop used in the inserts is a reasonable facsimile of the being seen in the Japanese footage (although an unverifiable online source claims that both suits were in fact the same, the Japanese prop having been sent to the U.S. for the insert scenes). In flashback, Carradine finally relates the sad story of the young monster's capture by circus folk, a somewhat ostentatious nod to *King Kong*. The death of the junior beast by mishandling precedes Armageddon, as the savage force of the "mountain man" is unleashed on humankind.

Due to the distancing effect of the various post-production conceits, the themes, plot points and even much of the exquisite photography are lost in a product which is extremely difficult to engage in, and one understands why *Half Human* was tucked at the bottom of a lackluster double bill with *Monster from Green Hell*, released by the tiniest of outfits, Distributors Corporation of America.

The Deadly Mantis

79 minutes, Black and White
Produced by Universal International Pictures
Distributed by Universal Pictures
Directed by Nathan Juran
Story: William Alland
Screenplay: Martin Berkeley
Produced by William Alland
Music by Irving Gertz, William Lava, Henry Mancini
Cinematography by Ellis W. Carter
Editing: Chester W. Schaeffer
Art Direction: Robert Clatworthy, Alexander Golitzen

Set Decoration: Oliver Emert, Russell A. Gausman
Gowns: Jay A. Morley, Jr.
Makeup Artist: Bud Westmore
Assistant Director: William Holland
Sound: Leslie I. Carey, Leon M. Leon
Special Effects: Fred Knoth
Special Photographer: Clifford Stine
Process Photographer: Tom McCrory
Music Supervisors: Joseph Gershenson, Harris Ashburn
Cast: Craig Stevens (Col. Joe Parkman), William Hopper (Dr. Nedrick "Ned" Jackson), Alix Talton (Marge Blaine), Donald Randolph (Gen. Mark Ford), Pat Conway (Sgt. Pete Allen), Florenz Ames (Prof. Anton Gunther), Paul Smith (Corporal), Phil Harvey (Lou), Floyd Simmons (Army Sergeant), Paul Campbell (Lt. Fred Pizar), Helen Jay (Mrs. Farley), Keith Aldrich (Jerry), William Anders (Sergeant, Archer Control), Marvin Bryan (Machine-Gunner), John Close (Engineer), Tom Cound (Group Capt. Hawkins), William A. Forester (Announcer), Paul Frees (Opening Narrator), Tom Greenway (Second Reporter), James R. Haskin (Civilian Announcer), Jess Kirkpatrick (Father), James Lanphier (Col. Harvey), Ned Le Fevre (Announcer), Harold Lee (Greenland Eskimo Chief), George Lynn (Bus Driver), Jack Mather (Officer), David McMahon (Capt. Frank Carver), Edward McNally (Policeman), Marvin Miller (Narrator), Madelon Mitchell (Mother), Ernesto Morelli (Italian Fisherman), Sigurd Nilssen (Prof. Harvey Pierce), Dick Paxton (Plotter), Bing Russell (State Trooper), Harry Tyler (Spectator), Sumner Williams (Pilot)

Synopsis: A giant prehistoric praying mantis, thawed out by nuclear tests in the Antarctic, comes alive and attacks humanity.

Universal-International tried to follow up their smash hit *The Incredible Shrinking Man* with a tired "giant monster" programmer, *The Deadly Mantis*.

This deadly dull, pedestrian and predictable programmer from Universal confirms that without an exemplary screenplay (aka *The Incredible Shrinking Man*), Universal had no idea what to do with the modern "science-horror" film (witness the dreadful *Creature from the Black Lagoon* series, as soulless a trio of thrillers as ever was made). This is especially odd, as Universal is considered the "father" of the modern horror film, thanks to expert adaptations of *Frankenstein, Dracula*, et al. Post-war, however, Universal-International just couldn't seem to get anything right — the same year's *The Land Unknown* was an embarrassing, lumbering behemoth, and the previous year's *The Mole People* was more joke than movie. One even wonders how a small gem like *This Island Earth* (1955, d: Joseph Newman) could have escaped from this hapless studio.

The Deadly Mantis is a good example of a "monster movie" with no redeeming qualities whatsoever, a cynical production so lacking in character it leaves no trace in the memory. The viewer knows he or she is in for trouble when assaulted by the most boring, pointless prologue in film history. The bulk of the film goes to extraordinary lengths to glorify the sinister military-industrial complex, amounting to little more than a love letter to the evil machine of war. Added to this is an embarrassing Neanderthal sexism that makes the whole film seem like some sort of throwback to a less enlightened age.

The film also indulges in a moment of overt racism via a montage of a tribe of Eskimos investigating the strange creature that has invaded its land; the montage is curiously sped up, turning the whole sequence into a mockery of old silent films, and painting this indigenous people as slapstick buffoons and their fight for survival as light comedy.

The monster, when seen as a marionette on the ground, is fairly effective, but this suspension of disbelief is nullified by the awkward, amateurish flying scenes. Some writers have taken great pains to call the title bug some sort of allegory for attacking Red Commies, but that comparison could be better made with any similar film of the decade. In sum, *The Deadly Mantis* is lifeless, lacking any sense of threat and creating no suspense whatsoever, and the exposition is so predictable that time seems to stand still while one waits for the highly-anticipated finale. As an example of Universal's cynical carelessness, *The Deadly Mantis* was double-billed with *Joe Butterfly*, a film about a washed-up boxer — just because both titles allude to *bugs!*

June

THE MONSTER THAT CHALLENGED THE WORLD
WITH *THE VAMPIRE* (UNITED ARTISTS)

Producers Arthur Gardner and Jules V. Levy, and director Arnold Laven, created this hot summer double bill through their Gramercy Pictures banner. Gardner, Levy and Laven had been working together as a production team since 1951, with their breakthrough picture being the crime-noir thriller *Without Warning!* (1952). Gardner-Levy-Laven would soon stake their claim in Hollywood as creators of the hit television series *The Rifleman* and *The Big Valley*. As always with these quick-run genre double bills, the marketing was key, as witness this Boxoffice magazine article entitled "Chill for Hot Weather":

In the midst of a warm spell, Paul Amadeo of the Pike Drive-In at Hartford, Conn., booked "The Monster That Challenged The World" and "The Vampire," with advertising copy carrying the line, "Feel Warm? Here's a combination that will positively chill you!"[26]

The Monster That Challenged the World

83 minutes, Black and White
Produced by Gramercy Pictures
Distributed by United Artists
Directed by Arnold Laven
Screenplay: David Duncan, Pat Fielder
Produced by Arthur Gardner, Jules V. Levy
Music by Heinz Roemheld
Cinematography: Lester White
Editing: John Faure
Casting: Kerwin Coughlin
Art Director: James Vance
Set Decoration: Rudy Butler
Makeup Artist: Abe Haberman
Hair Stylist: Olga Collings
Underwater Unit Director: Paul Stader
Assistant Director: Maurice Vaccarino
Sound Recordists: Charles Althouse, Joel Moss, B.F. Remmington
Special Effects Photographer: Robert H. Crandall
Special Effects Design: Edward S. Haworth
Special Effects: August Lohman
Photographer, Underwater Unit: Charles S. Welborn
Process Photographer: Paul Eagler
Wardrobe Supervisor: Allan Sloane
Conductor: Heinz Roemheld
Underwater Technical Advisor: Norman Bishop
Production Assistants: Virginia Mazzuca, Pat Fielder
Dialogue Director: Harlan Warde
Cast: Tim Holt (Lt. Cmdr. John "Twill" Twillinger), Audrey Dalton (Gail MacKenzie), Hans Conried (Dr. Jess Rogers), Harlan Warde (Lt. Robert "Clem" Clemens), Max Showalter (Dr. Tad Johns) (as "Casey Adams"), Mimi Gibson (Sandy MacKenzie), Gordon Jones (Sheriff Josh Peters), Marjorie Stapp (Connie Blake), Dennis McCarthy (George Blake), Barbara Darrow (Jody Simms), Robert Benevides (Seaman Morty Beatty), Michael Dugan (Clarke), Mack Williams (Capt. Masters), Jody McCrea (Sally) (as Eileen Harley), Wallace Earl (Seaman Fred Johnson), William Swan (Seaman Howard Sanders), Charles Tannen (Seaman Wyatt), Byron Kane (Coroner Nate Brown), Hal Taggart (Davis), Gil Frye (Deputy Scotty), Dan Gachman (Deputy Brewer), Milton Parsons (Lewis Clark Dobbs), Ralph Moody (Watchman), John Carlyle (Victim), John Close (Deputy), William Forrest (Admiral Greenhouse), Joseph Hamilton (Watchman), Charles Herbert (Boy), Ralph Littlefield (Gatekeeper), David McMahon (Patterson), Sarah Selby (Mrs. Simms)

Synopsis: Atomic testing unleashes gargantuan prehistoric snails.

This straightforward but well-crafted monster movie is unusually well photographed and features a terrific "creature" designed by Augie Lohman, possibly the best mechanical monster prop of the era. Although ostensibly a mammoth radioactive mollusk, the beast eerily symbolizes, in absurdly near-literal form, the inherent dangers of phallo-centric technology run amok. Specifically stated as being "unleashed" by accumulative atomic testing co-authored by the U.S. navy and various scientific concerns, the thing from the sea looks

Production team Arnold Laven, Arthur Gardner and Jules Levy hit pay dirt with *The Monster That Challenged the World* and *The Vampire*, an entertaining and successful drive-in double bill which was released through United Artists in mid-summer 1957.

like an immense erect penis, even to its sticky white effluence, which effectively mirrors human semen. Thus, in the scene's finale, when the mammoth cock-thing, dripping grotesque ejaculate, hovers menacingly over a tiny virgin girl, the symbolism could not be clearer: the joint efforts of the Military and Science creates diabolical extensions of male sexual violence, with destruction their only aim. This may explain the curiously lame title of the film, which does not do justice to the monster or the story, but alludes to something far darker — the "monster that challenged the world" is the Military-Industrial Complex, that diabolical postwar engine of systemic mass murder that will destroy us all.

One element which greatly enhances *The Monster That Challenged the World* is a rich, memorable score in the "classic horror" tradition by Heinz Roemheld (1901–1985). Roemheld had scored such horror classics as *The Invisible Man* (1933) and *The Black Cat* (1934), and the lush ambiance of a 1930s orchestral score is evident in *Monster*'s score. The score even includes a sappy romantic ballad called "Full of Love," scored both with and without vocals in the hopes that it might be released as a Top 40 hit![27] Needless to say, this 45 rpm record release never happened, but its existence in "pop vocal" form reveals how producers of the day had one eye always open to possible crossover merchandising opportunities. When United Artists began an 8mm home movie division in the early 1960s, selling 10-minute silent versions of their back catalog to film collectors, *The Monster That Challenged the World* was one of their first, and ultimately most successful, titles.

The Vampire

75 minutes, Black and White
Produced by Gramercy Pictures
Distributed by United Artists
Directed by Paul Landres
Story: Pat Fielder
Screenplay: Pat Fielder
Produced by Arthur Gardner, Arnold Laven, Jules V. Levy
Music by Gerald Fried
Cinematography: Jack MacKenzie
Editing: John Faure
Art Director: James Dowell Vance
Set Decoration: Rudy Butler
Hair Stylist: Carmen Dirigo
Makeup Artist: Donald W. Roberson
Assistant Director: Marty Moss
Sound: Charles Althouse, Lyle Cain, Joel Moss
Wardrobe Supervisor: Harry Black
Conductor: Gerald Fried
Production Assistant: Pat Fielder
Cast: John Beal (Dr. Paul Beecher), Coleen Gray (Carol Butler), Kenneth Tobey (Sheriff Buck Donnelly), Lydia Reed (Betsy Beecher), Dabbs Greer (Dr. Will Beaumont), Herb Vigran (George Ryan, Police Sergeant), Paul Brinegar (Willy Warner), Ann Staunton (Marion Wilkins), James Griffith (Henry Winston), Budd Buster, Arthur Gardner (Anesthetist), Raymond Greenleaf (Autopsy Surgeon), Hallene Hill (Mrs. Carrie Dietz), Mauritz Hugo (Joe, the Waiter), Louise Lewis (Mrs. Miller), Natalie Masters, Walter Merrill, Brad Morrow (Tommy), Anne O'Neal (Marion's Housekeeper), Christine Rees, Wood Romoff (Dr. Matthew J. Campbell)

Synopsis: A small-town doctor becomes habituated to a new medicine which turns him into a killer.

The Vampire is an effectively creepy thriller which mixes horror traditions willy-nillly, albeit to good effect. The monster, created by moral weakness as much as anything, is equal parts vampire and werewolf, with a touch of Jekyll and Hyde thrown in for good measure; but the effect is impressive, and John Beal gives a remarkable performance considering the absurdity of the role. Like other films of the era, the protagonist is also the villain of the piece via his involuntary "altered state."

As with so many other films of the late–1950s, the cause of the monstrous transformation of a simple man is failed experiments in age regression. Popular culture's obsession with age regression at this time may reflect at some level a collective wish to return to a simpler time before the so-recent horrors of World War II, and the American bombing of Hiroshima and Nagasaki. Yet in this scenario, as well as others, the effort to revert to an ancient, even prehistoric past proves foolhardy, traumatic, and fatal. To the primarily teenage audience, this notion of regression may reflect an even simpler wish — to return to the relative innocence of childhood. *The Vampire*'s screenplay seems virtually obsessed with youth, from the opening credits, which feature a young boy pedaling his bicycle down Main Street, to several scenes of the protagonist's coy 12-year-old daughter playing the piano, dancing or making a gymnastics move; each of these tableaus also hint at the creative energy of this first "atom age" generation.

The incisive scenario depicts a placid U.S. suburbia as victim to unleashed ancient forces which threaten to rent it asunder. In a highly symbolic eventuality, the pillar of the community, the kindly Dr. Beaumont, also turns out to be its mortal enemy. Yet Dr. Beaumont's personal struggle with the pills that turn him into a killer takes on all the traits of standard-issue drug addiction and withdrawal, a notion which further suggests something morally out of balance in this supposedly placid small town. Towards the film's end, a sign hanging over the office door reads "The Doctor is OUT," alluding to him being out of control, out of this world *and* out of his mind, as well as being a dangerous outsider.

One of the oddest characters in a film full of them is a scientist named Henry who wears a scowl and dark glasses, and refuses normal communication with his fellows (he may have been a conscious homage to Paul Johnson, the sunglasses-sporting misanthropic alien who graced Roger Corman's *Not of This Earth* several months earlier). In a nice gothic horror touch, Beaumont stuffs Henry's remains into an incinerator, a modern incarnation of the witch's cauldron or the biblical fiery furnace. Thanks to touches like these, plus a terrific score by Gerald Fried, *The Vampire* paints Small Town U.S.A. as a diabolical place with morbid secrets abounding, and grotesque horrors lurking in the shadows. It is not a fit place in which children can grow up or old folks retire — sort of like postwar America itself.

Producers Arthur Gardner and Jules Levy made *The Vampire* part of a package with *The Monster That Challenged the World*, selling it to United Artists who released the set as a double bill. As with so many cultural products packaged as a duo (45 rpm records are another good example), the B-side or the 2nd feature — in this case *The Vampire* — turns out to be far more interesting than the "main" product it was designed to support.

I Was a Teenage Werewolf with *Invasion of the Saucer Men* (American International Pictures)

American International Pictures had been releasing youth-centric films for almost a year before they had their industry breakthrough with this timely and topical double-bill,

American International Pictures had their breakthrough success with *I Was a Teenage Werewolf* and *Invasion of the Saucer Men*, a double bill which successfully caught the attention of the entire teenage moviegoing audience, as well as the movie industry in general.

which grossed over $2 million domestically, a record for this type of product.[28] The first film dealt obliquely with "troubled youth" — a theme resonating throughout U.S. culture at the time, and addressed in films such as *Rebel Without a Cause* (1955) — stitching this theme rather haphazardly to a common horror trope. The second movie playfully addressed the "flying saucer" craze of the period, again attaching it to a plot that revolved around how such a menace might affect the teenage population of a typical American community.

I Was a Teenage Werewolf

76 minutes, Black and White
Produced by Sunset Productions
Distributed by American International Pictures
Directed by Gene Fowler, Jr.
Screenplay: Herman Cohen, Aben Kandel (as "Ralph Thornton")
Produced by Herman Cohen
Music by Paul Dunlap
Cinematography: Joseph LaShelle
Production Design: Leslie Thomas
Set Decoration: Morris Hoffman
Makeup: Phillip Scheer
Hair Stylist: Fae Smith
Production Manager: Jack R. Berne
Assistant Director: Jack R. Berne
Property Master: Max Frankel
Sound Effects Editor: Henry Adams
Sound: James S. Thomson
Wardrobe: Oscar Rodriguez
Editorial Supervisor: George Gittens
Conductor: Paul Dunlap
Music Editor: Axel Hubert
Executive Producers: James H. Nicholson, Samuel Z. Arkoff
Script Supervisor: Mary Gibsone
Production Secretary: Donna Heydt
Cast: Michael Landon (Tony Rivers), Yvonne Lime (Arlene Logan), Whit Bissell (Dr. Alfred Brandon), Tony Marshall (Jimmy), Dawn Richard (Theresa), Barney Phillips (Detective Donovan), Ken Miller (Vic), Cindy Robbins (Pearl), Michael Rougas (Frank), Robert Griffin (Police Chief), Joseph Mell (Dr. Hugo Wagner), Malcolm Atterbury (Charles Rivers), Eddie Marr (Doyle), Vladimir Sokoloff (Pepe the Janitor), Louise Lewis (Principal Ferguson), John Launer (Bill Logan), Guy Williams (Officer Chris Stanley), Dorothy Crehan (Mrs. Mary Logan), Larry Carr (Diving Guy), Herman Cohen (Man with Crime Scene Photos), Steve Conte, Jaine DuPont, Patricia Merlin, Miss Johnson (Gym Teacher)

Synopsis: A disreputable hypnotist transforms a troubled adolescent into a monster.

This surefire mixture of juvenile delinquency, classic horror plot points, hypnosis and age-regression, combined with an iconic title, should have been a winner, but thanks to Herman Cohen's unfocused, lackadaisical screenplay, and the inexplicable miscasting of the two main characters, *I Was a Teenage Werewolf* falls as flat as a pancake, making a film that curiously refuses to remain in the memory even after multiple viewings. Even John Ashley's affected beatnik demeanor would have been preferable to Michael Landon's whiny, irritatingly "method" performance as an angst-tortured youngster; and even John Carradine's pompous summer-stock histrionics would have been an improvement over Whit Bissell's extraordinarily dull screen presence as mad scientist/surrogate daddy. But this stillborn dud went on to fame and fortune, proving that some folks will watch anything. Sam Katzman's *The Werewolf* (1956), seen by some as an inspiration for this film, was infinitely better and far less pretentious.

In his informative treatise on the youth film fad of the period, *Teenagers and Teenpics: The Juvenilization of American Movies in the 1950s*, Thomas Doherty takes a comprehensive, if flawed, look at the phenomenon, and rightly posits *I Was a Teenage Werewolf* as an iconic example of the trend. However, Doherty soon goes off-track, firstly by placing the picture as "riding the crest of the Hammer horror wave," a "wave" which had yet to occur. Secondly, Doherty bafflingly considers *I Was a Teenage Werewolf* a highly successful picture in its own right, stating, "Not to be discounted, however, is a narrative that takes teenage subculture on its own terms."[29] He further suggests that the AIP teen pics accurately reflected the feelings and concerns of the average American teenager of the day, a conspicuously indefensible argument. While the film does ostensibly address the role of the troubled outsider in modern American society, it does so in a superficial, clichéd, and ultimately failed way. As stated, the problem lies in the casting of two non-sympathetic personalities in the roles of surrogate father and son, a problem exacerbated by a screenplay which takes itself far too seriously in its somewhat infantile narrative pretensions. The result is a curious film which fails completely as cultural text yet succeeds wildly in symbolizing something iconic about the culture in which it was birthed. It is, perhaps, the *idea* behind *I Was a Teenage Werewolf,* and not what it ultimately became as an actual film, which has allowed this inferior work to nonetheless leave its mark on popular culture.

Invasion of the Saucer Men

69 minutes, Black and White
Produced by Malibu Productions
Distributed by American International Pictures
Directed by Edward L. Cahn
Screenplay: Robert J. Gurney, Jr., Al Martin
Story: Paul Fairman (from his story "The Cosmic Frame")
Produced by James H. Nicholson, Samuel Z. Arkoff
Executive Producer: Robert J. Gurney, Jr.
Music: Ronald Stein
Cinematography: Frederick E. West
Editing: Charles Gross
Art Director: Don Ament
Makeup Artist: Carlie Taylor
Production Manager: Bart Carre
Property Master: Karl Brainard
Sound Recordist: Josef von Stroheim, Philip Mitchell (as "Phil Mitchell")
Special Effects: Howard A. Anderson, Paul Blaisdell, Alex Weldon
Wardrobe: Marjory Corso
Editorial Supervisor: Ronald Sinclair
Script Supervisor: Judith Hart
Technical Advisors: Forrest J Ackerman, Bob Burns, Paul Blaisdell
Cast: Steven Terrell (Johnny Carter), Gloria Castillo (Joan Hayden), Frank Gorshin (Joe Gruen), Raymond Hatton (Farmer Larkin), Lyn Osborn (Artie Burns), Russ Bender (Doctor), Douglas Henderson (Lt. Wilkins, USAF), Sam Buffington (Col. Ambrose, USAF), Jason Johnson (Detective), Don Shelton (City Attorney Hayden), Scott Peters (USAF Sergeant with Bullhorn), Jan Englund (Diner Waitress), Kelly Thordsen (Sgt. Bruce), Bob Einer (Soda Jerk), Patti Lawler (Irene), Calvin Booth (Paul), Ed Nelson (Tom), Roy Darmour (Sgt. Gordon), Audrey Conti (Bobby's Girl), Jim Bridges (Bobby), Jimmy Pickford (Duke), Joan Dupuis (Liz), Buddy Mason (Policeman), Orv Mohler (Duke's Friend), Angelo Rossitto (Saucer Man), Floyd Hugh Dixon (Saucer Man), Dean Neville (Saucer Man), Edward Gibbons (Saucer Man), Paul Blaisdell (Saucer Man), Bob Burns (Saucer Man)

Synopsis: On a long Saturday night in a small town, a group of resourceful teenagers thwart an invasion of space monsters.

This early American International effort shows the fledgling production company at the top of its game. *Invasion of the Saucer Men* is a clever, always-surprising melodrama which stands as a small masterpiece of the genre, taking its lurid pulp fiction premise and running with it to create an unusual film that jumps deftly between light comedy, satire and straightforward thriller. The film pokes gentle but knowing fun at all authority figures, endearing itself to its teenage audience. Indeed, teenagers are clearly the heroes of the picture. Yet the movie divides this mocking of the parental universe into several interesting subsets. Both the military and the police (two groups teenagers would be intimately familiar with) are seen as inept, corrupt and obstreperous. Further, the film teases both rural culture, in the person of the cranky old farmer who chases horny youngsters off his property with a shotgun, and urban culture, via the two (quite possibly homosexual) hapless grifters who come to town in search of a quick buck.

Additionally, *Invasion of the Saucer Men* paints an astute, not uncritical portrait of small-town America, *as seen by teenagers* (the movie even takes place within a satire-infused fictional locale: *Hicksburg*). The film works well as a "great American fable," with courageous and highly moral teenagers saving their community (and, by extension, the country) from a potentially devastating invasion from without. The fact that the entire scenario takes place on one long, dark Saturday night also carries great import. Saturday night, of course, is the adolescent's holiday, when he can socialize with his peers and escape the rigors of school, work and parental tyranny. In addition, the fact that much of the film centers on a local "lovers' lane," in which horny couples smooch in their parked cars, suggests that the whole scenario functions as a sacred fertility ritual. This angle is reinforced by the revelation that the heroes of the piece were, that very night, planning to elope, determined to forge ahead into adulthood with or without their parents' permission.

As well, the struggle of the teenagers to cleanse their community of encroaching evil works as a symbolic "coming of age" ritual. Indeed, the whole film can be read as the teenage community's successful, albeit perilous, attempt to mature, literally overnight, when faced with the threat of extinction; their struggles, individually and as a unit, eerily echo the adolescent's painful transformation from child to adult, with its inherent responsibilities and rewards. The long Saturday night in which the film takes place may be seen as the teens' collective "dark night of the soul," a traumatic test for Hicksburg's adolescent community to see if they are worthy of advancement to the pleasures and horrors of the adult world. This "dark night" begins whimsically but quickly turns deadly serious when our heroes are falsely accused of murder; they must grow up *fast* or be lost forever to the corrupt machinations of the adult community to which they are still beholden.

And the adult community, as mentioned, is portrayed in anything but a sympathetic light: cops and soldiers are duplicitous buffoons; homeowners are paranoid misanthropes; city slickers are criminal and probably sexually perverse; parents are prejudiced, narrow-minded dictators. In contrast, the invading saucer men seem almost benign — until it is revealed that they have no qualms about random murder to further their agenda. Another curious bugaboo in the film is alcohol, which is used in a negative way by *both* the adults and the saucer men; it is only the teens who won't go near the stuff, although they are falsely accused of indulging.

The saucer men, when shown in deep shadow and quick edits, are alternately goofy and creepy "little green men from Mars," like something seen in a child's nightmare. Also like a child's nightmare, it is highly symbolic that it is light which evaporates the evil men from outer space, just as daylight vanquishes most bad dreams. These quirks reinforce *Saucer Men*'s claim to being a modern fable.

The film is deftly directed by Edward L. Cahn, with moody photography, great dolly work, and tight editing to maintain a rapid-fire pace. The entire movie takes place over one ink-black night, which greatly adds to a general air of malevolence. Enhancing this is an exceedingly creepy and memorable score by Ronald Stein, one of his best. The f/x work by unsung genius Paul Blaisdell is remarkable, considering the paltry fee received for his services and the shoddy treatment by Mssrs. Nicholson and Arkoff. Taking the sarcastic "little green men from Mars" motif then current in popular culture, Blaisdall created beings which simultaneously evoke ridicule and terror. Among Blaisdell's brilliant touches are protruding fingernails that inject poison alcohol into their victims; grotesque, bulbous heads which look like exploding brain-matter; sinister grimaces that carry on the famous tradition of the "Blaisdell scowl"; and a marvelous crawling hand with all-seeing eyeball. Blaisdell's Saucer Men are truly a child's horror nightmare come to life. Even more remarkable, the film indulges in some light gore, which adds immensely to the abiding creepiness of the piece.

Even the structure of *Saucer Men* is clever and somewhat unusual for its time and station. The film is bookended by sardonic narration from a person who reveals, at film's end, to have made the whole thing up! This wildly nihilistic revelation makes the preceding myth-infused scenario all the more allegorical. In fact, the narrator claims that the story he just related was a book he has written, and to couch potential criticism towards the far-fetched fable, he justifies his creation with the snide comment, "Ya *pay* before ya *read*!" This marvelous bit of self-reflexivity is a bold wink at the teenage audience, who likely went to see the film based on its deliciously lurid title and poster imagery, and may or may not have been disappointed by what actually transpired onscreen. To this important emerging consumer group, American International essentially invoked the cherished warning *caveat emptor*, i.e., "Buyer Beware!" This double bill proved to be another good example of the "flipside" being far superior to the main or "hit" feature.

Invasion of the Saucer Men took as its inspiration a short story by Paul W. Fairman entitled "The Cosmic Frame," which appeared in the May 1955 edition of the popular pulp science-fiction magazine *Amazing Stories*. Fairman (1916–1977) was a prolific writer of genre fiction, and also became the editor of several pulp fiction magazines, *Amazing Stories* included. The basic plot outline of *Invasion of the Saucer Men* follows that of the short story fairly faithfully, but screenwriters Robert J. Gurney and Al Martin made some portentous changes which made the film far more expansive and allegorical than the predictable, if effective source material. For instance, the story's locale, the laconic "Kensington Corners," becomes in the film the far more satirical "Hicksburg." The story's description of the alien being closely mirrors Paul Blaisdell's eventual screen creation:

> It was not more than four feet long and had a head far too large for the thin body. Its skin was green, the shades varying from deep to very pale. It had thin legs and two spiderlike arms ending in hands with thin delicate fingers and a thumb on either side. Its eyes were lidless and sank into bony pockets in the round, pale green skull. There was a network of dark veins all over the body and the feet were shapeless pads with neither toes nor heels.[30]

From this description, one can see that f/x designer Blaisdell added two crucial touches to his "Saucer Men"—the needles which protrude from the aliens' fingertips to inject its victims with poisonous alcohol, and the all-seeing eye that also adorned the hand. In the story, the aliens manage to mangle a Packard car by simply waving some sort of energy tubes over the vehicle, while in the film the Saucer Men must use more direct means to achieve "the cosmic frame." The story ends, rather grimly, with the protagonist being effectively framed by the aliens for their murder of Frank Williams; whereas in the movie the teens are eventually exonerated for the crime.[31] Yet, most importantly, the film's screenplay adds the crucial framing wherein an off-screen narrator informs the audience that the preceding melodrama was his own fictional fabrication, thus catapulting the scenario into the realm of "tall tale" or "urban legend," a most effective narrative device that makes *Invasion of the Saucer Men* a most charming atom-age fable—in effect, a science-fiction fairy tale.

As effective as *Invasion of the Saucer Men* is, Texas-based independent filmmaker Larry Buchanan brought the screenplay to dizzying new heights some eight years later with *The Eye Creatures* (1965). Commissioned by the newly-formed television arm of American International Pictures to create several color feature films specifically for TV syndication, Buchanan eventually made eight of these telefilms, all shot in 16mm color for under $30,000 apiece, producing them under his own Azalea Pictures banner. These micro-budget marvels, several of which are based on earlier AIP screenplays, are some of the finest examples of low-budget melodrama to come out of the 1960s, and *The Eye Creatures* is one of the best. Buchanan filmed the original story faithfully but also added an eerily Orwellian subplot wherein flunkies of the Military-Industrial Complex spy on local citizens, making the resultant film even more unworldly—and topical—than its progenitor.

THE GIANT CLAW WITH THE NIGHT THE WORLD EXPLODED (COLUMBIA PICTURES)

Certainly Columbia's strangest youth-market programmers of the year, this odd-duck combo nonetheless did respectable business in its late-summer run. Some interesting insight into "the horror business" comes from exhibitors' observations about this Columbia package deal. In the September 7 issue of *Boxoffice* magazine, manager Harry Hawksinson of the Orpheum Theater in Marietta, Minnesota (population: 380), had this to say:

> We played this [*The Night the World Exploded*] on a saturation basis, doubled with *The Giant Claw*. This one is good also. I know it would have fallen flatter yet if it hadn't been for the advertising on TV and radio. Played Wed., Thurs. Weather: Warm.[32]

Two weeks later, B. Bergland of the Trail Theatre in New Town, North Dakota (population: 1,200), noted:

> These horror pictures seem to jar them loose, although I believe that *The Giant Claw* and two Three Stooges comedies would have done just as well. *The Night The World Exploded* is the better of the two, but I don't believe in double bills, so I think *The Giant Claw* is the one that drew them in. Played Tues., Wed., Thurs. Weather: Warm.[33]

The Giant Claw

75 minutes / Black and White
Produced by Clover Productions

Trade advertisement for *The Giant Claw* and *The Night the World Exploded,* the second Sam Katzman "shocker" double bill released by Columbia Pictures in 1957, featuring one of the most memorably ridiculous monsters in the entire canon (conspicuously obscured in the poster art).

Distributed by Columbia Pictures Corporation
Directed by Fred F. Sears
Screenplay: Samuel Newman, Paul Gangelin
Produced by Sam Katzman
Music by Mischa Bakaleinikoff

Cinematography: Benjamin H. Kline
Editing: Anthony DiMarco, Saul A. Goodkind
Art Director: Paul Palmentola
Set Decoration: Sidney Clifford
Assistant Director: Leonard Katzman
Sound: Josh Westmoreland
Technical Effects Creators: Ralph Hammeras, George J. Teague, Lawrence W. Butler
Camera Operator: Emil Oster
Music Supervisor: Mischa Bakaleinikoff
Music by George Antheil, Jacques Belasco, Mario Castelnuovo-Tedesco, George Duning, John Leipold, Marlin Skiles, Max Steiner
Production Coordinator: Paul Sperling
Cast: Jeff Morrow (Mitch MacAfee), Mara Corday (Sally Caldwell), Morris Ankrum (Lt. Gen. Edward Considine), Louis Merrill (Pierre Broussard), Edgar Barrier (Dr. Karol Noymann), Robert Shayne (Gen. Van Buskirk), Frank Griffin (Pete), Clark Howat (Maj. Bergen), Morgan Jones (Lieutenant, Radar Officer), George Cisar (Man on Airliner), Fred F. Sears (Narrator), Robert Williams (State Trooper)

Synopsis: A mammoth vulture from outer space threatens humanity.

Another ingenious potboiler from Sam Katzman's Clover Productions mixes pedestrian science-fiction elements with some clever fantasy motifs, plus a "monster" which is not easily forgotten, especially when one realizes what it really represents. The title beast, first seen by a superstitious villager, is dubbed "La Kakanya," referring to an old French-Canadian legend of a mythical demon with "the head of a wolf, the body of a woman, and the wings of a bird theeese beeg!" This peculiar description of the as-yet-unseen beast will become important anon.

When finally seen, the monster is an extraordinary miniature creation, purportedly designed by Mexican artists, which may explain some of its fanciful folk-art qualities. Ostensibly a mammoth vulture or hawk-like creature, it does not have the head of a wolf nor the body of a woman, as the earlier observer insisted, but does evoke something out of fable or nightmare rather than the modern natural world. With its comical head, long scrawny neck, and weirdly flapping arms, the monster looks like a whimsical Dr. Seuss creation filtered through a child's nightmare memory, an evil cartoon of nature gone awry.

Yet as the scenario unfolds, the beast can clearly be seen as a curious manifestation of an antiquarian archetype — the malevolent elder woman, commonly known as "the Crone," part of the Triple Goddess of antiquity. Allied with her sisters, the Virgin and the Mother, the Crone is the figure who represents the end of life, and the magical transformation from death into new life, thus completing the circle started with the Virgin and the Mother in begetting and nurturing life. Most importantly, tradition states that any mortal who saw the face of the Crone was destined for immanent death. The Crone figure was maligned by modern patriarchal religious concerns, who demonized her and made her into the despised image of "the Old Witch." Derogatory male slang for old women, such as "the old buzzard" and "old crow" — a line actually used in the film — still amusingly evokes prejudices towards the Crone figure and more than clarifies that this is what the "Giant Claw" is supposed to represent.

The monster's existence is weakly explained by declaring it some form of "anti-matter"; this reference is also amusing in regards to the beast's Crone origins, and one wonders if the scenarists consciously used this phrase, which sounds remarkably like "Auntie Mater" (as in "Crone-Mother"). Regardless, the beast is clearly set against patriarchy and its agents, as it revels in chomping on little parachute men. Later on, the beast carries off a smoking freight train, which hangs from its beak like a string of sausage links, and later pecks away at the iconic Empire State Building as if it were a cob of corn. Both of these violated phallic targets serve well as techno-fetishist castration symbols par excellence. Scientists soon discover that "Auntie Mater" has a force field rendering her immune to man's killing cock-weapons, nicely symbolic again of the Crone analogy, as mortals certainly cannot "kill" any symbol or representative of Death.

Another recurring theme in 1950s fantastic cinema is the notion of undesired procreation, when monsters are found to have laid eggs that will breed more "monstrous young." A sly nod to eugenics aside, these scenes reinforce the notion that human overpopulation might itself not be the wisest move of an intelligent species with future survival on a planet of limited resources on its mind. It is thus highly symbolic when the heterosexual couple repeatedly fire rifle shots at one of the Crone-Beast's eggs until the placenta oozes out like monstrous blood; it is almost as if the soon-to-be-mated couple are effectively destroying *their own* fertility and future spawn with this highly symbolic act. Shortly thereafter, the Giant Claw attacks and maims a group of reckless teenagers on a joyride; this attack on cherished human adolescents is clearly meant as a vengeful response to the humans' attack on her own young. *The Giant Claw* uses the template of "monster movie" to invoke the defrocked spirit of the wise, magical elder woman of antiquity — only to demonize and demolish her with extreme prejudice so that woman-hating patriarchy may carry on uncontested.

The Night the World Exploded

Produced by Clover Productions
Distributed by Columbia Pictures
64 minutes/Black and White
Directed by Fred F. Sears
Screenplay: Jack Natteford, Luci Ward
Produced by Sam Katzman
Cinematography: Benjamin H. Kline
Editing: Paul Borofsky
Art Director: Paul Palmentola
Set Decoration: Sidney Clifford
Assistant Director: Willard Sheldon
Sound: Josh Westmoreland
Musical Director: Ross DiMaggio
Music by George Duning, Friedrich Hollaender, Arthur Morton, Leith Stevens
Cast: Kathryn Grant (Laura "Hutch" Hutchinson), William Leslie (Dr. David Conway), Tristram Coffin (Dr. Ellis Morton), Raymond Greenleaf (Gov. Chaney), Charles Evans (Gen. Bortes), Frank J. Scannell (Sheriff Quinn), Marshall Reed (General's Aide), Fred Coby (Ranger Brown), Paul Savage (Ranger Kirk), Terry Frost (Chief Rescue Worker), John Close (Soldier), Sam Harris (Governor's Board Member), Robert Kino (Scientist), Pierce Lyden, Dennis Moore (Radio Communications Man), Natividad Vacío (Hospital Physician), Otto Waldis (Professor Hagstrom), John Zaremba, Daniel J. Winters (Asst. Secretary of Defense)

Synopsis: A new element threatens the world with destruction.

This dreary programmer from Sam Katzman's Clover Productions boasts a good title and very little else, as it perfunctorily weaves the tale of yet another threat to Mankind, this time in the form of exploding rocks. The film is liberally sprinkled with newsreel footage of floods, earthquakes and other natural disasters, making it a most mundane stock-footage Armageddon. One unintentional highlight is a hilarious "demonstration" for the world's scientists in which Element 112 is put inside a model globe and everyone watches it explode; what sort of dopey professional would need such an infantile demonstration to convince him of a major world threat? (The bursting world-model does, however unwittingly, symbolize conformist U.S. culture at the breaking point, as accumulated socio-economic pressures threatened to "explode" society into neo-barbarism.)

Of minor interest is the sexist love story in which a mouse of a woman is about to marry "the wrong man" because she can't get her scientist co-worker to commit. During a crisis situation, the heroine freezes up, and her would-be paramour "rescues her" by haranguing the poor woman into some belated courage. It almost seems like the battle between Mankind and the Earth is played out in the "rocky" romance of the protagonists. The heroine even aligns herself with "Mother Earth" when she ponders, "It's almost like the Earth is striking back for the way we've robbed her natural resources," a sentiment which could have — and, in fact, soon did — come from Rachel Carson, of *Silent Spring* fame. Further, if the rock element represents the male principle — hard, unyielding and destructive — then water, eventually revealed to be the only thing able to vanquish the mineral's destructive power, may represent the female principle: healing, yielding, and creative. Indeed, perhaps the whole scenario of *The Night the World Exploded* is a sloppy metaphor for the potentially cataclysmic release of the decade's long-suppressed sexual tension, especially the patriarchal subjugation of the female, who seemed at this moment all but destined to burst forth and break her socio-political fetters, come what may.

THREE

Films Released July Through December

July

BEGINNING OF THE END WITH *THE UNEARTHLY* (REPUBLIC PICTURES)

These horror thrillers were produced, and originally slated for release, by AB-PT Pictures (a wholly-owned subsidiary of American Broadcasting and Paramount Theaters). In March of the year, talks were underway between AB-PT, Republic Pictures and United Artists to distribute features under the AB-PT banner, but this double bill was finally released by Republic Pictures, implying that the AB-PT distribution deal went sour somewhere along the line.[1] Regardless of the films' uneven quality, the double bill apparently did extremely well; in an article in *Boxoffice* magazine on September 21, 1957, analyzing the success of the "Summer Combos," Nathan Cohen singles out *Beginning of the End/The Unearthly* as doing business "well above average"—in fact, as well as Columbia's "hit" combo *20 Million Miles to Earth/The 27th Day*.[2] And in the August 10, 1957, issue of *Boxoffice* magazine Victor Weber, manager of the Center Theatre in Kensett, Arkansas, had this to say about the program:

> The two make a very good combo. It said on the advertising, "guaranteed to frighten" and it was telling the truth. It's one of the best horror shows in some time and business went up above average for once. Played Fri., Sat. Weather: Fair and hot.[3]

In addition to confirming that the "shocker" type of program was usually quite successful, the above quote also verifies that these double bills, aimed largely at the youth market, usually had very short runs (often no more than two days).

Beginning of the End

Produced by AB-PT Pictures Corporation
Distributed by Republic Pictures
76 minutes/Black and White
Directed by Bert I. Gordon
Screenplay: Fred Freiberger, Lester Gorn
Produced by Bert I. Gordon

Music by Albert Glasser
Cinematography: Jack Marta
Editing: Aaron Stell
Art Director: Walter Keller
Makeup Artist: Steve Drumm
Assistant Director: Melville Shyer
Second Assistant Director: Wilson Shyer
Property Master: James Harris
Set Dresser: George Milo
Stagehand: Duncan "Dean" Parkin
Sound Effects Editors: George J. Eppich, Douglas Stewart
Sound Mixer: Richard E. Tyler
Special Technical Effects: Bert I. Gordon
Special Effects: Flora M. Gordon
Chief Set Electrician: Austin Herick
Costume Jeweller: Joan Joseff
Conductor: Albert Glasser

Two apparently antithetical subjects — giant bugs and mad doctors — nonetheless provided Republic Pictures with a surprise summer hit with their release of two independently-produced films, *Beginning of the End* and *The Unearthly* (Newspaper advertisement).

Music Editor: Morrie McNaughton
Cast: Peter Graves (Dr. Ed Wainwright), Peggie Castle (Audrey Aimes), Morris Ankrum (Gen. John
  Hanson), Than Wyenn (Frank Johnson), Thomas B. Henry (Col. Tom Sturgeon), Richard Benedict
  (Cpl. Mathias), James Seay (Capt. James Barton), John Close (Maj. Everett), Don C. Harvey
  (Guard at Lab), Larry J. Blake (Illinois Highway Patrolman), Eilene Janssen (Girl Teenager in
  Car), Hylton Socher (Soldier), Frank Wilcox (Gen. John T. Short), Douglas Evans (Norman Tag-
  gart, News Editor), Paul Grant (Male Teenager in Car), Richard Emory (Lieutenant), Hank Pat-
  terson (Dave), Steve Warren (Soldier), Frank Connor (Soldier), Don Eitner (Soldier), Rayford
  Barnes (Chuck), Kirk Alyn (B-52 Pilot), Bill Baldwin (TV Announcer), Frank Chase (Helicopter
  Pilot), Patricia Dean (Red Cross Representative), James Douglas (Army Sentry), Paul Frees (Heli-
  copter Pilot), Lyle Latell (Police Lt. MacKenzie), Dennis Moore (Police Dispatcher), Zon Murray
  (National Guard Sergeant), Alan Reynolds (Insecticide Man), Ralph Sanford, Bert Stevens (Col.
  Hill), Alan Wells (Headquarters Sergeant)

Synopsis: Mammoth radioactive locusts invade Chicago.

This beloved "giant bug" movie from Bert I. Gordon stands today as an accomplished
example of the genre. The basic premise unfolds as a mystery when a whole town is suddenly
wiped off the face of the earth, seemingly overnight. Indeed, when the small village of
Ludlow is finally seen in a shambles, it eerily looks like an atomic wasteland and instantly
conjures up similar images of the recently "disappeared" cities of Hiroshima and Nagasaki.
It is significant that both of the film's main characters, the girl reporter and the noble
scientist, take time to relate to each other — and the audience — powerful and in some cases
traumatic stories of their service to humanity during World War II, with the shadow of the
so-recent atomic bombing of innocent peoples reinforced yet again. Indeed, the main message
here is that the attempted "peaceful" use of the atom, surely a guilt reaction to the horrible
destructive power of same, will ultimately end in the same tragedy and destruction as any
vile bomb — atomic power is an evil and uncontrollable demon in any form and should be
left alone. This notion is symbolized (albeit indirectly) by the villain of the piece, the U.S.
Department of Agriculture, who unwittingly poisoned insects with radioactive isotopes
during botanical radiological experimentation. It is thus significant that one of the workers
there is a deaf mute, his impairment a direct result of working with fissionable materials.
This character stands as a crude but effective depiction of the deleterious effects of low-
level radiation on animal life, and, more importantly, as metaphor for the awesome power
of the atom effortlessly "silencing" its foolhardy creator, mutating him into sullen, passive
impotence.

Yet it is the plucky heroine, newswoman Audrey Aimes (Peggie Castle), who eventually
solves the mystery and enables good scientist Peter Graves to save the world. Of course, the
ballsy "girl reporter" is a fixture of B-cinema almost since its infancy, a rare example of
female empowerment in a male-dominated art form; but as this heroine primarily fights
for and preserves phallocentric culture, she isn't a feminist figure at all but merely a good
servant of patriarchy. In the excellent *Women Scientists in Fifties Science Fictions Films*, Bonnie
Noonan astutely analyzes many aspects of the occurrence of the "professional" or "career"
woman in the decade's sci-fi films, and offers some fascinating insight into the character of
Audrey in *Beginning of the End*. Noonan identities the character as being inspired by real-
life photo-journalist Margaret Bourke-White.[4] Noonan observes that actress Peggie Castle,
although extremely attractive, was not perceived (especially by male reviewers of the film)
as "sexy" or "romantic," specifically due to her character's "manly" independence and pro-

fessional autonomy.[5] Further, Noonan positions Audrey — who, as noted, had a direct connection to World War II and its atomic horrors — as symbol of a distinct and specific threat to maledom in the post–Hiroshima era: "Thus, it is the masculinized woman and her connection to World War II and the atomic bomb that threatens traditional masculinity, to the extent of even pushing the American male into an implied undercurrent of homosexuality, that dark anathema of 1950s America."[6] Yet, as independent as Audrey is at the film's start, by the end she has, like all good fifties' heroines, been brought into line with the patriarchal order. Noonan describes this conscription well:

> At the beginning of the film, Aimes is in the driver's seat of her own life, aiming her way through a patriarchal system as an individual with an equal chance at participation in that system. Once romance and the cultural imperatives surrounding it inevitably enter the picture, Aimes begins to lose her mobility, function, and especially her voice. Her ultimate performance retains only a posture of courage and competence, devoid of any significant action to support it.[7]

When the giant locusts finally appear, they are effective optical blow-ups, one of producer-director Bert I. Gordon's specialties, and far better than similar attempts in Gordon's *The Amazing Colossal Man.* Gordon also wisely uses creepily enhanced sounds of chattering locusts to complete the picture of giant monsters, knowing well that sound is at least half the formula in creating a believable fantasy universe. As the locusts threaten to destroy Chicago (amusingly by walking all over various skyscrapers), at least one character takes pains to suggest that this may be a biblical plague come to life, an elementary but useful reference to religious culture and its obsession with world apocalypse. The military (an ever-present if problematic fixture in Gordon's films) suggests dropping an atomic bomb on Chicago in order to kill the giant insects. The patent absurdity of the suggestion does reveal the Military-Industrial Complex's infantile solution to everything: blow it up!

Luckily, the cooler head of Science prevails, and sound waves are used to lure the insects to a watery death. Yet culture's alternating worship, and horror, of the Atom is addressed well in this film, with commentary such as this, stated cynically by a soldier: "These days, they blame the atom for everything — bad health, bad crops, bad weather!" (Of course, it was eventually discovered that accumulation of low-level radiation is, in fact, responsible for *all* of the above, plus much more.) *Beginning of the End* is a most interesting film with some notable attributes, and perhaps the prototypical "giant bug" movie. (In a conspicuous effort to engage its target audience, the film opens with a pre-credits teaser in which two smooching teenagers are attacked by something unseen and off-screen, their horrific fate acting to draw in the viewer who could easily identify with such a weekend activity, and also triggering the mystery of who exactly the "villains" are.)

The Unearthly

Produced by AB-PT Pictures Corporation (American Broadcast-Paramount Theatres)
Distributed by Republic Pictures
73 minutes/Black and White
Directed by Boris Petroff (as Brooke L. Peters)
Story: Jane Mann
Screenplay: John D.F. Black (as Geoffrey Dennis), Jane Mann
Produced by Boris Petroff (as Brooke L. Peters)

Associate Producer: Robert A. Terry
Music by Henry Vars
Cinematography: W. Merle Connell
Art Director: Daniel Hall
Set Decoration: Mowbray Berkeley
Makeup Supervisor: Harry Thomas
Production Manager: Betty Sinclair
Property Master: Tony Portoghese
Sound: Phillip Mitchell
Sound Effects: Morton Tubor
Chief Electrician: Paul Grancell
First Grip: Art Manikin
Camera Operator: Ben Wetzler
Wardrobe Supervisor: William Zacha
Editorial Supervisor: Richard Currier
Musical Supervisor: Michael Terr
Conductor: Henry Vars
Cast: John Carradine (Dr. Charles Conway), Myron Healy (Mark Houston), Allison Hayes (Grace
   Thomas), Marilyn Buferd (Dr. Sharon Gilchrist), Arthur Batanides (Danny Green), Sally Todd

The Unearthly, one of the lowest-budgeted fantastic films of 1957, nonetheless proved to be surprisingly spooky, a worthy companion to Bert I. Gordon's giant monster apocalypse, *Beginning of the End.*

(Natalie Andries), Tor Johnson (Lobo), Roy Gordon (Dr. Loren Wright), Guy Prescott (Police Captain), Raymond Guta (Police Officer), Harry Fleer (Harry Jedrow), Gloria Petroff (Screaming Woman), Paul McWilliams (Police Officer), Karl Johnson (Monster)

Synopsis: At a lonely sanitarium a mad scientist uses human guinea pigs in his attempts to create eternal life.

This fun "spook show" bears so many similarities to Ed Wood's neglected *Night of the Ghouls* (ca 1957), one must assume that both filmmakers were aware of the other's project. Boris Petroff (who worked under the Anglicized pseudonym "Brooke L. Peters") was known to be a colleague of Wood's, and the two even worked together on at least one project, *Shotgun Wedding* (1963). In both Petroff's *The Unearthly* and Wood's *Night of the Ghouls*, a group of "lost souls" congregates at an isolated suburban setting, run by a fraudulent charismatic who is exploiting human beings for his own diabolical purposes. In each scenario the perpetrator of the ill-fated experiment promises his victims some sort of life extension, either via telepathic communication with the deceased (*Night of the Ghouls*) or the indefinite extension of physical life (*The Unearthly*). In each film the villain is "busted" by an undercover agent, and killed by a person (or persons) he had earlier exploited. And most conspicuously, in each film the villain's assistant is a giant named Lobo, played by Tor Johnson! Both of these fascinating low-budget programmers were shot in 1957, although *Night of the Ghouls* remained unreleased for many years. It would be enlightening to discover which script was shot first, so as to decide whom "borrowed" from who. (In *The Unearthly*, Petroff does take one possible "jab" at rival Wood when a young man laments to a young woman deeply immersed in a trashy sex novel, "Guys make a fortune scribbling junk like that!")

From a traditional entertainment point of view, *The Unearthly* is the better of the two films, although *Night of the Ghouls* has its champions, this author among them. *The Unearthly* unfolds as a somewhat anachronistic occurrence of a 1940s poverty row horror (they themselves often being updates on the time-honored "Old Dark House" horror film motif of the silent era). The somewhat predictable script benefits from having some very charismatic cast members, including Allison Hayes and Roy Gordon, both of whom assay roles not dissimilar to ones they played the next year in Nathan Hertz's fantastic proto-feminist fable *Attack of the 50-Foot Woman*. Posing John Carradine as a fake psychiatrist with an "unearthly" secret agenda may have been intended as a sly attack on the then-new psychiatric profession, seen by many at the time as mere quackery. In another playful jab at psychiatry, the extremely neurotic patients under the mad doctor's care are given drugs intravenously in order to suppress their frequent, often violent emotional outbursts.

The mad doctor's experiments involve exposing a synthetic gland to radioactive isotopes in an attempt to extend life. Of course, the experiments create only horrible monsters, including a beautiful young woman whose face is turned into a horrible mess via severe radiation burns. (Granted that facial deformity is a fantastic film staple, its curious emphasis in 1957 may have been, in some part, a nod to fears residing within the teenage audience who, in addition to being generally self-conscious about their appearance, may have been particularly sensitive to potentially devastating acne.) *The Unearthly* features an impressive finale that gives the audience a brief glimpse of its "cage of monsters," the doctor's cumulative failed experiments, in a gratuitous but highly effective coda to this affable and somewhat quirky "spook show."

CURSE OF FRANKENSTEIN AND
X THE UNKNOWN (WARNER BROTHERS)

Warner Brothers did extremely well with their U.S. release of *Curse of Frankenstein,* their first horror hit from Hammer Studios of England, and released it in many situations as a solo feature. However, in some later drive-in and grindhouse engagements, Warners released the film in tandem with *X the Unknown,* another Hammer production which had seen limited release on the bottom of other Warner double bills for some months previously.

Curse of Frankenstein

82 minutes, Color
Produced by Hammer Film Productions
Distributed by Warner Bros.
Directed by Terence Fisher
Screenplay: Jimmy Sangster
Story: Mary Shelley (from her novel *Frankenstein; or, the Modern Prometheus*)
Executive Producer: Michael Carreras
Produced by Anthony Hinds, Max Rosenberg
Associate Producer: Anthony Nelson Keys
Music by James Bernard
Cinematography: Jack Asher
Editing: James Needs
Casting: Dorothy Holloway
Production Design: Bernard Robinson
Art Direction: Ted Marshall
Costume Design: Molly Arbuthnot
Makeup Artist: Philip Leakey
Hair Stylist: Henry Montsash
Assistant Makeup Artists: Roy Ashton, George Turner
Production Manager: Don Weeks
Executive in Charge of Production: James Carreras
Assistant Director: Derek Whitehurst
Second Assistant Director: Jimmy Komisarjevsky
Third Assistant Director: Hugh Harlow
Master Plasterer: Arthur Banks
Draughtsman: Don Mingaye
Property Master: Tom Money
Construction Manager: Fred Ricketts
Sound: Jock May
Boom Operator: Jim Perry
Sound Camera Operator: Michael Sale
Matte Painter: Les Bowie
Stunts: Jock Easton
Lighting Technician: Steve Birtles
Still Photographers: Tom Edwards, John Jay
Camera Operator: Len Harris
Chief Electrician: Jack Curtis
Electricians: Harold Marland, Bob Palmer
Focus Puller: Harry Oakes
Assistant Editor: Roy Norman
Musical Director: John Hollingsworth

Continuity: Doreen Soan

Production Secretary: Faith Frisby

Cast: Peter Cushing (Victor Frankenstein), Hazel Court (Elizabeth), Robert Urquhart (Paul Krempe), Christopher Lee (Creature), Melvyn Hayes (Young Victor), Valerie Gaunt (Justine), Paul Hardtmuth (Professor Bernstein), Noel Hood (Aunt), Fred Johnson (Grandpa), Claude Kingston (Little Boy), Alex Gallier (Priest), Michael Mulcaster (Warder), Andrew Leigh (Burgomaster), Ann Blake (Wife), Sally Walsh (Young Elizabeth), Middleton Woods (Lecturer), Raymond Ray (Uncle), Josef Behrmann (Fritz), Henry Caine (Schoolmaster), Trevor Davis (Uncle), Marjorie Hume (Mother), Ernest Jay (Undertaker), Eugene Leahy (2nd Priest), Bartlett Mullins (Tramp), Raymond Rollett (Father Felix)

Synopsis: A mad scientist creates a living being from body parts of the deceased. The monster escapes the laboratory, and proceeds to bore the countryside.

Hammer Films of England purportedly jump-started the 1960s horror craze with this dreary postmodern gothic melodrama and its follow-up, *Horror of Dracula*, but it seems more likely that it was Alfred Hitchock's *Psycho*, along with the release of classic horror films to television, that did the trick. *Curse of Frankenstein* takes the vitality of Mary Shelley's timeless story and submerges it in a laborious faux–Dickensian universe. Even touches of the Burke and Hare and Sweeney Todd stories cannot raise this foul

Newspaper advertisement for Warner Brothers' double bill of the lachrymose *Curse of Frankenstein* and the thrilling *X the Unknown*, for a theater in New Haven, Connecticut. (Perhaps the tagline for the Frankenstein film should have read, "Please Try Not to Fall Asleep"?)

Peter Cushing tries desperately to transfuse life into *Curse of Frankenstein*, while Robert Urquhart looks on despairingly.

behemoth off the ground. One might posit that the birth of the beast from a warm tub of foggy liquid symbolizes a feminine-based notion of the womb, but this would be giving the film more credit than it deserves. The monster, when finally unleashed, is laughable; Christopher Lee with a mop-head and wrapped in gauze comes across as some sort of beatnik mummy, and elicits no emotional response whatever. The monster's attack on humanity is depicted via a ridiculous scene which combines two of the more poignant moments from the 1931 Universal classic *Frankenstein* into one hilarious misfire, as a small child leads a blind man into the woods, only to be confronted by the beatnik-monster. Honestly, the only good this film ever accomplished was to provide an amusing clip for Stanley Kubrick's classic black comedy *Lolita* (1962).

As noxious as it is, *Curse of Frankenstein* was nonetheless a huge hit in the United States, triggering a series of equally-lamentable "Hammer Horrors" which audiences were stuck with for decades to come, fatally poisoning the horror genre beyond repair. The reasons for the film's U.S. reception was likely twofold: firstly, something as novel as a "classic horror" story, hearkening back to the Universal horror classics of the 1930s and 1940s, probably seemed appetizing to filmgoers who may have been tiring of the sci-fi genre's obsession with the evils of atomic power. Sight unseen, the notion of a "new" Frankenstein movie might have seemed a breath of fresh air in an increasingly derivative "shocker" genre.

Secondly, and most importantly, Warner Brothers gave *Curse of Frankenstein* an elaborate and expensive advertising/marketing campaign which all but assured its success—and might have been applied to any other film with similar results.

The *Boxoffice* magazine of August 10, 1957, boasts no less than *four* articles reporting on various aspects of Warner Brothers' *Curse of Frankenstein* ballyhoo. The first, headlined "'Curse' Midnight Opening Draws Sensational Gross," chronicles the film's premiere on August 6 at the Paramount Theater in Times Square, where it took an impressive $6,904 its first showing. The article continues:

> The ballyhoo for the midnight opening included a headless Frankenstein monster parading up and down Broadway, arrival in a hearse of actor-members of 'Theatre Macabre,' attired in horror costumes, a nurses' aide in attendance at a complete 'first aid station' and Rocky Graziano on hand to offer his services to escort anyone home too frightened by the horror film to leave the theatre alone.[8]

Among other marketing gimmicks used at this premiere were the distribution of Frankenstein masks to patrons, free ticket giveaways, and even an "Ugliest Man in the World" contest! Celebrities in attendance at the opening included Julie Newmar, Miss New York State, Jack Durant and Alan Dale. In Anthony Gruner's "The London Report," it was reported that Hammer head honcho Jimmy Carreras was "bouncing with joy" over *Curse of Frankenstein*'s U.S. success, prompting him to engage scenarist Jimmy Sangster to deliver a finished script for a remake of *Dracula*, the next horror title in the Hammer pipeline.[9] A contest, called "My Most Terrifying Moment," encouraged participants to write a short essay on the aforementioned "moment," the winners to receive free passes to the movie.[10] Finally, the Stanley Theatre in Baltimore, MD, hatched a stunt in which a lone (unnamed) woman was invited to see *Curse of Frankenstein* by herself, sitting alone in the cavernous 3,000-seat theater. The young woman then reported her "terrifying experience" on several local radio stations.[11] Given the amount of effort used to promote this stinker, its boxoffice reception seemed all but guaranteed.

X the Unknown

81 minutes, Black and White
Produced by Hammer Film Productions
Distributed by Warner Bros. Pictures
Directed by Leslie Norman
Screenplay: Jimmy Sangster
Story: Jimmy Sangster
Executive Producer: Michael Carreras
Produced by Anthony Hinds
Associate Producer: Mickey Delamar
Music by James Bernard
Cinematography: Gerald Gibbs
Editing: James Needs
Casting by Joseph Losey
Art Director: Ted Marshall
Makeup Artist: Philip Leakey
Production Manager: Jimmy Sangster
Assistant Directors: Christopher Sutton, Hugh Harlow
Draughtsman: Don Mingaye

Sound Editor: Alfred Cox
Sound Mixer: Jock May
Boom Operator: Jim Perry
Special Effects: Jack Curtis, Les Bowie, Vic Margutti
Camera Operator: Len Harris
Still Photographer: Tom Edwards
Focus Puller: Harry Oakes
Wardrobe Supervisor: Molly Arbuthnot
Conductor: John Hollingsworth
Continuity: June Randall
Publicist: Bill Batchelor
Cast: Dean Jagger (Dr. Adam Royston), Edward Chapman (John Elliott), Leo McKern (Insp. McGill), Anthony Newley (LCpl. "Spider" Webb), Jameson Clark (Jack Harding), William Lucas (Peter Elliott), Peter Hammond (Lt. Bannerman), Marianne Brauns (Zena, the Nurse), Ian MacNaughton (Haggis), Michael Ripper (Sgt. Harry Grimsdyke), John Harvey (Maj. Cartwright), Edwin Richfield (Soldier), Jane Aird (Vi Harding), Norman Macowan (Old Tom), Neil Hallett (Unwin), Kenneth Cope (Sapper Lansing), Michael Brooke (Willie Harding), Frazer Hines (Ian Osborn), Max Brimmell (Hospital Director), Robert Bruce (Dr. Kelly), Angela Crow, Brown Derby (Vicar), Raymond Dudley, Archie Duncan (Sgt. Yeardye), Lawrence James (Gerard), Edward Judd (2nd Soldier), Stella Kemball (Nurse), Jack Lambert, Stevenson Lang (Reporter), Philip Levene (Security Man), Brian Peck (1st Soldier), Anthony Sagar (Gateman), Barry Steele (Soldier), John Stirling (Police Car Driver), John Stone (Jerry), French Taylor (PC Williams), Shaw Taylor (Police Radio Operator), Neil Wilson (Russell)

Synopsis: Intelligent mud from the center of the earth wreaks havoc while looking for radioactive food.

X the Unknown represents an anomaly from the British Hammer Film studios — a gripping, intelligent science-fiction tale. As usual, Man has made a Faustian bargain with the Devil, toying with forces far beyond his control (atomic energy), and his feeble attempts to harness this "genie in a bottle" once again go awry. Spooky photography, an abundance of atmosphere, and a crackling good script by Jimmy Sangster make this potentially trivial story entirely engaging. The oozing lava or mud which bubbles forth from a hideous gash in the earth is nothing more than the toxic (to man, that is) menstrual blood of a wounded Mother Earth pouring through a remarkably vagina-like orifice; and its attempts to retake its home can be seen, in sum, as the female principle manifest. The military, terrified en masse of the female genitals, tries desperately to blow up the monster hole, but, of course, fails miserably with their impotent phallo-centric weaponry.

The last reel of the film reveals the heretofore hidden "monster," an attractive crawling blob. Also memorable is the rather liberal (for its time) reliance on gore and shock effects: a small child dies of horrible radiation burns, which the audience witnesses; a soldier's back is covered with grotesque, festering welts; and an x-ray technician's face melts right off his skull in the film's most delightfully gruesome moment. The film ends with a big question mark, as the presiding doctor hears another mysterious explosion coming from deep below, suggesting that Mother Earth is not yet finished challenging the infantile death games of puny Man.

X the Unknown does owe something to the popular "Quatermass" stories of Nigel Kneale, the first two of which had already been made into television serials and theatrical features by the time of this film's production. While not up to the quality of *Enemy from Space* (the U.S. cut of *Quatermass II*), also released in 1957, *X the Unknown* covers much of the same territory in fine fashion.

20 Million Miles to Earth and *The 27th Day* (Columbia Pictures)

Ray Harryhausen (1920–2013) was one of the premiere f/x wizards of the era. After collaborating with animation legend Willis O'Brien on *Mighty Joe Young* (1949, d: Ernest B. Schoedsack) and other projects, Harryhausen went solo on what would be seen as his breakthrough picture, *The Beast from 20,000 Fathoms* (d: Eugene Lourie). Harryhausen soon caught the interest of Columbia producer Charles M. Schneer, the two starting an auspicious partnership which would make both of their fortunes. Effects-centric thrillers *It Came from Beneath the Sea* (1955, d: Robert Gordon) and *Earth vs. the Flying Saucers* (1956, d: Fred F. Sears) were both critical and boxoffice hits, and 1957's *20 Million Miles to Earth* was destined to follow suit. It was in 1958, however, with the release of the top-grossing *The 7th Voyage of Sinbad* (d: Nathan Juran)—the first Harryhausen animation spectacular to be filmed in color—that the Harryhausen/Schneer team really caught the eye of the industry. With *20 Million Miles to Earth* wedded to *The 27th Day*, probably the most cerebral sci-fi film of the year, this double bill was surely Columbia Pictures' biggest package of the year, making their other shock packages (*The Man Who Turned to Stone/Zombies of Mora Tau* and *The Giant Claw/The Night the World Exploded*) look positively pale in comparison.

20 Million Miles to Earth

82 minutes, Black and White
Produced by Morningside Productions
Distributed by Columbia Pictures Corporation
Directed by Nathan Juran
Screenplay: Robert Creighton Williams, Christopher Knopf
Story: Charlotte Knight
Produced by Charles H. Schneer
Music: Mischa Bakaleinikoff, Daniele Amfitheatrof, George Antheil, Mario Castelnuovo-Tedesco, Anthony Collins, David Diamond, George Duning, Louis Gruenberg, Werner R. Heymann, Friedrich Hollaender, Lucien Moraweck, Arthur Morton, David Raksin, Miklós Rózsa, Hans J. Salter, Marlin Skiles, Max Steiner, Leith Stevens
Cinematography: Irving Lippman, Carlo Ventimiglia
Editing: Edwin H. Bryant
Art Director: Cary Odell
Set Decoration: Robert Priestley
Assistant Directors: Octavio Oppo, Eddie Saeta
Sound: Lambert Day
Special Effects: Lawrence W. Butler
Technical Effects: Ray Harryhausen
Stunts: Dale Van Sickel
Cast: William Hopper (Col. Robert Calder), Joan Taylor (Marisa Leonardo), Frank Puglia (Dr. Leonardo), John Zaremba (Dr. Judson Uhl), Thomas B. Henry (Maj. Gen. A.D. McIntosh), Tito Vuolo (Commissario Charra), Jan Arvan (Signore Contino), Arthur Space (Dr. Sharman), Bart Bradley (Pepe), Sid Cassel (Farmer), James Dime (Felix Roy), Noel Drayton (News Correspondent), Darlene Fields (Miss Reynolds), Michael Garth, Ray Harryhausen, George Khoury (Verrico), Saverio LoMedico, Rollin Moriyama (Dr. Koruku), Don Orlando (Mondello), George Pelling (News Correspondent), Jerry Riggio, Barry Russo (American Embassy Aide), John Sorrentino, William Woodson (narrator)
Synopsis: A life form brought back from an excursion to Venus grows into a monster.

This lackluster SF meller is rescued from total failure by the unusual monster and its superb animation by stop-motion genius Ray Harryhausen. The otherwise infantile script is racist, sexist and unabashedly pro-military, but as it is just a vessel upon which to showcase the special effects, the lack of an abiding storyline can largely be forgiven. Harryhausen's animated f/x sequences are still impressive today, even after all the hubbub about the supposed superiority of CGI effects. Especially impressive is a fight between the "Ymir" (as his creator dubbed it) and a rampaging elephant. Yet even better than his animation of "organic" creatures are Harryhausen's animation of mechanical objects, such as the rocketship which crashes to earth at the film's opening, and the amazing spacecraft in *Earth vs. the Flying Saucers*. The unusual creature design of this film's beast borrows heavily from Greek mythology, combining the man/animal ethos of the Minotaur and the Centaur with a touch of Chinese dragon. The allusion to mythological sources is even evident in the film's first reel, with the Italian fishermen in their primitive sailing vessels looking like they could have come from ancient times. You can see where producer Charles Schneer and Harryhausen were heading with this film, as their breakthrough movie, *The Seventh Voyage of Sinbad* (1958), was a mythologically-infused fantasy of impressive proportions.

The 27th Day

Produced by Romson Productions
Distributed by Columbia Pictures Corporation
75 minutes, Black and White
Directed by William Asher
Screenplay: John Mantley
Story: John Mantley (based on his novel)
Produced by Helen Ainsworth
Executive Producers: Lewis J. Rachmil, Guy Madison
Music by Mischa Bakaleinikoff, George Antheil, George Duning, George Greeley, Louis Gruenberg, Werner R. Heymann
Cinematography: Henry Freulich
Editing: Jerome Thoms
Art Director: Ross Bellah
Set Decoration: Frank Tuttle
Assistant Director: Will Sheldon
Sound: Ferrol Redd
Sound Editors: Frank Bayes, Werner Kirsch
Cast: Gene Barry (Jonathan Clark), Valerie French (Eve Wingate), George Voskovec (Prof. Klaus Bechner), Arnold Moss (The Alien), Stefan Schnabel (The Soviet General), Ralph Clanton (Mr. Ingram), Friedrich von Ledebur (Dr. Karl Neuhaus), Paul Birch (Admiral), Azemat Janti (Ivan Godofsky), Monty Ash (Soviet Prison Physician), Irvin Ashkenazy (2nd Man), Charles Bennett (Gorki), John Bleifer (Spokesman), David Bond (Dr. Schmidt), Ralph Brooks (Pentagon Officer), John Bryant (Federal Agent Kelly), Hank Clemin (Hans), Tom Daly (Joe the Bartender), John Dodsworth (BBC Newscaster), Eric Feldary (Russian Sergeant), Paul Frees (Ward Mason, Newscaster), Jacques Gallo (French Newscaster), Michael Harris (FBI Agent), Ed Hinton (Commander), Jerry Janger (Officer), Weaver Levy (Chinese Sergeant), Arthur Lovejoy (Brakovich), Theodore Marcuse (Col. Gregor), Harold Miller (Pentagon Officer), Ralph Montgomery (Man in Bar), John Mooney (MP Captain), Peter Norman (Interrogator), Paul Power (Army Doctor), Don Rhodes (Television Technician), Grandon Rhodes (UN Presiding Officer), Emil Sitka (Newspaper Hawker), Don Spark (Harry Bellows), Sigfrid Tor (Gen. Zamke), Marie Tsien (Su Tan), Philip Van Zandt (Taxi Driver), Mark Warren (Pete), Mel Welles (Russian Marshal), Walda Winchell (Nurse), Doreen Woodbury (Woman)

This pre-release trade advertisement for *20 Million Miles to Earth* suggests that Columbia Pictures was aware it had a hit on its hands with this f/x driven sci-fi spectacular.

Synopsis: An emissary from outer space gives five ordinary citizens radioactive capsules which could destroy Mankind, all in order to see if humanity can work collectively towards peace.

The closest thing to a "cerebral" sci-fi offering in cinema's most fantastic year (and not a bad effort overall), this perfunctory but interesting thriller, based on a novel of the same name, posits a common populist fantasy of the day: what if the "Average Joe" were suddenly given the (atomic) power to save the world or to end it? Certainly the typical misanthropic teenager in the 1957 drive-in audience would say, "Blow the sucker up!" but in *The 27th Day* cooler adult heads prevail (by narrow margin). Unbearable pressures are put on the recipients of the alien capsules by their governments and peers, and the film uses this premise to paint a negative, even racist portrait of Communist Russia; the accruing tensions between the world powers make *The 27th Day*, if nothing else, a slice of Cold War agit-prop par excellence. Two of the recipients of the death-capsules are women, and both immediately discard their horrible burden, one through suicide, the message being that females want no part of the fearsome responsibility of life and death which is handed, in patriarchy, always to men. Too bad, that — as the film was produced by a woman (actress-turned-producer Helen Ainsworth), one might have hoped for a more powerful expression of female power — but sexist studio politics obviously ruled the day.

The bulk of the film concerns a man and a woman who must escape their sudden notoriety, taking refuge in a racetrack worker's shack; their involuntary exile mimics the

***The 27th Day* was by far the most thoughtful science-fiction film released in 1957, although it did succumb to certain race-centric Cold War prejudices.**

postwar heterosexual couple's desire to remain isolated and hidden from the awesome political turmoil swirling around them in the world at large. In their efforts to dodge the world's deadly tentacles by hiding in a tiny room, the film rather grimly repaints Suburbia as an armed compound within an intrusive police state.

With their awesome power and mysterious "lock" to which so few own the key, the alien capsules may remind us of the Greek myth of Pandora and her "Box" or "Jar," and the terrible power unleashed when foolishly opened. Yet in the highly improbable finale, it turns out that the capsules only destroy "the enemies of human freedom." Brief stock footage of the marvelous Harryhausen U.F.O. from the previous year's *Earth vs. the Flying Saucers* gives the film some of its minimal production value. The only false step in the whole picture may be the use of Paul Frees, whose ubiquitous cartoon voice seems to trivialize everything it touches. And it is somewhat sad to see two of Roger Corman's most talented stock players, Mel Welles and Paul Birch, in thankless small roles.

John Mantley's screenplay for *The 27th Day* follows his 1956 novel faithfully but for several interesting omissions and modifications, all understandable due to the meager budgetary restraints of the production (with some — in hindsight — probably being improvements). Firstly, the novel takes place in the (then) near future —1963 to be precise — for no apparent reason. Otherwise, the main characters are all transposed verbatim from the novel, retaining their original names and rendered quite faithfully from the source material. In the film, the five main characters are all approached on earth by alien beings depicted only as towering black shadows; the novel, playfully retaining a certain loyalty to pulp science fiction tradition, depicts these emissaries — described thus by the alien himself— as "being(s) about eleven feet tall with green hair and a third eye."[12] When the five poor souls soon awaken in the alien spacecraft, Jonathan is the first to express their common anxiety by quipping, "What we're all afraid to say is that we think we've been kidnapped by bug-eyed monsters!" Soon, the alien reveals himself; in the film, the alien is a garden-variety humanoid wearing a "regulation" silvery space suit and entering the antechamber via a sliding door. In the novel, however, the scene plays out quite differently: "Seated on an enormous chair on a low dais, backed by something that resembled black velvet, was an overpowering figure. But the fact which had drawn the incredulous reaction from all of them was that the figure was human. It was a man!" The alien begins his address to the earthlings with a rather significant revelation, one missing from the film version: "It may interest you to know that all the planets in the galaxy old enough to have produced life, and capable of supporting it, are inhabited."[13] Probably because the novel takes place in "the future," the alien refers to Man's most terrible weapon thusly: "Each capsule has many thousands of times the energy of an X-bomb, which I understand is your present most powerful weapon." Of course, the film version, taking place in the present day, names this super-weapon correctly as the "H-bomb."

Most amusingly, in the novel, when the alien begins his worldwide television transmission, he makes sure to "awaken" the zombies of the "boob tube" thusly: "People of Earth, this is *not* a commercial. May I repeat for those of you who may not have understood, this is not a commercial."[14] This is a wonderful comment on the mind-numbing aspect of TV, its tendency to dope viewers into an uncritical semi-slumber in which nothing is judged on its own merits and all programming blends somehow into a bland "sameness," so that an historical alien broadcast may look, at first glance, like just another soap commercial or bad sci-fi melodrama. And after the alien has finished his momentous "not-a-commercial" announcement, the novel offers a magical scene of alien visitation:

> And then, suddenly, with a speed that defied belief, something plummeted from the farthest reaches of the stratosphere beyond the range of human sight into the realm of visibility. The atmosphere above the world rolled and crashed in terrible earth-shaking thunder as the roiled air, rent by the ship's passage, rushed back into place. The star ships of the Aliens hung motionless in the sky. Vast, pulsating disks of ice-blue luminescence in the darkness and shimmering circles of silver incandescence in the light, they waited while humanity viewed them in fear and open-mouthed wonder. Then, as quickly as they had come, they flashed upward and vanished into space while the earth reeled again to the echoing thunder of their passage.[15]

Although the omission of this scene is understandable due to the film's budget, its absence is a shame, as it would have made a powerful impact; the scene as it stands in Mantley's novel may, in fact, have been "inspired" by a strikingly similar moment in Arthur C. Clarke's 1953 landmark sci-fi treatise *Childhood's End*. Sadly, the narrative void left by this scene's omission in the film is replaced by dopey Paul Frees as a newscaster reiterating the main points of the alien's message on a TV broadcast, a scene both redundant and grating.

In the novel, heroes Jonathan and Eve attempt to escape their otherworldly responsibilities not to a lonely racetrack in the off-season, as depicted in the film, but to a secluded cabin in the mountains near the High Sierras, which Jonathan shares with another writer who is currently off in Africa researching his next book. The couple are soon accosted by a deranged hermit who lives in the area (and collects music boxes!). Jonathan and the hermit engage in a fight, leaving the hermit seriously wounded and Jonathan with lesser injuries. Eve injects Jonathan with a sedative to ease his pain, and while under the influence of the sedative Jonathan proposes marriage to Eve. The couple soon decides that the hermit's injuries require professional medical assistance and so drive him to the nearest town, subsequently turning themselves in to the authorities. This entire sequence differs widely from the heroes' self-exile in the film, which is ended when Jonathan starts a fire in order to attract the authorities and surrender to his fate.

In both novel and film, a good deal of attention is given to the innocent soldier Ivan Godofsky's plight at the hands of a brutal, technocratic dictatorship, and here is where *The 27th Day*'s more racist tendencies come out. Although the film stops just short of naming the evil totalitarian regime which is at odds with the United States, referring to it obliquely as "the Iron Curtain" or "their government," the novel clearly and emphatically positions Soviet Russia as the bogeyman in no uncertain terms, and both novel and film are certainly fine examples of the decade's propensity towards Cold War agit-prop. Specifically, both the novel and the film take great pains to chronicle, in almost obsessive detail, Ivan's treatment at the hands of his superiors. Harsh interrogation and outright bullying devolve into physical and mental torture, and the use of psychological conditioning (the attempt to undermine a victim's mental defenses by radically altering his immediate reality) and narco-synthesis (the use of intravenous drugs to induce confession or mental collapse) is given especial prominence. This tendency towards the use of "science" in the service of totalitarian interests was a topic of concern at the time, as witness this passage from Aldous Huxley's scathing indictment of post–World War II society, *Brave New World Revisited* (1958):

Whatever may have happened in earlier years, it seems fairly certain that torture is not extensively used by the Communist police today. They draw their inspiration, not from the Inquisitor or the SS man, but from the physiologist and methodically conditioned laboratory animals. For the dictator and his policemen, Pavlov's findings have important practical implications. If the central nervous system of dogs can be broken down, so can the central nervous system of political prisoners. It is simply a matter of applying the right amount of stress for the right length of time. At the end of the treatment, the prisoner will be in a state of neurosis or hysteria, and will be ready to confess whatever his captors want him to confess.[16]

Another area in which the film glosses over a rather important element of the novel is the reaction of the world to the news of the aliens' plan for Earth, and the complicity of the five hapless human possessors of the awful death-capsules. Although hinted at in the film, primarily via radio and television news reports, the novel sketches a virtually apocalyptic collapse of the social order, such as this revelation: "Thirty-nine cities in the United States are now under martial law, and outbreaks of panic are spiraling."[17] Once they have surrendered, Jonathan and Eve are transported under heavy military guard to the White House, itself under siege by an angry mob. Indeed, the novel declares that "It was the most serious crisis in the history of the nation."[18] In the novel, Jonathan's observation on this mass panic is a somewhat tongue-in-cheek comment on the very genre to which his character owes its existence: "We have been fed on science fiction, invasions from space, and monsters from Mars for two generations and we're frightened!"[19]

As mentioned, the novel of *The 27th Day* takes a harsh look at modern Soviet Russia, declaring it a brutal dictatorship with no redeeming qualities, well in step with the xenophobic zeitgeist of the time. The Russian leader, clearly modeled on Joseph Stalin and called "the Great Leader" throughout the novel, is a cardboard stereotype of a villain-dictator, alternately quiet as a mouse and rabid with savage outbursts, and clearly insane as well. The Great Leader has one thing in mind, and one thing only: "Russian domination of the world." In addition to the merciless treatment of poor Ivan, the Great Leader also executes an intermediary, Gregor, who is a fully fleshed-out character in the novel (with a long-suffering wife and a fully staffed office). After Gregor fails to convince Ivan to share his otherworldly secrets with his comrades, Gregor and his wife are "disappeared." Even more ominously, the Great leader envisions a post–America world in which he is sole ruler and dictator, and the world is run by one immense, labyrinthine government, which he uncannily calls the "New World Order," a term with disturbing implications even today.

In both novel and film, the Americans decide they need to test one of the capsules to see whether the aliens are being honest in their assessment of the threat to mankind from the super-weapons. In order to do this, they need a "human sacrifice," someone willing to be in the target area and suffer the fate of whatever this miracle weapon has in store. For myriad moral and legal reasons, this sacrificial human is hard to acquire, with such obvious choices as the terminally ill and the perpetually incarcerated ruled out, essentially, for their potential "bad press." Seeing that the powers-that-be are at a stalemate, Bochner's colleague, Professor Neuhaus, quietly decides to be made available for that sacrifice. In the novel, Neuhaus claims that he has injected himself with poison in order to force himself into the running as the volunteer. But Neuhaus is bluffing — he had injected no poison — and told this little white lie in order to perform a difficult but heroic service for his fellow man. In the film, for reasons not made immediately clear but perhaps more "timely" regardless, Neuhaus exposes himself to a burst of deadly "gamma radiation." Assuming he was not lying about this act, Neuhaus certainly was doomed, and this brazen act of self-sacrifice forces his colleagues to reluctantly, but with great respect, allow Neuhaus to be the guinea pig for a new age of technological horror. (In the novel, shortly before his vaporization into history, Neuhaus ponders, "Think of it! Thirty thousand intelligent worlds out there and we are chained to the earth. Tragic!")

In the film version, when the test capsule is activated, Neuhaus just vanishes into thin air, leaving his jumpsuit to collapse onto the test raft, an effective if perfunctory illustration of personal dissolution. Yet, in another fine bit of prose — understandably untranslatable to the film — the novel chronicles the eventual "transformation" of Professor Neuhaus quite lyrically:

The professor spoke the last coordinate and the capsule disappeared. On the instruments, nothing happened. There was no explosion, there was no sound. On the seismograph, nothing changed. But at the tiny flag inside the lethal area, in a billionth of a microsecond, a battle was fought and lost. Countless billions of invisible rays flashed through the open mesh of massed molecules which formed the outline of Professor Neuhaus' body. Unerringly, each sought as its target one of the atoms which formed the basis of his physical entity, smashed with irresistible power intro the nucleus in the atom's heart, destroying the delicate balance of its electro-magnetic field. In that billionth of a micro-second, the microcosms which were in toto the form of Professor Neuhaus became a hundred different elements as electrons were battered out of their orbits, reaction induced counterreaction. And suddenly there was nothing.[20]

Professor Bochner is by far the most interesting and articulate character in the novel, and occupies at least as much narrative space as Jonathan and Eve. Working feverishly at a fully-equipped laboratory in Puerto Rico in order to find the secret of the alien hell-capsules — and living on "benzedrine and black coffee"(!) — Bochner comes across in the novel as a forceful, passionate hero-scientist, not the slightly befuddled "Alter kacher" that appears in the film. Bochner is also extremely wise — and not a little misanthropic — as he pontificates often and at length in the novel on the species he is forced to call his own: "Our history has been a manuscript of horror capped by the final exclamation points of Buchenwald and Hiroshima. The miracle is that, in this morass of criminal irresponsibility, we have still found time to build a few enduring monuments in the world of music, art, and science."[21] Later, Bochner calls his fellows' bluff by asking them a truly portentous — if rhetorical — question: "Try to imagine what would happen if we were *not* fundamentally a neurotic life form."

Post-transformation, Bochner clarifies a theory about human evil which had apparently been kicking around in his head for some time, now given validity by events transpired: "Perhaps what we call 'evil' in men is only the instinct of aggression developed to an abnormal degree. And it is possible that aggressive impulses are the product of a certain segment of the brain, like the speech or memory centers." And Bochner's final observation on the potential effects of the transformation of humanity from savage to world citizen is a fantasy almost too good to be true:

> It's too soon to tell, but we may discover we now live in a world where competitive sports do not exist any longer! Competitive sports are only a reflection of a competitive world. They prepare men to fight, and we have made 'fight' a proud word in our language.[22]

Most conspicuously, the novel features an epilogue entirely missing from the film version, taking place ten years hence (in 1973), describing an amazing new civilization built upon the carcass of the extinct "pre-intervention" one. Apparently, a huge paradigm shift in humanity's consciousness took place precisely at the moment when the bomb-capsules eradicated "the confirmed enemies of human freedom," and this portentous moment in time is known in the future as "the Transformation." The progressive society of 1973 features a one-world government, effortless space travel, a typical human lifespan of over 100 years, and a techno-industrial infrastructure run entirely on "cheap and unlimited atomic power." Even more exciting, the problem of human evil has finally been isolated and quarantined, and anyone suffering from "Power Sickness" may be easily cured by adjustment of errant brain chemistry. Further, the hapless Russian soldier Ivan has become an honored delegate to the World Federation, and Jonathan and Eve have married and have several children. Considering the low budget and humble origins of the film, *The 27th Day* captures the spirit of Mantley's quasi–Utopian novel well; regardless of its inevitable narrative and philosophical shortcuts, it is still one of the most successful fantastic films of the year.

THE CYCLOPS WITH *DAUGHTER OF DR. JEKYLL* (ALLIED ARTISTS)

Allied Artists continued its banner year (35 films released in 1957) with this pleasant if unexceptional mid-summer double bill. *The Cyclops* is an early f/x-driven spectacle by

As suggested by this newspaper advertisement, Allied Artists' mid-summer "horror chiller" release of *The Cyclops* and *Daughter of Dr. Jekyll* was an overt attempt to maintain the boxoffice buzz of their earlier 1957 release, Roger Corman's *Attack of the Crab Monsters* and *Not of This Earth*.

Bert I. Gordon, who would later that year hit the big-time (and earn the nickname "Mr. BIG") with his American-International hit *The Amazing Colossal Man*. The co-feature, *Daughter of Dr. Jekyll*, is an affable throwback to the gothic horrors of the 1940s by the always-interesting iconoclast Edgar G. Ulmer, director of such noir classics as *Detour* (1945). The coupling of these two otherwise unrelated films suggests a certain hetero-sexist presumption on the part of its creators in their emphasis on an overt "male/female" synergy; other double bills of the year which applied the same conceit were *Kronos/She-Devil* and *The Amazing Colossal Man/Cat Girl*.

The Cyclops

66 minutes, Black and White
Produced by B&H Productions Inc.
Distributed by Allied Artists Pictures Corporation
Directed by Bert I. Gordon
Screenplay: Bert I. Gordon
Produced by Bert I. Gordon
Associate Producers: Flora M. Gordon, Henry Schrage
Music by Albert Glasser
Cinematography: Ira Morgan
Editing: Carlo Lodato
Makeup Artist: Carlie Taylor
Special Makeup Creator: Jack H. Young
Production Manager: Henry Schrage
Assistant Director: Harry L. Fraser (as Harry O. Jones), Ray Taylor, Jr.
Properties: James Harris
Sound Effects: Douglas Stewart
Technical Effects Creator: Bert I. Gordon
Special Voice Effects: Paul Frees
Aeronautical Supervisor: Henry "Hank" Coffin
Animal Sequences: Jim Dannaldson
Snake Fight Supervisor: Ralph Helfer
Script Supervisor: Diana Loomis
Cast: James Craig (Russ Bradford), Gloria Talbott (Susan Winter), Lon Chaney, Jr. (Martin "Marty" Melville), Tom Drake (Lee Brand), Duncan Parkin (the Cyclops/Bruce Barton), Vicente Padula (the Governor), Marlene Kloss (the Salesgirl), Manuel López (the Policeman)

Synopsis: An intrepid group of explorers venture to Mexico to search for a missing pilot, only to discover a world of hideous radioactive monsters.

After honing his craft on *King Dinosaur* (1955), producer-director Bert I. Gordon hits his stride with this ludicrous but exciting SF fable, working out some f/x problems and plot fixations which would stand him in good stead for the four box-office hits he made for American International Pictures in 1957–58. The alluring Gloria Talbott, one of the decade's most singular actresses, plays a woman intent on finding her missing husband, an obsession that the males who surround her discount as "mania." With her short hair and conservative dress, Talbott almost looks like a religious figure, a nun perhaps who worships the memory of a man thought long dead, or perhaps never existed at all. After some exposition which is rendered useless due to the heavy accent of one of the characters, the film shifts into high gear in a desolate mountain valley filled with giant creatures, including a hawk who devours a giant rodent, and the obligatory lizards, seen before in Gordon's *King Dinosaur* and stealing a page from Hal Roach's stock footage goldmine, *One Million B.C.* (1940, d: Hal Roach, Hal Roach, Jr.). Gordon arguably got the most mileage out of the optical blow-up of real animals than any other filmmaker in history. Gigantism was all the rage in 1957, and these mutants, their pituitary glands affected by radiation, perfectly express the anxiety of the atomic age spun out of control.

When the title monster appears, it is, of course, the missing husband — grown to mammoth proportions by the abundance of uranium in the valley and sporting a hideously distorted face. Grotesque facial deformity is a fright-film staple, with many examples in the late 1950s, perhaps expressing in some fashion man's guilt and shame over his accrued crimes against nature, and illustrating his inner debasement and moral corruption, à la Oscar Wilde's *The Picture of Dorian Gray*. The most convincing scene in the film is the Cyclops' tangling with a mammoth python that, according to some sources, was really strangling stunt man Duncan "Dean" Parkin before crewmembers came to his aid.

The Cyclops is eventually felled, rather cruelly, by sticking a red-hot poker in its eye — a nod to Greek mythology and Homer's tales of the monstrous one-eyed beast Polyphemos, killed in similar fashion by Odysseus. Two of the film's down sides are the unfortunate cartoon voice of Paul Frees, whose monstrous grunts for the title terror always seem poised to lurch into vulgar parody, and Lon Chaney's inevitable drunken overacting. These flaws are almost obliterated by Albert Glasser's rousing score, one of his best. *The Cyclops* was Gordon's prototype for his two breakthrough "giant man" pictures, *The Amazing Colossal Man* and its sequel, *War of the Colossal Beast* (1958); yet this first of the trilogy is by far the best of the three films.

Daughter of Dr. Jekyll

Produced by Film Ventures
Distributed by Allied Artists Pictures Corporation
71 minutes, Black and White
Directed by Edgar G. Ulmer
Screenplay: Jack Pollexfen
Produced by Jack Pollexfen
Associate Producer: Ilse Lahn
Cinematography: John F. Warren
Editing: Holbrook N. Todd
Art Director: Theobold Holsopple
Set Decoration: Mowbray Berkeley
Makeup Artist: Lou Philippi
Production Manager: Joseph Boyle
Property: Irving W. Sindler
Sound Mixer: Fred Kessler
Special Photographic Effects: Louis DeWitt, Jack Rabin
Stunts: Ken Terrell
Wardrobe: Robert Martien
Music Supervisor: Melvyn Lenard
Script Supervisor Shirley Ulmer
Cast: John Agar (George Hastings), Gloria Talbott (Janet Smith), Arthur Shields (Dr. Lomas), John Dierkes (Jacob), Molly McCard (Maid Maggie), Martha Wentworth (Mrs. Merchant), Marjorie Stapp (Woman Getting Dressed), Rita Greene (Young Woman), Marel Page (Young Man), Ken Terrell
Synopsis: A descendant of the notorious Dr. Jekyll has reason to believe she has inherited her relative's murderous instincts.

This delightfully daffy modern gothic by sometimes-great director Edgar G. Ulmer starts off oddly and gets weirder. A somber narrator assures the audience that the legend of the horrible Dr. Jekyll has ended and will never rise again, to which a silhouetted figure in a laboratory setting turns towards the camera and cackles, "Are you sure?" in a demented, almost feminine-sounding voice. The always-engaging Gloria Talbott, as Janet, suffers gruesome dreams or hallucinations in which she believes she has killed, and when the people she dreams about turn up dead the next day, this confirms her worst fears. The killing sequences are artily filmed in deep shadow and convincingly portray the dream state. These somnambulistic states, which alternately evoke past lives and parallel universes, are induced via hypnosis by Janet's elder male guardian, who comes across as a suspicious character from the start. Thus the late 1950s bugaboo — age regression — comes to the aid of a scenario yet again. As Janet runs through her voluptuous mindscape, her flimsy nightgown fluttering in an unearthly breeze, the image seems a hardy projection of her suppressed libido, perhaps a useful metaphor for sexual awakening. Janet's first "victims" are both young women, easily seen as sexual rivals, reinforcing the notion that this "alter ego" of hers is fueled in part by sexual desire suppressed.

As Janet is led to believe she has the blood of Dr. Jekyll in her veins, she readily believes herself literally cursed by the "sins of the father." This notion follows a time-honored patriarchal script in which the female is blamed for the sins of the male, even unto potential self-destruction. Further, the fear of being "tainted" by toxic familial bonds suggests that among the curse of heredity are an innate moral weakness and uncontrollable inner depravity. At one point the elder explains to Janet that Dr. Jekyll believed that all men are "half good, and half bad, and that he wanted to separate the two," an odd notion in that one would think the goal of the social humanitarian would be to synthesize the antithetical tendencies in order to cancel out the excesses of both. Yet, ironically, the "curse" of Man's heredity is that he does indeed, whether he cares to or not, pass on the "evil" inherent in the species to subsequent generations.

As with many films of the era, horror traditions are mixed indiscriminately — here, apparently, a werewolf, not a vampire, can be killed only by a stake through the heart. (This convenient mixture of vampire, werewolf and Jekyll/Hyde lore is also brought into service in *The Vampire*, discussed elsewhere.) Additionally, the adult authority figure, first seen as benign and supportive, actually turns out to be the enemy, a none-too-subtle stroking of the teenage ego regarding parents, teachers, cops, etc. as malevolent authority figures. In a somewhat fuzzy last-reel turnabout, the old man turns out to be the real inheritor of Jekyll's evil, turning into a werewolf every night to kill unlucky villagers. Janet's hallucinations were just that — nightmares of familial guilt and sexual fear, not unreasonable reactions from an orphaned, soon-to-be-wed virgin. And although the woman is blamed for evil, and is brainwashed into believing her culpability, the real evil emanates from the male after all. The film ends as it began, with the narrator assuring the audience that evil is finally vanquished, and the silhouetted figure again teasing, "Are you sure?" — but this time in a distinctly *male* voice, for the face of evil has clearly been identified as male.

Daughter of Dr. Jekyll is an awful lot of fun thanks to Talbott's accomplished performance, Ulmer's quixotic direction and the rather carefree script. The main setting of the film, a lonely fog-enshrouded mansion, is nicely portrayed via a miniature by the f/x team of Jack Rabin and Louis DeWitt. The film well utilizes a stock music score, including recognizable themes from Phil Tucker's deranged *Robot Monster* (1953), whose score was credited to a young Elmer Bernstein. Producer Jack Pollexfen was also responsible for *Son of Dr. Jekyll* (1951), with which this film shares many plot points.

August

FROM HELL IT CAME WITH THE DISEMBODIED (ALLIED ARTISTS)

Hot on the heels of their early-year horror-show bonanza (*Attack of the Crab Monsters /Not of This Earth*), Allied Artists rushed into production another packaged horror bill which consciously, if superficially, alluded to the formula of earlier programs — i.e., one "giant monster movie" plus one "weird horror tale." Both films, despite their quickie genesis and opportunistic pretensions, have their merits, each rising above their intended function as "teenage time filler" in ways quite surprising. Yet *Boxoffice* magazine, in their August 31 review of the double bill, rather predictably meditated more on the phenomenon of the "packaged" double bills — and the horror genre itself — than on the films themselves, which seem to have made little impression on the reviewer:

(*From Hell It Came*): Cinematic creation of monsters has covered a wide range of possibilities — all the way from Frankenstein to giant, radiation-mutated sea pods. As a result, it is to be expected that the confirmed addicts of chills care but little about the form from which they come. Herein, believe it or not, it's a gnarled tree trunk that has grown out of the grave of an unjustly executed man. But for all its fantastic genesis, proportions and mutations, the object stalks through the film dispensing sufficient of violence and shudders to satisfy the customers who buy the all-horror program of which this is half. The spine chilling is hung on a yarn by Richard Bernstein, who further functions as an associate producer to Jack Milner. Because it has a science-fiction foundation, the story is as believable as most of its ilk, more so than many. Dan Milner directed competently and commanded acceptable performances from the cast of virtually unknown troupers. There's a thin thread of romance which will appeal to some spectators, but the feature's forte is horror — and that's what should be ballyhooed.[23]

(*The Disembodied*): Assuming that the market for so-called packaged horror films has not as yet reached the point of super saturation — which it may well have, in view of the number of such tandem deals that have recently been released — the bundle of which this is a half portion is certainly well equipped to match its share thereof. It differs from its contemporaries in one respect. Usually such packages constitute two features one of which is markedly superior to the other. Herein, however, both pictures rate about the same — slightly better than average for their category. Whether this evenness of quality will prove a booking and exhibition asset is problematical. Probably not on the supposition that the seekers of chills are happy to encounter a fair dosage and care not too greatly which member of the horrific team administers it. Veteran Ben Schwalb produced the offering and displayed his long-standing propensity toward squeezing the last drop of value from every budgetary buck. The movie is further noteworthy because it was creditably directed by Walter Grauman, a newcomer recruited from TV ranks, who extracted acceptable performances from a reasonably competent but name-light cast.[24]

From Hell It Came

Produced by Allied Artists Pictures Corporation, The Milner Brothers
Distributed by Allied Artists Pictures Corporation
73 minutes/Black and White
Directed by Dan Milner
Story: Richard Bernstein, Jack Milner
Screenplay: Richard Bernstein
Produced by Jack Milner
Associate Producers: Richard Bernstein, Byron Roberts

Allied Artists' third "science-chiller" double bill, *From Hell It Came* and *The Disembodied,* came close — in spirit if not in quality — to imitating their early–Spring cash cow *Attack of the Crab Monsters* and *Not of This Earth.*

Music by Darrell Calker
Cinematography: Brydon Baker
Editing: Jack Milner
Art Director: Rudi Feld
Set Decoration: Morris Hoffman
Costume Design: Frank Delmar
Hair Stylist: Carla Hadley
Makeup Artist: Harry Thomas
Production Supervisor: Byron Roberts
Assistant Director: John Greenwald
Property Master: Ted Mossman
Sound Recordist: Frank Webster, Sr.
Special Effects: James H. Donnelly
Key Grip: Charles Hannawalt
Chief Electrician: Wilbur Kinnett
Conductor: Darrell Calker
Monster Design: Paul Blaisdell
Script supervisor: M.E.M. Gibsone
Cast: Tod Andrews (Dr. William Arnold), Tina Carver (Dr. Terry Mason), Linda Watkins (Mrs. Mae Kilgore), John McNamara (Prof. Clark), Gregg Palmer (Kimo), Robert Swan (Tano), Baynes Barron (Chief Maranka), Suzanne Ridgeway (Korey), Mark Sheeler (Eddie), Lee Rhodes (Norgu), Grace Mathews (Orchid), Tani Marsh (Naomi), Chester Hayes (Maku / the Tabanga), Lenmana Guerin (Dori)

Published Synopsis: Kimo (Gregg Palmer), son of a deceased Kalai island chief, is put to death for his friendship with an American atomic research group, blamed by witch doctor Tano (Robert Swan) and Chief Maranka (Baynes Barron) for deaths caused by the black plague. Before he dies, Kimo swears to return from the grave to avenge himself on his wife Korey (Suzanne Ridgway), Maranka and Tano. Soon after, Dr. Terry Mason (Tina Carver) arrives to join Dr. WIlliam Arnold (Tod Andrews) in his work of caring for natives suffering from radiation burns. Before long, the two doctors discover a strange stump growing from Kimo's grave, and from Norgu (Lee Rhodes) they and Professor Clark (John McNamara) learn of the legend of Taranga, a monster which rises from the grave for vengeance. Although they know it may anger the natives, in the interest of science they determine to remove the monstrous growth. Meanwhile, the witch doctor and the island chief decide to kill Norgu, Korey and the Americans. Korey overhears the two plotting, learns a powerful medicine they will give the monster will make it their servant and helpful in the murders. Korey, frightened, rushes to the Americans, successfully pleads with them to let her remain with them. The monster-stump is removed and taken to the laboratory, given powerful injections but later escapes, and sets out for revenge. Korey is the first victim. The chief is the next victim. Now the Americans know they must find the Taranga and kill it. But before this is accomplished, the monster Taranga captures Terry. Only a well-placed bullet eventually drops the monster in quicksand in which it disappears. Natives, witnessing the death, rush to thank the Americans. The grateful Terry kisses Dr. Arnold, with more than just passing interest.

From Hell It Came was the "A" feature in Allied's third 1957 horror program, accompanied by the rather astounding *The Disembodied*. The film was produced by Jack and Dan Milner, whose previous effort, the moody horror-cum-murder mystery *The Phantom from 10,000 Leagues*, helped the fledgling American International Pictures get on their feet. Although lacking the intelligence and mystery of Corman's *Crab Monsters*, *From Hell It Came* is in some ways quite similar, adequately fulfilling its intended purpose as an entertaining if far-fetched monster movie.

The monster itself is one of those wonderful designs specific to the 1950s, when fantastic men-in-suit creations ensured that the beast would interact with the human characters, allowing a neo-realistic verisimilitude that makes the photoplay highly theatrical, with mythological overtones. The notion of a "monster tree" is something more likely to emanate from a fairy tale, or a child's nightmare, than from a sophisticated science-fiction premise, and indeed the tale here is more fantasy than horror, except for the sloppy and forced references to atomic energy.

Although master creature designer Paul Blaisdell declined the assignment to construct the monster — due, as usual, to the cheapness of the producers — luckily he was enlisted to fashion some preliminary sketches of the creatures design, which were then taken to a Hollywood prop shop for construction. The resulting creature, although not manifested literally by Blaisdell's hands, is truly a Blaisdell creation, one of those magical fantasy-beasts he created so well. A giant walking tree is one thing, but a giant walking tree with angry eyes, a beating heart, and a scowling, hangdog mouth could only come from an artist like Blaisdell, who rightly saw that modern horror creatures, to be effective, must tap into deep subconscious sources of collective fear and accumulated myth. Most striking in the "Tabanga," as with his other masterpieces, is the trademark "Blaisdell scowl," an overtly human face of anguish, dementia and rage superimposed onto the chosen beastly vessel. Seen by many today as silly or goofy, these unnervingly "human" faces are actually the brilliant heart of Blaisdell's creature design, an observation illustrated vividly when Blaisdell was talked out of using them, such as with the remarkably pedestrian headpiece of *It! The Terror from Beyond Space* (1958, d: Edward L. Cahn). Here, the Tabanga's gruesome frown, looking like an angry bulldog, adds immensely to the creature's mythological essence and narrative position, making it much more than an animated twig — making it, in fact, a character.

On the other hand, the confusing screenplay seems unable to decide on causes essential to the plot. U.S. scientists are visiting a Pacific atoll where the monster awakes, ostensibly to help the natives there deal with a mysterious "Black Plague." Alternately, there is the admission that the island was the unwitting recipient of a massive dose of radioactivity from a nearby H-bomb blast, and this is also blamed for the epidemic among the natives. The scientists, probably to cover their collective asses, insist that it is the plague and not atomic poisoning that is causing the illness. It is unclear, therefore, whether the radioactivity *is* the plague discussed, or whether there are two different forces ravaging these people simultaneously.

Likewise, when the monster comes to life it is alternately blamed on occult voodoo magic, radioactive mutation, *and* a new heart-enhancing serum created by one of the doctors. Perhaps this fuzziness is deliberate, intending to convey that significant socio-cultural events usually have more than one single traceable cause, or perhaps it is merely due to a hastily-concocted screenplay. Nevertheless, the effect is both to keep the viewer uncertain of where to place blame, and make the Caucasian scientists seem highly duplicitous, even if this was not intended.

What does comes across loud and clear, however, is the potentially negative force of Imperialism, that of an invading "white race" encroaching on a native peoples, ostensibly to "help" or "civilize" them, but in reality to overtake their resources and force them to assimilate to white cultural dictates. Well documented are the criminal activities of the U.S. military who, after evacuating native peoples from the Marshall Islands and poisoning their lands with radioactive bombs, encouraged the population to return. Insisting that the land was cleansed of radiological residue, the military of course lied, using these poor people as human guinea pigs in order to study the long-term effects of radiation exposure. Epidemics

EXPLOITATION

Transform Tree Trunk Into Movie Monster!

Your local park department or a lumber company can aid you in making a movie monster like "Taranga," the frightening tree in "From Hell It Came." Try and obtain the trunk of a tree about 7 feet high. If it has a few branches on it, all the better. If it has too many, prune the tree to resemble the illustration shown on the left. Then have your sign artist do the rest. Have him either paint or chisel out the eyes, mouth, etc., so when the job is done you will have a fairly good replica. Spot "Taranga" in front of your theatre, and light up to make it as eerie as possible. Naturally, tie-in both titles and playdate.

Typical bird-brained ballyhoo from the pressbook of *From Hell It Came*. Note the suggestion to find a 7-foot-tall tree trunk and then "prune the tree to resemble the illustration"! Also note that the monster is called "Taranga" here; it is referred to as "Tabanga" in the film itself.

of illness and death soon followed, with the military denying their possible complicity at every turn. This is Imperialism in its most virulent form, and *From Hell It Came*, perhaps in spite of itself, paints a not-uncritical portrait of this dark crime of postwar America. This emphasis on the toxic effects of Imperialism is reinforced by one of the characters, a comic buffoon named Mrs. Kilgore. Kilgore is a sex-starved, drunken Australian entrepreneur who, with her late husband, opened up a trading post on the island solely for the purpose of stealing precious commodities, such as rare pearls, from the gullible natives. Kilgore thus symbolizes the entire British Empire, portraying it as a comical, drunken, immoral force of utter depravity. Her casual disdain for all "dark" peoples is nicely summarized by one of her flippant asides: "They oughta drop a bloomin' hydrogen bomb on 'em all!" a comment which pretty much sums up the racist Imperialist mindset.

Another problematic aspect of the screenplay concerns the film's heroine, Terry, a scientist who starts out as a strong feminist ("I live by my *intellect!*") but is brought into line with subservient phallo-centric philosophy by film's end, collapsing into her brutish lover's arms and vowing never again to be a cold-hearted, independent female. This entirely retrograde, pre-feminist focus seems anachronistic even for the time, compared to the many proto-feminist characters which graced the fantastic 1957 screen. In fact, all the female characters in the film, including a duplicitous native wife, are fairly negative stereotypes, conforming to the dictates of an avowed sexism. Perhaps it is thus best to see the Tabanga as merely another fanciful extension of phallo-centrism — an enlarged, ambulatory penis that brutally reinforces the regressive socio-sexual agenda of its creators. This at times seems to be the film's stated agenda; for instance, it is exactly when the unforgivably feminist heroine first arrives on the island, descending from the skies like an angel (thanks to a helicopter), that the Tabanga begins its rebirth from the coffin of the slain warrior hero.

In their excellent treatise, *The Fifties: The Way We Really Were*, Douglas T. Miller and Marion Nowak discuss the phenomenon of the female as she appeared in the postwar popular culture of the decade, especially in film and television, and how the woman in these texts seemed somehow poised to reinforce the patriarchal status quo, even as they simultaneously railed against such gender-centric socio-political strictures. In their journey, the authors stumbled upon *From Hell It Came* and had some intriguing — if curious — things to say about the heroine:

> An excellent example is a cheap science-fiction film called *From Hell It Came*, probably inspired by the far more masterful success of *Creature from the Black Lagoon*. This film tells the story of a vicious possessed tree stump that walks about terrorizing the Polynesian islanders. There are two women prominent in the movie: a scientist with both M.D. and Ph.D (specializing in radiation studies and dermatology) and a trader who took over that post when her husband died some years before. The scientist is played by a pretty blond actress no more than 18 years old. The trader, who from all her dialogue is well into middle-age, looks about 30. The scientist finds herself pursued throughout the film both by the tree stump (which has worked up an inexplicable grudge against her) and a fellow researcher, a hefty male who embraces her and murmurs such scientific observations as "stop being a doctor first and a woman second.... Don't you want a husband and children like other women?"[25]

It is exceedingly curious that Miller and Nowak saw the film's heroine, Tina Carver, as being a "teenager" when she is clearly in her mid–20s (and, of course, perforce must be if she is a Ph.D). There are also several misinterpretations of minor plot points, understandable in someone unfamiliar with the genre casually pursuing a text such as this. Otherwise, the authors' assessment of the film's barbarian sexual politics is fairly accurate:

> At film's end, when the male researcher heroically kills the enraged stump (which is about to fling the teen-age scientist into the swamp), the two embrace and their colleagues note that it is time for "a stateside honeymoon." A foolish film, to be sure, but at the same time a great parable for attitudes about the competent woman in the fifties. When the scientist was assaulted by the stump, she only flailed the air with her hands, even though a means of killing the thing was more available to her than anyone. Women, the film seemed to say, just could not handle anything. They were safer married.[26]

As Miller and Nowak note, the "lesson" in *From Hell It Came* falls eerily in line with a generally perceived prejudice of the time — that the pursuit of knowledge, career or professional advancement was to be considered not only irresponsible and useless but actually harmful to those women foolish enough to seek them.[27] In *From Hell It Came*, it is only the "correction" of these errors on the part of patriarchy's ambulatory penis-surrogate that literally carries the film's heroine back into the arms of a loving and protective (if stifling) social order. Yet aside from its shamefully retrograde sexual politics, *From Hell It Came* still emerges as in some ways an exemplary example of the modern "monster movie," perhaps even an iconic example of the genre.

As with other science-fiction/horror titles from their back catalog, Allied Artists included *From Hell It Came* as part of its successful "Sci-Fi for the '60s" television syndication package. As mentioned in previous entries, the originally shorter theatrical running times were augmented by repeating a key scene from the film before the main credits, as well as adding an explanatory crawl, the text of which follows:

> In Haiti, a corpse walks, as
> a Zombi! In primitive India,
> the dead return as animals!
> On certain Pacific Atolls, a
> warrior treacherously
> murdered, may turn into a
> tree! Or so it is said by
> the Shamans ..
> Our story occurs on a savage
> island where a Prince is
> killed unjustly. The victim was
> buried upright in a hollow
> tree trunk. The legend says
> that "the tree walked to
> avenge its wrongs!"

As with the prologue crawls for other AATV offerings, this introductory text attempts to sketch the main narrative thrust of the ensuing story using wild splashes of lyrical, even hyperbolic prose — along with conspicuous typographical and grammatical errors — making the resultant passage in some wise a singular, even poetic annotation to the main filmic text. As mentioned previously, the textual prologue crawl was a fixture in low-budget filmmaking almost since the birth of the cinema, certainly a main fixture in silent film narratives but also used extensively in the first decades of sound film, often to legitimize or explain a low-budget exploitation-type film (and as in this case, to pad out a short running time). In the case of *From Hell It Came*, with its jungle-centric narrative, the prosaic excesses of the prologue crawl strongly reinforces the movie's debt to the "exotic film" craze of the 1920s and 1930s, independently-produced pictures which merged travelogue, documentary and narrative into a perplexing, lurid, and oftimes racist depiction of life in the "uncivilized" part of the world. Famous explorers such as Frank Buck (*Bring 'Em Back Alive*, 1932; *Wild Cargo*, 1934) and Martin and Osa Johnson (*Congorilla*, 1932; *Baboona*, 1935) made fortunes selling what were essentially their home movies to thrill-hungry audiences fascinated (as a self-proclaimed "modern" civilization) with anything considered "primitive."[28] This obsession in Western culture with what was soon dubbed "the third world" continued with a myriad of jungle-centric narratives in long-running film series featuring warrior-heroes such as Tarzan, Jungle Jim and others, including Allied Artist's own Bomba, the Jungle Boy (a series begun during the studio's poverty-row days as Monogram Pictures). As well, television series such as *Ramar of the Jungle* and *Sheena, Queen of the Jungle* garnered top ratings throughout the 1950s. For better or worse, *From Hell It Came* contains an abundance of the ethnocentric spirit of the jungle picture tradition, although the genre soon shrank from view in the face of increasing civil rights awareness, and a desire to present African-Americans and other dark-skinned ethnic groups in a more favorable, realistic light than their portrayal as "savages," a disgraceful racial bias allowed to fester unchallenged for so long in popular culture.

The Disembodied

Produced by Allied Artists Pictures Corporation
Distributed by Allied Artists Pictures Corporation
66 minutes/Black and White
Directed by Walter Grauman
Screenplay: Jack Townley
Produced by Ben Schwalb
Music by Marlin Skiles
Cinematography: Harry Neumann
Editing: William Austin
Art Director: David Milton
Set Decoration: Joseph Kish
Makeup Artist: Emile LaVigne
Production Manager: Allen K. Wood
Assistant Director: Austen Jewell
Property Master: Sam Gordon
Sound Recordist: Ralph Butler
Wardrobe Master: Bert Henrikson
Script Supervisor: Richard Michaels
Cast: Paul Burke (Tom Maxwell), Allison Hayes (Tonda Metz), John Wengraf (Dr. Carl Metz), Eugenia Paul (Mara), Joel Marston (Norman), Robert Christopher (Joe), Dean Fredericks (Suba) (as Norman Frederic), A.E. Ukonu (Lead Voodoo Drummer), Paul Thompson (Gogi), Otis Greene (Kabar)

Published Synopsis: Tom Maxwell (Paul Burke), author-lecturer; Norman Adams (Joel Marston), photographer, and Joe Lawson (Robert Christopher), Tom's assistant, are in a jungle when the latter is seriously wounded by a lion. He is taken by his friends and Gogi (Paul Thompson), native guide, to Dr. Karl Metz (John E. Wengraf) who, with his young wife, Tonda (Allison Hayes), lives on the edge of the jungle. Despite the doctor's dislike for strangers, he treats Joe. Tonda, who secretly practices voodoo and entices a native servant, Suba (Norman Fredric) and has attempted to cast a spell over her husband, is immediately attracted to Tom. Suba becomes jealous. Meanwhile, Tonda is threatened by her husband when he discovers her practicing voodooism over the unconscious Joe. Later, at night, as Tom, Norman and Gogi spy upon her, she is seen plunging a knife into the heart of a doll as part of a strange ritual in which Suba lies frozen in terror atop an altar. Later Suba is found dead, his heart having been cut out. His wife, Lara (Eugenia Paul), accuses Dr. Metz of murder. Joe miraculously recovers, but under a mesmeric spell assumes Suba's characteristics and attacks Tom when he discovers him making love to Tonda. Tom knocks Joe unconscious. Tonda, disclaiming voodoo power, accuses the doctor of creating deadly evils, and begs Tom to kill him. She becomes enraged when Tom repulses her. Now the adventurers' guns disappear, their gasoline is spilled and Gogi is slain. In a moment of hate, Tonda stabs the doctor and casts a fatal spell on Kabar (Otis Greene), a native, when he leaves to summon help for the physician. However, Tonda is tricked into believing Kabar lives. Now believing her voodoo had failed, she begins another wild voodoo ritual and Tom is captured by natives as he again spies on her. Joe, still in a hypnotic spell and under Tonda's orders, attempts to stab Tom. He recovers from his trance just as Lara arrives and knifes Tonda to death. Tom, Norman and Joe now bid farewell to Dr. Metz and return to civilization.

Director Walter Grauman and scenarist Jack Townley bring the shop-worn, and soon obsolete, jungle melodrama genre to dizzying new heights with this extraordinary melodrama, which pits two oppressed females against each other in a battle to the death, and in so doing makes some rather progressive remarks about female empowerment and class struggle. First, there is Tonda Metz, a young slut who is the virtual prisoner of her elder, impotent husband-doctor. She responds to her forced exile by becoming a very powerful person in the jungle hierarchy — a voodoo priestess, an avocation which positions her as an alternately negative and sympathetic proto-feminist character. Although Tonda's newfound power is used primarily for evil purposes — to vanquish enemies and silence rivals — it does illustrate an impressive case of female empowerment; one could argue as well that since Tonda is trapped in a loveless partnership with an old-world tyrant, a bitter hack who refuses her any personal autonomy, she is more than justified in seeking personal fulfillment elsewhere, even if it be a whole world apart from her fallow patriarchal prison.

Tonda's rival is Lana, a courageous native woman who takes matters into her own hands when the "evil" white woman kills her rival's husband via a voodoo curse. Lana's killing of Tonda at a crucial moment in a voodoo ceremony is not only an act of personal courage and incipient empowerment — eerily mirroring those same traits in her enemy — but an act of class defiance, as the natives are considered the inferior servants of the visiting "white men." Here *The Disembodied* radically defies a time-honored jungle melodrama taboo: the native underlcass may not threaten or harm their (invariably white) rulers — except when narratively framed as a crime committed against the prevailing social order, a crime swiftly and unmistakably identified and punished. Yet here Lana, representing the native underclass, defends herself and her community against Tonda, representative of the ruling class, by killing her, and yet is seen in the narrative as being entirely justified, even heroic, in doing so. Surely, an underclass standing up against, and defeating, an oppressive

Allison Hayes beats patriarchy at its own game with the conspicuously "phallic" stabbing of petty tyrant John Wengraf in Walter Grauman's astounding proto-feminist fable *The Disembodied.*

governance from a "ruling class" would become a common trope in popular culture of the 1960s and beyond, but it jumps seemingly out of nowhere in *The Disembodied* and may be, like the film's unabashed feminist leanings, a sort of cultural "canary in the coal mine," picking up on the progressive cultural zeitgeist which was at that very moment in time poised for radical alteration.

In this author's opinion, nobody could pull off the role of the completely amoral, schizophrenic, yet wholly charismatic — and arguably sympathetic — Tonda better than Allison Hayes, one of the most underused and underappreciated actors of the era. Tonda as played by Hayes is an extraordinary amalgam of silent-film villain, sultry femme fatale, and shockingly post-modern woman of power and vision. Like many of the "monsters" in fantastic cinema of the time, as the ostensible "villain" of the piece she must die in order to restore sacrosanct patriarchal order; still, Tonda remains in memory as a curiously sympathetic character, a tragic heroine of the old school, perhaps even a sacrificial victim slain on the altar of justice so that her community might evolve and mature. Luckily, the utterly remarkable Hayes essayed one more indelible parable of female empowerment during her too-short reign as B-movie queen: 1958's *Attack of the 50-Foot Woman*.

The Disembodied harkens back to the back-lot jungle pictures mentioned previously, including Allied Artists' own long-running series featuring Bomba, the Jungle Boy, even more than *From Hell It Came* — primarily for the reason that it looks exactly like many of those poverty-row programmers, in that it was filmed entirely on interior studio-built sets (just like most of the cheaper jungle films of the era). In contrast, *From Hell It Came* had exterior scenes which were, almost exclusively, actually filmed outdoors, giving the film a somewhat expansive (if not exactly epic) quality. In contrast, *The Disembodied*, like its Kiddie Matinee cousins, comes across as downright claustrophobic, with actors cavorting in comparatively tight physical spaces, the jungle always closing in around them. In the case of *The Disembodied*, this stifling stage-bound quality actually adds to the film's uncanny allegorical charm, as the scenario seems to take place (not unlike Roger Corman's *The Undead* or Ed Wood's *Plan Nine from Outer Space*, 1959) in a spiritual limbo, a stifling artificial space in which characters are trapped as if sentenced to purgatory. And as a (possibly inadvertent but nonetheless effective) proto-feminist fable, this sense of suffocating space uncannily mirrors the general observation that many a woman of the era felt "trapped" or "imprisoned" in her house, her community, her society, even her world by that omnipresent "benevolent dictatorship," the patriarchal order.

As with its co-feature, *The Disembodied* was added to Allied Artists' "Sci-Fi for the '60s" television syndication package and padded (as were its companions) with a most evocative prologue crawl for its TV incarnation, as follows:

> In Africa there exists
> remote islands of savagery
> where the ancient rites of
> Voodoo are still practiced.
> The African Witch Doctor
> does not know the
> meaning of "psychology,"
> yet he has mastered
> its art for centuries.
> It is an established fact

> that with primitive peoples,
> a native can die by
> power of "suggestion."
> White men, as a rule, are
> not susceptible to Voodoo.
> Yet there are recorded
> instances of lost travelers
> "losing their minds"
> to the "Black Magic."
> Our story is concerned
> with such events.

The prologue crawl for *The Disembodied* takes the same authoritative tone as that for *From Hell It Came* and other Allied Artists TV offerings, attempting to combine fact and fiction into one unassailable hypothesis upon which to rest the surely fantastic story to follow. In fact, all of the Allied Artists TV prologue texts appear documentary in spirit but veer off carelessly into wildly implausible stretches of narrative imagination. In addition, *The Disembodied*'s prologue crawl is quite racist, carefully differentiating the logical "White Man" from the superstitious "native"—and managing to take a swipe at the psychiatric profession at the same time. It would be unfair to suggest that the anonymous author of this passage had any sort of personal agenda, but the text does reflect some of the cultural prejudices of the time.

THE UNKNOWN TERROR AND *BACK FROM THE DEAD* (TWENTIETH CENTURY–FOX)

Certainly a minor package compared to Twentieth Century–Fox's summer blockbusters *Kronos* and *She-Devil*, this horror show nonetheless probably did fair business just based on the momentum of the teenage double bill phenomenon. The official *Boxoffice* magazine reviews sum up the films' chances for survival in the marketplace succinctly:

(*The Unknown Terror*): Quite probably the current booming market for the so-called package deals will win for this somewhat unhorrific horror play a number of bookings that otherwise it would not enjoy. Along with its running mate feature, "Back from the Dead," analyzed elsewhere on this page, the picture will get by, but little more. Its many weaknesses are the more accented because it is upon this one that the tandem bill obviously depends for the quota of chills that the program promises, through the very nature of the title and the scare 'em ballyhoo on which it will have to be sold. Failure of the film to generate such spine-tingling is initially attributed to the story which is basically the shopworn yarn about the mad medico whose screwball experimentations loose dire forces that threaten the life of the entire world. This hackneyed device has given the screen everything from Frankenstein to giant man-eating ants. But the monsters that are developed herein are illy defined and they'll certainly not frighten many ticket buyers. Perhaps the picture's brightest spot is a musical interlude supplied by the King of the Calypso, Sir Lancelot.[29]

(*Back From the Dead*): As a single entry, this rather unusual celluloid venture into the intricacies of occultism could find a place and a reasonable amount of favor as the supporting feature on the average dual bill. Whether the fact that it is teamed with "Unknown Terror" as a package will prove an asset or a liability will probably be a matter of geography. In product-starved situations where three program changes per week are routine, the former can well obtain. The picture is praiseworthy if for no other reason than the impressive, authentic and artistic production mountings with which Robert Stabler endowed it. This asset manifests itself principally in set dressings and location exteriors. Moreover, the cast boasts names, especially on the distaff side, that can add some merchandising weight to all but the deluxe programs. Under able direction by Charles Marquis Warren the troupers, most of them in exacting roles, perform admirably, especially topliner Peggie Castle. While the screen story is eerie and suspenseful, it can hardly be termed a horror play which is hinted by the fact that the offering is being teamed to form an averred chill-dispensing bundle booking.[30]

The Unknown Terror

76 minutes, Black and White
Produced by Emirau Productions, Regal Films
Distributed by Twentieth Century–Fox Film Corporation
Directed by Charles Marquis Warren
Screenplay: Kenneth Higgins
Produced by Robert Stabler
Music by Raoul Kraushaar, Dave Kahn
Cinematography: Joseph F. Biroc
Editing: Michael Luciano
Production Design: James W. Sullivan
Set Decoration: G.W. Berntsen
Makeup Artist: Glen Alden
Hair Stylist: Pat Whiffing
Production Manager: Nathan Barragar
Assistant Director: Nathan Barragar
Property Master: Mike Gordon
Sound: Hugh McDowell
Special Effects: Norman Breedlove
Optical Effects: Louis DeWitt, Jack Rabin
Wardrobe Supervisor: Vou Lee Giokaris, Robert O'Dell
Conductor: Raoul Kraushaar
Script Supervisor: Mary Chaffee
Cast: John Howard (Dan Matthews), Mala Powers (Gina Matthews), Paul Richards (Peter Morgan), May Wynn (Concha Ramsey), Gerald Milton (Dr. Ramsey), Duane Grey (Lino), Richard Gilden (Raoul Koom), Martin Garralaga (Villager), Patrick O'Moore (Dr. Willoughby), William Hamel (Mr. Trainer), Charles Gray (Jim Wheatley), Charles Postal (Higgs), Sir Lancelot (Himself)

Synopsis: A bacteriologist working with slime molds for antibiotics unwittingly creates a monster fungus.

A "white" expedition into "native" territory is the ostensible framework for this most diverting drive-in potboiler. While the basic scenario harkens back to hundreds, if not thousands, of "jungle safari" films, the plot is used here as a springboard for some most interesting ruminations on issues of class, race and mortality. Guest singing star Sir Lancelot, billed as "King of the Calypso," is inserted awkwardly into the first reel in order to cash in on the stupid "Calypso" craze of that year (clueless Hollywood "trendspotters" absurdly predicted that calypso music would be the next big fad after rock and roll died away); however, his songs are well used as purveyors of taboo folk wisdom, with one line, "He's got to suffer to be born again," vividly foreshadowing the ensuing religious emphasis of the film. Through the songs, the audience learns that the natives consider the nearby "Cave of Death," the object of the expedition, to be a literal purgatory for man awaiting judgment before leaving this earthly plane.

The expedition arrives at the location they seek, encountering an odd character called Ramsey, an exiled scientist who is conducting sinister biological experiments in an ersatz private kingdom far removed from the scrutiny of his peers. Ramsey immediately reminds us of Kurtz in Joseph Conrad's *Heart of Darkness*, a white megalomaniac who has the natives cowed and terrified. (Even the name "Ramsey" suggests "Ramses," famed Egyptian pharaoh who ruled his people as a god-like tyrant.) Ramsey is first seen stirring a boiling cauldron, amusingly reinforcing his role as some sort of white witch doctor with diabolical powers. When a member of the expedition asks him for the exact location of the coveted "Cave of Death," Ramsey chuckles, "I can show you how to find that — it's their purgatory...." as he points his spoon towards the flames under his boiling pot. A more literal reference to the fiery flames of the Christian Hell cannot be imagined, and the audience knows now that what the natives fear, and what the white men seek, is access to death. The mission then becomes one of self-destruction, even race suicide.

Ramsey's sexy native wife is named Canja, alluding to both "conjure" (reinforcing her role as supernatural witch-mate) and "conjugal" (marking her as the sexual slave of her mad husband). Ramsey's possessive stance towards his wife is soon revealed when he brutally whips her for some minor faux pas, causing protest from the others which he silences by bellowing, "It's *my* wife!" Ramsey clearly considers his mate mere property, without rights or soul.

In an extraordinary later scene, one of the expedition members, a female, runs through

Paul Richards and May Wynn discuss their options in escaping the rule of a jungle tyrant in *Unknown Terror*.

the night jungle in a filmy white nightgown, looking like a phantasm of virginal innocence. She is soon surrounded by menacing, dark males who peer at her from behind the foliage. The woman faints in horror and awakens sometime later to find that her attackers have vanished. Did she dream the whole thing, or did she lose consciousness, and later memory, of a brutal sexual attack?

When the expedition finally reaches the cave, it contains a carved godhead used as a sacrificial altar — the cave is literally a gateway to primitive gods, a sublime purgatory for fallen man on his road to the bowels of Hades. The cave floor is strewn with dead bodies in all stages of decay, another marvelous illustration of some sort of Dante-esque inferno to which all mortals eventually succumb.

Deep in the bowels of the hell-cave the explorers encounter some hilarious Indian fungus-men, at which point the film earns its claim as a bonafide "monster movie." The mass of dripping fungus which threatens our protagonists comes across as some sort of "primordial ooze" that swallows men whole, absorbing their souls into the cosmic void. The monster is merely a convenient *deus ex machina* for the real boogeyman of the piece, for by now it is clear that the "unknown terror" refers to the unfathomable mysteries of Death.

The film ends as the sacred white couple escapes through an amazingly womb-like tunnel into the healing waves of the ocean. This highly symbolic faux-birth suggests that the couple, and perhaps the whole White race, has been "born again" — as Sir Lancelot foretold — repentant of their grievous mistakes against non–White races and Mother Nature, and, drawing from the primordial strength of the female earth elements, is ready to forge a new egalitarian society. As this film's remarkable companion feature, *Back from the Dead*, will soon underscore, that achievement can only be brought about by a rejection of deadly phallo-centric culture and a resurgence of the healing, life-affirming matriarchal principle embodied in the noble mission of female empowerment.

Back from the Dead

Produced by Emirau Productions, Regal Films
Distributed by Twentieth Century–Fox Film Corporation
79 minutes, Black and White
Directed by Charles Marquis Warren
Story: Catherine Turney (from her novel *The Other One*)
Screenplay: Catherine Turney
Produced by Robert Stabler
Music: Raoul Kraushaar, Dave Kahn
Cinematography: Ernest Haller
Editing: Leslie Vidor
Art Director: James W. Sullivan
Set Decoration: G.W. Berntsen
Hair Stylist: Madine Danks
Makeup Artist: William Woods
Production Manager: Nathan Barragar
Assistant Director: Nathan Barragar
Property Master: Ted Cooper
Sound: Jack Goodrich
Optical Effects: Louis DeWitt, Jack Rabin
Wardrobe Supervisors: Joseph Dimmitt, Vou Lee Giokaris
Supervising Editor: Fred W. Berger

Conductor: Raoul Kraushaar
Script Supervisor: Mai Dietrich
Cast: Peggie Castle (Mandy Hazelton Anthony), Arthur Franz (Dick Anthony), Marsha Hunt (Kate Hazelton), Don Haggerty (John Mitchell), Marianne Stewart (Nancy Cordell), Otto Reichow (Maitre Renault), Helen Wallace (Ada Bradley), James Bell (Mr. Bradley), Evelyn Scott (Molly Prentiss), Jeanne Bates (Agnes), Ned Glass (Doctor), Jeane Wood (Nurse), Joan Bradshaw (Redhead), Frances Turner (Baby Sitter)

Synopsis: A young woman is possessed by the spirit of a witch.

Back from the Dead portentously opens where its companion feature, *The Unknown Terror*, ends — the ocean, with its eternal crashing waves and abiding female presence. The credits are accompanied by a bizarre orchestral theme that features a vaguely female voice in the lead, hinting that the following scenario will be unabashedly gyno-centric. The film's long-suffering protagonist is a young woman named Mandy, whose travails against a clearly homicidal patriarchy posit her as some form of Victorian heroine battling gruesome predators who conspire against her on all sides. Mandy is a curious name for the protagonist, considering her overriding agenda of breaking free from male-dominated culture and embracing a matrist outlook (one might say her goal is to "de-man").

Over a shot of a dark mansion, Mandy narrates: "Before I knew what went on in that house, behind those dark walls, I wouldn't have believed it could happen in twentieth–Century America." Although she is referring to subsequent occult-oriented revelations, she could as easily be referring to the systemic subjugation and exploitation of the female in postwar America, symbolized by the suburban prison-house.

Soon, two hooded figures toss a female corpse over a cliff; this human sacrifice clearly stands as symbol of the targeting and extermination of the autonomous female in modern patriarchal culture, with the killers being both the male *and* the female who subscribes to, aids and abets a phallo-centric socio-political agenda — in short, the typical bourgeois heterosexual couple.

Throughout the film's opening moments, voices "talk" to Mandy; is she merely a hallucinating neurotic or is she hearing voices from within, urging her to rebellion and emancipation? At one point the voice tellingly taunts Mandy: "You can't get away from me...."— that is, she cannot permanently avoid her repressed subconscious, her inner (possibly better) voice, which desires above all to emancipate Mandy from her present sociological shackles. At one point Mandy declares of the voices, "I think something's trying to get at me," and later, "It's almost as if it were inside my head," again suggesting that these voices are repressed elements of her conscience, with urgent words of wisdom for her short-term survival and long-term happiness. Of course, to the male medical establishment, Mandy is mentally disturbed; Mandy reveals that regarding the voices, her (male) doctor "just smiled and said I imagined it"— that is, imagined her own potential emancipation from patriarchal bonds.

Mandy is invited to stay with two relatives, Dick and Kate, for a much-needed rest. (Significantly, Mandy's relationship to Dick and Kate are alternated throughout the film. Mandy is first identified as Kate's sister, then later as her sister-in-law. Even more troubling is the notion that Dick is established as Mandy's husband for much of the film, but also identified as her brother-in-law, implying that Kate is Dick's wife! This odd shuffling of easy role identification, although likely nothing more than sloppy continuity problems

Charles Marquis Warren's *Back from the Dead* was one of the first fantastic films to address the notion of devil worshippers working out of modern suburbia, using their conformist public facades to hide nefarious antisocial activities.

inherent in a rushed production schedule, eerily adds to the emphatic social dissociation of Mandy from her peers, as she seems to be largely "not of this earth.")

The aptly-named "Dick," for one, seems determined to suppress the revolutionary potential of Mandy. After one of her frequent emotional outbursts, Dick quips, "What you need is a good, hot cup of coffee, *and a fire....*" Is the fire Dick recommends the historical fire which cleansed the male-dominated earth of uppity witch-women? As soon as Mandy is ensconced in the couple's house, Dick immediately attacks her by playing, against her wishes, a strange record. The angry, atonal, even violent piece blares out of Dick's newfangled stereo system at an ungodly volume. This "devilish" composition, by Raoul Kraushaar, is the same tune played over the opening credits, an odd combination of tribal rhythms, harsh brass melodies, the aforementioned strange, theremin-like "voice" that sounds vaguely female — all in all, sort of a cross between avant-garde jazz and exotica, two popular music genres of the period. (In the original novel *The Other One*, this music is amusingly identified as the 3rd movement of Rachmaninoff's 2nd Symphony, a lilting melody that couldn't trigger seizures in anyone!)[31]

When Dick finally relents and ends the aural torture, he does not apologize but merely quips, "You *used to* like it." (Mandy's psychological hazards are compounded when it is revealed that she is pregnant with child — she has the evil curse of patriarchy growing inside her. Conceivably then, what Mandy "used to like" was being the servant of men, the vessel

Marsha Hunt, Arthur Franz and Peggie Castle suffer a most auspicious "love triangle" in *Back from the Dead.*

for their progeny, and perhaps this is exactly what she is trying to rebel against now.) As Mandy seizes, due to the deep psychological impact of the "devil music," the family dog suddenly growls at her; he does not care for the animalistic urges which are boiling up inside the poor woman. Post-seizure, it is revealed that Mandy has miscarried, a traumatic event certainly (and an unusual one in 1950s mainstream cinema), but an essential step in Mandy's eventual rejection of her role of phallo-centric servitude.

Dick and Kate (and the audience) watch in horror as, after the seizure, Mandy's face transforms into an entirely new being, a simple but remarkable optical effect which carries much allegorical import, as Mandy is literally "changing face" before our eyes. The fantasy plot kicks in at this point, as Mandy reveals that she is now actually "Felicia," Dick's former wife, who died mysteriously some years ago. As Felicia, Mandy "sees" the world with new eyes. Although Felicia is drawn as an evil character (a witch who managed to manifest an occult return to the mortal plane), her symbolic role is that of the "new" Mandy, allergic to any obsolete patriarchal notions.

Felicia/Mandy visits the Bradleys, who turn out to be Felicia's parents. The Bradleys are portrayed as an archetypal old-money American couple — until it is revealed that they are actually devil worshippers! The Bradleys thus function nicely as symbols of the moral evils which so often lie hidden beneath the ostensibly vapid facade of suburbia. Felicia's mother especially is the evil power figure in the proceedings; at one point she quips to Kate, "You believe in your god, and I'll believe in mine...." The father, who is weak and walks with a cane, is portrayed as an enervated patriarch, virtually obsolete and ready for extinction. Mandy's sister (or sister-in-law) Kate sees the evil that is Felicia and vows to destroy her, being the good little servant of male-dom that she is, but Felicia sees the threat and tries to kill her as well; after all, in terms of gender-centric politics, they are now enemies. Felicia cruelly kills the family dog with a garden sickle, a death that goes conspicuously unaddressed during the remainder of the film, implying that the dog's presence as an identifier of incipient evil was more symbolic than literal.

Meanwhile, down the road a piece, a creepy foreigner named Reynaud runs a "club" which worships a "new religion," and all the bored women in town have foolishly joined the club, which is, of course, just a front for a murderous cult of devil worshippers. The somewhat timid finale depicts the beginnings of one of Renault's satanic high masses, replete with what appears to be a virgin sacrifice, which is interrupted before it can be completed. Soon, Felicia leaves her host body, and a sadder, wiser Mandy sighs, "I've been having the most awful dream," referring to the necessarily traumatic but ultimately emboldening trans-formation from phallo-centric girl-slave to autonomous female. Although sketchy in some key areas and philosophically problematic in spots, *Back from the Dead* largely works as an intriguing proto-feminist text in which a conscripted woman is brought to the brink of death so that she can be born anew, free of the toxic bonds of male servitude. As its title alludes, *Back from the Dead* celebrates the imminent return of the long-suppressed Goddess image, icon of matrist culture, so long buried by patriarchal interests.

The remarkable screenplay is by Catherine Turney, based on her 1952 novel *The Other One*. In addition to the copious gender-centric material in the scenario, *Back from the Dead* must rank as one of the first (and few) mainstream films of the decade to deal with the then-obscure subject of devil worship, albeit somewhat timidly — it would not be until 1958's *Curse of the Demon* and 1959's *The Devil's Partner* that the subject was brought up again, and, of course, devil worship was de rigueur in many horror films of the 1960s and beyond.

The Land Unknown

Produced by Universal International Pictures
Distributed by Universal Pictures
78 minutes, Black and White
Directed by Virgil Vogel
Story: Charles Palmer
Screenplay: Laszlo Gorog
Adapted by William N. Robson
Produced by William Alland
Music by Henry Mancini, Heinz Roemheld, Hans J. Salter, Herman Stein
Cinematography: Ellis W. Carter
Editing: Fred MacDowell
Art Directors: Alexander Golitzen, Richard H. Riedel
Set Decoration: Russell A. Gausman, Ray Jeffers
Makeup Artists: Bud Westmore, Irving Berns
Production Manager: Norman Deming
Assistant Director: Joseph E. Kenney, Ray DeCamp
Sound: Leslie I. Carey, Corson Jowett

Sound Technician : Donald Cunliffe
Special Effects: Orien Ernest, Jack Kevan, Fred Knoth
Optical Effects: Roswell A. Hoffmann
Stunts: Sol Gorss
Special Photography: R.O. Binger, Clifford Stine
Still Photographer: Rollie Lane
Assistant Camera: Lew Schwartz
Camera Operator: Lloyd Ward
Wardrobe: Seth Banks, Nevada Penn
Music Supervisor: Joseph Gershenson
Dialogue Coach: Irvin Berwick
Lizard Handler: Jim Dannaldson
Stand-In: Pete Dunn
Script Supervisor: Dorothy Hughes
Unit Publicist: Don Morgan
Cast: Jock Mahoney (Harold Roberts), Shirley Patterson (Margaret Hathaway) (as Shawn Smith),
    William Reynolds (Jack Carmen), Henry Brandon (Carl Hunter), Douglas Kennedy (Capt. Burn-
    ham), Phil Harvey (Steve Miller), Ralph Brooks, Kenner G. Kemp (Officer), Bing Russell (Radio
    Operator), Bert Stevens (Officer)

Synopsis: An Antarctic expedition discovers a valley of dinosaurs.

Even great poster art could not save the lifeless bore known as Universal-International's *The Land Unknown*.

It is hard to decide whether Universal-International's laughable attempt at a big-budget science-fiction "epic," their clumsy effort to top *Forbidden Planet* (1956, d: Fred MacLeod Wilcox) or *The Beast from 20,000 Fathoms* (1953, d: Eugene Lourie), is more pathetic or repulsive. It takes some sort of talent to make an expansive Cinemascope production look like a sloppy no-budget snoozer, but here they succeeded brilliantly. The threadbare, clichéd storyline doesn't help, nor do the disastrous special effects, including a clumsy man-in-suit dinosaur. Even the elaborate prehistoric settings are rendered lifeless in monochrome — apparently the penny-pinching genii at U-I didn't think this giant spectacle even warranted color film! Yet as bad as this film is, it is also mean: live lizards are forced to fight to the death, certainly an act of animal cruelty; an adorable monkey-like creature is eaten by an evil-looking monster plant; a kooky hermit tries to burn an aquatic dinosaur alive. *The Land Unknown* is as dimwitted as a prehistoric bird, and as slow-moving as a lumbering behemoth. Lippert's *The Lost Continent* (1951) covered the same "prehistoric world discovered" territory at a fraction of the budget.

September

Enemy from Space

(aka *Quatermass II*)
85 minutes/Black and White
Produced by Hammer Film Productions
Distributed by United Artists
Directed by Val Guest
Story: Nigel Kneale
Screenplay: Nigel Kneale, Val Guest
Produced by Michael Carreras, Anthony Hinds
Music by James Bernard
Cinematography: Gerald Gibbs
Editing: James Needs
Art Director: Bernard Robinson
Makeup Artist: Phil Leakey
Production Supervisor: Anthony Nelson Keys
Production Manager: John Workman
Assistant Directors: Don Weeks, Stanley Goulder, Hugh Harlow
Master Plasterer: Arthur Banks
Draughtsmen: David Butcher, Don Mingaye
Property Master: Tom Money
Construction Manager: Fred Ricketts
Sound Editor: Alfred Cox
Sound: Cliff Sandell
Boom Operator: Claude Hitchcock
Special Effects: Frank George, Henry Harris, Bill Warrington, Brian Johnson
Matte Painter: Les Bowie
Camera Operator: Len Harris
Electrician: Steve Birtles
Chief Electrician: Jack Curtis
Clapper Loader: Alan Gatward
Still Photographer: John Jay
Focus Puller: Harry Oakes

Wardrobe: Rene Coke
Assistant Editors: Alfred Cox, Michael Hart
Conductor: John Hollingsworth
Continuity: June Randall
Publicist: Bill Batchelor
Cast: Brian Donlevy (Professor Quatermass), John Longdon (Lomax), Sydney James (Jimmy Hall), Bryan Forbes (Marsh), William Franklyn (Brand), Vera Day (Sheila), Charles Lloyd Pack (Dawson), Tom Chatto (Vincent Broadhead), John Van Eyssen (the P.R.O.), Percy Herbert (Paddy Gorman), Michael Ripper (Ernie), John Rae (EJ "Mac" McLeod), Marianne Stone (Secretary), Ronald Wilson (Young Man), Jane Aird (Mrs. McLeod), Betty Impey (Kelly), Lloyd Lamble (Inspector), John Stuart (Commissioner), Gilbert Davis (Banker), Joyce Adams (Woman M.P.), Edwin Richfield (Peterson), Howard Williams (Michaels), Phillip Baird (Lab Assistant), Robert Raikes (Lab Assistant), John Fabian (Intern), George Merritt (Super), Arthur Blake (Constable), Michael Balfour (Harry), Leslie Crawford (Guard), Vernon Greeves (First Man), Jan Holden (Young Girl), Alastair Hunter (Labour MP), Barry Lowe (Chris), Henry Rayner (Drunk), Joan Schofield (Woman Shopper)

Published Synopsis: Professor Bernard Quatermass (Brian Donlevy) is a scientist, engaged on [sic] interplanetary research. Quatermass gets his first eperience [sic] of the nameless horror that hides under the guise of a Government research station, when his car is hit by another vehicle driven by a young man strangely disfigured by an object from outer space. His efforts to investigate the mysterious research establishment are thwarted until, at last, accompanied by Inspector Lomax (John Longden) of Scotland Yard, and Jimmy Hall (Sidney James), an ace newspaperman, he gains entrance to the research station. Here, with the local townsfolk in rebellion, against the station's brutal security guards, they route [sic] the intruders from another world.

This second theatrical film based on Nigel Kneale's popular "Quatermass" sci-fi stories is a stunningly dark and paranoid thriller, far superior to the previous year's

Nigel Kneale's "Quatermass" science fiction stories were a hit in Great Britain, both in television and film versions. The stunningly dark theatrical feature *Quatermass II* was released in the United States as *Enemy from Space*.

The Quatermass Experiment. The discovery of an occlusive, top-secret government project in the hinterlands, complete with armed guards, scared local citizens and even a creepy corporate logo, is like something out of a George Orwell nightmare. Much of the film takes place at a massive industrial complex (in fact, a Shell oil refinery), underscoring the essentially diabolical nature of heavy industry and vividly illustrating the threat inherent in the unchecked growth of the Military-Industrial Complex. When the project is revealed to actually be of alien design, with the goal of brainwashing humans towards alien invasion, the film shifts gears and becomes a most interesting take on Jack Finney's *Invasion of the Body Snatchers*, arguably the biggest sci-fi movie hit of 1956. The somewhat hasty inclusion of an amazingly strange protoplasmic creature in the film's final minutes may cause some to dismiss it as just another "monster movie," but the relentless fixation on sinister government conspiracy, evocatively filmed in a menacing, bleak industrial landscape, makes the film most memorable, and one wonders why it seems to have largely been forgotten. Indeed, some have stated that scenarist Kneale withdrew the film from circulation due to misgivings about casting Brian Donlevy as Quatermass, but the chances of a writer having that kind of power over a film's destiny seems unlikely; and furthermore, Kneale didn't seem to have any problem with Donlevy playing the *same* role in the first Quatermass film![32] It is far more probable that the film was withdrawn due to its relentlessly pessimistic nature, which shines a harsh light on collusion between government and industry towards manipulating the populace, a popular concern that would reach fruition in films such as Joseph Losey's *These Are the Damned* (1962), with which *Enemy from Space* has a good deal in common. Regardless, this second installment of the Quatermass saga stands as by far the most mature of the fantastic films released Stateside in 1957, as well as being the darkest by far. Even the usually unmoved *Boxoffice* magazine applauded *Enemy from Space*, even while acknowledging its absurdist "monster movie" ending:

> One of the best of the recent science-fiction programmers, this British-made film produced by Anthony Hinds has an awesome and suspenseful quality throughout and the terrifying climax, though completely unbelievable, will live up to most patrons' shuddery expectations. Brian Donlevy, veteran Hollywood character actor, is the only marquee name but some of the English players, notably Sidney James, will be familiar to those who patronize English films. The fanciful story, well directed by Val Guest from his own screenplay in collaboration with Nigel Kneale, deals with visitors from another planet who have managed to delude the British government, as well as the public, into thinking that their gigantic research plant is manufacturing synthetic food — instead of a deadly substance which may destroy the earth. Donlevy, as a scientist engaged in interplanetary research, decides to investigate the factory, but he is refused help from all except a member of Parliament — who comes to a horrible end. The townspeople who helped construct the plant finally aid Donlevy in destroying it. There is no romance, but blond Vera Day adds a bright touch as a chatty barmaid. A likable youngster, Bryan Forbes, and sinister John Van Eyssen are the best of the others.[33]

THE AMAZING COLOSSAL MAN AND CAT GIRL (AMERICAN INTERNATIONAL PICTURES)

Arguably American International's "biggest" release of the year, this crowd-pleasing double bill did sensational boxoffice despite the fact that the combo included one terrible picture (*The Amazing Colossal Man*) and one slow-moving, contemplative picture (*Cat Girl*) that was unlikely to engage slap-happy American teens. The *Boxoffice* magazine reviews of the pair reflects at least this flaw on the part of *Cat Girl*, although the author seems to have thoroughly enjoyed *The Amazing Colossal Man*:

> (*The Amazing Colossal Man*): Devotees of science-fiction desire but scant credibility in their screenfare, because as believability increases, thrills decrease in direct proportions. Despite the fact that it is not wanting in the scientific double talk that is standard equipment for features of its category, this "sci-fi" entry boasts more plausibility than most — and without sacrifice of excitement and suspense. While the picture is going forth in double harness — it is being teamed with "Cat Girl" as a package deal — there probably will be plenty of situations where the picture will be bought by itself to furnish sterling support on the more important double bills. And it is amply qualified to perform such service. Lion's share of the credit for the feature's high evaluation goes to Bert I. Gordon. His name completely dominates the main title — producer, director, collaborative scripter and special technical effects, in which last-named chore imaginative Mr. Gordon especially excels. While it lists no names that will set the marquee aflame, the cast, individually and collectively, delivers sincere, ingratiating performances with a particular nod due to Glenn Langan, title roler, and Cathy Downs, the only femme in the acting lineup.[34]

> (*Cat Girl*): When a strictly-from-formula, Hollywood-type screenplay encounters a cast of British actors, almost anything can happen. And in this import from England it does. The story is acceptable, although it undertakes to blend two standard themes hallowed by countless preceding chill dispensers. Moreover, there is not great lack of talent to be found among the troupers, individually or collectively. But all of the horrification — and there is aplenty thereof to satisfy the seekers of chills — doesn't seem to ring true when handled in the polite, restrained manner characteristic of overseas troupers. Nonetheless, the feature can depend upon widespread consideration and bookings if for no other reason than its being teamed with "Amazing Colossal Man" (yep, it's still another package deal) appraised elsewhere on this page. And having been brought to the screen in that runningmate capacity, the picture will serve satisfactorily. There will be some customers that are impressed by title-roler Barbara Shelly. Considering that the film was made on a comparatively limited budget, producers Lou Rusoff and Herbert Smith mounted it intelligently, while direction by Alfred Shaughnessy extracts everything possible from the unimaginative screenplay.[35]

The Amazing Colossal Man

80 minutes/Black and White
Produced by Malibu Productions
Distributed by American International Pictures
Released in September
Directed by Bert I. Gordon
Screenplay: Mark Hanna, Bert I. Gordon, George Worthing Yates, Arthur C. Pierce
Produced by Bert I. Gordon
Executive Producers: Samuel Z. Arkoff, James H. Nicholson
Music by Albert Glasser
Cinematography: Joseph F. Biroc
Editing: Ronald Sinclair
Production Design: Bill Glasgow
Set Decoration: Glen Daniels
Costume Design: Bob Richards
Makeup Artist: Bob Schiffer
Hair Stylist: Joan St. Oegger
Production Supervisor: Jack R. Berne
Assistant Directors: Jack R. Berne, Nate D. Slott
Property Master: James Harris

Property Constructor: Paul Blaisdell
Sound Recordist: Jack Solomon
Sound Editor: Josef von Stroheim
Sound: Charlie King
Special Technical Effects: Bert I. Gordon
Special Effects: Norman Breedlove
Electrician: Joe Edessa
Conductor: Albert Glasser

Trade advertisement for American-International's *The Amazing Colossal Man* promised "amazing colossal grosses." Doubled with the British-lensed *Cat Girl*, the gender-centric duo indeed went on to become one of AIP's biggest hits.

Music Editor: Lloyd Young
Assistant Technical Effects: Flora M. Gordon
Assistant to Producer: Henry Schrage
Cast: Glenn Langan (Lt. Col. Glenn Manning), Cathy Downs (Carol Forrest), William Hudson (Dr. Paul Linstrom), Larry Thor (Maj. Eric Coulter, MD), James Seay (Col. Hallock), Frank Jenks (Truck Driver), Russ Bender (Richard Kingman), Hank Patterson (Henry), Jimmy Cross (Sergeant at Reception Desk), June Jocelyn (Nurse Wilson), Stanley Lachman (Lt. Cline), Harry Raybould (MP at Main Gate), Jean Moorhead (Woman in Bathtub), Scott Peters (Sgt. Lee Carter), Myron Cook (Capt. Thomas), Michael Harris (Police Lt. Keller), Bill Cassady (Lt. Peterson), Richard Nelson (Sgt. Hansen), Edmund Cobb (Dr. McDermott), Paul Hahn (Attendant), Diana Darain (Hospital Receptionist), Lyn Osborn (Sgt. Taylor), Jack Kosslyn (Lieutenant), William Hughes (Bombsite Officer), Keith Hetherington (TV Anchorman), John Daheim (Soldier), Harold Miller (Official)

Synopsis: After being exposed to a plutonium explosion, Colonel Glen Manning inexplicably mutates into a giant.

The new kid in town, American International Pictures, really hit its stride in 1957 with eight fantastic film releases, all aimed at the teenage drive-in market. This Bert I. Gordon production cynically cashed in on Universal's smash hit *The Incredible Shrinking Man,* even tweaking the former film's title to its own designs. Unlike the earlier film, *The Amazing Colossal Man* is a clumsy, lumbering movie that carries none of the subtlety of its prototype, but then again, AIP was concerned only with short-term boxoffice results, not quality entertainment. Producer/director Gordon had gotten his feet wet with this type of picture with *King Dinosaur* (1955) and *The Cyclops* (1957), and released another "gigantic" picture this same year, *Beginning of the End.* Gordon's obsession with gigantism made for some pleasant if myopic B-movie entertainments. *The Amazing Colossal Man* tries to make the case that being a giant freak is as emotionally stressful as being a shrunken midget, but neither the elementary basic premise nor the perfunctory performances carry off the conceit. Possibly the film's one claim to greatness is a one-second-long shot at the film's start, so quick as to be almost subliminal, which shows the titular man being burned alive by the initial blasts of an atomic explosion. This rather gruesome shot effectively conveys the collective horror of puny man standing naked against a hell-force he cannot control, and is a far better moment than anything which follows it. For sure, the film's disappointing climax, wherein Manning is struck by gunfire and falls to his death over a dam, is so badly filmed via Gordon's patently awful optical effects, that it sours the viewer who previously had any sympathy for the film. This shameless "get it in the can" attitude on the part of AIP ruined several potentially good films, at least in the early years of the firm.

Most likely coincidentally, the tragic fate of the "Amazing Colossal Man" functions nicely as a simplistic allegory for the trajectory of America following World War II. When Colonel Glen Manning is "exposed" to the burst of plutonium at Ground Zero he is irrevocably changed, and can never return to his innocent, "pre-atomic" self. Manning mutates into a giant: fearsome and seemingly invincible. Likewise, when America first unleashed the horrors of atomic power on the world, with the unfathomable crimes of Hiroshima and Nagasaki, it quickly evolved into the premiere world power, with the frightful power of the mighty atom used both to silence the citizenry at home and terrify other nations into abject obedience to America's newfound global supremacy on the world political stage. But both Manning and America are also made grotesque freaks by their atomic apotheosis, and both grow perhaps "too big" for their own good. Significantly, the reason that Colonel Manning is doomed to certain death after his miraculous transformation is that his *heart* has not grown as quickly or effectively as the rest of his being, and so cannot pump the blood needed for continued survival. This most intriguing condition of Manning's personal tragedy may serve as a sloppy yet not ineffective symbol of America's "overnight" growth into a fearsome juggernaut of technocratic world power, with the Military-Industrial Complex being the most visible extension of this neo-imperialist force. This force, growing exponentially due to rapid scientific and technical advancement beyond its sponsors' wildest dreams, was expanding — according to at least some observers — at a rate faster than its accompanying ethical maturation. In short, America's "heart" — that is, its moral sense — did not grow on equal footing with its intellectual progress, allowing it to commit the crimes of a dumb, blind, lumbering beast with no moral center or overarching ethical purpose. As Manning clutches his failing heart, one may also sense America's pain at growing too fast for its collective health, of forgoing its humanitarian responsibilities.

The use of the "Amazing Colossal Man" as symbol for postwar America is given an even more portentous — and virtually comical — aspect due to the bizarre fact that the bald, glowering Manning-as-giant bears an uncanny physical resemblance to then–U.S. president Dwight Eisenhower, certainly *the* preeminent emblem of postwar America as a techno-military state. Thus, Manning's slow personal disintegration due to a failing heart may eerily mirror that of Eisenhower himself, who had heart problems throughout his presidency and, in fact, suffered a significant stroke on November 25, 1957 — the exact moment when *The Amazing Colossal Man* hit its stride in national release. As Eisenhower also represented (literally as well as figuratively) the forces of conservatism in American socio-political affairs for almost the entire decade, one might even see the eventual death of the "Amazing Colossal Man" as a metaphor for the end of conservatism in American life, as liberal forces were gathering on the horizon, preparing to catapult America into the convulsive yet cathartic 1960s.

As noted, it would be difficult to prove that the screenplay for *The Amazing Colossal Man* addressed any of these themes in a conscious, deliberate way, and it is best to see these parallels as amusing coincidences. However, it may be worth noting that scenarist Mark Hanna would soon pen a superficially similar screenplay — *The Astounding Giant Woman* (which would eventually morph into *Attack of the 50-Foot Woman*) — which treated the same subject matter as clever, conscious satire. Hanna's "giant woman" screenplay also included another most conspicuous male giant, here almost certainly intended to evoke the specter of President Eisenhower as representative of a antediluvian neo-militaristic empire spiraling completely out of control and threatening the world with utter annihilation through its vapid, infantile excesses.

Cat Girl

76 minutes/Black and White
Produced by Insignia Films
Distributed by American International Pictures
Directed by Alfred Shaughnessy
Screenplay: Lou Rusoff
Presented by Nat Cohen, Stuart Levy
Executive Producer: Peter Rogers
Produced by Lou Rusoff, Herbert Smith
Cinematography: Peter Hennessy

Young "cat girl" Barbara Shelley is haunted as much by her burgeoning sexuality as her inherited tendency towards sociopathology in the moody and contemplative *Cat Girl*.

Editing: Jocelyn Jackson
Production Design: Jack Stevens
Art Director: Eric Saw
Hair Stylist: Nina Broe
Makeup Artist: Philip Leakey
Production Manager: John W. Greene
Assistant Director: William Hill
Sound Recordist: Len Page
Camera Operator: Paddy A'Hearne
Wardrobe Mistress: Vi Murray
Music by: John Addison, Kenneth Essex, Robert Gill, Frank Spencer
Continuity: Olga Brooks
Animal Trainer: Frank Farrar
Cast: Barbara Shelley (Leonora Johnson/Brandt), Robert Ayres (Dr. Brian Marlowe), Kay Callard (Dorothy Marlowe), Ernest Milton (Edmund Brandt), Lily Kann (Anna), Jack May (Richard Johnson), Paddy Webster (Cathy), John Lee (Allan), Edward Harvey (Doorman), Martin Boddey (Cafferty), John Watson (Roberts), Frank Atkinson (Guard), John Baker (Male Nurse), Selma Vaz Dias (Nurse), Geoffrey Tyrrell (Caretaker)

Synopsis: A young woman suffers from a familial curse in which she becomes a predatory feline at night that kills human prey.

American International was hungry for product in its first two years of existence, and so courted Anglo-Amalgamated, a low-rent British distribution outfit, to supply a second feature for their showcase offering, *The Amazing Colossal Man*. Leaving the creation of a monster movie for dumbed-down American teens to the Brits might not have been such a great idea, for while *Cat Girl* is an intriguing rip-off of producer Val Lewton's immortal *Cat People* (1942, d: Jacques Tourneur), it is far too mature and contemplative to be the "spook show" that drive-in teens were looking for.

Still, the film as it stands today is remarkable in its portrayal of some rather complex adult situations, and Barbara Shelley is marvelous in the lead role. Shelley plays Leonora, a sublimely tragic figure — a mentally fragile newlywed who has a devastating family background (which may include incest with a creepy uncle) as well as a two-timing bounder for a husband. In short, Leonora's life under patriarchy has been nothing but torturous suffering and servitude, and her periodic lapses into a bloodthirsty spotted leopard, although seen as a curse, in many ways seems a badly-needed release for the timid, repressed soul. Indeed, Leonora is essentially conspired against by all of humanity, so her "other self" seems a downright justified connection to the maligned animal kingdom.

A common theme in fantastic films of the day, seen as well in *Blood of Dracula* and *She Devil*, is the ritual transformation of a "normal" female into a sinister, savage, and homicidal creature. Useful as simple metaphor for the emergence of formerly suppressed autonomous urges within the subject, it is, in effect, an ill-fated effort to birth what might be considered a proto-feminist archetype. Of course, in these vehicles the "female monster" is considered a bad, evil, dangerous thing, as her existence and freedom threatens society — specifically, established phallo-centric culture, which expects women to serve or ignore but never subvert or challenge maledom. This primary message is reinforced by the fact that the heroine's killer self often, if not always, targets male enemies and female sexual rivals as her victims. Yet the "message within the message" — that being the inevitability and/or advantage of bursting one's patriarchal shackles to forge an independent creature — can be seen by anyone caring to look. As well, the split between "civilized" woman and "primitive" animal mirrors the observed psychological split between rational man and savage beast existing in potential within every human being, and exemplified simplistically in parables such as *Dr. Jekyll and Mr. Hyde*.

As with other films designed primarily for teens, in *Cat Girl* it is the elders who consciously conspire against the young generation. This is seen both in Leonora's "curse," clearly depicted as something passed down from the older generation to the younger, and Leonora's sinister, daft uncle, who acts the part of a domineering father figure without the compassion or mercy a real parent would (ideally) have. The uncle, in fact, seems duty-bound by ancient dictates to terrify Leonora and further weaken her already shaky constitution; he drags the poor girl, virtually against her will, into a "secret room" full of grotesques dioramas depicting savage felines devouring terrified humans.

In a plot twist which mirrors a recurring theme in the year's fantastic cinema, Leonora is told that under no circumstances may she bear young, or her "curse" will continue in the next generation. This notion of the evil of breeding by accursed individuals loudly echoes eugenist sentiments of the period, which decried the indiscriminate breeding of mental inferiors and criminal personalities. Further, this taboo also mirrors the greater harm of procreation by all human beings — that being the indefinite perpetuation of a species seen by many as defective, dangerous, and even downright evil. Certainly the "curse" of mankind is carried on by every child birthed by indifferent or oblivious parents, a "curse" that will continue until Man is no more.

In the final reel, Leonora, who seems to have accepted her bestial self, stalks and attempts to kill another woman, following her into a lonely part of town before summoning her feline self to attack. Here, Leonora's targeting of a rival takes on the sinister aspect of a sexual stalking, as if she wants not to eliminate but mate with this mirror of her better sexual self. Another subtle, undeveloped moment which suggests thwarted lesbian longing occurs earlier when a creepy old female servant stares at Leonora as she undresses, taking great pains to comment on her apparently lithesome naked body. These unfocused, awkward moments also suggest an ill-conceived attempt by Leonora to connect politically with her sisters in spirit, a task doomed to failure because patriarchy has successfully convinced her that all women are enemies and rivals for the attentions of men, not potential sources of friendship, love or solidarity.

American International undoubtedly knew that this slow-moving, complex film had limited audience appeal as submitted, so they commissioned effects wizard Paul Blaisdell to quickly come up with a "cat monster," which ended up being one of Blaisdell's trademark ghoulish headpieces worn by an uncredited actor in leotards. Oddly, the two brief scenes of the Blaisdell beast are so fuzzy that one can hardly see a thing; was this yet another example of Nicholson and Arkoff's absolute disregard for quality control in the early days, or was this optical sabotage deliberate, an attempt to obfuscate what may have been an especially primitive monster mask? Either way, the effect on the viewer is one of dreamlike disorientation — one wonders what, if anything, he actually saw, and in spite of themselves, the awkward inserts actually enhance the trance-like quality of this most intriguing film.

October

The Black Scorpion

88 minutes/Black and White
Produced by Amex Productions, Frank Melford-Jack Dietz Productions
Distributed by Warner Bros. Pictures
Directed by Edward Ludwig
Screenplay: David Duncan, Robert Blees
Story: Paul Yawitz
Produced by Jack Dietz, Frank Melford
Music: Paul Sawtell, Jack Cookerly
Cinematography: Lionel Lindon
Editing: Richard L. Van Enger
Art Director: Edward Fitzgerald
Assistant Directors: Jaime Contreras, Ray Heinze
Sound Effects: Mandine Rogne
Sound: Rafael L. Esparza
Special Effects: Willis O'Brien, Wah Chang
Animator: Peter Peterson
Additional Effects: Ralph Hammeras
Conductor: Paul Sawtell
Orchestrator: Bert Shefter

Cast: Richard Denning (Hank Scott), Mara Corday (Teresa Alvarez), Carlos Rivas (Artur Ramos), Mario Navarro (Juanito), Carlos Múzquiz (Dr. Velazco), Pascual García Peña (José de la Cruz), Fanny Schiller (Florentina), Pedro Galván (Father Delgado), Arturo Martínez (Major Cosio), Bob Johnson (Narrator)

Synopsis: Volcanic eruptions unleash mammoth, carnivorous scorpions in Mexico.

Perfunctory exposition mars this potentially thrilling monster movie, which only comes to life when the title beasts appear. When the scorpions do emerge, they really knock your socks off. Brought to life via a winning combination of exquisitely-rendered animation (by Willis O'Brien, of *King Kong* fame) and an adequate prop headpiece (replete with rolling eyes and drooling mandibles), the scorpion's creepy look and even creepier slithering around make the monster scenes nightmarish. Best of all, several scenes show the monster brutally stinging and preparing to eat (miniature) people, an act of horror that is often implied but rarely shown in fantastic '50s cinema. There is also a nightmarish scene in a dank cave, where giant scorpions, spiders and earthworms fight each other for dominion. Too bad the rest of the film is so very pedestrian. Still, this is far better than the overrated *Them!* (1954, d: Gordon Douglas), and shows that Warner Brothers had by now at least figured out how to make a believable prop headpiece! Like *Kronos*, much of *The Black Scorpion* is set in Mexico, featuring several sympathetic "Latin-flavored" characters. This may have been the movie studios' pathetic attempt to pander to a new segment of their audience — the postwar influx of Puerto Rican immigrants. The Mexicans here are patronizingly portrayed as primitive, superstitious but good-hearted simpletons. A better screenplay might have made *The Black*

Expressionistic poster art for *The Black Scorpion*, Warner Brothers' attempt to repeat the success of their previous giant monster hits *The Beast from 20,000 Fathoms* (1953) and *Them!* (1954).

Scorpion a classic, but it is still a somewhat entertaining entry in the 1957 "monster movie" sweepstakes.

Boxoffice magazine liked *The Black Scorpion* quite a bit — understandable, as it was a relatively "big" offering from a respected studio rather than a low-budget "quickie" from an upstart independent distributor:

Another demonstration — and an impressive one — of the growing trend toward decentralized production, this hair-raiser was fabricated by Frank Medford and Jack Deitz, a pair of filmmakers who long since established their respective abilities for making every budgetary buck do yoeman's service. Because the picture was filmed in its entirety in Mexico, against breathtakingly beautiful scenic backgrounds, and inasmuch as most of the footage resulted from out-of-doors photography, its physical mountings are exceptional for a feature of its category. It is a cross between science-fiction and horror-play and as such should exert a strong appeal to those sizable segments of ticket buyers who relish film fare of either classification. Resultantly, the offering assays as prime supporting fare and in many instances can top a dual program without any apologies necessary from the exhibitor who so books it. Particularly praiseworthy are the special effects which make more realistic than usual the outsize monsters indicated by the title, which in this instance get away from the overworked mutation approach. Performances — generally competent and noteworthy in the case of Richard Denning — and Edward Ludwig's direction is geared to action, chills and suspense rather than finesse.[36]

The Invisible Boy

90 minutes/Black and White
Produced and distributed by Metro-Goldwyn-Mayer
Directed by Herman Hoffman
Screenplay: Cyril Hume
Story: Edmund Cooper
Produced by Nicholas Nayfack
Music by Les Baxter
Cinematography: Harold Wellman
Editing: John Faure
Art Director: Merrill Pye
Set Decoration: Darrell Silvera
Production Manager: Gus Schroeder
Assistant Director: Bert Chervin
Recording Supervisor: Fred Lau
Sound Editor: Cathey Burrow
Special Effects by Irving Block, Louis DeWitt, Jack Rabin
Casting Supervisor: Lynn Stalmaster
Conductor: Les Baxter
Orchestrator: Albert Harris
Cast: Richard Eyer (Timmie Merrinoe), Philip Abbott (Dr. Tom Merrinoe), Diane Brewster (Mary Merrinoe), Harold J. Stone (Gen. Swayne), Robert H. Harris (Prof. Frank Allerton), Dennis McCarthy (Col. Macklin), Alexander Lockwood (Arthur Kelvaney), John O'Malley (Prof. Baine), Robby the Robot (Robby), Rayford Barnes (Capt. McLaren), Gage Clarke (Dr. Bannerman), Helen Kleeb (Miss Vandergrift), Alfred Linder (Martin/Computer), Marvin Miller (Robby the Robot), Michael Miller (MP at Gate), Alvy Moore (Scientist), Jefferson Dudley Searles (Prof. Foster), Gary Vinson (Young Soldier), Ralph Votrian (MP at Gate), Than Wyenn (Prof. Zeller)

Synopsis: An omniscient super-computer creates its own evil consciousness and attempts to take over the world.

Although the more creative science-horror films usually emanated not from the big studios but relatively low-budget independent filmmakers, there are always exceptions to

Two-page trade advertisement for MGM's magnificent *The Invisible Boy*, successful follow-up to the previous year's hit sci-fi spectacular, *Forbidden Planet*, and featuring that film's undeniable "star" — Robby the Robot — here misleadingly shown as a behemoth crushing men in its mammoth claws, an understandable if spurious allusion to 1957's obsession with gigantism.

the rule. Hollywood powerhouse MGM really hit the mark with this fantastic serio-comic fantasy, which ruminates thoughtfully on the postwar American family, the perilous bridge between childhood and maturity, the Homeric seeking of wisdom, and, of course, the fatal seduction of technology. Thanks to a hell of a screenplay, a solid cast and the marvelous f/x work of Rabin, Block and DeWitt, *The Invisible Boy* stands as the unquestioned champion of fantastic 1957 cinema.

A scientist-dad has created a massive, nuclear-powered super-computer, which is ensconced deep underground in a top-secret military installation, nicely symbolizing the inherently secretive nature of the Military-Industrial Complex that has consistently used obfuscation and deceit to hide its size, whereabouts and goals. The "boy" of the film, Timmy, is a precocious, terribly average child until the supercomputer brainwashes him for its own nefarious purposes, after which Timmy has miraculously gained several IQ points. One of "super–Timmy's" first acts is to create a working robot out of a pile of discarded techno-rubbish in his father's closet, a remarkable feat which clarifies the robot's role as allegorical character.

The star of the film (even receiving top billing) is Robby the Robot, the beautiful man-machine first featured in *Forbidden Planet* (1956). The voluptuous curves of the metallic giant give it a profoundly soft, even quasi-feminine look, alluding both to the soft planes of a favorite stuffed animal and a mother's comforting breasts. As mentioned elsewhere, the very "50s" paradigm of "boy and robot," of which *Tobor the Great* (1954) may be the first cinematic example, involves a young boy who becomes emotionally, even sexually attached to a mechanical man that was essentially "birthed" by the child's father. The resultant "boy toy" thus stands as both surrogate father and surrogate sibling, as well as a highly fetishized emblem of the youngster's budding sexuality, often combining phallic imagery with other assorted technological symbology to fashion a metallic "uber-penis" that mirrors in concrete form the boy's potential psycho-sexual power on the cusp of puberty. Indeed, the ubiquitous robots of 1950s cinema and television were clearly intended as subliminal sex objects for American kids (males primarily, but not exclusively), erotic icons which neatly encapsuled the highly sexual fetishizing of technology (especially military), an overt agenda of popular postwar culture.

As Timmy is not only a son of patriarchy, but literally a "son" of the Military-Industrial complex, it follows that he would embrace technology almost as a religion and thus be vulnerable to the evil forces which lurk behind all technological advances, waiting for opportunities to spring and ambush their always-naive creators. Technology is truly the boy's "toy," just as modern technology, in all its evil glory, is seen by its creators as nothing more than their collective plaything.

Yet the father-inventor is even more naïve, truly believing that a project so monstrous as his atomic super-computer could be held in check against all possible mutation. After unsuccessful attempts to pass on knowledge to his reluctant student, Dad foolishly uses his super-computer to psychoanalyze his supposedly "troubled" child, giving the machine cherished personal information which it is able to use to blackmail its creator.

The prime directive of Robby is to do no harm to its creators and/or charges, a fine allegory for the essential moral structure of the human mind, without which all hell breaks loose and cruel barbarism is unleashed upon the world. Infantile phallo-centric culture wishes always to find a way to avoid or remove its own "prime directive" — that is, to eliminate all moral consideration from the use of technologically-based science. In other words, big "boys" seek to play recklessly with their monstrous "toys" without being chastised by "mother" (i.e., the moral self). Here, Timmy succeeds in circumventing Robby's basic directive and, in so doing, engages in increasingly dangerous acts of reckless folly, leading up to a potential "non-existence."

Timmy soon achieves a goal of the gods — invisibility — and uses his cloak of secrecy to further run roughshod over the rules of good behavior. Invisibility here is used primarily as a metaphor for the child wanting to escape adult notice and scrutiny, and thus avoid the terrifying prospect of adult responsibility, of having to "grow up," which certainly involves being "seen" and counted as a responsible member of adult society. In one of the most problematic but memorable scenes in the film, Timmy's parents take their son's newfound "non-existence" casually in stride, barely batting an eyelash when they first discover the horrible secret. The parents are thus portrayed as either entirely too permissive, or possibly even uncaring, towards their charge. Either way, the effect is chilling, as the adults seem indifferent, even happy, about this possible "removal" of the burden of caretaking. This somewhat duplicitous perspective towards child-rearing goes even one step further, as the film depicts several instances of corporal punishment (spanking and hitting), a common child-rearing tactic of the day but one not usually shown in graphic detail on film. There is even some gruesome reference to (unfulfilled) child torture. Childhood may be central to *The Invisible Boy*, but it is certainly not worshiped or glorified.

The monster computer eventually takes over several key military and scientific personnel, again tapping into common fears of "good" citizens turned into soulless automatons
dictated to by evil technocratic forces — a none-too-subtle stab at the then-current "bogey,"
Red Communism, but also clearly expressing subconscious fears of Americans becoming
slaves to an increasingly labyrinthine and sinister military-science cabal. Even Timmy and
Dad are ultimately powerless to stop the continued plans of their evil creation; it is significantly the child's robot-toy-penis surrogate, with its prime directive (i.e., moral center)
restored, which can intervene and finally destroy the otherwise unstoppable juggernaut of
technology run amok. The message could not be clearer: only a constantly maintained
morality can keep dangerous scientific and technological advances from becoming our worst
nightmares.

In a truly inspired coda, Dad — still not having learned his lesson — goes to slap Timmy
for some perceived infraction of the patriarch's hopelessly obsolete "law," but Robby the
moral guardian stops him cold, signaling that civilization must now progress beyond the
primitive barbarism of physical punishment, even when practiced "lovingly" as "discipline"
towards the young. As if to verify that Dad has got the message, he bequeaths Timmy a
shiny red apple, the preeminent symbol of transferred knowledge since ancient times, clar-
ifying that the passage of knowledge occurs not only from old to young but, more importantly, from the enlightened to the uninformed. By film's end it is clear that it was the
father, not the child, who needed to "mature" into a moral being, and it was the child who
lead the father to his moment of ethical awakening, demonstrating that wisdom may bloom
at any age and that it is never too late to "get smart."

Boxoffice magazine noted an interesting marketing technique used to ballyhoo *The
Invisible Boy*:

> Producer Nicholas Nayfack and director Herman Hoffman will promote their MGM release,
> "The Invisible Boy," with a direct tie-in with the International Geophysical Year. The science-
> fiction feature, follow-up to Nayfack's "Forbidden Planet," will highlight a space platform in its
> ads, much the same as that being publicized in connection with the Geophysical Year published
> plans. Trailer material will mention the current world scientific cycle, highlighting the similarity
> of the new space travel discoveries that are included in the plot of the picture.[37]

The Man of a Thousand Faces

Produced by Universal International Pictures
Distributed by Universal Pictures
122 minutes/Black and White
Directed by Joseph Pevney
Story: Ralph Wheelwright
Screenplay: R. Wright Campbell, Ivan Goff, Ben Roberts
Produced by Robert Arthur
Music by Frank Skinner, Milton Rosen, Edward Ward
Cinematography by Russell Metty
Editing by Ted J. Kent
Art Directors: Alexander Golitzen, Eric Orbom
Set Decoration: Russell A. Gausman, Julia Heron
Costume Design: Bill Thomas
Makeup Artists: Jack Kevan, Bud Westmore
Unit Manager: Edward Dodds

This trade advertisement for *The Man of a Thousand Faces*, a treacly biographical portrait of make-up genius Lon Chaney, boasts astounding boxoffice business in early playdates, proving only that aggressive marketing can sell almost anything.

Assistant Director: Phil Bowles, Ray DeCamp
Sound Recordists: Leslie I. Carey, Robert Pritchard
Sound Editors: Robert L. Bratton, Edward L. Sandlin
Special Effects by Clifford Stine
Wardrobe: Marilyn Sotto
Orchestrator: Joseph Gershenson
Technical Advisors: Clarence Kolb, Marjorie Ramsey
Cast: James Cagney (Lon Chaney), Dorothy Malone (Cleva Creighton Chaney), Jane Greer (Hazel
    Bennet Chaney), Marjorie Rambeau (Gert), Jim Backus (Clarence Locan), Robert Evans (Irving
    Thalberg), Celia Lovsky (Mrs. Chaney), Jeanne Cagney (Carrie Chaney), Jack Albertson (Dr. J.
    Wilson Shields), Roger Smith (Creighton Chaney at 21), Robert Lyden (Creighton Chaney at 13),
    Rickie Sorensen (Creighton Chaney at 8), Dennis Rush (Creighton Chaney at 4), Nolan Leary (Pa
    Chaney), Simon Scott (Carl Hastings), Clarence Kolb (Clarence Kolb), Danny Beck (Max Dill),
    Philip Van Zandt (George Loane Tucker), Hank Mann (Comedy Waiter), "Snub" Pollard (Comedy
    Waiter)

Synopsis: A highly fictionalized biography of the movie make-up genius Lon Chaney.

This sappy and empty Hollywood bio-pic gets everything wrong from the word "go,"
including using as a male lead someone (James Cagney) who doesn't look a thing like the
person he was portraying (and is about twenty years too old for the part!). In addition,
several sources claim that the chronology of Chaney's life is highly fabricated and contains
only a very minor amount of historical truth. The focus on the various famous make-ups
compensates for some of these flaws, but overall this film, which falls into the "fantastic"
category only peripherally due to its subject matter, could not have been of much interest
to anyone but the diehard classic horror fan. Yet as lackluster as it is, the picture did well
in several premiere showcase situations, with *Boxoffice* magazine reporting U.S. grosses well
above average.[38] In addition, there was an auspicious premiere in London, "to which were
invited Boris Karloff, a long list of exhibitors and all the Chaneys in the London telephone
directory. U-I's drum-beater, John Nelson Sullivan, should have been more than amply
rewarded by the turnout of photographers for what was not an essentially glamourous
evening and by the space he received in the following day's press."[39]

The Abominable Snowman of the Himalayas

85 minutes/Black and White
Produced by Hammer Film Productions
Distributed by Twentieth Century–Fox Film Corporation
Directed by Val Guest
Story: Nigel Kneale (from his story "The Creature")
Screenplay: Nigel Kneale, Val Guest
Produced by Aubrey Baring
Executive Producer: Michael Carreras
Associate Producer: Anthony Nelson-Keys
Music by Humphrey Searle
Cinematography: Arthur Grant
Editing: Bill Lenny
Production Design: Bernard Robinson
Art Director: Ted Marshall
Costume Design: Beatrice Dawson
Makeup Artist: Phil Leakey

Trade advertisement for the deeply disappointing Hammer production *The Abominable Snowman of the Himalayas.* For honesty's sake, the tagline, "What did they see?" should have been followed by "Absolutely Nothing!"

Hair Stylist: Henry Montsash
Production Manager: Don Weeks
Assistant Directors: Robert Lynn, Hugh Harlow
Sound Recordist: Jock May
Camera Operator: Len Harris
Gaffer: Steve Birtles
Wardrobe: Molly Arbuthnot
Dress Designer: Beatrice Dawson
Musical Director: John Hollingsworth
Continuity: Doreen Soan
Cast: Forrest Tucker (Tom Friend), Peter Cushing (Dr. John Rollason), Maureen Connell (Helen Rollason), Richard Wattis (Peter Fox), Robert Brown (Ed Shelley), Michael Brill (Andrew McNee), Wolfe Morris (Kusang), Arnold Marlé (Lhama), Anthony Chinn (Majordomo), Fred Johnson (Yeti), John Rae (Yeti)

Synopsis: A group of explorers seek the legendary "Yeti" in the Himalayas.

Another dreadful bore from poor Hammer Films, who can't seem to get anything right. The dialogue-heavy exposition is marred by the thick accents of all involved. Much of the film is shot in medium to long shot, presumably to take advantage of the widescreen process, but succeeding only in distancing the audience even further from the scenario. The simplistic script by Nigel Kneale pits clashes of cultures, ideologies and moral values against each other to no avail; even a potentially interesting discussion of humanism versus misanthropy is botched by tedious delivery. It's hard to decide which is more risible: Peter Cushing's shameless scene-stealing or Forrest Tucker's clumsy scenery-chewing. Alas, the promised beast proves elusive to the explorers, and thus to the audience, depriving them even of this tiny thrill. When the beast is finally shown, it appears more like a hermit or caveman than a missing link, and one moody close-up does not a monster movie make. Even the revelation of the creature's capacities for mental telepathy comes too little, too late. The nihilistic ending, in which the local Lama either coerces or hypnotizes Cushing into denying what he saw, falls flat as a pancake, because after all the tedious drudgery which went before, we couldn't care less.

November

Rodan, the Flying Monster

(original production, *Sora no daikaijû Radon*, 1956)
70/72/74 minutes/Color
Produced by Toho Film Co. Ltd.
Distributed by Distributors Corporation of America (DCA)
Directed by Ishirô Honda
Screenplay: David Duncan (English-Language Version)
Screenplay: Takeshi Kimura, Ken Kuronuma
Story: Takeo Murata
Produced by Frank King, Maurice King (English-Language Version)
Produceed by Tomoyuki Tanaka
Music by Akira Ifukube
Cinematography: Isamu Ashida
Editing: Robert S. Eisen (English-Language Version)
Editing: Kôichi Iwashita

Production Design: Tatsuo Kita
First Assistant Director: Jun Fukuda
Sound Recordist: Masanobu Miyazaki
Director of Special Effects: Eiji Tsuburaya
Special Effects Art Director: Akira Watanabe
Special Effects Opticals: Hiroshi Mukoyama
Special Effects Assistant Camera: Sadamasa Arikawa
Cast: Kenji Sawara (Shigeru Kawamura), Yumi Shirakawa (Kiyo), Akihiko Hirata (Professor Kashiwagi), Akio Kobori (Police Chief Nishimura), Yasuko Nakata (Female Honeymooner), Minosuke Yamada (Chief Osaki), Yoshifumi Tajima (Izeki), Kiyoharu Ohnaka (Male Honeymooner), Ichirô Chiba (Police Chief), Mike Daneen (American Soldier), Tazue Ichimanji (Haru), Saburo Iketani (News Reader), Saburô Kadowaki (Sunagawa's colleague), Tateo Kawasaki (miner), Kanta Kisaragi (miner), Jirô Kumagai (Policeman Tashiro), Saeko Kuroiwa (Nurse), Tsuruko Mano (Osumi,), Mitsuo Matsumoto (Professor Isokawa), Hideo Mihara (Commander of JASDF), Kiyomi Mizunoya (Otami), Jun'ichirô Mukai (Military Officer), Toshiko Nakano (Kiyo's Neighbor), Rinsaku Ogata (Goro), Keiji Sakakida (Miner), Yasuhiro Shigenobu (Miner), Junnosuke Suda (Coroner), Shigemi Sunagawa (Pilot), Jirô Suzukawa (Miner), Masaaki Tachibana (Policeman), Bontaro Taira (Laborer), Kiyoshi Takagi (Dr. Minakami), Kamayuki Tsubono (Policeman of the Crime Laboratory), Mitsuo Tsuda (Takeuchi), Hideo Unagami, Akira Yamada (Radio Operator), Shôichi Hirose (Pilot), Ren Imaizumi (Sunagawa), Keiichirô Katsumoto (Employee), Fuyuki Murakami (Professor Minami), Haruo Nakajima (Rodan), Ichirô Nakatani (Senkichi), Yutaka Oka (Pilot), Tadashi Okabe (Journalist), Katsumi Tezuka (Hotel Manager), Yasuhisa Tsutsumi (Pilot), Kôji Uno (Reporter), Ren Yamamoto (Soldier)
Voices (English-Language Version): Paul Frees, Art Gilmore, Keye Luke, George Takei, James Yagi

Synopsis: Reckless mining excavations unleash prehistoric monsters.

After the success of Toho's inaugural behemoth epic *Gojira* (1954), the studio began a series of "monster movies" which lasted, in its first incarnation, for decades. Following the box-office success of the English-Language release of *Godzilla, King of the Monsters*, U.S. producers scrambled for more Japanese fantasy product to customize for American audiences. The King Brothers (Frank, Herman and Maurice) licensed the Toho production *Radon* (1956) for U.S. release. As opposed to the extensive surgery done to *Godzilla*, including the addition of expositional scenes with Raymond Burr, the Kings left the bulk of *Radon* intact, adding only a superfluous stock-footage prologue, implicating the H-Bomb for the horrors unleashed in the subsequent film. Hal Roach Jr.'s distribution company Distributors Corporation of America released *Radon* in 1957 as *Rodan, the Flying Monster* on a curiously racial-centic double bill with *Hell in Korea* (a misleadingly retitled British war film called *A Hill in Korea*).

Rodan is an exciting postwar fable marred only somewhat by an overzealous narrator and the recognizable cartoon voices of Paul Frees. Some of the dubbed dialogue lends towards the gruesome: "He was almost hacked to pieces!" The most interesting portion of the film is the first half, which concentrates on a small mining village and the socio-economic upheaval that occurs when one of the mine shafts becomes home to some fanciful monsters (giant carnivorous millipedes). Early scenes in the creepy, dreary mines are quite unnerving, possibly some of the best mine disaster footage ever committed to film (fantastic storyline notwithstanding). The protagonist, a miner called Shigeru, soon gets trapped in a cave-in and witnesses an event so horrible he blocks it from memory: giant eggs hatching, the birth of monsters, the unspeakable horror of new life. Two mammoth reptile birds, a male and a female, soon emerge from the caves and begin their assault on the modern world.

The second half of the film, which centers on the giant birds' attack on major Japanese cities, is far less emotionally engaging but still a worthy diversion. As do most of the Japanese monster movies, *Rodan* works best as spectacle, with Eiji Tsuburaya's special effects excellent throughout. An orgiastic military battle features endless rocket launchings and voluptuous explosions, a pure release of the phallo-centric death wish and illustrating vividly the Military-Industrial Complex's one great wish — to destroy everything in sight. The later destruction of a mammoth miniature city, primarily through wind effects, is nothing short of dazzling.

The finale, in which the two Rodans convulse in their death throes amidst the sputtering flames and lava of a raging volcano, are visual poetry of the purest kind, quite possibly one of f/x designer Tsuburaya's greatest single set pieces. The graceful movements of the twin bird marionettes evoke an aerial ballet, and as Shigeru and his mate watch this prehistoric couple dying together in a holy sacrifice, one senses the impending doom of the heterosexual social construct, buried alive by the raging fire-semen which gushes forth from the bowels of a tortured and enraged Mother Earth.

The Brain from Planet Arous and
Teenage Monster (Howco International)

Producers C. Francis White (aka J. Francis White) and Joy N. Houck (aka Joy M. Houck) had cut their production teeth on the long-running western film series starring "Lash" LaRue in the late 1940s and early 1950s. White and Houck each owned and operated successful movie theaters in Louisiana, Mississippi, Arkansas, Virginia, and North and South Carolina. In the early 1950s, along with filmmaker Ron Ormond, Houck and White formed a distribution company named Howco Productions (headquartered in New Orleans), which soon entered the exploitation market with films such as *Mesa of Lost Women* (1953, d: Herbert Tevos, Ron Ormond) and Ed Wood's notorious *Jail Bait* (1954). The company changed their corporate banner to Howco International in 1957, a nod to would-be competitors Universal-International and American International. In addition to this popular "weird horror" double bill, Howco released another youth-centric package the same year: *Carnival Rock,* produced and directed by Roger Corman, and *Teenage Thunder* (d: Paul Helmick).

An indication of how quickly these films were conceived and produced is offered by a blurb in the August 31 issue of *Boxoffice* magazine which stated that make-up genius Jack Pierce had just been signed to create the monster make-up for *Teenage Monster* (mentioned here under its working title *Monster on the Hill*), and which had yet to begin production.[40] As the double bill seems to have been available for bookings in late November or early December, it would imply that *Teenage Monster,* and probably *The Brain from Planet Arous* as well, were created entirely within a 12-week period.

The Brain from Planet Arous

71 minutes/Black and White
Produced by Marquette Productions
Distributed by Howco International Pictures
Directed by Nathan Juran (as Nathan Hertz)
Screenplay: Ray Buffum
Produced by Jacques Marquette
Associate Producer: Dale Tate

Louisiana-based Howco International Pictures had a national hit in 1957 with the wild horror-science fiction double bill of *The Brain from Planet Arous* and *Teenage Monster*.

Executive Producers: Joy N. Houck, J. Francis White
Music by Walter Greene
Cinematography: Jacques Marquette
Makeup Artist: Jack Pierce
Assistant Director: Bert Chervin

Bizarre Mexican lobby card for *The Brain from Planet Arous* which (as did much film advertising South of the border) utilized generic, pulp-oriented artwork unrelated to the actual movie being promoted.

Properties: Richard M. Rubin
Sound: Philip Mitchell
Stunts: Gil Perkins, Ken Terrell
Supervising Film Editor: Irving Schoenberg
Conductor: Walter Greene
Technical Advisor: J.L. Cassingham
Cast: John Agar (Steve March), Joyce Meadows (Sally Fallon), Robert Fuller (Dan Murphy), Thomas B. Henry (John Fallon), Kenneth Terrell (Colonel), Henry Travis (Colonel), E. Leslie Thomas (General Brown), Tim Graham (Sheriff), Bill Giorgio (Russian), Kenner G. Kemp (Military Man at Meeting), Dale Tate (Professor Tate/Gor/Vol)

Synopsis: An evil brain from outer space inhabits the body of a nuclear scientist in an effort to conquer the Earth.

This terrific SF melodrama goes to show that even the most tawdry and fantastical science-fiction premise can be successfully brought to life with brisk direction, a good screenplay, accomplished photography and a rousing music score. In this case Nathan Juran (who made his two most interesting "experimental" works under the pseudonym Nathan Hertz), Ray Buffum, Jack Marquette and Walter Greene, respectively, provided the talent which raises this pulp fiction nightmare to the level of low-brow film art.

In one of the movie's most notorious plot points, the alien possession of the protagonist makes him *more*, not less, sexual than before, an ironic twist on the emotionless alien takeovers in films such as *Invaders from Mars* (1953), *Invasion of the Body Snatchers* (1956) and *It Conquered the World* (1956). (Even the brain's home planet, "Arous," is an overt reference to the sexual goddess Eros, as well as sexual "arousal.") Actually, this film is more sociologically accurate in its assumption that sexual appetite in 1950s men (and women) was largely repressed, needing an outside force to energize it. However, it is also shown that an unbridled libido quickly turns violent, so a healthy sexual appetite ends up being the bogeyman after all.

The title brain is a magnificently absurd creation, purportedly a giant balloon illuminated from within, which is most effective in the finale when seen as a solid object interacting with the actors. Amazingly, *The Brain from Planet Arous* touches on almost *all* of the salient themes in 1957 fantastic cinema: guilt/fear regarding the atom bomb, atomic mutation, transformation of the personal self, fear of sexual expression, facial deformity, the consequences of runaway technology, fear of alien invasion, and the immanent destruction of planet earth. Only the long-suffering, sexually retrograde heroine seems a step backwards. This film's production team (Hertz, Marquette, and producer Dale Tate) would get together once more to create what is perhaps the quintessential social satire of the 1950s: *Attack of the 50-Foot Woman* (1958), a stunning proto-feminist fairy tale which was years ahead of its time, eerily foreshadowing in stark symbolist terms the emergence of feminism into the cultural mainstream.

Teenage Monster (aka *Meteor Monster*)

65 minutes/Black and White
Produced by Marquette Productions
Distributed by Howco International Pictures
Directed by Jacques R. Marquette
Screenplay: Ray Buffum
Produced by Jacques Marquette
Associate Producer: Dale Tate
Executive Producers: Joy N. Houck, J. Francis White
Music by Walter Greene
Cinematography: Taylor Byars
Makeup Artist: Jack Pierce
Assistant Director: Kenneth Walters
Properties: Richard M. Rubin
Sound: Philip Mitchell
Supervising Film Editor: Irving Schoenberg
Conductor: Walter Greene
Technical Advisor: J.L. Cassingham
Wardrobe Supervisor: Jerry Bos
Cast: Anne Gwynne (Ruth Cannon), Stuart Wade (Sheriff Bob Lehman), Gloria Castillo (Kathy North), Charles Courtney (Marv Howell), Gilbert Perkins (Charles Cannon), Norman Leavitt (Deputy), Gabe Mooradian (Fred Fox), Stephen Parker (Charles Cannon as a Boy), Jim McCullough (Jim Cannon), Frank Davis (Man on Street), Arthur Berkeley (Man with Burro)

Synopsis: In the 1880s, a meteor from outer space kills a father and turns his son into a hideous monster.

In this delightfully absurd take on the Oedipal dynamic of lusting sons and sexually controlling mothers, all logic is thrown to the wind in exchange for some preposterous ruminations on the sexual tension between the sexes, and the generations. Taking place for no apparent reason in the back-lot Old West of a bad B-movie, the scenario thus becomes somewhat symbolic, lending a pseudo-historic authenticity to a plot which might have come across as unbearably perverse were it set in the present day. The odd setting also reframes the postwar ideal of the nuclear family (father-mother-child) as historical myth, making the subsequent events take on greater import.

The source of the family's meager income is a uranium mine, and the *deus ex machina* of the ensuing drama is a (presumably radioactive) meteor from outer space which kills the father and irradiates the son; thus the 1950's obsession with atomic energy is evoked, even in this antediluvian setting. After the father's divinely-inspired death, a classical Oedipal dynamic ensues, with the widow and her now-teenage son forming a conspiratorial alliance, an unholy pact triggered by the father's involuntary absence. The teenaged Charles is hilariously portrayed as a retarded, whining, buck-toothed, drooling idiot of a thing, hairy and hunched over like an ape or a caveman. In short, Charles is meant to symbolize the pubescent teenage male, both as he often appears to his own, self-loathing person, and equally as often to his detractors. Hiding in the dark, skulking and complaining, attacking authority when he is able to, and mumbling indecipherable gibberish in response to Mother's constant commands—this is clearly meant to be an expressionist manifestation of the proverbial "tortured adolescent."

The classically dominating Mother uses shame as her main control tool, yet also perversely holds out the possibility of incest with promises like, "You can have anything you want ... *anything*." Yet the deranged matriarch makes her poor son work the uranium mine like a day laborer, forcing him to live in the caves like a lowly animal—Charles is literally her slave, sexual and otherwise. Periodically, Charles escapes his torturous confinement to go out and murder, apparently choosing all male victims, a predilection which nicely symbolizes expressed anger towards the father for abandoning him to this monstrous female dictator. Yet the murders are also posited as releasing some sort of thwarted sexual urges— as killer, Charles also represents the potentially destructive force the sexually repressed teenager can have in the community.

Eventually, Mother and Charles move to a new house "in town" in a hilarious nod to the presumptuous American notion of "upward mobility," and in this faux-suburban setting the couple become an amusing grotesquerie of the iconic postwar "nuclear family," a notion made even more comical by the fact that their worldly "success" is directly due to the divine intervention of "nuclear" assets (the uranium mine and the atomic meteor). Soon, Mother tries to raise her social station by dating the town's Sheriff, making him (and thus all authority figures) literally, as well as figuratively, Charles' rival for Mother's attentions, and his primary nemesis. In a subsequent fit of rebellion which smacks of Freudian castration, Charles beheads his horrible little clown doll, nicely underscoring the sociopathic nature of this eternally adolescent male. Finally, Charles can contain his thwarted Mother-lust no longer, so he kidnaps a local tart and brings her home, ostensibly as a plaything to replace his broken dollie. To hide his new "toy" from Mother, Charles stuffs the poor girl in the closet, a rather hilarious metaphor for suppressed sexual urge.

Yet in one of the screenplay's best plot twists, the young innocent Charles kidnaps is anything but—Kathy is the town slut, as debased and mercenary as any seasoned grifter.

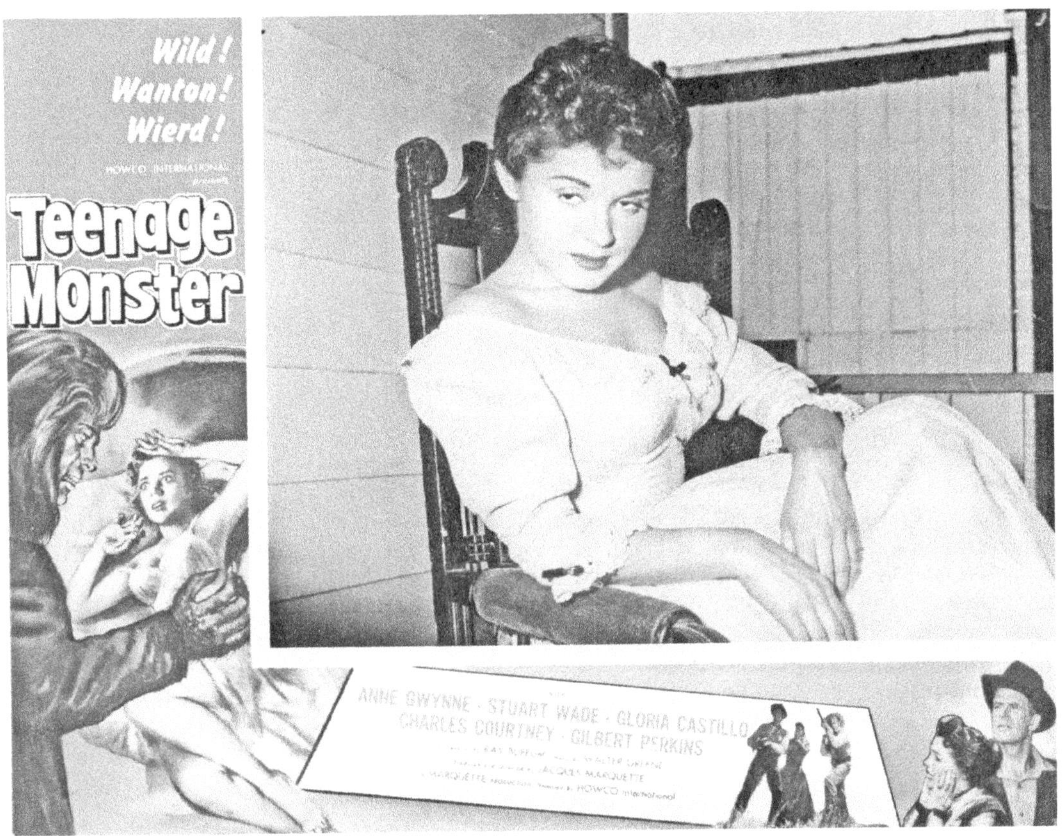

Sexy Gloria Castillo as she appeared in *Teenage Monster*, playing a most unusual 1957 archetype —the completely amoral female teenager.

The scenario thus repositions Charles not as a diabolical force unleashed against a moral community, but merely another player in a corrupt social environment; indeed, perhaps Charles is the only "innocent" in town. Like Mother, conniving Kathy easily dupes poor Charles into doing her bidding, which quickly escalates to murder. Kathy is a true sociopath — she watches a gruesome murder with unabashed glee. Her rationalization: "Because I've been used. I've been cheated and robbed by everybody...." This confession likely also refers to sexual violation, probably starting at an early age, by all the local males. With the introduction of Kathy, women *in toto* are painted as evil, crafty creatures who can easily harness male sexual energy to their own advantage. Yet the unabashedly sexist scenario additionally portrays women as inferior, even comic villains, because they are not smart enough to keep their "trap" shut, to refrain from spilling their plans to the enemy!

In a most perverse incarnation of the clichéd "star-crossed lovers," Charles and Kathy both eventually fall off a cliff to their deaths, mimicking the timeless tale of teenage tragedians Romeo and Juliet and their terrible mutual fate. *Teenage Monster* is a most absurd atomic fable, with unusually strong sexual subtext and a dark-as-pitch perspective on the "modern" family, greatly enlivened by moody photography, an anachronistic but appealing western milieu, and an emphatic score by Walter Greene which cannily mirrors Charles' sexual energy by alternating strident martial cues with lusty polka-esque tempos.

The Story of Mankind

Produced by Cambridge Productions
Distributed by Warner Bros. Pictures
100 minutes/Technicolor
Directed by Irwin Allen
Story: Henrik Van Loon (from his novel)
Screenplay: Irwin Allen, Charles Bennett
Produced by Irwin Allen
Associate Producer: George E. Swink
Music: Paul Sawtell
Cinematography: Nicholas Musuraca
Editing: Roland Gross, Gene Palmer
Art Director: Art Loel
Costume Design: Marjorie Best
Assistant Director: Joseph Don Page
Sound Mixer: Stanley Jones
Music Editors: Leon Birnbaum, Robert Tracy
Cast: Ronald Colman (the Spirit of Man), Hedy Lamarr (Joan of Arc), Groucho Marx (Peter Minuit),
    Harpo Marx (Sir Isaac Newton), Chico Marx (Monk), Virginia Mayo (Cleopatra), Agnes Moore-
    head (Queen Elizabeth I), Vincent Price (Scratch), Peter Lorre (Nero), Charles Coburn (Hip-
    pocrates), Cedric Hardwicke (High Judge), Cesar Romero (Spanish Envoy), John Carradine
    (Khufu), Dennis Hopper (Napoleon Bonaparte), Marie Wilson (Marie Antoinette), Helmut Dan-
    tine (Marc Antony), Edward Everett Horton (Sir Walter Raleigh), Reginald Gardiner (William
    Shakespeare), Marie Windsor (Josephine Bonaparte), George E. Stone (Waiter), Cathy O'Donnell

**Francis X. Bushman in the role he was born to play — Moses of the Old Testament — from Irwin
Allen's stupendous pseudo-historical omnibus *The Story of Mankind*.**

(Christian Woman), Franklin Pangborn (Marquis de Varennes), Melville Cooper (Major Domo), Henry Daniell (Bishop of Beauvais), Francis X. Bushman (Moses), Jim Ameche (Alexander Graham Bell), David Bond (Christian), Nick Cravat (Devil's Apprentice), Dani Crayne (Helen of Troy), Richard Cutting (Court Attendant), Anthony Dexter (Christopher Columbus), Toni Gerry (Wife), Austin Green (Abraham Lincoln), Eden Hartford (Laughing Water), Alexander Lockwood (Promoter), Melinda Marx (Child), Bart Mattson (Cleopatra's Brother), Don Megowan (Early Man), Marvin Miller (Armana), Nancy Miller (Early Woman), Leonard Mudie (Chief Inquisitor), Burt Nelson (Early Man), Tudor Owen (High Tribunal Clerk), Ziva Rodann (Egyptian Concubine), Harry Ruby (Indian Brave), William Schallert (Earl of Warwick), Reginald Sheffield (Julius Caesar), Abraham Sofaer (Indian Chief), Bobby Watson (Adolf Hitler), Sam Harris (Nobleman), Angelo Rossitto (Dwarf)

Synopsis: A cosmic tribunal decides the fate of Mankind.

This truly amazing, if failed, attempt at high-concept fantasy was purportedly based on a history book, but the story source is merely used as an excuse for numerous vignettes of notable moments in world history. The pretentious framing device has a court of law residing in the heavens, with Ronald Colman as an angel defending Man, and Vincent Price as the Devil, decrying him. According to the judge, Man has come to a fateful crossroads since he invented "the Super H-Bomb" 60 years before he was supposed to! The Gods must decide if Mankind is mature enough to handle such awesome power, in a plot device so common to SF films of the 1950s, where the "gods" were played by benevolent (or malevolent) space creatures who worried not only for the Human Race, but the fate of the Universe as well.

Nancy Miller and Don Megowan play "Early Woman" and "Early Man" in Warner Brothers' epic historical-fantasy flop *The Story of Mankind*.

The bulk of the film consists of truly horrendous re-enactments of major world events, with the heroes or villains of the event portrayed by big name stars such as Hedy Lamarr, Cesar Romero and Groucho Marx. The film comes across largely as an errant, foppish spectacle with highly Christian overtones, probably influenced by Cecil B. DeMille's box-office smash of the previous year, *The Ten Commandments*. Liberal use of Warner Brothers stock footage lends the film a bigger air than its medium-sized budget deserves, but the awkward juxtaposition of straightforward melodrama, satire and parody never gels, and some of the portrayals are downright embarrassing. Especially egregious are John Carradine as an apparently retarded Pharaoh, Agnes Moorehead as a frumpy Queen of England, and Dennis Hopper, who plays Napoleon like a mumbling beatnik doofus. More amusing are Robert Watson as a nerdy Hitler and Peter Lorre as a truly deranged Nero.

The overt Christian propaganda in the film grows tiresome after a while; for instance, Moses is canonized as the man who found the "one true god," while the angel Colman offers the fantastic notion that every single god Man worshipped before Jesus came was a "false god!" Several times throughout the film Colman utters an absurd disclaimer to the effect that "whether this is history or myth, it still stands as testimony to Man's greatness!" And indeed, fables like Moses on the mountain are treated as equal in historical import to the French Revolution and the U.S. Civil War, making *The Story of Mankind* a very heavy-handed piece of Christian propaganda if nothing else. Also treated very badly are women, who are largely portrayed via historical figures like Helen of Troy and Cleopatra as being inherently evil and the ruiner of men.

After what seems like a millennium, the whole thing ends in a stalemate, with some hasty "Man of Tomorrow" pleading for the continuance of the species. Throughout the fiasco the Devil gets all the good lines, and his arguments are far more convincing than the angel's pathetic attempts to balance centuries of wanton slaughter with some pleasant artwork and clever inventions. As the Devil rightly states, "Man is a charlatan and a fool!" (The ongoing debate between angel and devil would be repeated to good effect in Taylor Caldwell's strange novel *Dialogues with the Devil*, a correspondence between Satan and Saint Peter in which the Dark One wins his argument that Man is inherently evil and should no longer be allowed to contaminate the universe.)

Indeed, perhaps one of the reasons *The Story of Mankind* failed so miserably during its holiday season release is not that it is embarrassing to its many stars, and fails both as comedy or spectacle, but the fact that the Devil's arguments are so hard to refute. You come away from this film really seeing that Man is a lunatic maniac and should be immediately eradicated from the face of the Earth. Maybe this wasn't the "happy holiday" message 1957 audiences wanted. There must be some reason why Warner Brothers has consistently refused to release this film on home video, and only this year offered it in a pricey, made-to-order DVD "archive" edition. Still, producer Irwin Allen learned much from this notorious debacle; he would go on to great fame as a creator of TV series such as *Lost in Space*, and all-star disaster epics such as *The Poseiden Adventure*. Who knew back then that *The Story of Mankind* would be Allen's first "epic disaster?"

The Hunchback of Notre Dame

(original production, *Notre-Dame de Paris*, 1956)
104 minutes/France-Italy/Color

Produced by Panitalia, Paris Film Productions
Distributed by Allied Artists Pictures Corporation
Directed by Jean Delannoy
Story: Victor Hugo (from his novel)
Screenplay: Jean Aurenche, Jacques Prevert, Ben Hecht
Produced by Raymond Hakim, Robert Hakim
Music by Georges Auric
Cinematography by Michel Kelber
Editing by Henri Taverna
Production Design: René Renoux
Costume Design by Georges K. Benda
Makeup Artist: Louis Bonnemaison, Georges Klein
Wig Maker: Huguette LaLaurette
Hair Stylist: Jean Lalaurette
Production Manager: Ludmilla Goulian
Unit Manager: Paul Laffargue
Second Assistant Directors: Joseph Drimal, Alain Kaminker
Assistant Director: Pierre Zimmer
Set Dresser: Maurice Barnathan
Assistant Decorators: Alfred Marpaux, Jean Taillandier, Pierre Tyberghein
Sound: Jacques Carrère
Special Effects by Gérard Cogan
Assistant Camera: André Delille, André Domage
Camera Operator: Wladimir Ivanov
Still Photographer: Raymond Voinquel
Grip: Victor Lanoux
Wardrober: Emmanuel Bourassin, Léon Zay
Dress Maker: Catherine, Raymonde
Dresses: Veniero Colasanti
Assistant Editors: Marie-Louise Barberot, Ginou Bretoneiche
Dance Music: Angelo Francesco Lavagnino
Musical Director: Jacques Métehen
Choreographer: Léonide Massine
Administrator: Léo Spohr
Script Girl: Claude Vériat
Cast: Gina Lollobrigida (Esmeralda), Anthony Quinn (Quasimodo), Jean Danet (Phoebus de
    Chateaupers), Alain Cuny (Claude Frollo), Robert Hirsch (Pierre Gringoire), Danielle Dumont
    (Fleur de Lys), Philippe Clay (Clopin Trouillefou), Maurice Sarfati (Jehan Frollo), Jean Tissier
    (Louis XI), Valentine Tessier (Aloyse de Gondelaurier), Jacques Hilling (Maitre Charmolue), Jacques
    Dufilho (Guillaume Rousseau), Roger Blin (Mathias Hungadi), Marianne Oswald (La Falourdel),
    Roland Bailly (the Hangman), Piéral (the Dwarf), Camille Guérini (the President), Damia (the
    Beggar), Robert Lombard (Jacques Coppnole), Albert Rémy (Jupiter), Hubert de Lapparent (Guil-
    laume de Harancourt), Boris Vian (the Cardinal), Georges Douking (Thief), Paul Bonifas (Master
    Lecornu), Madeleine Barbulée (Madame Outarde), Albert Michel (Night Watchman), Daniel
    Emilfork (Andry le Rouge)
Synopsis: Paris, 1482: An unemployed playwright is rescued from certain death by a gypsy woman,
    who agrees to marry him as he is about to be executed by a band of thieves. Elsewhere, a deformed
    misfit is bullied by an evil alchemist who becomes obsessed with the gypsy woman and uses the
    poor hunchback to lure her into his clutches.

The Hunchback of Notre Dame was an attempt by Allied Artists to "go big" with a
classy, large-budget production in 1957, considered by some to be the "major-minor's" best
overall year. Although low-cost double bills such as *Attack of the Crab Monsters/Not of This*

Gina Lollobrigida undergoes torture in Allied Artists' big-budget interpretation of Victor Hugo's *The Hunchback of Notre Dame*.

Earth and *Teenage Doll/Undersea Girl* were still the studio's "cash cows," garnering the bulk of boxoffice receipts, the studio was attempting at this time to compete with the major studios by producing and releasing what might be called "little big pictures," such as *Hunchback* and *Love in the Afternoon*. *The Hunchback of Notre Dame* was also one of the first films to capitalize on a new phenomenon, the European film production created for an international market. Many consider Roger Vadim's *And God Created Woman* (U.S. release 1957) to be the first "foreign" production to hit it big in U.S. theaters, and there soon followed a veritable wave of such releases, primarily from France, Italy, Germany and Spain. Although the 1957 U.S. fantastic film release schedule shows a preponderance of domestic product, "foreign" cinema was well represented thanks to *The Hunchback of Notre Dame, Unnatural: The Fruit of Evil, The Blonde Witch, Rodan, the Flying Monster* and *Half Human*, making 1957 a somewhat "international" year. As the 1950s blossomed into the 1960s, the foreign film in America became an increasingly important part of the marketplace, and the 1960s was definitely the decade of what might be somewhat derisively called "the cheap foreign import" — a tag which could be applied to cars, appliances and pop songs as well as films — in which a quality product with relatively high production values could be obtained from overseas sources more cheaply than a comparable product procured from domestic U.S. sources.

This version of Victor Hugo's story is mounted as a giant spectacle, played as a broad comedy-opera, and offers lavish production values. Unfortunately, as the production features many non–English actors, they are overdubbed in cartoony voices spouting hyperbolic dialogue, trivializing what might have otherwise worked as a very "Shakespearean" costume drama. Perhaps the big-budget European historical spectacle, or costume drama (an admirable genre on many levels), was a form doomed to became dated and anachronistic almost at the moment of its birth due to the inevitable cultural lag time between its Eurocentric conception and (for instance) American exhibition. Popular culture, especially in the U.S., was accelerating ever faster as the decade waned, too fast to hold onto the more traditionalist narrative anchors of the typical European film. Although desperately trying in many cases to be universal in its appeal, the European film created for the international market was all but certain to appear quaint, even backwards, to more trendy "nationalistic" audiences such as those in the U.S. The death knell for many of these films was the hasty, careless, and often almost satirical dubbing of the script into English which, while making the story easily accessible to U.S. audiences, tended to distance the film from the viewer, who was constantly reminded that this was a "foreign" movie due to the strange, often cartoon-like voices coming out of the actors' mouths. *The Hunchback of Notre Dame* is a good example of a film which — despite its many charms — likely appeared somewhat "odd" to its original U.S. audience, and may appear downright antediluvian to viewers today. Still, from this moment through the mid–1970s, the "foreign import" film was a viable, salable and entertaining clone of similar domestically-produced products.

Italian sexpot Gina Lollobrigida is the "star" of this film, illustrating how (as Vadim did so successfully with Brigit Bardot in *And God Created Woman*) European producers sweetened their product for the international marketplace by creating a comely, identifiable "star" and using this person as a "brand" to ensure interest in subsequent films featuring same. Yet Lollobrigida's earthy charms are completely negated by the film's one bad — indeed fatal — casting choice, understandable in hindsight yet still lamentable. Aside from his assuredly good intentions, Anthony Quinn turns the character of Quasimodo into a pathetic cartoon freak, overtly gruesome and entirely unlovable. Quinn's manic pantomime is off-putting enough, but for some unknown reason the producers also allowed the character to speak often and liberally, with an embarrassing "special needs" voice that reduces the spectacle to the level of a Saturday Matinee cartoon.

Still, Allied Artists went all out with this "prestige" production — one of the bigger pictures in their 1957 release schedule — even creating a four-page "Photoplay Study Guide" which theater exhibitors were encouraged to purchase in bulk and offer gratis to local schools as an "educational resource" for students of classic literature. The comprehensive guide, prepared by Frank A. De Lisi of Rutgers University, discusses the film in detail, including setting, main characters and director Jean Delannoy, even taking care to underscore novelist Victor Hugo's main theme in the book, translated faithfully to the screen version: the malefic forces of Fate trump the pretentious aspirations of free will every time.[41] Elsewhere, theater owners launched such predictable marketing gimmicks as a "Nickname for Gina Lollobrigida" contest in which, according to *Boxoffice* magazine, "A $25 savings bond went for the best suggestion, with 15-runnersup getting pairs of guest tickets. A truck float toured the downtown section of the city for three days."[42]

For the Discussion and Appreciation of

THE HUNCHBACK OF NOTRE DAME

An Allied Artists Production

Prepared by FRANK A. DE LISI, Rutgers University

Edited by WILLIAM LEWIN, Ph.D.

Esmeralda, out of pity, offers water to the suffering Quasimodo.

THE AUTHOR

A man of extraordinary versatility and almost unbelievable luxuriance of imagination, Victor Hugo, for sheer quantity and power in writings of every description, stands among the giants of world literature. His triumphs in the fields of poetry, drama, and fiction, exhibiting his resources of fertility, inspiration, and creation, have given the world some of its greatest classics.

Hugo was not only a writer; he plunged headlong into the politics of France, using the power of his pen to advance his liberal principles.

At the age of 39, Hugo was elected to the French Academy in recognition of his genius. At 69, he was elected to the National Assembly in recognition of his patriotism. At 74, he was elected to the French Senate in recognition of the esteem with which he was held by the French people. At his death in 1885, he was given the funeral of a hero of France and was buried in the Pantheon in Paris.

THE SETTING

The awe-inspiring Cathedral of Notre Dame casts its brooding shadow over the square which becomes in the photoplay a stage where scenes of violence, terror, pity, and pathos, play out their action.

What scenes of life, love, and death have those gargoyles witnessed throughout the centuries! At once majestic and sublime, formidable and wondrous, Notre Dame stands unruffled and unperturbed in all its ancient, Gothic splendor against the impacts of human passion.

CHIEF PLAYERS

Esmeralda	GINA LOLLOBRIGIDA
Quasimodo	ANTHONY QUINN
Phoebus	JEAN DANET
Claude Frollo	ALAIN CUNY
Clopin Trouillefou	PHILIPPE CLAY
Fleur de Lys	DANIELLE DUMONT
Gringoire	ROBERT HIRSCH
Mathias Hungadi	ROGER BLIN
La Falourdel	MARIANNE OSWALD
Louis XI	JEAN TISSIER
Jehan Frollo	MAURICE SARFATI

CHIEF PRODUCTION CREDITS

Producers, Robert and Raymond Hakim for Allied Artists. **Director,** Jean Delannoy. **Photographer,** Michael Kelber. **Production Manager,** Ludmilla Goulian. **Film Editor,** Henri Taverna. **Sound Engineer,** Jacques Carrire. **Art Director,** Rene Renoux.

TYPE AND THEME

SET in medieval Paris, THE HUNCHBACK OF NOTRE DAME is the tragic, melodramatic story of Esmeralda, a beautiful gypsy girl; of Quasimodo, a deformed bell-ringer; and of Frollo, a sinister archdeacon—all of whose lives become inextricably entangled through the queer workings of fate. His imagination fired by the Greek word for doom, ANAGKA, which he saw carved in one of the towers of Notre Dame Cathedral, Victor Hugo shaped a story to show this theme: evil destiny, not free will, influences the lives of people.

THE STORY

In 15th-century Paris, on the day of The Feast of Fools, boisterous students interrupt the performance of Pierre Gringoire's morality play, *The Quest for Beauty.* Then they participate in the festivities where Esmeralda (Gina Lollobrigida), a gypsy, is singing and dancing for the people of Paris.

Claude Frollo (Alain Cuny), archdeacon of Notre Dame Cathedral and an alchemist, tries to clear the noisy throng from the square because the merry-makers disturb his work. When Frollo is roughly handled, his servant, Quasimodo (Anthony Quinn), the hunchbacked bellringer of the cathedral, rescues him from the mob.

The people then begin to select the King of Fools, a title awarded to the ugliest man in Paris. Esmeralda spies the malformed Quasimodo and suggests he be crowned.

Front page of a "study guide" created for Allied Artists' *The Hunchback of Notre Dame.* **Theater managers were encouraged to order these by the thousands and pass them out to local schools as education-oriented publicity.**

December

THE MAN WITHOUT A BODY AND FRIGHT
(BUDD ROGERS RELEASING CORPORATION)

This double bill consisted of pick-ups of two independently-produced films, released in tandem by one Budd Rogers, a most enigmatic player in the low-budget movie distribution market. It may be merely coincidental that both films were either directed or produced by W. Lee Wilder, or it may suggest that Wilder owned U.S. rights to both films and licensed them to Rogers for distribution; Rogers also mounted a limited 1956 re-release for Wilder's *Phantom from Space* (1953). Very little is known about Rogers, other than the fact that he held the rights to a small library of late–1940s Hollywood productions, such as *The Dark Mirror* (1946, d: Richard Siodmak), *Magic Town* (1947, d: William Wellman), *Secret Beyond the Door* (1948, d: Fritz Lang) and *Mr. Peabody and the Mermaid* (1948, d: Irving Pichel), all of which he graced with 1955 theatrical releases before leasing them to National Telefilm Associates some time later for television syndication purposes. Oddly enough, however, neither *The Man Without a Body* nor *Fright* seem to have made it into any known TV syndication package, languishing for decades before turning up unceremoniously on budget DVD labels. It is likewise difficult to pinpoint the exact release dates of this double bill, as no mention of it was made in the major trade publications. From the National Screen

The body of a megalomaniac plus the head of Nostradamus — *The Man Without a Body*.

Service numbers on the poster material, however, it may be surmised that the package was released late in the year, possibly as late as December.

The Man Without a Body

80 minutes/Black and White
Produced by Filmplays Ltd.
Distributed by Budd Rogers Releasing Corporation
Directed by Charles Saunders, W. Lee Wilder
Screenplay: William Grote
Produced by Guido Coen
Music by Albert Elms
Cinematography: Brendan Stafford
Editing: Tom Simpson
Art Director: Harry White
Hair Stylist: Ivy Emerton
Makeup Artist: Jim Hydes
Production Manager: John "Pinky" Green
Assistant Director: William Lang
Sound Recordist: Cyril Collick
Camera Operator: Tony Heller
Conductor: Albert Elms
Continuity: Splinters Deason
Cast: Robert Hutton (Dr. Phil R. Merritt), George Coulouris (Karl Brussard), Julia Arnall (Jean Cramer), Nadja Regin (Odette Vernet), Sheldon Lawrence (Dr. Lew Waldenhouse), Peter Copley (Leslie), Michael Golden (Nostradamus), Norman Shelley (Dr. Alexander), Stanley Van Beers (Madame Tussaud's Guide), Tony Quinn (Dr. Brandon), Maurice Kaufmann (Chauffer), William Sherwood (Dr. Charot), Edwin Ellis (Publican), Donald Morley (Stock Broker), Frank Forsyth (Detective), Kim Parker (Maid — Suzanne), Ernest Bale (Custom's Officer)

Synopsis: A wealthy industrialist with a brain tumor enlists the aid of a mad doctor in order to extend his life.

This wildly implausible yet utterly engaging melodrama, co-directed by the iconoclastic W. Lee Wilder, is perhaps the most inherently absurd "fantastic" film released in 1957, deftly juggling adult themes (adultery, murder, betrayal) with a preposterous sci-fi premise. The main character, Karl Brussard (well played by George Colouris) is a self-made Capitalist, and his subsequent breakdown and ruin stands as apt metaphor for the pitfalls inherent in the expansionist philosophy of that troubled socio-economic system. Brussard encounters a local mad doctor who claims that he can, in theory at least, abate his death sentence with a revolutionary new brain transplant experiment.

A most disturbing early scene in the doctor's lab shows a living monkey's head grimacing in agony over its diabolical fate at the hands of human monsters. Thus begins the wonderfully ludicrous science-fiction angle of the film, as Brussard first travels to Madame Tussaud's Wax Museum to sample some of history's most brilliant minds. The megalomaniac decides that French philosopher/prophet Nostradamus is the head for him and miraculously finds an alcoholic medico willing to exhume the ancient's perfectly reserved noggin! Brussard smuggles the famed seer-head into Great Britain under a plaster bust and soon has his mad doctor regenerating the head via his laboratory gizmos. The head comes to life and tele-pathically communicates with his captors, deduces that Brussard is a lunatic, and sabotages him with faulty financial advice.

George Coulouris undergoes brain testing under the guidance of Julia Arnall in W. Lee Wilder's fantastic horror fable *The Man Without a Body*.

As if the scenario couldn't get nuttier, another implausible plot twist necessitates the grafting of Nostradamus' head onto the body of a fallen lab assistant, creating a truly absurd creature and catapulting the film right into "monster movie" territory. Nostradamus' head is encased in an immense, bandage-wrapped contraption which makes the resultant creature look like a walking molar tooth; yet this grotesque "giant head" stands well as a metaphor for man's immense, insatiable ego bursting out of his tiny cranium to wreak all sorts of havoc on himself and his world. The creature, and Brussard, soon fall to their timely deaths in an old school building; as the monster falls, it is conveniently beheaded, and Nostradamus' severed head may once again find peace, removed from the lunatic designs of modern man. The grim, noirish quality of this highly allegorical film, in harness to a silly pulp-fiction plot, make it a most affable and interesting entry in the 1957 fantastic film canon.

Fright

(aka *Spell of the Hypnotist*, original production released in 1956)
68 minutes/Black and White
Produced by Planet Filmplays
Distributed by Budd Rogers Releasing Corporation
Directed by W. Lee Wilder

Screenplay: Myles Wilder
Produced by W. Lee Wilder
Music by Lew Davies
Cinematography: J. Burgi Contner
Editing: Robert Gardett, L. Robert Harris
Makeup Artist: Josephine Cianelli
Sound Mixer: Walter Wood
Optical Effects: Arthur Jackson
Lighting Technician: Harold Kraus
Wardrobe Supervisor: Bernard Shapiro
Conductor: Lew Davies
Cast: Nancy Malone (Ann Summers), Eric Fleming (Dr. James Hamilton), Dean L. Almquist (Cullen), Frank Marth (George Morley), Humphrey Davis (Prof. Charles Gore), Elizabeth Watts (Lady Olive Fitzmaurice), Walter Klavun (Warden), Amelia Conley (Miss Ames), Tom Reynolds (City Editor), Robert Gardett (Managing Editor), Norman MacKaye (Inspector Blackburn), Ned Glass (Taxi Driver), Donald Douglas (Inspector II — Lt. White), Sid Raymond (Van Driver), Philip Kennealy (Cop), Chris Bohn (TV Announcer), Norman Burton (Reporter), Alney Alba (Guest), Jimmy Little (Joe the Bartender)

Synopsis: A disreputable psychiatrist encounters a neurotic young woman and a convicted killer, and brings them together for a diabolical experiment.

Certainly the grimmest film inspired by the notorious "Bridey Murphy" regression case of 1952, *Fright* features a ludicrous premise that creates a fascinating and morbid story

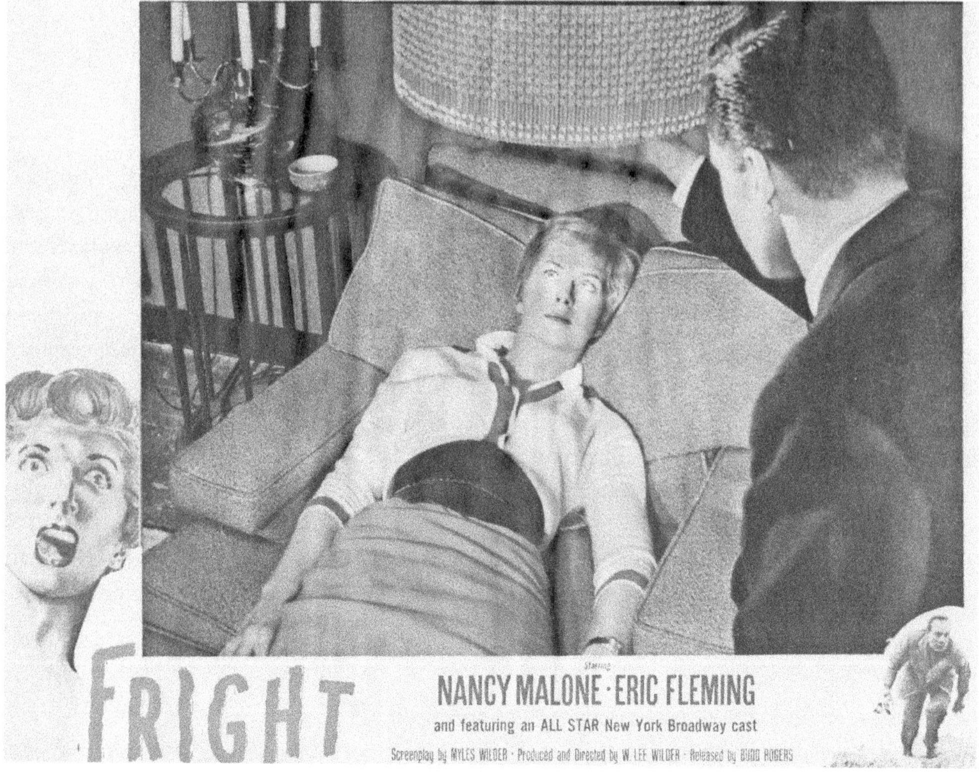

Nancy Malone falls under the spell of a hypnotist with decidedly ambiguous morals in W. Lee Wilder's exemplary *Fright*.

about the fragility of identity and the burden of conscience. Opening sequences are filmed on location in Manhattan, prominently featuring landmarks like the Brooklyn Bridge and the United Nations. In this way, *Fright* aligns itself with other "New York Noir" films of the period like *Violated* (circa 1953) and *Killer's Kiss* (1955). However, the bulk of the film is shot in a nondescript urban environment which is as generic as it is lackluster.

The screenplay takes a most problematic view of the new science of psychiatry by presenting as its main protagonist a severely conflicted professional whose womanizing past and nihilistic present make for a most unstable force. He crosses path with a disturbed young woman (Nancy Malone in a marvelous performance) who appears to be channeling memories of a past life as a teenage German girl forced to commit suicide by a brutal lover. The doctor is unclear whether the woman is actually accessing a past life or merely suffering a trauma-induced split personality, so he decides to try a daring experiment to seek the truth; he brainwashes a convicted killer to think of himself as the spurned historical lover of which the woman speaks of.

In a startling finale, the doctor traps the mad killer in a small room with the neurotic innocent, even leaving a gun for the killer to use against his prey. Through the cathartic and highly metaphoric fake murder of the woman's alter ego by the killer-under-hypnosis (the gun holds blanks), the woman is "cured" of her delusions and/or real ancient memories, and the killer is returned to death row. One may consider this act as merely cruel and reckless, or demonstrably immoral and illegal, but it paints a most ruthless picture of the psychiatric profession. The loss of self affected by the young woman's frequent lapses into her "other self" are consciously foisted upon the criminal via the doctor's machinations, implying that the psychiatric profession was ruled by a bunch of opportunistic hacks. The portrayal of a predatory, highly intrusive press is not much better, with W. Lee Wilder depicting modern society as rife for exploitation by those very forces supposedly dedicated to the service of the community. The real monster in *Fright* is the medical profession, and its victims appear to be the whole of society.

I WAS A TEENAGE FRANKENSTEIN WITH *BLOOD OF DRACULA* (AMERICAN INTERNATIONAL PICTURES)

American International's biggest year to date continued with these late releases designed to ride the momentum of AIP's hit *I Was a Teenage Werewolf/Invasion of the Saucer Men* double bill. Production of the two films started in mid–September, and they were ready for market a mere eight weeks later, as was true of so many of the so-called "quickie" pictures. (According to *Boxoffice* magazine of September 7, 1957, another AIP production slated to film in September was "She Came from 5,000 AD," to be produced and directed by Roger Corman! This project, of course, evolved into *Terror from the Year 5000*, produced and directed by Robert Gurney, Jr., and released in 1958.)[43]

I Was a Teenage Frankenstein

74 minutes/Black and White, and Color
Produced by Santa Rosa Productions
Distributed by American International Pictures
Directed by Herbert L. Strock

Screenplay by Herman Cohen, Aben Kandel (as Kenneth Langtry)
Produced by Herman Cohen
Executive Producers: James H. Nicholson, Samuel Z. Arkoff
Music by Paul Dunlap
Cinematography: Lothrop B. Worth
Art Director: Leslie Thomas
Set Decoration: Tom Oliphant
Makeup Artist: Phillip Scheer
Production Manager: Austen Jewell
Assistant Director: Austen Jewell
Property Master: James R. Harris
Sound: Al Overton
Sound Effects Editor: Kay Rose
Wardrobe Master: Einar Bourman
Editorial Supervisor: Jerry Young
Music Editor: George Brand
Script Supervisor: Mary Gibsone
Production Secretary: Barbara Lee Strite
Cast: Whit Bissell (Frankenstein), Phyllis Coates (Margaret), Robert Burton (Dr. Karlton), Gary
    Conway (Bob), George Lynn (Sgt. Burns), John Cliff (Sgt. McAffee), Marshall Bradford (Dr. Ran-
    dolph), Claudia Bryar (Arlene's Mother), Angela Blake (Victim), Russ Whiteman (Dr. Elwood),

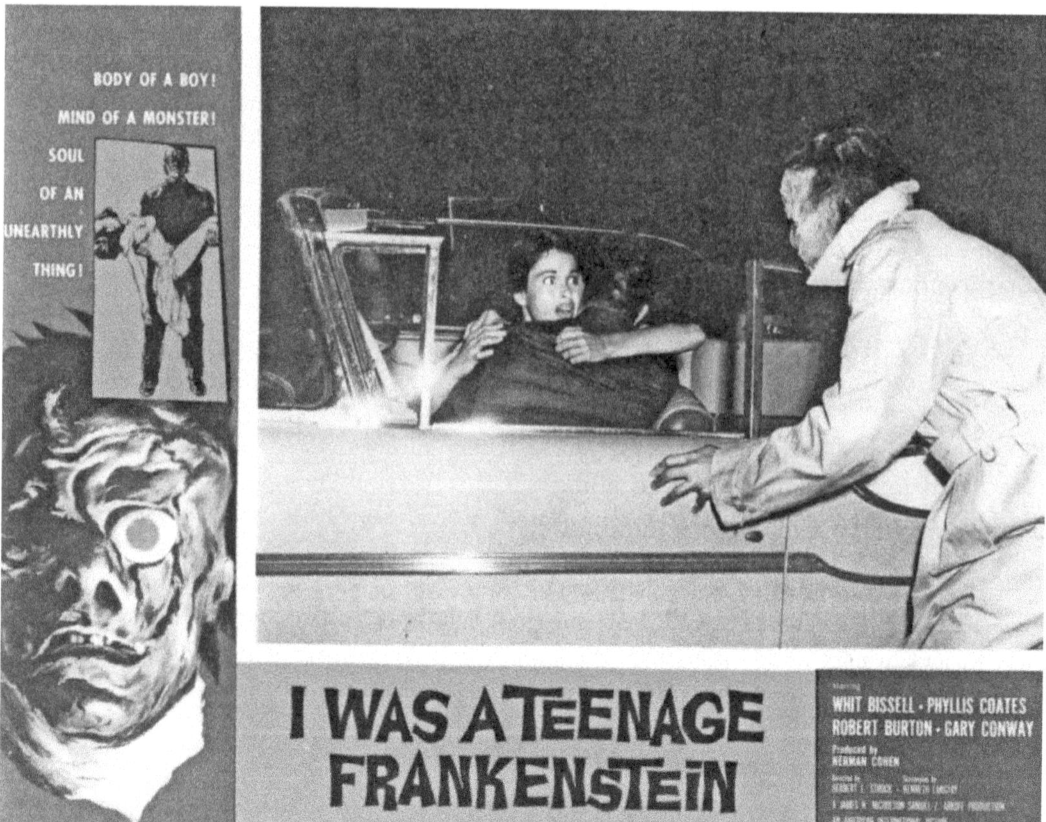

Gary Conway (or, more likely, a stunt double) attacks teenage smoochers in American International's smash hit *I Was a Teenage Frankenstein*.

Charles Seel (Sexton), Paul Keast (Man), Gretchen Thomas (Woman), Patrick Miller (Police Officer), Joy Stoner (Arlene), Larry Carr (Young Man), William H. O'Brien (Boarder)

Synopsis: A mad doctor makes a monster out of dead teenagers.

American International Pictures' cynical follow-up to *I Was a Teenage Werewolf* was rushed into theaters to take advantage of the current Frankenstein fad brought on by Hammer's inexorable *Curse of Frankenstein*, and Screen Gems' release to television of many of the Universal horror film classics, including James Whale's exemplary *Frankenstein* (1931). *Teenage Frankenstein* is even worse than its predecessor, a mean feat in that the scenario was promising enough: a mad doctor stitches together a new being from the limbs of teenage auto-crash victims. This gruesome premise is buried by the predictable, sterile Herman Cohen production, and for some ungodly reason the remarkably dull Whit Bissell was brought back to play the villainous adult. Also, Gary Conway isn't as irritating as Michael Landon, but he ain't much better. The monster's facial deformity accurately, if simplistically, acts as metaphor for the teenage audiences' self-consciousness concerning the scourge of acne and other assorted pubescent horrors. A laughably truncated electrocution finale, filmed for no apparent reason in color, also fails miserably, proving that even in B-Movie Land, the right combination of screenplay, production and performance is everything.

Blood of Dracula

68 minutes/Black and White
Produced by Carmel Productions
Distributed by American International Pictures
Directed by Herbert L. Strock
Screenplay: Aben Kandel (as Ralph Thornton)
Produced by Herman Cohen
Executive Producers: James H. Nicholson, Samuel Z. Arkoff
Music by Paul Dunlap
Cinematography: Monroe P. Askins
Editing: Robert Moore
Production Design: A. Leslie Thomas
Set Decoration: Tom Oliphant
Makeup Creator: Phillip Scheer
Production Manager: Austen Jewell
Assistant Director: Austen Jewell
Property Master: James Harris
Sound: Herman Lewis
Sound Effects Editor: Kay Rose
Wardrobe Supervisor: Florence Hayes
Music Editor: George Brand
Conductor: Paul Dunlap
Script Supervisor: Mary Gibsone
Production Secretary: Barbara Lee Strite
Cast: Sandra Harrison (Nancy Perkins), Louise Lewis (Miss Branding), Gail Ganley (Myra), Jerry Blaine (Tab), Heather Ames (Nola), Malcolm Atterbury (Lt. Dunlap), Mary Adams (Mrs. Thorndyke), Thomas B. Henry (Mr. Paul Perkins), Don Devlin (Eddie), Jeanne Dean (Mrs. Perkins), Richard Devon (Det. Sgt. Stewart), Paul Maxwell (Mike), Shirley De Lancey (Terry), Michael Hall (Glenn), Craig Duncan (Police Officer), Edna Holland (Miss Rivers), Carlyle Mitchell (Stanley Mayther), Voltaire Perkins (Dr. Lawson), Barbara Wilson (Ann), Jimmy Hayes (Joe), Lynn Alden (Linda)

Synopsis: A troubled teenage girl is sent to a boarding school where a manipulative older woman turns her into a homicidal maniac.

This third and final installment in American International Picture's canny "teenage monster" series is by far the best, another example of early AIP product having some profound adult themes haphazardly mixed in with adolescent hi-jinks. In this entry the emphasis is on female empowerment, with repressed same-sex urges a major subtext. Indeed, the whole scenario can be seen as a treatise on unrequited lesbian longing, told in simplistic, allegorical fashion through the horror-lens of vampirism. The oftimes overt homosexual overtones of *Blood of Dracula* is even hinted at in the film's two working titles, *I Was a Teenage Dracula* and *I Was a Daughter of Dracula*. One wonders why this exemplary psycho-sexual horror fable was buried at the bottom of a double bill with the woeful *I Was a Teenage Frankenstein* and saddled with a dreary, generic title; perhaps the steamy sexual subtext was seen as a little over-the-top for teenage drive-in audiences, and AIP wanted to "underplay" the film's existence.

The film starts off strongly, as troubled young Nancy (a veritable "Nancy-Boy" of same-sex mythos) is being driven to boarding school by her emotionally distant father and sleazy stepmother. Nancy desperately wants to stay at home and not be forced into this premature adult adventure; she grabs the automobile's steering wheel from the father, attempting to drive the car off the road and kill them all. Nancy thus represents the archetypal proto-feminist female "taking the wheel," as it were, away from a corrupt and uncaring patriarchal system which has thus far failed her. When male-dominated balance is regained shortly, mother, father and daughter share an adult conversation about the perils of emotional maturity, as each smokes a cigarette; the fact that Nancy is allowed to smoke with her parents is a significant, potentially scandalous concept.

Upon arriving at school, Nancy is immediately "hazed" by her classmates, forced into a humiliating initiation in which all of her personal belongings are picked over and mocked. The leader of this secret sorority, hilariously dubbed the "Birds of Paradise," tells Nancy in no uncertain terms that no rebels are allowed, and only utter conformity to the group will ensure her subsequent survival here. It is revealed anon that these "Birds of Paradise" take turns dating the only male on campus, a dullard handyman named Eddie; this revelation clearly positions the female collective as politically omnipotent and sexually predatory.

Next we meet the villain and/or *deus ex machina* of the piece, depending on your point of view, a middle-aged educator named Miss Branding who comes across from the beginning as a fierce iconoclast. She tells a pupil, "We live in a world ruled by men, for men," thus announcing herself as the female principle personified. It turns out that Branding is working on some mysterious alternative energy sources, and although her theses are constantly rejected by patriarchal interests, she believes that her new energy has the power to save the world from the horrors of male-dominated science, which is essentially just big bombs. When Branding coos to her protégé, "There is a power strong enough to destroy the world within each of us," we know that she means to destroy the *male* world, and that the power she speaks of is the power of female-female love. Branding reveals her agenda when she comments to her all-female class, "We have a bouquet of *very* pretty girls!"

Branding soon zeroes in on Nancy, who she sees as a "disturbed girl, but with a will of her own," presumably the kind of young female who is easily seduced. What ensues is a "master-slave" psycho-sexual dynamic quite similar to the male-centric ones in *I Was a*

Teenage Werewolf and *I Was a Teenage Frankenstein*, in which a secret pact between a charismatic elder and a vulnerable youngster alludes to some potentially disturbing sexual situations. Branding soon has young Nancy under her spell, thanks to an ancient cats-eye amulet. Branding thus "seduces" Nancy into accessing her inner self, in which the suppressed female rage of this victim of patriarchal tyranny can be unleashed, with powerful social and sexual implications.

The film stops dead in its tracks to revel in a silly choreographed scene in which a young male sings "Puppy Love," possibly one of AIP's first movie–pop song tie-ins. Yet the song does suggest that heterosexual love is "puppy love" — that is, immature (and presumably obsolete) "kid stuff" — whereas mature, highly evolved women seek the arms of other women.

Soon, Nancy is turning nightly into a fanged monster, killing her classmates left and right, as Branding stands by her window and sends powerful telepathic messages to her mental slave, clearly in a state of high sexual arousal. The killings — referencing the vampire mythos — are highly sexualized, as Nancy lustily bites the necks of her male and female victims with all the fervor of a hot kiss. The power of this sexualized violence is not lost on

This hilarious production still from American International's *Blood of Dracula* shows Louise Lewis donning makeshift radiation protection gear in anticipation of undermining patriarchy by appropriating the awesome energy of the split atom to her own gender-centric ends. The scene vividly illustrates the confusion with which the film's creators — and society in general — viewed the somewhat threatening notion of "the woman scientist."

Nancy's "master." After one such crime, Branding enters Nancy's dorm room to awaken her and sits coyly on the bed next to her, gently consoling her and saying, "How *pretty* you are after the night!"

The film's finale pivotally takes place during Halloween night, traditionally a time of great significance for all matrist societies. Originally called the Season of the Crone, Halloween was the time when high priestesses gathered their communities to celebrate the spirits of the deceased, the abundance of the harvest, and the perpetuation of the species via the children; in short, it was the pivotal event for celebrating female empowerment. The girls all prowl a spooky graveyard during a highly ritualistic "Scavenger Hunt," looking for all the world like witches cavorting in the ancient moonlight, honoring their dark gods. Meanwhile, Nancy commits two more ritual murders. The next morning one of the cops even states exasperatedly, "According to you, we oughta start a *witch hunt!*" cleverly intuiting the real motivation behind these murders.

Nancy and Branding soon have their inevitable confrontation in which Nancy breaks from her master's hypnotic (sexual) spell long enough to claim, "I feel a strength that's almost frightening!" referring to her burgeoning homosexual awareness. Nancy even confesses to Branding, when she tries to clear her mind, "All I see is you!"—about as clear a reference to sexual preference as one could hope for in this kind of vehicle. As if to verify these searing "flames" of aggressive sexuality which Branding transmits to her poor charge, a close-up of the elder woman dissolves into the image of a raging fire. Nancy's boyfriend finally shows up in the last reel to inquire why she hasn't written him. He finds her distant, aloof, and cold as a fish—he doesn't know that she has crossed the bridge to homosexual love. Nancy easily resists both the urge to kiss and to kill her boyfriend—the male holds no interest for her whatsoever.

In the final confrontation, Branding insists that Nancy continue to finish "their experiment," which by now is all but declared sexual in nature. Nancy, however, has seen the sexual agenda for what it is, merely a sophisticated pick-up: "I know who you are...." Slave kills master, and good Nancy returns to her dull heterosexual world, none the wiser for the experience. In an amusing parting shot, the schoolmistress intones, "There is a power greater than Science that rules the earth." One wonders if she knows that this power is the sacred fluid of the female, the menstrual blood of the daughters of Lesbos—i.e., the "Blood of Dracula."

Blood of Dracula awkwardly—but not unsuccessfully—juggles two main conflicts. The first is generational, which is understandable considering the film's intended audience. As with several other films targeted primarily at teenagers, parents and teachers in *Blood of Dracula* are overtly portayed as "the enemy" in several pieces of dialogue, the film clearly attempting to align itself with its target demographic. Yet the teens are not the only ones who feel this way about authority figures—it is eventually revealed that the middle-aged Branding is actually rebelling against *her* elder, the head of the school, and so illustrating a generational war between male and female, and female against female, each generation vying for political and sexual control.

Yet the overriding theme in *Blood of Dracula* is surely that of a failed but noble grasp at female empowerment within entrenched power structures. Early in the film Branding breathlessly tells Nancy of her ultimate goal: the transformation of power from "a lower sphere to a higher sphere"—that is, from the male sphere to the female sphere. Later, Branding confirms this goal, restating that her experiments involve "substance changed from one physical state to another," yet again a metaphor for shifting sexual identity, in effect the attempted overthrow of the patriarchal paradigm for a matriarchal one. Branding has one foot firmly planted in her avowed womanhood and the other uneasily set within the male scientific establishment, an uncomfortable stance which leads to much frustration and confusion, and ultimately encourages her demise. This ill-fated desire to be "of both worlds" is nicely illustrated in a scene wherein Branding conducts an experiment with dangerous isotopes; she amusingly wears only the helmet of a radiation suit, leaving her dress and jewelry visible below, a somewhat awkward yet visually compelling expositional anomaly which aptly underscores Branding's chronic gender confusion. Does Branding desire to be a nurturing lesbian mother figure or an omnipotent male tyrant figure? For either goal, the would-be alchemist knows that she would need to locate and extract that magical fluid which lifts all mortals to immortality and omniscience. Her failure in this quest is but a small step in Woman's journey towards locating the source of true, abiding power, towards discovering the legendary "Blood of Dracula."

Sabu and the Magic Ring

Distributed by Allied Artists Pictures Corporation
61 minutes/Color
Directed by George Blair
Screenplay: Benedict Freedman, John Fenton Murray, Samuel Roeca
Produced by Lonnie D'Orsa
Associate Producer: Maurice Duke
Music by Harry Sukman
Cinematography: Harry Neumann
Editing: William Austin
Art Director: Dave Milton
Set Decoration: Hal Gausman
Costume Design: Eileen Younger
Makeup Artist: John G. Holden
Production Manager: Allen K. Wood
Assistant Director: Ned Dobson, Grayson Rogers
Props: Ted Mossman
Construction Supervisor: James West
Recording Engineer: Ralph Butler
Sound Editor: Del Harris
Sound: B.J. Remington
Special Effects: Augie Lohman
Camera Operator: Archie R. Dalzell
Wardrobe: Bert Henrikson, Sid Mintz
Music Editor: Neil Brunnenkant
Cast: Sabu (Sabu), Daria Massey (Zumila), William Marshall (Genie), Peter Mamakos (Mazufar), John Doucette (Kimal), Vladimir Sokoloff (Old Fakir), Robin Morse (Magician), George Khoury (Assassin), Bernard Rich (Ali), Robert Shafto (Caliph), Cyril Delevanti (Abdul), John Lomma (Soldier), Ken Terrell (Guard)

Published synopsis: Sabu (Sabu), the Caliph's (Robert Shafto) stable boy, finds a ring which he decides to give to Zumeela (Daria Massey), who works in the market place. As Sabu rubs the ring to clean it, Ubal (William Marshall), a genie, appears and explains he is the slave to anyone possessing the magic ring. Muzafar (Peter Mamakos), of the Caliph's staff, learns Sabu has the ring and determines to gain possession of it. Yunan (Robin Morse), the magician, after convincing Muzafar that only he is capable of getting the ring from Sabu, kidnaps Zumeela and it is then that Sabu calls upon Ubal for aid. At Yunan's home they find the magician has turned the girl into stone. Yunan then uses magic to render Ubal powerless while Sabu unsuccessfully tries to go it alone as the ring does not work while Ubal is under Yuan's [sic] influence. Finaly Ubal breaks through Yunan's evil spell, forces him to return Zumeela to her normal self and makes possible again the magic power of the ring. But hard luck continues to be Sabu's lot. He loses the ring, and is in constant danger of capture by Muzafar's soldiers who are hot after it. As Sabu and Zumeela search the market place for the ring, they see a goose eat it. Later the ring is found in an egg the goose lays, and Zumeela takes charge of it. At her command, Ubal sends to the Caliph's palace Sabu, disguised as a prince of Damascus, an ally of the Caliph's, who with his retinue has been waylaid and slain by henchmen of Muzafar, who covets the Cailph's throne. With Ubal doing their bidding, Sabu and Zumeela save the Caliph from Muzafar's clutches. This done, they return the ring to Ubal, who returns Sabu and Zumeela to their original stations in life to enjoy happiness in normal surroundings.

Sabu and the Magic Ring is a strange little curio, a combination of an Arabian Nights–type adventure film with some light comedy thrown in. Considering its episodic nature, it is not surprising to find that the film is composited from three episodes of an unsold television series, perhaps Allied Artists' attempt to break into TV series production. The stage-

Allied Artists stitched together several episodes of an unsold television series and released it to theaters in late 1957 as *Sabu and the Magic Ring*. Yet the advertising for this Arabian Nights fantasy still took care to allude to the fearsome atomic age via its tagline, "In a World Bewitched by Wizards..."

bound, well-scrubbed film looks very much like similar TV product of the day, such as *African Patrol* and *Ramar of the Jungle*. An older, wiser Sabu essentially reprises the role he started almost twenty years previous in the Kordas' excellent adaptation of Rudyard Kipling's *The Jungle Book* (1940, d: Alexander Korda). According to publicity materials, *Sabu and the Magic Ring* was released theatrically in color, but only black and white television prints appear to have survived. The film was originally released on the bottom of a drive-in double bill with the Bowery Boys feature *Up in Smoke*, making the pair only a marginally "fantastic" 1957 entry.

THE MONOLITH MONSTERS WITH LOVE SLAVES OF THE AMAZONS (UNIVERSAL INTERNATIONAL)

Universal-International released their last bonafide science-fiction film alongside an obscure potboiler called *Love Slaves of the Amazons*, a curious December double bill which suggests that the studio had no more qualified fantastic films available. This seems extremely odd for the studio that had made a name for itself with classic films of terror, ranging from *Frankenstein* (1931) to *This Island Earth* (1955). However, it also seems apparent that U-I did not generally go along with the current fad of releasing pre-packaged double bills, as did the other B-Studios. U-I released its other science-thrillers of the year primarily (not exclusively) as single bills — making this odd-duck pairing stand out all the more.

The Monolith Monsters

Produced by Universal International Pictures
Distributed by Universal Pictures
77 minutes/Black and White
Directed by John Sherwood
Story: Jack Arnold, Robert M. Fresco
Screenplay: Norman Jolley, Robert M. Fresco
Produced by Howard Christie
Music by Irving Gertz, Henry Mancini, Herman Stein, William Lava
Cinematography: Ellis W. Carter
Editing: Patrick McCormack
Art Directors: Alexander Golitzen, Robert E. Smith
Set Decoration: Russell A. Gausman, William Tapp
Gowns: Marilyn Sotto
Makeup Artist: Bud Westmore
Unit Production Manager: Lew Leary
Assistant Directors: Joseph E. Kenny, Ray DeCamp
Sound: Leslie I. Carey, Frank Wilkinson
Sound Editor: Robert L. Bratton, Alvin Todd
Sound Technicians: Ed Hall, William Lambert, James F. Rogers
Special Photography: Clifford Stine
Special Effects: Frank Brendel
Still Photographer: Rollie Lane
Assistant Camera: Robert Pierce
Camera Operator: Harry L. Underwood
Wardrobe: Seth Banks, Martha Bunch
Music Supervisor: Joseph Gershenson

Striking poster art for Universal-International's sci-fi programmer *The Monolith Monsters*, one of a few fantastic films of 1957 — along with *Kronos*— to feature intriguing "abstract" menaces.

Orchestrators: Charles Maxwell, David Tamkin
Script Supervisor: Bob Forrest
Unit Publicist: Lon Jones
Cast: Grant Williams (Dave Miller), Lola Albright (Cathy Barrett), Les Tremayne (Martin Cochrane), Trevor Bardette (Prof. Arthur Flanders), Phil Harvey (Ben Gilbert), William Flaherty (Police Chief), Harry Jackson (Dr. Hendricks), Richard Cutting (Dr. Reynolds), Linda Scheley (Ginny Simpson), Dean Cromer (Highway Patrolman), Steve Darrell (Joe Higgins), Troy Donahue (Hank Jackson), Paul Frees (Narrator), Paul Petersen (Paperboy), Elizabeth Russell (Telephone Operator), William Schallert (Weatherman)

Synopsis: Monstrous towers of rock, borne of a meteor, devastate a desert community.

Nineteen fifty-seven ended with a literal "bang," with this extremely clever revision of the tired "monster movie" formula, in which, like the earlier *Kronos*, the "monster," although giant, deadly and menacing, is an abstract, largely inorganic thing whose presence lends itself to all sorts of interpretation. Here, malignant rock formations, when introduced to water, grow into monstrous, toppling towers of doom. Stunning miniature work brings this strange premise to life quite handily, and the film is a visual delight from start to finish. The extraordinarily phallic monoliths, grown to mammoth proportions by the introduction of water, acts as almost comical metaphor for male sexual arousal when the penis is surrounded by female vaginal secretions. As well, the monoliths, which came from a renegade meteor and target a small desert town that has thrived on heavy industrialization, act as some sort of divine punishment for the community's exploitation of natural resources (salt primarily). Further, there is the theme of man, subsequent to the industrial revolution, being punished and trapped by his own technology, nicely symbolized in a disturbing scene of a small child encased in a creepy, coffin-like iron lung.

When the silicate-based alien mineral contacts human flesh it turns the person into stone, an apt metaphor for encroaching conformity in an increasingly techno-centric, potentially emotion-free police state. Interestingly, the fourth estate is glorified as one of the few vital social lifelines left in an increasingly technologically-based culture. And the evacuation of Saint Angelo mirrors well the Cold War fears of America being invaded by sinister "alien forces." The casting in the film is adequate, with Grant Williams playing a shadow of his former tragic self as *The Incredible Shrinking Man*. Most odd is seeing William Schallert as a neurotic meteorologist. The only false step in the whole movie is in the prologue, which suffers from the cartoon-like droning of Paul Frees. Still, *The Monolith Monsters* stands as one of the exemplary films of the year, most surprising as it emerged from cynical hack-factory Universal-International.

Love Slaves of the Amazons

81 minutes, color
Produced by Jewel Productions
Distributed by Universal-International Pictures
Filmed at Vera Cruz Studios, Sao Bernardo
Directed by Curt Siodmak
Story and Screenplay: Curt Siodmak
Produced by Curt Siodmak
Associate Producer: Terry O. Morse
Cinematography: Mario Pagés
Editing: Oswald Hafenrichter, Terry O. Morse
Art Director: Pierino Massenzi
Set Decoration: Carlos Jacchieri
Makeup Artist: Flavio Torres
Production Manager: Luiz Francunha
Assistant Director: Ray Endsleigh
Second Unit Director: Terry O. Morse
Sound: Leslie I. Carey, Spiros Saliveros
Camera Operator: Honorio Marin
Music Supervisor: Joseph Gershenson
Songs: Radames Gnattali
Vocalist: Jara Lex
Choreography: David Condi, Fernanda Condi
Jewelry: R. Simon, Cia Ltda.
Cast: Don Taylor (Dr. Peter Masters), Gianna Segale (Gina Vanni), Eduardo Ciannelli (Dr. Crespi), Harvey Chalk (Aldemar Silva), Wilson Viana (Fernando), Eugenio Carlos (Carlos), Tom Payne (Dr. Mario Dellamano), Gilda Nery (Guard), Ana Maria Nabuco (Queen Conori), John Herbert (Desk Clerk), Louis Serrano (Rescue Pilot)

Synopsis: Explorers stumble upon a tribe of women warriors deep in the heart of the Amazon jungle.

Love Slaves of the Amazons is a late entry in an avowedly sexist film genre endemic to the 1950s known colloquially as the "wild women" or "amazon woman" melodrama. In these sophomoric male fantasies a group of male explorers on a journey to a remote or "forbidden" land stumbles upon an obscure or lost tribe of primitive natives largely—if not wholly—comprised of women. These female collectives have either inadvertently circumvented or specifically prohibited the male gender, making them, for all intents and purposes, examples of a most noxious concept to entrenched patriarchy, the "malevolent matriarchy." These gyno-centric societies not only run efficiently in spite of the absent "benefit" of the male gender, but in fact function all the more brightly and autonomously due to this lack. In almost all cases, however, these utopian matriarchies are doomed by one very "Old Testament" flaw—lust. These female tribes are invariably "tamed," if not outright decimated, by their weak collective admission that all they ever really wanted was a good ... male. The proud warrior women in these films inevitably fall in love with the dumbest pricks in the invading group, thus surrendering their hard-won power to the ominous male collective in exchange for hugs and kisses. The message is simple and brutal in these films: a woman who does not allow herself to become a slave to her lust in trade for male sexual favors is a cold, heartless monster, an enemy of (male) society ripe for extermination. The genre, aimed almost certainly at the young, single, male audience member, had its most prolific period at the beginning of the postwar era, with films such as *Prehistoric Women* (1950), *Wild Women* (1951), *Untamed Women* (1952), *Mesa of Lost Women* (1953) and *Cat-Women of the Moon* (1953). The genre petered out by decade's end with increasingly surreal entries like *Queen of Outer Space* (1958), *The Wild Women of Wongo* (1958) and *Island of Lost Women* (1959).

Love Slaves of the Amazons fits somewhere right in the middle of this phenomenon. While it expectedly depicts its utopian Amazons primarily as drooling, man-hungry idiots, there are other, more intriguing aspects to this curious female collective. Their virulently anti-male, isolationist agenda mirrors the basic tenants of radical feminist ideology, which would rise to prominence for a brief time in the subsequent decade. At least it is clear that these Amazons see males as inferior, slave-like beings, fit only for casual copulation and domestic servitude, never to be considered as socio-political equals. In short, they see males exactly as postwar culture saw womankind.

The film opens with a green-faced goddess singing; a close-up of her head hovers over the jungle—a fertility goddess reigning supreme over the natural world—hinting at the pre-eminence of the female principle over the ensuing scenario. The hero of the piece, an archaeologist called Masters, represents a most woeful example of the "master" gender, a virtual "tool" of phallocentric culture. His subsequent encounter with the warrior tribe is framed, significantly, as possibly unreal, a fever dream resulting from his catching malaria on the journey up the Amazon river. When the Amazon women are revealed, they too are green-skinned like the goddess, reinforcing that they are—unlike their enemy, Man—part of the natural world. As Masters is taken captive by the tribe, he acts like the tool of maledom he is, immediately pawing and ogling the attractive young warriors, a knee-jerk chauvinist reaction he soon lives to regret, as he learns that predatory sexual lust cuts both ways. Soon a gaggle of dumpy Amazon matrons attack Masters, forcibly disrobing and bathing him in an act which the terrified male—now a *victim* of unsolicited sexual advances—sees as virtual rape. From another male prisoner Masters learns that the Amazons keep one, and only one, male as a sexual slave for breeding purposes. Once a new generation of children are sired, the male drone is put to death. Even more threatening to patriarchal ideology is the revelation that only female children are allowed to live, all male infants being ritually slaughtered. Masters is given hallucinatory drugs in order to disable him mentally, preparing him to be the next breeding drone of the female savages. He manages to escape, however, and, once rescued, decides to keep his otherworldly "experience" a secret. The viewer may then wonder if Masters' decision was based on a desire to save mankind from the exterminating forces of radical feminism or to save sacred radical feminist ideology from the corrupting influence of phallocentric culture? In either case, the "secret" of this well-oiled, if anti-male, socio-political system is safe from threat until the next unlucky "tool" of patriarchy lets curiosity lead him to what will be certain death.

Although fitfully filled with a risible sexism, there is an almost unwitting insistence throughout *Love Slaves* to depict the male as a weak and flawed creature, in contrast to the female, who is depicted as omniscient if ruthlessly efficient in decimating unwanted "members" of society. One remarkable scene which underscores this thematic contrast between male and female depicts pirates and explorers fighting each other in shallow, muddy waters. As the men grope each other and slosh around in the thick mud, they look strikingly like primitive marine vertebrates crawling out of the primordial slime, as might have been witnessed in earth's prehistory; the scene thus suggests the evolutionary lowness of the male animal, in stark contrast to the highly evolved Amazons.

Love Slaves is, in many ways, an indirect sequel to *Curucu, Beast of the Amazon* (1956). Both films were written and directed by Curt Siodmak, both were filmed in Brazil and the Amazon jungle, and both were released by Universal-International a mere year apart. Although there is no direct narrative connection between the two films, there are so many aesthetic and thematic consistencies that one is tempted to call the pair two parts of what might be called Siodmak's "Amazon period." *Curucu's* expositional template borrows heavily from that of *Creature from the Black Lagoon* (1954), understandable in that *Creature* was a stunning recent success for Universal.

As with its counterpart, the plot of *Curucu* awkwardly balances some truly retrograde old-world sexism with fitful stabs at progressive, proto-feminist ideology, igniting a dialectic which energizes both films' considerable sexual and political *frisson*. The main thrust of *Curucu* concerns Andrea, a woman doctor (played with trenchant "pluck" by Beverly Garland) who ventures deep into the Amazon in an attempt to procure a native folk medicine which she believes may cure cancer, that scourge of the atomic age. Along the way she encounters a ferocious "beast" which is decimating the native population. It is significant that Andrea is a doctor, *not* a nurse. She is not a handmaiden to a male professional but an independent, autonomous individual in her own right.

Through several life-threatening ordeals, Andrea grows out of patriarchal dependence to become something vaguely proto-feminist by film's end. There are several scenes of predators devouring prey, all of which Andrea, as well as the audience, witnesses. In response to one of them, Andrea quips, "I'll get used to it; I'll *have* to," suggesting that she must radically and briskly mature if she wants to participate in male culture, let alone conquer it. Yet Andrea is also used (i.e. exploited) by male society in an attempt to forge progressive social relations with the unruly natives. At one point the film's ostensible male hero, having come to terms with a potentially threatening tribe, quips, "Peace—thanks to your attributes," reinforcing woman's role in maintaining order in a dangerous world.

The beast "Curucu" is revealed at midpoint to be merely a man in disguise, underscoring not only that Man himself is the lowest, vilest beast in all creation, but also that the beast was a peripheral red herring after all. (This may be why *Curucu* was a relative failure at the box office, as it was erroneously marketed as a "monster movie," which it most assuredly is not.) Indeed, the real villain of the piece is a man called Tupinico (translated as "small god"), an exiled native who donned the monster-bird costume in order to frighten his peers into returning to their primitive, superstitious ways. Tupicino has effectively gathered a gaggle of renegade warriors, lording over them as an omnipotent, if mad, demigod, making him a most conspicuous analog of Colonel Kurtz in Joseph Conrad's immortal *Heart of Darkness*; this aspect of the scenario gives *Curucu* a slight anti-colonialist flavor.

Late in the film a native dancer performs a sexy, highly erotic dance with a large snake wrapped around her. This titillating, if sexist, moment underscores the regressive (pre-feminist) female's subservience to "serpentine" phallocentric society, her role being to stroke, massage and otherwise worship (and thus excite) male lust; she must never challenge or deny it. Yet, portentously, at the film's climax Andrea battles for her life against a monstrous boa constrictor that threatens to literally squeeze the life out of her, this primordial serpent aptly acting as symbol of the potentially soul-crushing forces of phallocentric culture. In contrast to the native dancer who literally "embraced" phallocentric culture with her erotic dance, Andrea intuits that in her case, to engage this monstrous serpent on its own terms would mean certain death. Freed from this last onslaught by tyrannical patriarchal interests, Andrea is finally empowered when given the cure for cancer by a grateful native, who also offers her, as a most portentous gift, the shrunken head of Tupicino, that alternately fearsome and comical emblem of failed patriarchal omniscience, now rendered grotesque, trivial, and harmless. Through the unmasking of the beast, Andrea has "de-clawed" the male universe and is now positioned to heal it. Both *Curucu* and *Love Slaves* are interesting early examples of U.S. film productions shot largely, or entirely, in another land using (relatively cheap) foreign labor in many cast and crew positions. *The White Orchid* (1954), discussed elsewhere in its 1957 re-release incarnation, *Creatures of the Jungle*, and *The Living Idol* (1956), are other examples of a trend which would expand exponentially in the subsequent decade. A minor release at the time, and rarely seen since, *Love Slaves of the Amazons* is nonetheless a fitting finale to film's fantastic year, as it illustrates in bold relief some of the contradictions — primarily in the area of gender — being toyed with in the films of 1957. In regards to the role of women in society, *Love Slaves* pits an antediluvian, misogynist sexism against a proud, if barbaric, proto-feminism, offering one possible prototype of a gyno-centric culture with the potential to function flawlessly without the aid — or hindrance — of the predatory male animal. As does its co-feature, *The Monolith Monsters*, *Love Slaves of the Amazons* suffers only from the grating cartoon-voice of Paul Frees, used here to overdub several of the male characters.

Beast of Paradise Isle with *Creatures of the Jungle* (Mutual Productions of the West)

Mutual Productions of the West — one of several tiny distribution outfits to crop up during the mid–1950s to re-release older film product — released *Beast of Paradise Isle* and *Creatures of the Jungle* in early December 1957 (based on the National Screen Service numbers on extant posters), making this the last, and quite possibly the most cynical, attempt to cash in on the year's hot teenage horror-sf craze, a particularly desperate attempt to catch some of the wake of Allied Artists' astonishingly popular double bill *Attack of the Crab Monsters/Not of This Earth*. Indeed, this re-release possibly stands as the biggest "cheat" of 1957; although the advertising for this double bill claimed to offer "2 Super-Shock Hits!" neither film was particularly "super-shocking." The posters also prominently featured a "crab monster" threatening a buxom beauty, an overt rip-off of *Attack of the Crab Monsters'* iconic poster art. When unwary patrons sat down to the films, however, they were treated to lackluster, recycled product from several years previous. *The Beast of Paradise Isle* is a re-titling of a 1953 RKO release, *Port Sinister*, which only peripherally features a giant crab. The co-feature, the provocatively-titled *Creatures of the Jungle*, is a re-titled 1954 United Artists potboiler, *The White Orchid*, which contained no fantastic elements whatsoever, despite its tagline "Fantastic Terror Rites!" This double bill stands as an example of cynical opportunism at its most desperate, and one wonders if Albert Zugsmith, the original producer of *Port Sinister*, aka *Beast of Paradise Isle*, had a hand in this quickie cash-in project, as he did for the other "recycled" release of the year, *1,000 Years from Now/Invasion U.S.A.*

Beast of Paradise Isle

(originally released as *Port Sinister* in 1953)
Produced by American Pictures Company
Distributed by RKO Radio Pictures (1953), Mutual Productions of the West (1957)
65 minutes/Black and White
Directed by Harold Daniels
Screenplay: Aubrey Wisberg, Jack Pollexfen
Produced by Jack Pollexfen, Aubrey Wisberg

Possibly the largest "cheat" of 1957 was this late-year release of *Beast of Paradise Isle* and *Creatures of the Jungle*, reissues of earlier productions, both melodramas with minimal fantastic content. Note the crude attempt to invoke the memory of Roger Corman's crab monster, certainly one of the most indelible pop icons of the year.

Associate Producer: Albert Zugsmith
Music by Albert Glasser
Cinematography: William Bradford
Editing: Fred R. Feitshans, Jr.
Production Design: Theobold Holsopple
Set Decoration: Clarence Steensen
Makeup Artist: Harry Thomas
Production Manager: Carl Hiecke
Sound: Roy Meadows
Mechanical Effects: Rocky Cline
Special Photographic Effects: Jack Rabin
Wardrobe: Einar H. Bourman
Cast: James Warren (Tony Ferris), Lynne Roberts (Dr. Joan Hunter), Paul Cavanagh (John Kolvac), William Schallert (Collins), House Peters, Jr. (Jim Garry), Marjorie Stapp (Technician), Helen Winston (Florence), Eric Colmar (Christie), Norman Budd (Akers), Anne Kimbell (Nurse), Robert Bice (George Burt), Merritt Stone (Nick), Ken Terrell (Hollis), Charles Victor (Coast Guard Lieutenant), Edward Hearn (Capt. Crawley), Dayton Lummis (Mr. Lennox)

Synopsis: Explorers to a volcanic island encounter buried treasures protected by a mammoth crustacean.

As noted, *The Beast of Paradise Isle* is a re-titling of *Port Sinister*, a 1953 melodrama. The film concerns an expedition to the fabled "Port Royal" near Jamaica, a sunken island

The crew of a doomed expedition are trapped on a volcanic island overrun by monster crabs in *Beast of Paradise Isle*, the 1957 re-release of a 1953 RKO melodrama, *Port Sinister*. William Schallert is pictured third from right.

which is supposedly due to rise up out of the sea to reveal untold buried treasures. The legend of Port Royal as an island sunk by a massive 1692 earthquake gained popularity with 1952's release of a book called *Port Royal: Ghost City Beneath the Sea* by Harry Reisling, which was the story source for a major motion picture, *City Beneath the Sea* (d: Budd Boetticher), starring Anthony Quinn. *City* was released in March of 1953, and *Port Sinister* snuck in behind it, released in April of the same year. Truth be told, *Port Sinister* is the more entertaining treatment of the story, albeit in a ridiculous, pulp-fiction manner.

The sparse "fantastic" elements, an early effort by '50s f/x wizard Jack Rabin, consist of a fairly impressive miniatures scene wherein the "ghost island" bubbles to the surface of a studio-tank ocean, along with two brief sequences wherein the "crab monster" menaces the heroine and eats one of the sailors. The crab f/x alternate awkwardly between optical blow-ups of a real crab and a few shots of a puppet-crab; neither effect is terribly convincing. This early Albert Zugsmith production is nonetheless interesting on its own, although comparing it to Corman's groundbreaking crab opus is like pitting *Citizen Kane* against *Star Wars* —no contest.

Creatures of the Jungle

(originally released as *The White Orchid* in 1954)
Produced by Cosmos Productions, Producciones Eduardo Quevedo S.A.
Distributed by United Artists (1954), Mutual Productions of the West (1957)
81 minutes/Eastmancolor
Directed by Reginald Le Borg

Lobby card for *Creatures of the Jungle*, a 1957 retitling of a 1954 melodrama, *The White Orchid*, which contained no fantastic elements whatsoever yet was dishonestly marketed as a "science-shocker," along with its co-feature, *Beast of Paradise Isle*. (Stars William Lundigan, Peggie Castle and Armando Silvestre are seen at center.)

Story: David Duncan, Reginald Le Borg
Screenplay: David Duncan, Reginald Le Borg
Produced by Reginald Le Borg
Associate Producer: James O. Radford
Music by Antonio Díaz Conde
Cinematography: Enrique Wallace (as Henry Wallace), Gilbert Warrenton
Editing: Jose W. Bustos
Art Director: Ramón Rodríguez
Production Manager: Manuel Rodriguez
Assistant Directors: Francis Kowalski, Valerio Olivo
Sound Engineer: Nicolás de la Rosa
Sound Director: James L. Fields
Conductor: Antonio Díaz Conde
Production Coordinator: Frank Fox
Production Assistant: Manuel Bernal Salas
Cast: William Lundigan (Robert Burton), Peggie Castle (Kathryn Williams), Armando Silvestre (Juan
   Cervantes), Rosenda Monteros (Lupita), Jorge Treviño (Arturo), Alejandro de Montenegro (Miguel),
   Miguel A. Gallardo (Pedro), Ramon S. Fernandez (Baytab), Amalia Fernández (Lead Dancer),
   Ballet Moderno de Mexico (Dancers)

Synopsis: Explorers in Mexico stumble upon a bloodthirsty lost tribe, presumed to be the direct
   descendents of the Aztecs.

As mentioned, *Creatures of the Jungle* is actually a 1954 film, *The White Orchid*. While
an interesting melodrama, *The White Orchid* doesn't fall into the "thriller-diller" category
by any means. An early Mexican–U.S. co-production, the feature boasts a few qualities
which raise it above the norm. Firstly, it ironically stands as one of few color releases of
1957 to fall into the supposed "fantastic" category. Also, it contains some marvelous location
shooting of the ancient Aztec temples. And finally, in the film's finale, the primitives attempt
a virgin sacrifice via the kidnapping of the heroine, Peggie Castle; this may be the "Fantastic
Terror Rites!" referred to in its advertising. Colorful and exotic, but not "fantastic," *Creatures*
stands as a good example of clever marketing used to fill a product void with any available
commodity. (Trivia note: the memorable music score by Antonio Diaz Conde was recycled
for the 1957-lensed Mexican horror hit *La Momia Azteca*.)

The Thing from Another World

(original production released in 1951)
Winchester Pictures Corporation/RKO Radio Pictures
81 minutes (1957 reissue), black and white
Directed by Christian Nyby
Story: John W. Campbell, Jr. (based on his story "Who Goes There?")
Screenplay: Charles Lederer
Produced by Howard Hawks
Associate Producer: Edward Lasker
Music by Dimitri Tiomkin
Cinematography: Russell Harlan
Editing: Roland Gross
Art Directors: Albert S. D'Agostino, John Hughes
Set Decoration: Darrell Silvera, William Stevens
Hair Stylist: Larry Germain
Sound: Phil Brigandi, Clem Portman

Special Effects: Donald Steward, Linwood G. Dunn, Harold E. Stine
Wardrobe: Michael Woulfe
With: Margaret Sheridan (Nikki), Kenneth Tobey (Patrick Hendry), Robert Cornthwaite (Dr. Arthur Carrington), Douglas Spencer (Scotty), James Young (Lt. Eddie Dykes), Dewey Martin (Crew Chief), Robert Nichols (Mac MacPherson), William Self (Corporal Barnes), Eduard Franz (Dr. Stern), Sally Creighton (Mrs. Chapman), James Arness (the Thing)

Synopsis: A group of scientists and military personnel at an Arctic research station discover a spacecraft buried in the ice, along with its frozen pilot.

Last, but definitely not least, the fantastic year of 1957 ended with the wide national re-release of *The Thing from Another World*, one of the earliest and most successful "alien invasion" films of the decade. With its impressive box-office history, abundant thrills, and iconic pulp-fiction title, *The Thing* was a natural to bring to a close a most bizarre and wonderful year for fantastic film. The bleak locale of the film — a frigid outpost somewhere near the North Pole — is eerily suggestive of a certain form of purgatory, a place for sinners to reflect on their transgressions. In keeping with the general narrative template of "a Howard Hawks film," it may also suggest the male universe, emotionless without love, and cold unto death. As in much of producer Hawks' work, the all-male group represents patriarchy in microcosm, a male collective working in solidarity towards common goals and keeping out anyone considered an "outsider." These "outsiders," of course, could be anything from foreign enemies to intellectuals to women to anyone who threatens the avowedly phallo-centric nature of the Hawksian "boy's club." In this and other Hawks films the homo-erotic dream of an all-male society is maintained only by safely corralling and/or exterminating any threat to that desired goal. Here the male club is physically (and voluntarily) cut off from "normal" society, another hint that the club desires to separate itself from women, children, the animal world, etc., in order to carry on unfettered with members of its own elite club. (Considering the pathological fear men in Hawks' films have for women, one might posit that the goal of these males-only enclaves is to protect its members from what man subconsciously fears most: the sexual mother.)

In *The Thing*, the threat is an alien from another planet (or "another world"), but the strongly isolationist setting of the desolate outpost suggests that "the other" could be anything or anyone set against entrenched male hegemony. When analyzed, the "Thing" is described as an intelligent vegetable (dubbed a "super carrot" by one observer), seen as lacking all emotion, a convenient verdict clearly in line with its role as an alien "other," interchangeable with any chosen foreign enemy. Even the alien's eventual death by electrocution seems destined to reflect the fate of other American "enemies," such as atomic spies Julius and Ethel Rosenberg, who were sentenced to death in 1951 even as *The Thing* first slithered across U.S. movie screens, and who were subsequently electrocuted for perceived crimes against U.S. maledom. Even the film's tagline, "Keep Watching the Skies!" is surely meant to suggest that the audience constantly troll the heavens for evil Soviet war planes, making *The Thing* in some ways the quintessential Cold War agitprop piece. And *The Thing* expresses clearly, if inadvertently, that the male collective's program is always self-serving and always quantifiably hazardous to all "others"; when the "boys" locate the alien saucer, the first thing they think to do is blow it up, a reckless and destructive — but wholly predictable — reaction to what might be considered a threat to the fragile, infantile ego of the group. Later, in an attempt to immolate the alien, the gang almost burns down their own dwelling as well, so

Poster art for RKO's 1957 reissue of Howard Hawk's 1951 Cold War classic, *The Thing from Another World*.

short-sighted and ruinous is patriarchy's agenda. As well, *The Thing* shares similar narrative affects with other melodramas depicting a harsh life on the American frontier. In this narrative template, "the unknown"—be it Indians, bandits, monsoons, mountains, or monsters—threatens the group and forces it to eschew individual prejudices and flaws in an effort to function harmoniously as a viable socio-political unit. Many have thus seen this general genre of film, with its avowedly nationalistic flavor, as allegorical treatises on the growth of America, and its attempt to forge and maintain a working democracy, a woefully isolationist stance which nonetheless had (and has) many champions.

As noted by other observers, the place of the woman in a Hawks film is problematic and portentous. In *The Thing*, the "token" female, Nikki, is used primarily as symbol of the female principle abstracted from the male group, acting more as catalyst than character in the scenario proper. (A second female appears so infrequently, and always in the background, as to become invisible to the narrative.) Yet as peripheral as Woman is to the male group, to the hero, Hendry, she is also a muse, an enigma, a breathing Chinese Puzzle, something desired yet perplexing and perhaps unattainable. And the Hawks male will go to great lengths in order to solve this mystery of the feminine, an entire subset of the world which has thus far eluded him. In a somewhat astounding scene, after Nikki and Hendry have flirted, and Hendry suggests that Nikki tie him up, the next scene shows Hendry actually tied to a chair, voluntarily becoming a passive (and assuredly masochistic) partner, temporarily switching the sacred Hawksian power dynamic of "male over female." Hendry momentarily surrenders his power to Nikki via this strange bondage ritual in which the chosen leader of the male pack allows himself the shame of sexual humiliation in order to gain ground with "the enemy"—that is, Woman, symbol of the natural world and avowed foe of phallocentric ideology. Yet in the film's finale, when Nikki and Hendry seem to be pushed together by the hero's buddies, it appears that even the conquest of the female in a Hawks film is done not to balance the yin-yang of the universe, but to further stabilize and balance the immutable and unassailable male-centric society, to enhance and solidify maledom's omniscience.

The villain of the piece, a scientist named Carrington, is an almost caricaturist depiction of several prejudices of the era. He is first and foremost a scientist, and interested in knowledge for its own sake. As any viewer of the film was acutely aware, Science, left to its own devices, may come up with horrible entities such as the atomic bomb—a connection made explicit when Carrington is noted as having been part of the atom-bomb tests at Bikini atoll. Furthermore, Carrington is an intellectual, an affliction seen as an aberration—or worse—in a fearsomely anti-intellectual era. Finally, Carrington is presented as far more "feminine" than Nikki (his female assistant), being always shown wearing ridiculous garments such as frumpy slacks, foppish turtlenecks and frilly fur collars. Indeed, he symbolizes "the female" far more effectively than the two actual females in the film. All of these deadly "flaws" paint Carrington as an enemy of male America, one more than likely to conspire with "the enemy," whomever that may be. Indeed, this loathsome "egghead" states that he actually wants to communicate with, to reason with, the horrible alien, to align himself with "the enemy," and thus is painted as a coward and a traitor. When Carrington later in the film sputters, "Knowledge is more important than life!" one can surely imagine those same, or similar, words emanating from any straw-dog tyrant labeled as an enemy to democracy. Yet Carrington's unforgivable sin is his attempt to reproduce the alien in a laboratory setting, painting this "egghead" as not only supporting but gleefully breeding legions of foreign monsters in order to vanquish America. The message is clear, if a bit reactionary: Science absolutely refuses moral responsibility and thus is an enemy of Man. As well, Carrington illustrates another recurring Hawksian theme in which the free-thinking individual is invariably targeted, ostracized and banished in deference to the survival of the group (and its retrograde, oddly socialist mindset).

Curiously, the main premise of *The Thing* mirrors that of an incident which supposedly occurred near an Air Force base in Roswell, New Mexico, in the summer of 1947, when an unidentified flying object — originally reported by the press officer as being of extraterrestrial origin — crash-landed on a nearby farm. Further anecdotal reports maintained that one or more deceased occupants of the craft were recovered and kept under wraps for years by the military under "top secret" conditions. *The Thing* may have thus safely fictionalized a real-life incident which the powers-that-be did not want scrutinized or addressed in other forums. RKO, the original producer and distributor of the film, had all but collapsed by 1957, with their last original production wrapping up in January of that year. Former CEO Howard Hughes had sold RKO to General Teleradio in 1955, and production had dwindled rapidly since then. Remaining RKO product, including the infamous fiascoes *Jet Pilot* and *Public Pigeon No. 1* (both 1957), along with *The Thing*'s re-release, were distributed by Universal-International through 1957 and early 1958. Seven minutes were snipped from the original 87-minute version of *The Thing* for its 1957 re-release, although it is unverified which scenes were excised. Although no month of release has been verified, it would appear that *The Thing* was unleashed upon the nation's screens late in 1957 — possibly as late as December — in order to garner some badly needed holiday-season revenue for RKO's new handlers.

It is impressive to observe that *The Thing* is as strong a film today as it was 60 years ago — and looks even better when compared to the laughably inferior 1987 remake by the talent-free John Carpenter. The grim, wholly existential horror essayed by the grotesque "super carrot" in the original shines even more brightly when compared to the dumbed-down, shape-shifting, cartoon nonsense of the remake. (To those who argue that the creature's multiple transformations in the remake adhere more closely to the beast as drawn in John Campbell's original short story, one need only remind them that the more fanciful aspects of pulp fiction prose were never intended to be literally brought to life through the "magic of motion pictures," some things being far better left to the imagination.) In short, the original boasts abundant intelligence and imagination, traits completely lacking in the remake — and, one might dare say, its many sad fans. Thankfully, the original remains in print on DVD and is often aired on classic movie channels, so there is no need to fear its imminent obscurity or settle for the feeble Reagan-era clone.

Conclusion

Either by omniscient prophecy or diabolical invocation, the fantastic films of 1957 predicted much of the cataclysmic upheaval of the subsequent decade. The problematic nature of an industrialized, conformist culture and its attempts to create a space for individual human expansion, addressed in primitive, even simplistic terms in many of the fantastic offerings of 1957, became a veritable cultural mantra in ensuing years thanks to the coming of age of a group of citizens unlike any which had come before. As well, the role of the woman in society, hinted at in several films discussed, became in a very few years a cause celebre and ralling cry for an entire generation. Elsewhere, the awesome impact of the Military-Industrial complex could be seen in the ongoing nuclear arms race and the triumph of war mentality, which soon succeeded in sinking the United States into a socio-political quagmire via an obscure Asian country called Vietnam. And hovering over it all, like a monstrous specter determined to haunt its host into paralysis, was the horrible reality of the split atom, a Faustian bargain with Evil which will torture mankind until his final days on this accursed globe.

As for the film industry, 1958 proved to be the last gasp of the teen-oriented "science-chiller" craze, with roughly 40 genre films released, many of them shoddy, independently-produced filler like *Giant from the Unknown* (d: Richard Cuhna) and *Terror from the Year 5,000* (d: Robert Gurney, Jr.). Only two exceptional genre films emerged from 1958 — *The Colossus of New York* (d: Eugene Lourie) and *The Space Children* (d: Jack Arnold) — and even a big-budget "blockbuster" like Allied Artists' *Queen of Outer Space* (d: Edward Bernds) could not revive what was a quickly dying market. By 1959, the short-lived teenage double bill fad was largely dead. B-movie factories such as Columbia Pictures, Allied Artists and American International turned their attention to making fewer, larger-budgeted productions, more often than not in color, attempting to reach a wider target audience than the short-lived-but-effective teenager "niche" market.

In the following decade the science-fiction film took two distinctly separate paths. There was still a market for entertaining "pulp" sci-fi, and films such as *Mutiny in Outer Space* (1965, d: Hugo Grimaldi) and *Women of the Prehistoric Planet* (1966, d: Arthur C. Pierce) did respectable business in drive-in and grindhouse engagements, as well as enjoying successful afterlives in television syndication. More interesting, however, was the trend towards what might be termed "cerebral" science fiction, a cinema which emphasized ideas and concepts over mere serial-type thrills. Films such as *The Angry Red Planet* (1960, d: Ib Melchior), *Creation of the Humanoids* (1962, d: Wesley Berry), and *The Time Travelers* (1964, d: Ib Melchior) offered the audience some relatively "deep" philosophical substance along with their traditional narrative conceits, and expanded the possibilities of the genre immensely. Certainly this trend had its apex in 1968 with Stanley Kubrick's astonishing *2001: A Space Odyssey*, which was a revelation at the time of its release, and today still comes across as something created far out of its time. The stunning success of this outré film led to a brief renaissance of cerebral sci-fi films that produced a veritable cornucopia of such entries, including such high watermarks as *Silent Running* (1971, d: Douglas Trumbull), *Zero Population Growth* (1972, d: Michael Campus), *Phase IV* (1974, d: Saul Bass) and *Zardoz* (1974, d: John Boorman). Sadly, this promising trend was brought to a crushing halt in the late 1970s when Twentieth Century–Fox single-handedly killed the science-fiction genre with two lamentable, sophomoric franchises—*Star Wars* and *Alien*—both of which jettisoned all conceivable philosophy, wit or intelligence to return with a vengeance to the "whiz-bang" school of infantile Saturday-morning cliffhanger serials such as *Flash Gordon* and *Buck Rogers*. The ascent of this action-packed, brain-dead junk has created a phenomenon far greater than anything *2001* or the *Star Trek* television series could ever boast. These woefully transparent cultural texts, which in most cases amount to nothing more than "Cowboys and Indians in Space," almost invariably feature two or more alien civilizations fighting it out with spectacular futuristic techno-weaponry, armed combat being the prevalent motif. Indeed, since the release of the aptly-titled *Star Wars*, the modern science-fiction film has become nothing more than a war movie clumsily disguised in futuristic or otherworldly garb. These immensely popular films have thus become quite effective as propaganda, indoctrinating the undiscriminating to accept the supposed inevitability of "endless war" unto eternity, shamelessly fetishizing the super-technology needed to fight these perpetual battles. In rather conspicuous comparison, the "intelligent," contemplative science-fiction picture, which might actually suggest how peoples and civilizations could theoretically get along, has by now become an endangered species. The occasional anomaly, such as *City of Lost Children* (1995, d: Jean-Pierre Jeunet, Marc Caro), is all too quickly obscured by the lumbering assault of the newest installment of the *Star Wars* or *Alien* cinematic thrill-ride, proudly proclaimed by their makers as having "no boring parts"—meaning no contemplative ideological dialogue exchanges which would make the audience actually have to think. Ultimately, *Star Wars*, *Alien* and their ilk may be little more than infomercials for the Military-Industrial complex, disingenuously positing an ungodly glorification of technology-fueled perpetual war as the natural state of man.

As for the horror film, it, too, went in two distinctly different directions. During the 1960s the horror film seemed to be on its way to a real renaissance, with stunning works like *Psycho* (1960, Alfred Hitchcock), *The Haunting* (1963, d: Robert Wise) and *Night of the Living Dead* (1968, d: George Romero). Alongside these most original works was the continuation of the lamentable Hammer gothic horror series from England, that hapless studio which churned out endless turgid retreads of the Frankenstein, Dracula and Zombie tropes in increasingly inferior productions that—even some fans were forced to admit—began to look indistinguishable from one another. Luckily, the late 1960s and early 1970s were saved from complete suffocation by the import of a plethora of foreign horror films from Spain, Italy and elsewhere, thanks to talents such as Jess Franco, Dario Argento, Jean Rollin and Lucio Fulci. Sadly, in the late 1970s, as they had simultaneously done with the science-fiction film, the major film studios decided to appropriate the horror movie as their own corporate product, creating dull, predictable horror franchises such as *Friday the 13th*, *Halloween* and *A Nightmare on Elm Street*, which glutted the nation's screens, swiftly bullying out all lower-rent competitors both foreign and domestic. Although the independent horror film has managed to achieve a hard-won "mini-renaissance" in the 21st Century, with strikingly original films like *Mum & Dad* (2008, d: Steven Sheil), *The Woman* (2011, d: Lucky McKee) and *The Human Centipede II: Full Sequence* (2011, d: Tom Six), it is impossible to calculate the damage done to the genre by the conspiratorial tactics of the major studios who effectively exterminated the creative independent horror film for over twenty years.

Returning to the fantastic films of 1957, these pictures entertained generations of audiences in both theatrical and television incarnations, and made impressive profits for their creators. Yet their final lesson, mounted in simplistic terms but still accessible for those who care to look, may be a grim awareness of the awful power of the atom, nurtured and coddled by the military and industry without citizen oversight, sprung without warning or consent on a world that had no use for it. The "nightmare fables" of 1957 strikingly, if allegorically, conveyed the brutal, savage horror of the atomic bomb's, and its big brother, the hydrogen bomb's, capacity to vaporize entire civilizations.

In the real world the horrible reality of these awful engines of destruction was deliberately diluted by the more furtive — yet equally pernicious — promise of "peaceful" atomic energy to create supposedly unlimited electrical power. Hiroshima and Nagasaki showed Man at his most monstrous, while Chernobyl and Fukushima showed Man at his most ignorant. It is the eternal toxic repercussions of these ungodly industrial accidents — and the many more which are sure to follow — which has, after all, pronounced the death sentence for man on earth. For, sadly, the atom once unleashed cannot be reined in. The freed genie will not be rebottled. The cat is out of the bag. One might say that 1957 is the year in which the earth began in earnest its long, painful metamorphosis into a hellish atomic wasteland full of disease, mutation and strife, a noxious legacy hastily forged in a desperate time — one which will prevail until the last living creature has succumbed and the earth becomes a barren radioactive graveyard of the dead.

For thanks to mankind's illimitable capacity for blindness and folly, the atomic age received a precipitous boost in 1957, an occurrence most ironically annotated by that year's fantastic film output. In that year the U.S. military tested a record number of thermonuclear weapons, with the resultant devastating environmental impact. This same year can be seen as a key one also for the nascent atomic energy industry, that foolhardy gamble to harness this most deadly of technologies to boil water for generating electrical power. Currently, over 400 atomic power plants worldwide continually spew out their invisible poisons through their regular, daily operations (as well as the ever-more-frequent catastrophic accident). This egregious error on the part of humanity has doomed it to a legacy of radiological contamination of the biosphere and all its inhabitants — human and otherwise — which will last as far into the future as one can envisage. Millennia from now, when archaeologists root through the charred scraps of our deceased civilization and ponder whence came the malefic spirit which cursed it to atrocious extermination, they might most accurately speculate, "It Came from 1957."

Chapter Notes

Chapter 1

1. David Halberstam, *The Fifties* (New York: Fawcett Columbine, 1993), 700.
2. Ibid., 244.
3. Ibid., 405.
4. Ibid., 704.
5. Ibid., 36.
6. The Office of the Historian, Joint Task Force One, *Operation Crossroads: The Official Pictorial Record* (New York: Wm. H. Wise & Co., 1946), 8.
7. Ibid., 108.
8. Ibid., 67.
9. John May, ed., *The Greenpeace Book of the Nuclear Age* (New York: Pantheon, 1989), 86.
10. Howard Ball, *Justice Downwind: America's Atomic Testing Program in the 1950s* (New York: Oxford University Press, 1986), 25.
11. Lewis Strauss, ed., *Atoms for Peace* (Washington: U.S. Atomic Energy Commission, 1955), 3.
12. Halberstam, 39.
13. Douglas T. Miller and Marion Nowak, *The Fifties: The Way We Really Were* (Garden City: Doubleday, 1977), 22.
14. Ibid., 55.
15. Ibid., 52.
16. The Pacific War Research Society, *The Day Man Lost: Hiroshima, 6 August 1945* (Tokyo: Kondansha International, 1972), 240.
17. Miller and Nowak, 55.
18. Ibid., 60.
19. The Manhattan Engineer District, *The Atomic Bombing of Hiroshima and Nagasaki* (Washington: United States Department of Defense, 1946), 47.
20. Ibid., 53.
21. Samuel Glasstone, ed., *The Effects of Nuclear Weapons* (Washington: United States Department of Defense, 1957), 473.
22. The Manhattan Engineer District, 30.
23. Halberstam, 347.
24. Miller and Nowak, 62.
25. Ibid., 57.
26. Ibid., 65–66.
27. Ibid., 67.
28. John W. Campbell, Jr., "Brookhaven Sketches," *Astounding Science Fiction* (July 1949): 4.
29. Miller and Nowak, 61.
30. Ernest Sternglass, *Secret Fallout: Low-Level Radiation from Hiroshima to Three-Mile Island* (New York: McGraw-Hill, 1981), 119.
31. Ibid., 121.
32. Ibid., 141.
33. Ibid., 145.
34. Ibid., 150.
35. Ibid.
36. Ibid., 171.
37. Jay M. Gould and Benjamin A. Goldman, *Deadly Deceit: Low Level Radiation, High Level Cover-Up* (New York: Four Walls Eight Windows, 1990), 158.
38. May, 86–87.
39. Ibid., 122.
40. Alexander Zaitchik, "Inside the Zone," *The Exile* 12, October 12, 2007, archived at http://www.exile.ru/ARTICLE_ID=13122&IBLOCK_ID=35, 4.
41. May, 121.
42. Lorna Arnold, *Windscale 1957: Anatomy of a Nuclear Accident* (Dublin: Gill and Macmillan, 1992), 55.
43. May, 115.
44. Robert Hastings, *UFOs and Nukes: Extraordinary Encounters at Nuclear Weapons Sites* (Bloomington: AuthorHouse, 2008), 39.
45. Ibid., 82.
46. Ibid., 83.
47. Ibid., 120.
48. Halberstam, 625.
49. Ibid., 609.
50. Miller and Nowak, 344.
51. Aldous Huxley, *Brave New World Revisited* (New York: Harper & Brothers, 1958), 97.
52. Miller and Nowak, 270.
53. Ibid., 271.
54. Ibid., 334.
55. W.T. Lhamon, Jr., *Deliberate Speed: The Origins of a Cultural Style in the American 1950s* (Washington: Smithsonian Institution Press, 1990), 147.
56. Miller and Nowak, 138.
57. Huxley, 31.
58. Ibid., 33–34.
59. Miller and Nowak, 152.
60. Halberstam, 590.
61. Ibid., 598.
62. Miller and Nowak, 174.
63. Ibid., 155.
64. Halberstam, 590.
65. Eugenia Kaledin, *Mothers and More: American Women in the 1950s* (Boston: Twayne, 1984), 39.
66. Kaledin, 41.
67. Bonnie Noonan, *Women Scientists in Fifties Science Fiction Films* (Jefferson, NC: McFarland, 2005), 48.
68. Ibid., 49.
69. Ibid., 58.
70. Lhamon, 28.
71. Ibid., 7.
72. Ibid., 33.
73. Miller and Nowak, 314.
74. "Telemovies Ready to Project First Runs into Living Rooms," *Boxoffice*, August 31, 1957, 7.
75. Jim Ridenour, *Secrets of the Spook Show* (Seattle: Something Weird Video, 2001), 2.
76. Ibid., 3.
77. Ibid., 6.
78. Ibid., 3.
79. Miller and Nowak, 335.
80. In addition to the fantastic films discussed in Chapter 2, Allied Artists also released four entries in their long-running "Bowery Boys" series in 1957, all of which contained some element of fantasy or horror, yet another nod to the popularity of "fantastic films" that year. In *Hold That Hypnotist* (released in February), Sach allows himself to be regressed to a past life by a hypno-

tist — which he discovers was as a tax collector who gets a map of buried treasure from Blackbeard the Pirate. In *Spook Chasers* (released in June), the Bowery Boys get stuck during a thunderstorm in a spooky mansion, where they run into ghosts, gorillas and various "apparitions." In *Looking for Danger* (released in October), Sach recalls his days as a spy during World War II when he was sent to an Arabian kingdom disguised as a Nazi officer to engage an underground leader known only as "the Hawk." In *Up in Smoke* (released in December), in order to get the names of winning horses at the track, Sach sells his soul to the devil.

Chapter 2

1. Eric Schaefer, *Bold! Daring! Shocking! True! A History of Exploitation Films, 1910–1959* (Durham: Duke University Press, 1999), 208.
2. *Film Bulletin,* February 18, 1957, 20.
3. Roger Corman and Jim Jerome, *How I Made a Hundred Movies in Hollywood and Never Lost a Dime* (New York: Delta, 1991), 39.
4. Ibid., 37.
5. Philip J. di Franco, *The Movie World of Roger Corman* (New York: Chelsea House, 1979), 78.
6. Randy Palmer, *Paul Blaisdell: Monster Maker* (Jefferson, N.C.: McFarland, 1997), 112.
7. D. Earl Worth, *Sleaze Creatures: An Illustrated Guide to Obscure Hollywood Horror Movies 1956–1959* (Key West: Fantasma, 1995), 112.
8. Palmer, 136–138.
9. Di Franco, 78.
10. W.T. Lhamon, Jr., *Deliberate Speed: The Origins of a Cultural Style in the American 1950s* (Washington: Smithsonian Institution Press, 1990), 147.
11. Ibid., 137.
12. Beverly Garland performed many similar roles in films of the time period (Corman's 1956 western *Gunslinger* is another great one); and later in 1957 Garland secured the lead in a wonderful syndicated television series, *Decoy: Police Woman,* which enabled her (as a cop in disguise) to essentially play a different character every week.

13. Di Franco, 79.
14. *Motion Picture Herald,* March 16, 1957, 299.
15. Ibid.
16. *Film Bulletin,* February 18, 1957, 15.
17. Ibid., 17.
18. David Halberstam, *The Fifties* (New York: Fawcett Columbine, 1993), 347.
19. Halberstam, 348.
20. *Boxoffice,* September 7, 1957, BG-14.
21. Some sources claim this double bill as having a December 1958 release date, but the National Screen Service log numbers, and extant newspaper ads, confirm that the films were first released in May 1957.
22. *Boxoffice,* September 7, 1957, 27.
23. Ibid., BG-7.
24. Hal Erickson, *Syndicated Television: The First Forty Years, 1947–1987* (Jefferson, NC: McFarland, 1989), 9.
25. Ibid., 20.
26. *Boxoffice,* August 31, 1957, SH-207.
27. David Schecter, *The Monster That Challenged the World,* audio CD liner notes (Chatsworth: Monstrous Movie Music, 2011), 12–13.
28. Thomas Doherty, *Teenagers and Teenpics: The Juvenilization of American Movies in the 1950s* (Boston: Unwin Hyman, 1988), 160.
29. Ibid., 161.
30. Paul W. Fairman, "The Cosmic Frame," *Amazing Stories* (May 1955), 66–67.
31. Fairman, 74.
32. *Boxoffice,* September 7, 1957, BG-13.
33. Ibid., BG-12.

Chapter 3

1. *Motion Picture Herald,* March 16, 1957, 29.
2. Nathan Cohen, "Good Summer, with Combos Offering Surprising Help," *Boxoffice,* September 21, 1957, 9.
3. *Boxoffice,* August 10, 1957, 11.
4. Bonnie Noonan, *Women Scientists in Fifties Science Fiction Films* (Jefferson, NC: McFarland, 2005), 105.
5. Ibid., 108.

6. Ibid., 112.
7. Ibid., 113.
8. *Boxoffice,* August 10, 1957, E-5.
9. Ibid., E-8.
10. *Boxoffice,* "Showmandiser" section, August 10, 1957, 189.
11. Ibid., 193.
12. John Mantley, *The 27th Day* (Greenwich: Fawcett, 1956), 19.
13. Ibid., 20.
14. Ibid., 45.
15. Ibid.
16. Aldous Huxley, *Brave New World Revisited* (New York: Harper & Brothers, 1958), 75.
17. Mantley, 98.
18. Ibid., 126.
19. Ibid., 122.
20. Ibid., 150.
21. Ibid., 129.
22. Ibid., 171.
23. *Boxoffice,* August 31, 1957, 2131.
24. Ibid.
25. Douglas T. Miller and Marion Nowak, *The Fifties: The Way We Really Were* (Garden City: Doubleday, 1977), 163–164.
26. Ibid.
27. Ibid., 160.
28. Eric Schaefer, *Bold! Daring! Shocking! True! A History of Exploitation Films, 1919–1959* (Durham: Duke University Press, 1999), 265.
29. *Boxoffice,* August 10, 1957, 2120.
30. Ibid.
31. Catherine Turney, *The Other One* (New York: Dell, 1952), 23.
32. Tim Lucas "*Quatermass 2* DVD review," *Video Watchdog* 52, 15.
33. *Boxoffice,* August 31, 1957, 2130.
34. *Boxoffice,* September 7, 1957, BG-2133.
35. Ibid.
36. *Boxoffice,* September 21, 1957, 2140.
37. *Boxoffice,* "Showmandiser" section, August 31, 1957, 208.
38. *Boxoffice,* August 31, 1957, E-2.
39. Ibid., E-8.
40. Ibid., 18.
41. *Boxoffice,* September 21, 1957, 27–30.
42. *Boxoffice,* "Showmandiser" section, November 30, 1957, 285.
43. *Boxoffice,* September 7, 1957, 22.

Bibliography

Arnold, Lorna. *Windscale 1957: Anatomy of a Nuclear Accident.* Dublin: Gill and Macmillan, 1992.

Ball, Howard. *Justice Downwind: America's Atomic Testing Program in the 1950s.* New York: Oxford University Press, 1986.

Campbell, John W., Jr. "Brookhaven Sketches." *Astounding Science Fiction,* July 1949.

Corman, Roger, and Jim Jerome. *How I Made a Hundred Movies in Hollywood and Never Lost a Dime.* New York: Delta, 1991.

Di Franco, Philip J. *The Movie World of Roger Corman.* New York: Chelsea House, 1979.

Doherty, Thomas. *Teenagers and Teenpics: The Juvenilization of American Movies in the 1950s.* Boston: Unwin Hyman, 1988.

Erickson, Hal. *Syndicated Television: The First Forty Years, 1947–1987.* Jefferson, NC: McFarland, 1989.

Fairman, Paul. "The Cosmic Frame." *Amazing Stories,* May 1955.

Ford, Daniel. *Meltdown: The Secret Papers of the Atomic Energy Commission.* New York: Touchstone, 1986.

Glasstone, Samuel, ed. *The Effects of Nuclear Weapons.* Washington: United States Department of Defense, 1957.

Gould, Jay M., and Benjamin A. Goldman. *Deadly Deceit: Low Level Radiation, High Level Cover-Up.* New York: Four Walls Eight Windows, 1990.

Halberstam, David. *The Fifties.* New York: Fawcett Columbine, 1993.

Hastings, Robert. *UFOs and Nukes: Extraordinary Encounters at Nuclear Weapons Sites.* Bloomington: AuthorHouse, 2008.

Hawley, Gessner G. *Atomic Energy in War and Peace.* New York: Reinhold, 1945.

Heffernan, Kevin. *Ghouls, Gimmicks, and Gold: Horror Films and the American Movie Business, 1953–1968.* Durham: Duke University Press, 2004.

Huxley, Aldous. *Brave New World Revisited.* New York: Harper & Brothers, 1958.

Kaledin, Eugenia. *Mothers and More: American Women in the 1950s.* Boston: Twayne, 1984.

Kashner, Sam, and Jennifer MacNair. *The Bad and the Beautiful: Hollywood in the Fifties.* Old Saybrook: Konecky & Konecky, 2002.

Lhamon, W.T., Jr. *Deliberate Speed: The Origins of a Cultural Style in the American 1950s.* Washington: Smithsonian Institution Press, 1990.

Lifton, Robert Jay, *Death in Life: Survivors of Hiroshima.* New York: Random House, 1967.

Manhattan Engineer District, The. *The Atomic Bombing of Hiroshima and Nagasaki.* Washington: United States Department of Defense, 1946.

Mantley, John. *The 27th Day.* Greenwich: Fawcett, 1956.

Martin, Len D. *The Allied Artists Checklist: The Feature Films and Short Subjects, 1947–1978.* Jefferson, NC: McFarland, 1993.

Masters, Dexter, and Katharine Way. *One World or None.* New York: The New Press, 2007.

May, John, ed. *The Greenpeace Book of the Nuclear Age.* New York: Pantheon, 1989.

McGee, Mark Thomas. *Fast and Furious: The Story of American International Pictures.* Jefferson, NC: McFarland, 1984.

Miller, Douglas T., and Marion Nowak. *The Fifties: The Way We Really Were.* Garden City: Doubleday & Company, 1977.

Noonan, Bonnie. *Women Scientists in Fifties Science Fiction Films.* Jefferson, NC: McFarland, 2005.

The Office of the Historian. *Joint Task Force One, Operation Crossroads: The Official Pictorial Record.* New York: Wm. H. Wise & Co., 1946.

Pacific War Research Society, The. *The Day Man Lost: Hiroshima, 6 August 1945.* Tokyo: Kondansha International, 1972.

Palmer, Randy. *Paul Blaisdell, Monster Maker: A Biography of the B Movie Makeup and Special Effects Artist.* Jefferson, NC: McFarland, 1997.

Ridenour, Jim. *Secrets of the Spook Show.* Seattle: Something Weird Video, 2001.

Schaefer, Eric. *Bold! Daring! Shocking! True! A His-*

tory of Exploitation Films, 1919–1959. Durham: Duke University Press, 1999.

Sternglass, Ernest. *Secret Fallout: Low-Level Radiation from Hiroshima to Three-Mile Island.* New York: McGraw-Hill, 1981.

Turney, Catherine. *The Other One.* New York: Dell, 1952.

Warren, Carol A.B. *Madwives: Schizophrenic Women in the 1950s.* New Brunswick: Rutgers University Press, 1987.

Worth, D. Earl. *Sleaze Creatures: An Illustrated Guide to Obscure Hollywood Horror Movies 1956–1959.* Key West: Fantasma Press, 1995.

Index

Numbers in *bold* italics indicate pages with photographs.

www.ingramcontent.com/pod-product-compliance
Ingram Content Group UK Ltd.
Pitfield, Milton Keynes, MK11 3LW, UK
UKHW051853150726
7214IPUK00021B/402

9 780786 477777